LEVELED BOOKS (K–8)

Matching Texts *to* **Readers** *for* **Effective Teaching**

IRENE C. FOUNTAS
GAY SU PINNELL

HEINEMANN
PORTSMOUTH, NH

KH

Heinemann
A division of Reed Elsevier Inc.
361 Hanover Street
Portsmouth, NH 03801–3912
www.heinemann.com

Offices and agents throughout the world

© 2006 by Gay Su Pinnell and Irene C. Fountas

Library of Congress Cataloguing-in-Publications Data

Fountas, Irene C.
    Leveled Books (K-8): matching texts to readers for effective teaching / Irene C. Fountas, Gay Su Pinnell
        p. cm.
    Includes index.
    ISBN 0-325-00818-3 (alk. paper)
    1. Book Leveling. 2. Reading (Elementary) 3. Reading (Middle school) 4. Children-Books and reading. 5. Classroom libraries. 6. Effective teaching. Pinnell, Gay Su. II. Title.
LB1573.F643 2005
372.41–dc22

Cover photos (center and far right) copyright © by Robert Mirani

Printed in the United States of America on acid-free paper

10 09 08 07 06   VP   2 3 4 5 6 7

The authors and publisher wish to thank those who have generously given permission to reprint borrowed material:

Text *from* Horrible Harry in Room 2B *by Suzy Kline, copyright © 1988 by Suzy Kline. Used by permission of Viking Penguin, A Division of Penguin Young Readers Group. A Member of Penguin Group (USA) Inc., 345 Hudson Street, New York, NY 10014. All rights reserved. "Illustrations" by Frank Remkiewicz, copyright © 1988 by Frank Remkiewicz.*

"July 29, 1920, Dear Tovah" from Letters from Rifka *by Karen Hesse, © 1992 by Karen Hesse. Reprinted by permission of Henry Holt and Company, LLC.*

Reprinted with the permission of Atheneum Books for Young Readers, an imprint of Simon & Schuster Children's Publishing Division from Henry and Mudge: The First Book of Their Adventures *by Cynthia Rylant, illustrated by Sucie Stevenson. Text copyright © 1997 Cynthia Rylant. Illustrations copyright © 1987 by Sucie Stevenson.*

From Harry's Mad *by Dick King-Smith, copyright © 1984 by Dick King-Smith. Illustrations copyright © 1984 by Jill Bennett. Used by permission of Crown Publishers, an imprint of Random House Children's Books, a division of Random House, inc.*

Excerpt from Spider Boy *by Ralph Fletcher. Text © 1997 by Ralph Fletcher. Reprinted by permission of Clarion Books, an imprint of Houghton Mifflin Company and by permission of Marian Reiner for the author. All rights reserved.*

From Baking Bread *by Natalie Lunis. Pelham, NY: Benchmark Education, 2002. Used by permission of the publisher.*
From Making a House *by Rebecca Weber. Pelham, NY: Benchmark Education, 2003. Used by permission of the publisher.*

From Balloon Ride *by Theresa Bryson, Illustrated by Sandra Cammell. Pelham, NY: Benchmark Education Company, 2003. Used by permission of the publisher.*

From Batteries *by Cynthia Swain. Pelham, NY: Benchmark Education, 2003. Used by permission of the publisher.*

From Big Rocks, Little Rocks *by Margie Burton, Cathy French, and Tammy Jones. Pelham, NY: Benchmark Education, 2003. Used by permission of the publisher.*

Going to the Dentist *by Helen Frost. Copyright © 1999 by Capstone Press. All rights reserved. Photo used by permission of David Clobes.*

From The Mirror *by June Melser. Copyright © 1998 Wright Group Publishing, Inc. Used by permission of The McGraw-Hill Companies and Shortland/McGraw-Hill Australia.*

From Earth and Moon *by Fred and Jeanne Biddulph. Copyright © 1992 Wright Group Publishing, Inc. Used by permission of The McGraw-Hill Companies and Wendy Pye Ltd. Photo page 12: NASA. Photo page 13 by permission of AANT Photo Library.*

From Incredible Places *by Erin Haniflin et al. Copyright © 1999 Wright Group/McGraw-Hill. Used by permission of The McGraw-Hill Companies and Shortland/McGraw-Hill Australia*

From Ocean Life *by Sharon Dalgleish. Weldon Owen Inc © 1999. Used by permission. Photo of Johan and the Whale: The Granger Collection*

From Under a Microscope *by Jan McPherson. Copyright © 1996 The Wright Group Publishing, Inc. Used by permission of The McGraw-Hill Companies and Wendy Pye Ltd.*

From The Sleepover *by Carrie Waters, Illustrated by Hector Borlasca in* Houghton Mifflin Leveled Readers. *Copyright © 2004 by Houghton Mifflin Company. Reprinted by permission of Houghton Mifflin Company. All rights reserved.*

Excerpt from Anastasia Krupnik *by Lois Lowry. Copyright © 1979 by Lois Lowry. Reproduced by permission of Houghton Mifflin Company. All rights reserved.*

From Grandparents are Great *by Margie Sigman in* Houghton Mifflin Leveled Readers. *Copyright © 2004 by Houghton Mifflin Company. Reprinted by permission of Houghton Mifflin Company. All rights reserved.*

From Landslides, *by Linda Hartley in* Houghton Mifflin Leveled Readers. *Copyright © 2004 by Houghton Mifflin Company. Reprinted by permission of Houghton Mifflin Company. All rights reserved.*

From Rachel Carson, *by Ellen Jean Peters, Illustrated by Jerry Tiritilli. in* Houghton Mifflin Leveled Readers. *Copyright © 2004 by Houghton Mifflin Company. Reprinted by permission of Houghton Mifflin Company. All rights reserved.*

From Cactuses *by Lesley Pether, Copyright © 2001 National Geographic Society. Page 6 photo: Walter Meayers Edwards/National Geographic Image Collection. [Photo page 7: see last column]*

From Weather Watch *by Ina Cumpiano. Copyright © 1992 Hampton-Brown Books. Used with permission of the publisher. All rights reserved. Photo: Mick Roessler/SuperStock.*

"Creatures of the Night," written by Kath Murdoch and Stephen Ray, from Mondo's BOOKSHOP Literacy Program. Text © 1997 by Kath Murdoch and Stephen Ray. Photograph credits Kathie Atkinson, P. 15 (center); Minden Pictures/Australian Picture Library, P. 14 (bottom); C & S Pollitt/ANT Photo Library, P. 14 (top); Cyril Webster/ANT Photo Library, P. 14 (bottom); Norbert Wu/ANT Photo Library, P. 15 (left); reprinted by permission of Mondo Publishing, 980 Avenue of the Americas, New York, New York 10018. All rights reserved.

8/16/06

Dedicated to the memory of

Susan E. Hundley,

a dear colleague who loved children and books

CONTENTS

ACKNOWLEDGMENTS

Creating this and preparing the booklist that is its companion gave us the opportunity to have many pleasurable hours discussing good books with our colleagues.

Our special appreciation goes to Carol Woodworth, who has helped us manage this complex process. She has devoted countless hours to helping us keep up with new books and our complex systems of analysis. We also thank Patty Federow, who is another important member of our team.

The highly expert Heinemann editorial team has been especially involved in the creation of this book. Throughout the process Lois Bridges has offered good advice and superb editing. As always, we appreciate Michael Cirone's expertise and artistry in layout and design, and Lisa Fowler's excellence in cover design. Leigh Peake's work on the website was integral to the production of this volume, and we would like to acknowledge her valuable advice. We are especially grateful to Lesa Scott for constant encouragement and support. We thank everyone at Heinemann for their patience. This "small" project grew into a large one, as projects often do. They have been flexible, patient, and willing to solve problems.

Our university colleagues in the Literacy Collaborative continue to challenge us through research and dialogue; we learn so much from their work. At Lesley University, we wish to recognize the work of Jill Eurich, Margaret Crosby, Toni Czekanski, Helen Sisk, Mechelle Abney, Diane Powell, Leslie Ryan, and Meredith Teany. At Ohio State University, we acknowledge the work of Andrea McCarrier, Lynda Mudre, Justina Henry, Joan Wylie, Kecia Hicks, and Marsha Levering.

We also acknowledge the contributions over the years of leaders in Reading Recovery: Emily Rodgers, Mary Fried, Susan Fullerton, Diane E. Deford, Carol Lyons, and Eva Konstantellou. We also wish to recognize the work of Barbara Peterson, who used the Reading Recovery levels, developed by Marie Clay and Barbara Watson, to do groundbreaking work. Barbara analyzed books that were leveled by Clay and Watson, discovering detailed text factors that assisted teachers in leveling early books for readers. We thank her for her contributions to teachers' understanding of text factors in early books.

Good work can be accomplished when people with many areas of expertise come together to work on the details. We wish to thank Sharon Freeman for her many organization skills in supporting the writing process. We also recognize our friend Salli Oddi who constantly shares her knowledge of books with us.

Our families are an important part of every writing process. We thank Ron Melhado and Ron Heath for the humor, patience, love, and good times that make writing go a little easier. As always we acknowledge Catherine Fountas and Elfrieda Pinnell for helping us become readers ourselves.

Finally, we rededicate this book to Susan E. Hundley, a collector of wonderful books for children. In the years we worked with her, she was unfailingly generous in contributing her insights about texts. We will always miss her.

INTRODUCTION

Technology has made important differences in just about every aspect of our work as educators and we, as book lovers, are no exception. When faced with the need to update our leveled book lists for primary, intermediate, and middle grades, we realized that just the first update would approach a list of about 20,000 books; and it would grow from there. The volume would be massive and the list would take up all of the space, leaving no room for information on readability, the text gradient, and suggestions for creating and using a leveled book collection. At the same time, we knew that constant updating would be more useful to teachers than waiting for a new list every five or six years. We had the additional problem of storing thousands of books!

With those concerns in mind, we created the website called *fountasandpinnellleveledbooks.com* to serve the ongoing needs of teachers in kindergarten through grade eight who are using leveled books for guided reading instruction. This website currently stores a searchable list of over 18,000 leveled books, A to Z, and more are added each month. Additionally, we have placed a variety of professional development resources on the website: DVD clips of guided reading, frequently asked questions and answers, analysis of running records, and recommendations of books to read aloud. While the list is available in hard copy, the website is a convenient way to access materials and other information.

Over the years, we have found it extremely helpful to work with our colleagues to level books. When we are analyzing texts for ourselves, we are actually thinking about the demands texts make on processing. We find that performing this analysis, talking about it with others, and tentatively assigning a level provides a strong foundation of information when we plan introductions to texts for guided reading lessons because we have already thought about the potential demands. So, while it would be a huge job to level all of the books used in guided reading, we have always encouraged teachers to level some books for themselves. In the two previous books, there are prototypes, descriptions, and page layouts for each level that can be used as a guide.

In addition, both volumes provided background information about the gradient of text and described its role in a literacy program. Factors related to readability and accessibility were also included, as well as some practical information on creating classroom and school collections and ways to acquire more books, including grant writing.

We made the decision to update the information in both volumes, including information on grades kindergarten through three as well as providing more detail for grades four through eight.

The result is *Leveled Books (K–8): Matching Texts to Readers for Effective Teaching*. In chapter 1 you will find a rationale for matching books to readers, and in Chapter 2 the gradient of text is described. These two chapters gave us an important chance to clarify our perspective of the use of leveled texts in classrooms; for example, we describe what a gradient is and what it is not. Chapter 3 presents a picture of comprehensive approaches to language and literacy teaching, kindergarten through grade eight.

In Chapter 4, we examine the "text base" that is needed in a classroom for effective language literacy instruction. If they are to become proficient citizens who use reading and writing for both professional and personal goals, year after year students need to engage in reading, listening to, discussing, and writing about a rich array of books. Leveled books have their place because they offer a ladder of support for intensive small group instruction; however, we also describe other components of the text base, for example books to read aloud and to read independently. In Chapter 5, we explore the concept of readability and the various ways it is calculated, and in Chapters 6 and 7, we present ten factors related to accessibility and readability, as well as examples of text analysis at many levels.

Chapter 8 provides guidelines for creating a high-quality leveled book collection. Chapter 9 focuses on how to match books to readers by using benchmark assessment and ongoing analysis of reading. This assessment is an important base for effective teaching in guided reading because if books are too hard or too easy, it is difficult to help students expand the systems of strategic actions they need to develop. Once you find the right levels for instruction, you can then easily place stu-

dents into small groups and select texts that will make it possible to do effective teaching in guided reading. In Chapter 10, we discuss using leveled books in guided reading from kindergarten through grade 8.

Chapters 11, 12, 13, and 14 will help you understand the gradient and text factors in detail and to analyze and level books for yourself. We present level by level descriptions and include prototypes and page layouts for both fiction and nonfiction texts, A to Z.

In Chapters 15, 16, and 17, we return to descriptions of the kinds of texts teachers need in primary, intermediate, and middle school classrooms and resource rooms. In Chapter 15 we discuss the classroom library, including the collections from which students choose books for themselves. Chapter 16 focuses on the classroom collection for guided reading. In Chapter 17, you will find guidelines for creating and using a school bookroom. In all of these chapters, there are guidelines and cost estimates for building the needed collections over time.

In the last two chapters, we focus on ways to increase your collection of books. Chapter 18 provides practical information on cost-effective planning as well as how to acquire books free through book clubs and gifts. In Chapter 19, you will find examples of letters, concept papers, and proposals that you can use to seek funding. In the Appendixes for this book, we provide ordering information on publishers and addresses.

We hope you'll find our book an important resource for developing your understanding of texts and their implications for effective teaching.

—I.C.F. and G. S. P.

CHAPTER ONE

WHY MATCH BOOKS TO READERS?

Good readers read regularly, voluntarily, and voraciously. They read a wide variety of material with confidence and enjoyment. They read for many purposes—to become informed, to improve their lives, to escape to other worlds, to learn about themselves, to revel in adventures, and to understand others who are distant in time, space, and culture. They collect books, talk about books, and recommend books to their friends. They have favorite books and favorite authors. They know their tastes and preferences but are willing to try something new. They remember what they read, reflect on the ideas and experiences they've gained from books, and make connections between and among books. They read actively, bringing their imagination and past experiences to bear on their reading; and they read critically, evaluating what they read for objectivity, completeness, authenticity, and quality. All of these characteristics are part of being a reader, and developing those characteristics is the goal of the language and literacy program throughout schooling.

As teachers, we want our students to lead literate lives and discover for themselves the adventure, knowledge, and wisdom readers experience. Not everything about learning to read comes easily, but we want the dream to be always within reach. For many children, it will take repeated efforts on their part and ours to reach the necessary levels of competence. We want these efforts to be successful, the kind that become their own reward.

In this chapter we discuss the importance of matching books to readers and the role of leveled books in literacy programs.

Matching Books to Readers

Matching books to readers depends on three interrelated sets of understandings, all of which are critical to effective teaching:

■ Knowing the readers.

■ Knowing the texts.

■ Understanding the reading process.

In this book we will provide information that will help you know the texts that children read as part of an effective instructional program in literacy. But we must always consider these texts in relation to the readers and the processes they are learning. We refer you to our other publications for detailed explanations of readers and the reading process (Fountas and Pinnell 1996, 1998, 2006).

Why Is Matching Books to Readers So Important?

Much has been written about providing simple, suitable texts for beginning readers. Matching books to readers is critical for children who are beginning to build a reading process; and it is also important to use a gradient of text to be sure that older readers have the support and challenge they need to expand their reading powers as they engage with more complex texts over time.

PRIMARY STUDENTS

The young children we teach are building a network of strategic actions that make up an early reading process. They develop successful processing strategies as they learn to read for meaning and use the language and print of texts. When children are reading a book that they can read with success, they are able to use many different sources of information in a smoothly operating processing system. While focusing on the meaning of the story, they might:

- Make predictions about what will happen next.

- Interpret characters and form opinions about their nature.

- Notice and use word groups or phrases and language patterns to anticipate what will follow.

- Recognize a large number of words quickly and easily.

- Take words apart efficiently to read them.

- Notice a word that is unfamiliar or that they don't see very often and solve it—that is, think about its meaning or how to pronounce it (often ignored in silent reading).

- Reread part of the text to confirm information that is essential to understanding the rest of the text.

- Notice how the information is organized.

- Connect the text to others they have read or to their own life experiences.

Intermediate and Middle School Students

Older students continue to expand their network of strategic actions as texts become more challenging. They need to broaden their experience with texts, becoming more sophisticated in reading a wide range of informational texts. As they do so, they will acquire content knowledge; but the goal of reading instruction is to help them learn *how* to read more complex nonfiction texts that require integration of information from increasingly complex graphics as well as using readers' tools such as indexes, pronun-ciation guides, glossaries, and many different kinds of headings.

More proficient readers will explore difficult social issues in realistic fiction, and they also take on difficult works of fantasy that require entering entire worlds where the struggle between good and evil is symbolically portrayed. Historical fiction requires readers to consider the customs, attitudes, and perspectives of people living in former times. Across narrative texts, even though the settings are different from reality or distant in time and geography from their own, readers need to use ideas from texts to gain insight into the human condition and to apply them to their own lives. We want to assure that intermediate and middle school readers learn to understand, analyze, and think critically about this wide range of texts.

Texts in Relation to Readers

Terms like "hard" and "easy" are always relative. "Hard" for whom? "Easy" for which readers? When we use those terms in reference to books, we are always thinking from the perspective of the readers. A book is easy or difficult only in terms of a particular reader or even a group of readers. So, when we know the readers, we can think of any text as "hard," "easy," or "just right." Each kind of text has important implications for the behavior of the reader and the potential to "learn on the text."

Hard Texts

Think about reading a text that is very difficult for you as an adult. It might be a legal document, a technical manual (such as the tax code), or a novel by an author with an unusual style completely unfamiliar to you. How would reading that diffi-cult text limit your ability to bring what you know to the process of reading? Your understanding might be impaired; if you attempted to read it aloud you might even stumble over some words or use expressions in awkward ways. You might find yourself reading some sections over and over in an attempt to make sense of them. You might even skip some words altogether because you are unsure of pronunciation, of meaning, or of both. If you have to skip too many words, you may become confused. Chances are, after a while you would not continue to read. You would simply discard the text or seek the information in some other way.

Elementary students are in exactly the same position with the too-hard texts they encounter in school. If they are struggling, they cannot use what they know in efficient, strategic ways. In fact, forcing students to read too-hard texts has devastating results:

- They begin to think that reading is simply a matter of saying one individual word after another. Reading may, in fact, sound like a laboriously pronounced list of isolated words.

- They lose the meaning of the text. Older students spend so much energy on word solving that they have little attention to give to remembering details, following a plot, thinking beyond a text, and other critical aspects of comprehension. Young children may even conclude that reading doesn't have to make sense and will "tune out" deeper thinking altogether as they focus on figuring out each word.

- They find it difficult to bring their knowledge of language structure to the process and may not recognize larger units, such as phrases. They cannot anticipate the next word because they are unaware that reading should sound like language.

- They practice inappropriate reading behaviors, such as the laborious "sounding out" of words in a way that makes no sense. As they grow older, they may even give up searching for meaning.

- They become frustrated with reading and avoid it altogether. Motivation is severely undermined. Reading becomes a task to be avoided.

EASY TEXTS

What about books that readers find easy? How do such books fit into a reading program? Easy reading is actually beneficial for elementary age readers, just as it is for adults. Reading a book that is very easy for you requires less intensity and energy. Most of what you do is fully automatic. You read quickly and easily. You feel in control. You are probably in a very relaxed state, and you can simply enjoy the reading experience. You are able to enjoy faraway places—almost as though you are there. You can anticipate events in the text; you enjoy thinking about the plot and characters. You may become completely engaged, blocking out everything around you. You meet few problems in terms of words, and you understand the text with little effort. Many of us use this "easy reading" to while away the time in airports or to help us fall asleep at night.

Easy reading allows students to enjoy the process and to use what they know in a smoothly operating system. With harder books, children may be reading a text accurately but not processing it in a smooth, fluent way. With easy books, they are unhindered by the demands of reading because they automatically—or almost automatically—use the skills they control.

Easy books also allow readers to focus on the meaning of the text and enjoy humor or suspense. They can ask questions and find answers. They can think in a deeper way about aspects of text such as characters, settings, or plots. They may encounter challenging issues that offer a foundation for discussion after the reading.

Easy reading gives students "mileage" as readers and builds confidence. They process a great many words and build up rapid word recognition as well as fluency in processing. Easy reading frees them to attend to new aspects of print and thus engage in new learning. They can read for meaning and use language in an orchestrated way.

So, texts that are easy to read are appropriate for some aspects of literacy learning. We recommend that in the classroom children have the opportunity to engage every day in a large amount of easy reading. But to help readers learn more about how to read increasingly challenging texts, they need more than easy reading.

"Just Right" Texts

Our purpose in literacy education is to help readers learn more as readers—to nudge them beyond their current development and help them expand their processing systems. We want to support their efforts to stretch as they successfully meet the challenges of more demanding texts.

To help readers build an effective network of reading strategies, you will want to select texts that allow individuals to read for meaning, draw on the skills they already control, and expand their current processing strategies. In other words, the text used for learning "how to read" must have the right mixture of support and challenge.

The reader must be able to process or read the text well with the support of the teacher. That means:

- Using knowledge of what makes sense, sounds right, and looks right—simultaneously—in a smoothly operating system.

- Knowing or taking most of the words apart quickly with a high level of accuracy (above 90 percent).

- Reading at a good rate with phrasing and intonation (that is, putting words together in groups so they sound more like oral expression) but also slowing down occasionally to engage in successful problem solving (independently and/or supported by the teacher).

- Grasping the literal meaning of a text by searching for and using information and remembering details.

- Using prior knowledge to understand the text.

- Thinking beyond the text, making inferences.

- Synthesizing new information learned from the text.

- Noticing the way the text is organized or the way the writer has used language to craft the text.

- Thinking critically about any aspect of the text.

The texts you choose for new learning must both support and challenge your students because children—like adults—learn best when the task is achievable. By matching books to readers, you make it possible even for young children to use their strengths and extend their control of the reading process.

The instructional level text should be just demanding enough to provide a few opportunities to work out problems so they can expand their reading systems. The goal is not just to learn new words and add them to a reading vocabulary, although that will inevitably happen. It's about the processing, the "working out," that helps readers develop the skills and strategies that will make them independent—strategic actions that they can apply again and again as they read other texts. The "just right" book provides the context for successful reading work and enables readers to strengthen their "processing power."

Readers in Relation to Texts

As teachers we encounter a wide range of readers, from those who are just beginning to learn about print to those who can read just about anything we give them. Meeting students where they are developmentally requires that we assess their understandings of what reading is and how they go about it. We analyze reading behaviors to assess what they control, almost control, and do not yet control.

As we observe readers' behaviors, we need to keep in mind a broad continuum of learning. As we accompany and guide their literacy development, we need to be ever mindful of definitive characteristics and behaviors. Our goal is to support them in using what they already know to get to what they do not yet know. That means knowing our students and working "on the cutting edge" of their learning.

In Figure 1–1, we have described general characteristics of readers at five levels so we can think broadly about how readers change over time.

The "advanced" category encompasses another continuum of progress. Advanced readers continue to expand their processing powers across increasingly demanding texts in terms of:

- Complex structures.
- Demanding content.
- Literary features.

These categories are generally useful in helping us think about the broad characteristics of readers. No one child will exactly fit one of these categories, and many students will evidence behaviors in more than one.

This is the art of teaching: we observe and describe children's reading behaviors and, in so doing, build a working understanding of each child as a reader at a particular point in time. In this way, we can trace changes in behavior as students learn and grow, and we can plan sensitive instruction that supports them every step of the way.

Books, Readers, and the Reading Process

The purpose of matching books to readers is to find the right books—those that provide reading opportunities that will help students develop an effective reading process. There are many opportunities in the school day for students to choose their own books, for example during independent reading, but in instructional reading the teacher does the matching so that the learners can expand what they know how to do. Our goal is to help them develop the kind of processing system that makes it possible to learn a great deal more—a system that extends itself (Clay 1991).

As indicated in Figure 1–1, "self-extending" and "advanced" readers use many different sources of information in an orchestrated way. A competent reader reads the words and does so with high accuracy, but processing a text involves much more. It means engaging in a set of strategic actions for picking up text information, working on it, and putting it together while reading.

Since reading is a complex process that brings together a reader and a text, competent readers must bring everything they know how to do as readers to the process, including:

- The use of language knowledge (an aural and reading vocabulary, the structure or syntax, and the subtle nuances of language and how they are interpreted).

- The use of background knowledge (from life experiences that include both direct and vicarious learning through books, film, television, etc.).

- The use of literary experiences (the books and other print materials they have read throughout their history as readers).

Readers are active in that they are constantly accessing information from this experiential base (invisible information), which they connect to the information in the text at hand (visible information) (Clay 2000). Effective readers put together the two kinds of information in a smooth processing system that expands or extends with the increasing demands of text.

Moreover, a proficient processing system means that you are using strategic actions in flexible ways. You gain the information or content of the reading material, and simultaneously you learn more about the reading process itself. In other words, you extend the knowledge and skill of the reading simply by engaging proficiently in the act. Most adults control a proficient system; children are developing the system. From the moment we hand a young reader a book, our teaching goal is to help the reader engage in successful processing which will build an effective system. Not

Characteristics of Readers: Change Over Time

EMERGENT

Emergent readers rely on language and meaning as they read simple texts with only one or two lines of print. They are just beginning to control early reading behaviors such as matching spoken words one by one with written words on the page, recognizing how print is arranged on pages, and moving left to right in reading. They are just figuring out what a word really is, how letters go together, and how letters are different from each other. They may know a few high frequency words that can be used as anchors as they learn to focus their attention on specific aspects of print. As they read, they notice aspects of print such as first letters of words, and they begin to pay closer attention to letters and sounds. They are learning how to use picture information to help them learn about print. They point under each word to develop word-by-word matching.

EARLY

Early readers have achieved control of early reading behaviors such as directionality and word-by-word matching. Their eyes are beginning to control the process of reading, so they do some of their reading without pointing. They have acquired a small core of high frequency words that they can read and write, and they use these words to monitor their reading. They can read books with several lines of print, keeping the meaning in mind as they use some strategies to solve unfamiliar words. They have developed systems for learning words in reading and can use simple letter-sound relationships in conjunction with their own sense of language. They consistently monitor their reading to make sure that it makes sense and sounds like language. Early readers use several sources of information to check on themselves. They use language structure along with the text meaning and are able to check with the print.

TRANSITIONAL

Transitional readers have early reading behaviors well under control. They can read a variety of texts with many lines of print. While they notice pictures and enjoy them, they do not need to rely heavily on illustrations as part of the reading process. They read fluently with some expression, using multiple sources of information while reading for meaning. They have a large core of frequently used words that they can recognize quickly and easily. They are working on how to solve more complex words through a range of word-analysis techniques. They can use language structures to anticipate the text and can begin to make sense of some literary language structures. They can attend to the meaning of texts that are longer and contain a few episodes.

SELF-EXTENDING

Self-extending readers use all sources of information flexibly in a smoothly orchestrated system. They can apply their strategies to reading fiction and nonfiction texts that are much longer and more complex. They have a large core of high frequency words and many other words that they can quickly and automatically recognize. Self-extending readers have developed systems for learning more about the process as they read so that they build skills simply by encountering many different kinds of texts with a variety of new words. Self-extending readers can analyze and make excellent attempts at new multisyllable words and can attend to and use more literary language structures. They are still building background knowledge and learning how to apply what they know how to do as readers to longer and more difficult texts.

ADVANCED

Students who are advanced in reading have moved well beyond the early "learning to read" phases of literacy learning. They are still learning and developing a complex network of strategic actions while they have varied experiences in reading a wide variety of fiction and nonfiction texts. Through using reading for many different purposes, they acquire important tools for learning. There is virtually no text that an advanced reader cannot "read," but using prior knowledge, sophisticated word-solving strategies, and understanding the nuances of a complex text are still under development. Advanced readers sustain their interest and understanding of long texts over extended periods of time.

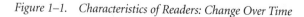

Figure 1–1. Characteristics of Readers: Change Over Time

surprisingly, independence and confidence are highly related to the development of such a system.

Knowledge of the reading process is a critical element in matching books to readers for guided reading lessons. This knowledge helps us examine texts from two perspectives: (1) we note the demands of the text on the reader or what the reader will need to be able to do to process the text well; and, (2) we consider what the particular reader knows how to do with a text. With this information we can begin to make a match:

- If we know the challenges in a text and we understand the reading process, then we can think about what this particular text requires the reader to do.

- If we know what readers control and we understand the reading process, then we can also think about what they need to learn how to do next.

- Finally, we can intervene and teach to support new learning before, during, and after students read a text.

When we match books to readers, we become more effective teachers. A good match enables readers to engage in the successful processing that builds the self-extending system—the network of understandings that all competent readers control.

Suggestions for Professional Development: Observing the Characteristics of Readers

Work with colleagues to explore the difficulty levels of texts in relation to students' diverse needs.

1. Select a book that students at your grade level typically read.

2. Observe three to six different children as they read this text (or about 250 words of it). For primary children, take running records. For older children, note the error behavior on a photocopy of a section of text. For all ages, make notes on fluency and phrasing. Have an informal conversation with each student about the text after reading and make notes about fluency and comprehending from your observations and discussion.

3. Bring your notes and a copy of the text to a meeting with colleagues. Discuss the challenges in the book. It will be an easy text for some students, a "just right" text for other students, and a hard text for still others. Talk about text difficulty in relation to the individual readers.

4. Using the Characteristics of Readers chart, discuss what you have learned about each reader. Ask:
   - Which readers did you learn the most about?
   - What specific reading behaviors did you notice?
   - From these behaviors, what can you infer about the strategic actions the reader controls?
   - What are the implications for the level of the text for the particular reader?
   - What happened when the text was too hard? too easy? just right?

5. Talk, in general, about applying your knowledge of individual readers to the creation and use of a gradient of text for instructional reading.

CHAPTER TWO

A GRADIENT OF TEXT: WHAT, WHY, AND HOW?

You need a large and varied collection of books to foster variety and quality in students' reading. As your students read widely and develop a sophisticated understanding of texts and how they "work," they extend and refine their comprehending strategies. In order to use these books most effectively, you need to determine accessibility to readers at different points in their development as they learn how to meet the demands of different kinds of texts. Looking closely at a book's characteristics, you consider: *How easy or how difficult will this text be for readers? What makes it easy or hard? What are the challenges and supports?*

Using Books for Different Purposes

If we expect students to read voluntarily and with ease and understanding, the texts we present to them must be accessible. Accessibility is provided in two ways—by teacher selection of a text that is within the reach of the readers, and by the instruction that accompanies the reading of the text. Consider several different levels of support. Sometimes you read a text to students and briefly discuss it before, during, and after reading it, making the text meaning and language more available to the readers through the read aloud. At other times, in small group instruction, you introduce them to a text, support them as they read, and teach following the reading. You may guide their independent reading choices, and sometimes listen to students read and talk with them about the meaning of texts in individual reading

conferences. In your minilessons you may help readers think about the meaning, language, and print in texts that you have read to them. These texts can serve as a resource for thinking together. When you have a reliable guide to text difficulty you can select texts that have the appropriate level of accessibility in relation to the level of support you provide. You can select levels for small group instruction that require your support and guide students to choices for independent reading that require no teacher support. You will not need to consider level when you read aloud to students. Of course you will always want to consider the appropriateness of content and the complexity and sophistication of plot and theme.

A Gradient of Text

To support your work in guided reading lessons, we recommend using a gradient of text to select the most appropriate text for instruction. A gradient of text is an arrangement of books from easiest to hardest, defined by a set of characteristics. The books are grouped in levels so that you can select from within a particular group. You can access our comprehensive list of thousands of leveled books on the website *www.fountasandpinnellleveledbooks.com* or in print form—*Leveled Book List, K–8* (Fountas and Pinnell, Heinemann 2006). You can also follow the guidelines in this book, leveling and adding books to our list as you read and use them with students. We strongly recommend, however, that you and your colleagues work together to understand the gradient, becoming aware of the range of text characteristics used to determine the levels. A common leveling system is very helpful in communicating across classrooms and grade levels about the complexity of texts and students' progress over time as they read a variety of increasingly challenging texts.

A Gradient Is . . . and Is Not

A gradient of text is a defined continuum of characteristics related to the level of support and challenge that a reader meets in a text. Terms like *easy* and *hard* are not helpful to teachers in the upper elementary grades. Texts are easy or hard with regard to a wide range of factors, including the individual reader's foundation of background knowledge.

By its nature, a gradient is *relational* and *categorical*. Texts are grouped into categories along a continuum because they offer readers a similar level of support and challenge. The level is an approximation of its difficulty, and within a level there is some variation. The challenges are not the same in every text in a level. One text may offer a challenge because of its technical language; another at the same level may be challenging because of its long sentences, archaic language, or mature content. This variety is good because while reading many texts at a level, a developing reader meets many different demands, becoming more flexible in the process. A given level is always seen in relation to the levels below and above it. As you move up the gradient, the texts are harder; as you move down, the texts are easier.

The gradient we have developed is illustrated in Figure 2–1, along with approximate corresponding grade levels. Grade levels are not the important factor when you are selecting books for students. You must start where students are in their development of reading abilities, and that may or may not be their grade level. The grade-level designations are useful, however, because they help you know the student whose instructional levels are below their expected grade level and need intensive daily instruction that moves

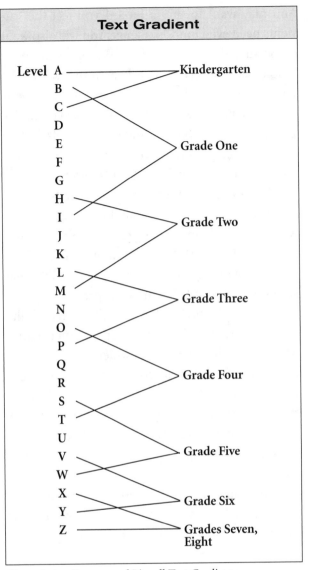

Figure 2–1.   Fountas and Pinnell Text Gradient

them into increasingly challenging texts. The only way to bring the students to grade-level goals will be to begin the teaching where they are and take them forward, step by step. When you begin the teaching where the learners are, they can feel success and take small steps forward.

A gradient is not a precise sequence through which all students move. We do not recommend making students read all the books in a collection at one level before moving to the next. When students are reading books at a level with ease, fluency, and understanding, encountering very few problems, it's time to increase the text difficulty.

You may want to skip a level if you feel the students need even more challenge. You will also want to be sure that students have the opportunity to read a wide variety of texts at a given level. As the levels of difficulty increase, readers need to experience a greater range of genre within each level. The point is not simply to "move up" levels but to increase their breadth of reading by applying their strategies to many different kinds of texts.

In our text gradient, the upper grades have fewer levels within them than do the early grades. Most intermediate students reach a point at which they can decode texts at just about any level, no matter how difficult, although their reading may sound choppy and they may mispronounce quite a few words. Texts that they can read with ease, fluency, and deep understanding are another matter. Much more flexibility and a wider range of strategies across a greater variety of genres are required of advanced readers. Again, the point is not simply to move up the gradient but to expand the students' breadth of experience with different types of texts and a range of content, authors, formats, and genres.

You will want to be cautious about using texts at levels that are more than about a year beyond the student's present grade level. Texts at grade levels on the gradient contain content that is developmentally appropriate for and/or interesting to the age group, so when your students are working at levels too far up, they will not be able to gain the full text meaning and may encounter content less appropriate for them. Just because you can read a hard book does not necessarily mean you will find it interesting or meaningful.

Figure 2–2 presents a clear summary of what a gradient is—and is not.

A gradient is not and was never intended to be a way to categorize or label students, whose background experiences and rate of progress will vary widely. We have never written about leveling students. Such interpretations are intentionally or unintentionally erroneous. The text levels are designed for teachers to use along with their knowledge of students to make good instructional decisions.

In our view, the level of a text has no place on a report card. Although parents do need to know their child's progress in relation to grade-level expectations, text levels are too narrow a measure. Parents have not been taught to understand the complexities involved in analyzing and selecting texts for different purposes and may see a text level too simplistically. We advise you to help parents understand whether

What the Text Gradient Is and Is Not	
THE TEXT GRADIENT IS . . .	*THE TEXT GRADIENT IS NOT . . .*
❖ A tool for matching books to readers	❖ A complete "reading program"
❖ A guide for making good instructional decisions	❖ A set of books that every student must read
❖ A tool to consider in relation to readers' abilities and experience	❖ A rigid sequence that defines reading progress
❖ A support for teachers as they work with readers	❖ A way of labeling readers
❖ A support for teachers in analyzing the demands of a text on readers	❖ A label or grade on a report card
	❖ A list to send to parents
	❖ A way to organize a school or classroom library from which students choose books

Figure 2–2.   *What the Text Gradient Is and Is Not*

the student is reading in the expected grade-level range, above it, or below it and to understand continuous progress over time. In a conference, you can help a parent understand that a student is far from reaching grade-level reading goals, but explain that the child is making progress by showing a sample text the student was reading upon entry and one that the student is currently reading, pointing out the differences in challenge. The gradient contains a large collection of titles that are categorized by level of difficulty. It is meant solely to support the effectiveness of the reading program.

The gradient is neither a precise sequence of texts that everyone must read nor a reading "program." During independent reading a student can read across a range of levels. In fact, classroom libraries need to be organized around topics, themes, genres, and authors rather than by levels (see Chapter 15). The text gradient is designed to be a flexible tool to help the teacher choose texts for reading instruction, not for the students to define themselves. While in general all students read some books at most levels, it should be clear that:

- They are not expected to read every book on a level.

- There is no prescribed "order" to the books at any given level.

- Students making fast progress will skip levels.

- You can always move up or down the gradient as you see the need for easier or more challenging texts for your students.

- For independent reading, students do not choose from books organized into levels.

In other words, the text gradient is a tool for the teacher, not the student. It helps the teacher select better texts to support improved reading achievement. While it can be used very effectively to document a student's progress over time, the gradient is not the sole definition of achievement in reading. You will also need to look closely at oral reading behaviors as well as at how students talk and write about their reading in relation to the gradient. It is the combination of the range of observations about reading that informs and defines an individual's continued progress.

Value of a Gradient

Your leveled collection should be in an unobtrusive area to which you alone have access, since you will be using it to make choices for guided reading. These books will not be among the books students peruse as they make their own choices. For many teachers, most of the books you use for guided reading will be in a school bookroom which houses a large shared collection (see Chapter 12).

The gradient serves some important purposes in your instructional program (see Figure 2–3). If some students consistently choose books that are too hard and find it difficult to make good selections, you'll want to guide them through the process. You can accompany the student to the book baskets and make several possible choices together. You can place a small collection of books at the right independent reading level in a basket that is not labeled and ask students to limit their selections to those books for a while. Then, talk with the students about

---

Value of an Established Gradient of Text

- ❖ Provides guidance in selecting books for instruction in guided reading.

- ❖ Serves as a teacher's guide for helping students choose books for independent reading and home reading.

- ❖ Helps in documenting students' reading progress over time.

- ❖ Provides a basis for teachers to talk with one another about text difficulty and text selection.

- ❖ Helps in planning and evaluating the range of books in a classroom library and a school leveled book collection.

Figure 2–3. Value of an Established Gradient of Text

what made these books "just right," so that they learn to monitor their own choices.

The gradient will also be helpful as you work with your grade-level colleagues and teachers at other grade levels. Having a common leveling system and gradient will help you document change over time and understand student records of reading progress as they are passed along (see Chapter 9). Also, your conversations about texts for each grade level will be more comprehensible, because you are working from the same basic definitions. Having a common language will help you as you teach and communicate with one another about your students. Finally, the gradient will help you make wise expenditures when you do have resources to spend. You can identify the gaps in your classroom libraries and in your leveled collections and fill in the levels that are most needed.

Relationship of the Text Gradient to the Reading Process

Each successive level of the gradient makes greater and more varied demands on the reading process. (In *Guiding Readers and Writers* and *Teaching for Comprehending and Fluency, K–8* we discuss in detail the strategies for comprehending written texts and level-by-level teaching goals.) By the time students enter the intermediate and middle grades, most have developed a full and rich range of in-the-head strategic actions that operate simultaneously as they process continuous texts. These in-the-head actions for sustaining the reading process we call thinking within the text. They include:

- Using a range of strategic actions for decoding and understanding the meaning of the words (*solving words*).

- Checking on their reading to be sure of the meaning and correcting themselves when needed (*monitoring and self-correcting*).

- Picking up the important information from print and illustrations as the eyes move across the page (*searching for and using information*).

- Putting together and remembering the important information as an ongoing statement of what the text is all about (*summarizing*).

- Sustaining smooth, phrased reading that reflects rapid word solving while thinking about the meaning of the text (*maintaining fluency*).

- Varying reading style and rate according to purpose for reading and the type of text (*adjusting*).

These strategic actions are not employed or learned one at a time. Instead, readers apply them simultaneously to every text they read if the text calls for them. The process is easier to orchestrate for simple texts, of course, and becomes much more demanding for complex texts. For example, it is easy to search for and use information in a straightforward and easy-to-remember text like *Henry and Mudge: The First Book* (Rylant 1996, Level J). It becomes much harder in books like *Stone Fox* (Gardiner 1980, Level P), because there are more difficult words, language, and concepts and much more to remember and think about while reading. While they are sustaining their reading of a text, readers are also required to think beyond it. They develop strategic actions for expanding meaning. We call these actions for thinking beyond and about the text. They include:

- Anticipating what will follow—at the word, phrase, sentence, and text level (*predicting*).

- Searching for, noticing, and making connections to their own personal experience, to their knowledge of the world (content knowledge), and to other texts they have read (*connecting*).

- Thinking about what the writer implies but does not tell explicitly (*inferring*).

■ Revising their own background knowledge as new understanding is acquired (*synthesizing*).

Readers also consider the text as an object. They think about the writer's style or craft and they evaluate it by:

■ Closely examining elements of the text to know more about the writer's craft and the construction of text (*analyzing*).

■ Evaluating and critiquing a text for quality or authenticity (*critiquing*).

All of these strategies for thinking within, beyond, and about a text are employed at lower text levels. Even texts like the *Henry and Mudge* (level J) series require the reader to infer what characters are thinking or feeling, pick up important details and use them to understand the problem and the characters. You might also notice some ways the writer helps you understand how characters feel. But, in general, more is required of the reader as you move up the text levels. Concepts are more complex and less familiar to students; new ideas must be synthesized, more ideas must be inferred. This ability to cope with text complexity is built over time and through experience.

Looking at Readers—Change Over Time

Earlier, we described broad changes in students' development. Figure 2–4 summarizes the shifts we see in readers over time in several broad phases and also coordinates these changes with the guided reading levels used in this book, with grade levels, and with the traditional basal reading levels found in commercially produced reading programs.

The chart follows readers from their entry into school through the end of elementary school, which is typically either grade five or six, and through middle school levels.

In the first years of school, children gradually learn how written language sounds when it is read aloud. They learn the alphabetic principle (that there is a relationship between sounds and letters); and, through many early experiences with print, they learn how written language works. An important step for *emergent readers* is learning to match the print word by word and learning to hear the sounds in words and connect them with a few letters (one spoken word to one cluster of letters with white space on either side). These readers are able to process text levels A and B.

Early readers generally have word-by-word matching under control and can read fluently, with appropriate phrasing, books from about level C through about G. They no longer need to point to words but control the process with their eyes. Early readers have learned to use several sources of information to check on their reading—for example, whether it makes sense, sounds right, or looks right in terms of the visual or print information (letter-sound coordination). They also are rapidly building a core of frequently encountered words and high utility words that they recognize automatically. Early readers can process simple texts, mostly narratives, that require following a story line and recognizing storytelling characteristics. While the stories are not complex, they offer opportunities to make personal, world, and book-to-book connections.

Transitional readers are moving from mostly oral to primarily silent reading and have a large core of known words that they recognize rapidly and automatically. They have a broad range of word-solving skills and can handle multisyllable words by taking them apart. These word-solving strategies are used "on the run" while processing continuous texts. They are learning to use simple graphic illustrations in informational texts and extending their knowledge of texts to a wider range of genres. They are reading books from level H to about M.

			Change in Reading Over Time
F&P Level	*Grade*	*Approximate Basal Level*	*Shifts in the Reading Process*
A	Kindergarten Grade One	Readiness	Emergent Readers are just becoming aware of print. They enjoy listening to stories and begin to understand the differences in syntax and vocabulary that are likely to appear in written (versus oral) language. They read orally and are learning to match word by word and to read left to right. At first, they point with their fingers, but their eyes will start to take over the process. They use information from pictures and rely on meaning and language to interpret simple texts. They use word matching, spaces, and some visual information to check on themselves while reading. They are learning to hear sounds in words and connect them with letters; they recognize a few frequently encountered words.
B	Kindergarten Grade One	PP1	
C	Kindergarten Grade One	PP1	Early Readers read orally, mostly without finger pointing, and are beginning to read very softly or silently some of the time. They are familiar with most easy frequently encountered words, and quickly recognize them while reading. They know many letter-sound relationships, and use letter-sound information to solve words while reading. They can use this knowledge of words to check on themselves as readers. On easy texts they read fluently with phrasing, using the punctuation. They are able to use several sources of information (meaning, syntax, and visual aspects of print) in combination as they process longer pieces of text. They still rely on pictures as an important source of information, but they are beginning to process print with less picture support.
D	Grade One	PP2	
E	Grade One	PP3	
F	Grade One	Primer	
G	Grade One		
H	Grade One/Grade Two	Grade One	Transitional Readers read silently much of the time; when reading aloud, they read with fluency and phrasing on appropriate levels of text. They have a large core of known words that they recognize automatically while reading continuous text. They use multiple sources of information (letter-sound relationships, word structure, syntax, and meaning) to check on their reading and solve problems. They do not rely on illustrations but use them to enhance understanding, and they can draw information from graphic illustrations in informational texts. They have a range of flexible word-solving strategies and are beginning to read in several different genres. They are beginning to expand their range in reading simple informational texts on topics that are accessible to them. They are also learning to sustain their reading over longer texts, including easy chapter books.
I	Grade One/Grade Two		
J	Grade Two	Grade Two	
K	Grade Two		
L	Grade Two/Grade Three		
M	Grade Two/Grade Three		

Figure 2–4.   Change in Reading Over Time

		Change in Reading Over Time *(continued)*	
F&P LEVEL	**GRADE**	**APPROXIMATE BASAL LEVEL**	**SHIFTS IN THE READING PROCESS**
N	Grade Three	Grade Three	Self-Extending Readers read silently most of the time and are fluent in oral reading. They use all sources of information (word structure, syntax, and meaning) in a smoothly orchestrated way. They can sustain reading over longer texts requiring several days. They enjoy illustrations and use them to enhance comprehension. They analyze words in flexible ways and make excellent attempts at new, multisyllable words, even technical ones. Self-extending readers are in a continuous process of building background knowledge, which they bring to their reading of texts. They have systems for learning more about the reading process, building higher-level skills as they encounter a wide variety of texts. They become absorbed in books and identify with characters; they connect texts with others they read.
O	Grade Three/Grade Four		
P	Grade Three/Grade Four		
Q	Grade Four	Grade Four	
R	Grade Four		
S	Grade Four/Grade Five		Advanced Readers read silently; when asked to read aloud they exhibit fluency phrasing and some expression that reflects their interpretation of the text meaning. They effectively use their understanding of how words work; they employ a wide range of word-solving strategies, including making analogies to known words and using word roots, base words, and affixes. They constantly acquire new vocabulary through reading and use reading as a tool for learning in the content areas. As they read a wide variety of texts, they constantly develop new strategies and knowledge. They consistently go beyond the text to form interpretations and apply understanding to other areas. They are able to sustain interest and understanding over long texts; they read for extended periods of time. They notice and comment on aspects of the writer's craft and read to explore their world, including philosophical, ethical, and social issues. They actively work to connect texts. They develop favorite topics, genres, and authors that form the basis of life-long reading preferences.
T	Grade Four/Grade Five		
U	Grade Five	Grade Five	
V	Grade Five/Grade Six		
W	Grade Five/Grade Six		
X	Grade Six/Grade Seven/Grade Eight	Grade Six	
Y	Grade Six/Grade Seven/Grade Eight	Grade Seven	
Z	Grade Seven/Grade Eight	Grade Eight and Beyond	Middle school and junior high school readers approach adult competency in processing texts, but they are still expanding their content knowledge and their ability to read more sophisticated and complex texts. They have developed strong opinions about their reading. They are aware of and can talk about their tastes and preferences across genres. They have a store of memorable texts that they can draw on while reading. They know writers and have favorites, demonstrating a literate stance.

Figure 2–4. Change in Reading Over Time (continued)

Self-extending readers read silently most of the time, but are fluent and smooth in their oral reading of texts at about levels N through S. They have a broad range of flexible word-solving strategies, although they are still learning more about how words work. They have developed interconnected systems that allow them to expand their reading abilities as they successfully process more difficult and varied texts. Levels N through S contain substantially longer and more complex texts than earlier levels. There is also a greater range of genres. In a sense, texts have become "transparent" for these readers. They are very seldom aware of their own reading processes, but concentrate instead on the meaning and purposes for reading.

Advanced readers are in their final years of elementary school or are reading at the middle school level. Their word-solving abilities approach adult levels, although over the next few years they will become more skilled by delving into the study of words (for example, word roots). Reading texts at levels T through Z, they are required to employ a full range of strategies and to sustain interest and understanding over long periods of time. Through experience, they have increased their rate of reading as well as their ability to make quick connections, predictions, and inferences. They use reading to learn about themselves and their world as they explore important social problems and issues through both fiction and nonfiction. They take on very complex literary texts, such as Lloyd Alexander's works of high fantasy. At the same time, they increase their ability to read a wide variety of nonfiction, and are able to use reading as a tool for learning.

Analyzing the texts at each level of this gradient is a way of increasing your understanding of reading. One of the questions that helps us think about the reading process is: *What does this text require of the reader?* Or, to put it another way: *to read this text with accuracy, fluency, and understanding, the reader must do such-and-such.* So another way a text gradient helps us as teachers is by providing a

kind of road map of the reading process. Learning to read is not a linear process, with one discrete "skill" being learned at a time. It is a matter of developing complex, interrelated systems that can be applied to the reading of increasingly difficult texts. (See Fountas and Pinnell 1996, 2001, 2006.)

Creating a Gradient of Text

To create a leveled collection of books, you evaluate texts against the characteristics established for each level and you also think about the likely levels of reader knowledge. A high-quality literacy program requires thinking about what makes texts difficult in relation to your students and recommending texts for their use. A gradient of text makes it easier for you to select books for readers that meet their needs and allow them to use their strengths.

To create a gradient of text you need to pay attention to all of the factors that contribute to reading difficulty. It means classifying books along a continuum based on the combination of variables that support and confirm readers' strategic actions and offer the problem-solving opportunities that continue to expand the reading process.

Again, the gradient *is not a precise sequence* through which all students move as they progress in their reading development. It is a group of categories arranged in levels of difficulty from which you can select texts that are suitable for groups and individuals. The gradient is not a rigidly defined set of categories. We recognize that a student's background knowledge will vary widely according to the experiences that he or she has had at home, in the community, and in school.

As individuals, readers cannot be strictly categorized (for example, as a "level M reader"). They will be developing reading ability in many dimensions. As they gain reading experience, for example, they learn how texts are organized; they also develop content knowledge as part of their experiences and study. All of this knowledge has an impact on the level of text a student can read, and it does so *differentially*. In other words, for an individual student, background experience will affect reading level. Any given student will probably feel comfortable reading a range of levels independently. This range is based on the reader's background knowledge, general understanding of vocabulary, experience in reading texts with different structures, experience in reading different genres, and interests.

Your expertise in understanding your students will also be a factor in helping students begin to take control of their own reading development. For example, we want students to learn how to select texts that they:

- will enjoy.
- can read with understanding and fluency.
- can read with confidence and competence.
- will increase their content and literary knowledge.
- will expand the range of genres that they read and enjoy.
- will help them understand themselves and their worlds.

The gradient is a classification system—nothing more. At the risk of presenting simplistic metaphors, we ask you to think about articles of clothing. In general, you probably have a size that you start with when shopping for clothes. As you start trying on garments, however, you may find that you need a smaller or larger size depending on the style, cut, fabric, and type of clothing. You can wear some more close fitting garments and you'll want some particular pieces to be loose fitting. In addition, you may have preferences based on color, personal image, or texture. Finally, particular kinds of clothing are worn on particular occasions. Even with all these variations, however, we still need to consider a basic "size range."

This size range is analogous to the gradient of text. Bottom line, no matter how interested students are in the topic, the text must be within a range that is accessible to them. No matter how engaging a plot or character might be, the reader must be able to access the information in the print. So when you consider text difficulty, be aware of the limitations and make cautious selections. Test decisions against students' reading behaviors (as you sample oral reading), their conversation about texts, and their evidence of understanding in written responses.

Factual and Fiction Texts Along the Gradient

We use this gradient to categorize both fiction and factual texts. These genres pose different challenges for students. Examining fiction is likely to require looking at features such as plot complexity, literary language and devices, multisyllable words, poetic vocabulary, character development, and sophistication of the problem or theme.

When examining nonfiction texts, you look at slightly different factors. Vocabulary will always be a concern, but here the difficulty may be related not just to the length or connotations of a word but to its technical meaning. Nonfiction texts often incorporate the language of a particular discipline to communicate information. Also, nonfiction is likely to be organized in sections or chapters, each focusing on a different topic (rather than a "story"). It may include graphic features that communicate some of the meaning and must be examined. Factual texts present particular difficulties to students because of the amount of "content" and the number of organizational features; that is why it is hard to find appropriate informational books for children who are just beginning to build a reading process. Factual texts can be deceptive, so it is important to look closely at the particular features that challenge young readers. It is perfectly possible for the same reader to find a longer chapter book of fiction quite a bit easier than a short informational text, and that is true of adults as well.

In placing fiction and nonfiction along the gradient of difficulty, we considered a wide range of features for both genres. These features are described in depth in Chapter 3. However, if we are to use a common gradient to support our work in guided reading, levels must be consistent for both fiction and nonfiction. In other words, a G is a G, regardless of genre. A factual text may at first glance *look* easier than a fiction text at the same level but nonetheless be of comparable difficulty.

Getting Started

You can create a gradient using the books that are available in your school. We engaged in a process that took place over many years, with primary-level teams working first and intermediate and middle-level teams joining the work. Here's the process we used to level books:

1. We gathered a selection of books to consider for elementary and middle school students. We also included some "short reads," or short stories at intermediate and middle school levels.

2. Then we convened "leveling teams" composed of expert teachers of literacy. The groups selected those books they thought were appropriate for including in the collection for guided reading.

3. Working together, we read, discussed, and placed books in groups by difficulty and talked about the characteristics of each of the books, focusing on characteristics such as:
   - Genre and format.
   - Structure or text organization.
   - Content.
   - Themes and ideas.
   - Language and literary features.
   - Sentence complexity.
   - Vocabulary.
   - Words to decode.
   - Illustration support.
   - Print features such as layout.

4. We selected several prototype texts for each level we had identified and created some formal descriptions for each group. We tried to include fiction and nonfiction among the prototypes and thought about what the texts require of the reader as well as how the texts offered support.

5. Teams of teachers tested the prototypes with students at several grade levels.

6. We reconvened the teams and shared our observations of students' reading behaviors while reading and discussing the various texts. We found that we needed to make some adjustments in our prototypes.

7. We eliminated some texts and selected others, and then started comparing a larger group of texts against the prototypes, creating categories.

8. We tested the prototypes again, meanwhile adding to the texts in each category along the gradient.

9. Over the next several years, the leveling teams met periodically to reevaluate the prototypes and place texts within the various level categories. The reexamination and adjusting of levels of particular books is an ongoing process (see the form in Appendix 3).

10. Within categories along the gradient, we sorted texts by genre and discussed the range of texts within each level to assure variety.

Prototypes and Benchmarks

A useful prototype or benchmark text is one that you have tested again and again and that has proved to be highly reliable and stable for the level. It is a book that will be appropriate for the large majority of students who are demonstrating similar behaviors at a certain point in time. It can serve as a benchmark against which other books can be compared, and it can also be helpful in assessing students' reading so that you can find other books for them.

Assessing students' reading levels requires sampling oral reading and also some conversation with the student about the text. Accuracy is part of the picture. The foundation of reading at any level or in any genre is being able to process the print with an acceptable level of accuracy; but accuracy seems to be a *contingent* factor, meaning that it is necessary *but not sufficient* for comprehension. We all know that sometimes students can say the words but don't understand what they read; certainly, however, they cannot understand if they cannot read the words.

There are a number of ways besides accuracy that you will want to consider when assessing whether students understand what they read. You may use the range of assessment procedures we describe in other texts (Fountas and Pinnell 2001, 2006). Day to day, however, you will want to gather evidence of understanding by:

- Observing what kinds of information from the text readers use as they read aloud.

- Observing how students talk with one another about the texts.

- Observing how readers work to make meaning as they process a text.

- Examining the kinds of comments and questions students share in reading conferences and group share.

- Looking at what students write about their reading.

- Involving students in analysis and critique.

- Talking with students about their interests and responses.

- Observing phrasing and fluency in oral reading.

As you gather information about the way students respond to texts, you will also be gaining insight into text difficulty.

The prototypes or benchmarks that you identify can be integrated into a more formal assessment system that will help you group students initially for guided reading. (See Fountas and Pinnell 2001, 2006, conference protocols.) First, select a passage of about 200 words from a benchmark text to use for assessment. Next, while the student reads the passage, note accuracy and other important aspects of reading behavior such as repeats and self-corrections. Then have a discussion or ask the student some questions that prompt literal recall as well as draw out inferences and predictions about what will happen next or what information one is likely to find in the text. Answers to those questions will provide important evidence about how well the student comprehended the text. The student's written response will provide added information.

Ten Suggestions for Creating a High-Quality Leveled Collection

1. Purchase texts from a variety of publishers.

2. Select texts that do not have racial or cultural stereotypes.

3. Include texts by a widely diverse group of authors.

4. Select books by authors who are popular with students.

5. Include books on topics that are interesting to today's students.

6. Include a variety of fiction genres.

7. Include informational texts with a variety of organizational structures and on a variety of topics.

8. Select books that have high-quality illustrations and interesting and useful graphic features.

9. Include many short stories or texts that can be read in one session.

10. Select some books in series that have the same characters and/or topics.

Figure 2–5. Ten Suggestions for Creating a High-Quality Leveled Collection

Assuring High Quality in the Leveled Text Collection

The leveled books your students read, like the other texts that support your literacy program, should be of high quality. Because a book is leveled does not mean it is a good book. The important work you do with students in guided reading depends on the suitability and variety of the titles available. In Figure 2–5, we suggest ten principles to keep in mind as you create your leveled collection.

In addition, it is essential for students to enjoy their reading. Upper elementary and middle school students are unlikely to be motivated to read simply to "practice" reading. They need texts that not only are accessible to them but that pique their interest and give them something enjoyable and important to talk and think about afterward.

A Universal Gradient

As we have worked with classroom and school collections, it has become increasingly clear that no one publisher can supply the great variety of texts needed. Publishers offer many different kinds of books and some have created their own leveling systems. You will want to check levels that publishers give their own books with those on our list if you want to use books leveled with the characteristics we describe.

What we provide here is a "universal gradient," one that allows you to select and level texts from a wide range of publishers. We encourage you to get to know the characteristics in our leveling system and then add new books as you get to know them. You can also suggest titles for us to level or level changes using the form in Appendix X or at *fountasandpinellleveledbooks.com*. Bringing your own thinking to categorizing texts has several benefits:

- You will think deeply about the characteristics of texts.

- You will become more skillful at analyzing texts for the supports and challenges they offer the readers in your classes.

- In the process, you will find that you are also preparing to introduce texts, discuss them with students, and support them in comprehending texts.

Selecting high-quality texts and organizing them into a gradient of difficulty allows you to create your own instructional sequences. Since students expand their processing systems by meeting the demands of increasingly difficult texts, your selections are very important. There will be better and weaker books illustrating various text characteristics. The important thing is to provide high-quality texts that support the development of literacy.

Remember that the task of finding good books is ongoing. The collection is always being revised; you add excellent books as you find them and remove books that are less effective. You will select a relatively limited number of books for guided reading. Those selections should be the ones with the strongest potential to achieve your goals.

Summary

The concept of a gradient of text is based on the way in which children build a reading process. This helpful "ladder" is a tool with many benefits; the most important is to provide appropriate texts for guided reading. In the process of creating a text gradient, you will find yourself delving into texts and noticing aspects that you may have missed before. This deep look at texts will help you talk with your students about texts and support their learning.

Suggestions for Professional Development: Analyzing Texts

1. Work with colleagues to begin exploring texts that you plan to include in the leveled collection. You'll find that you bring a great deal of expertise to the process. (This beginning examination will ground your thinking as you work with the text leveling process in Chapter 3.)

2. Ask each member of your grade-level group to bring to a meeting five books that are just about right for most readers in that grade at your school, paying attention to variety in difficulty and genre. All books should have been read by the person who brings them.

3. Working as a whole group or in pairs, look at each text. Ask:

   Meaning
   - What information do readers need to bring to the text in order to read it with understanding? (Think about personal knowledge, world knowledge, and literary knowledge.)
   - Are there places in the text that are likely to lead to confusion? If so, what strategies will readers need to resolve the confusion?
   - How appropriate is the content for the level?

   Language
   - Are there language structures in the text that students may never have heard or said before?
   - Are there long and/or complex sentences that will be challenging?

   - Are there idioms that may make understanding difficult?
   - Is there literary or technical language that will be challenging?
   - Are there vocabulary words that are challenging and essential to the meaning?

   Organization
   - Are there any challenges in the way the text is organized?
   - Does the print layout assist readers?
   - Are there graphic features that readers will have to examine and get information from?

   Words
   - What word-solving challenges does this text provide?
   - How many new vocabulary words will the reader encounter?
   - Does the text contain words that students know but must understand in new ways (word connotations) in order to comprehend the text?
   - Are there multisyllable words that students will need to break apart and relate to other words or parts of words that they know?

4. Use these questions to prompt a good discussion of texts and identify the characteristics that you will need to know about in order to select and introduce texts effectively. Once you have had this discussion, try placing the texts along a continuum of difficulty. It may help to consider your grade level and decide which would be best for most students at the beginning of the year, which in the middle of the year, and which toward the end of the year.

CHAPTER THREE

A COMPREHENSIVE AND EFFECTIVE LITERACY CURRICULUM

Students do not develop sophisticated reading and writing systems by receiving one, or even two-dimensional instruction. They need to process texts across many different learning contexts. In this chapter, we briefly describe a range of language and literacy contexts across the elementary and middle school grades. The framework is described in great detail in these books:

- *Guided Reading: Good First Teaching for All Children.*

- *Guiding Readers and Writers: Teaching for Comprehension, Genre, and Content Literacy.*

- *Teaching for Comprehending and Fluency (K–8): Thinking, Talking, and Writing about Reading.*

- *A Continuum of Reading Progress, K–8*

Goals of a Language and Literacy Program

Normally, we don't develop skill in doing something we dislike. A high-quality literacy program is designed to help students expand their reading skill and at the same time build their interest in and love for books. Becoming a good reader requires thousands of hours of engaged reading. It means coming to know authors and illustrators in a variety of genres, developing readerly tastes, and gaining a wide range of skills while refining literate knowledge and growing in confidence as a reader.

Within a broad language and literacy framework designed to support student learning in reading, writing, and word study books assume a key role in five instructional reading contexts: interactive read-aloud, independent reading, guided reading, literature study (book clubs), and investigations or research. Big books or enlarged picture books will be key in shared reading. A teacher's understanding of leveled books is particularly helpful in independent and guided reading.

Components of a Language/Literacy Framework

The integrated elements of a comprehensive language and literacy framework work together to develop broad-based and effective reading, writing, thinking, and speaking skills.

As shown in Figure 3–1, we conceptualize this framework within three blocks of time, which may be scheduled anywhere within the school day.

Transitions Across Time

The way you create and apply these instructional contexts will vary according to the needs of your students and the demands of your schedule. Looking across the grades there are some important transitions across time.

Across kindergarten and early grade one, children are learning how print "works," as well as how to monitor and check their reading through using early understandings about letter-sound relationships. They need short, easy-to-understand texts so that they can concentrate on these

A Comprehensive Language and Literacy Framework

Grades K–2		Grades 2–6		Grades 6–8	
LANGUAGE/WORD STUDY		**LANGUAGE/WORD STUDY**		**LANGUAGE/WORD STUDY**	
30–45 minutes	*Select from:* ❖ Interactive Read-Aloud ❖ Modeled/Shared Reading ❖ Phonics/Word Study/Handwriting Lesson	**30–45 minutes**	*Select from:* ❖ Interactive Read-Aloud ❖ Model/Shared Reading ❖ Poetry Sharing/Response ❖ Readers Theater/Process Drama ❖ Choral Reading ❖ Interactive Vocabulary ❖ Interactive Edit ❖ Handwriting ❖ Current Events ❖ Test Reading & Writing ❖ Word Study Lesson/Application/Share	**as time allows**	*Select from:* ❖ Interactive Read-Aloud ❖ Poetry Sharing/Response ❖ Interactive Vocabulary ❖ Interactive Edit ❖ Test Reading & Writing ❖ Word Study Lesson/Application/Share
READING WORKSHOP				**READING WORKSHOP**	
60–90 minutes	❖ Guided Reading ❖ Independent Work ▪ Reading ▪ Writing ▪ Word Study ▪ Sharing			**as time allows**	❖ Independent Reading ❖ Guided Reading ❖ Literature Study
		READING WORKSHOP		**WRITING WORKSHOP**	
WRITING WORKSHOP		**60 minutes**	*Select from:* ❖ Independent Reading ❖ Guided Reading ❖ Literature Study	**as time allows**	❖ Independent Writing ❖ Guided Writing ❖ Investigations
30–45 minutes	❖ Minilesson ❖ Interactive/Guided or Independent Writing and Conferring ❖ Sharing	**WRITING WORKSHOP**			
		60 minutes	*Select from:* ❖ Independent Writing ❖ Guided Writing ❖ Investigations		

Figure 3–1. A Comprehensive Language and Literacy Framework

important learnings, but they soon become fluent readers of much longer texts. They need to read and reread many texts and talk to others about their reading. By second grade, they have made the important transition to silent reading and can hold much more in memory so that they can sus-tain reading over longer periods of time. They can do much more writing about their reading and expand their knowledge of genres. Over the next four years, they will use a full range of strategies to process a wide variety of short and longer texts. Complex thinking will be required.

One of the best ways to support your students in making these transitions over time is to become an expert analyzer and selector of texts. Children are, in fact, working their way up a "ladder of support" (Clay 1991) when they read books of slightly increasing difficulty along a gradient of text. Your teaching enables them to reach out further than they could without your support. While our educational system is organized into "grades," readers' progress is actually continual. While they do gradually go "up the levels," the progress is not completely linear. Students may read more difficult texts when the content or text organization is quite familiar; yet, in a new topic area they may drop down to an easier text. And it is true that avid readers tend to read both challenging and easy texts for different reasons. The key is to provide many opportunities to think, talk, and write about reading.

Language/Word Study

The language and word study block consists of a number of instructional techniques from which you may select according to the needs of your students and the curriculum in your district. Most teachers place higher priority on large, uninterrupted blocks of time for reading workshop and writing workshop and use smaller time segments for the types of activities in this block. All activities include learning more about oral and written language, and generally include the whole class in a community meeting. Brief descriptions of these activities are presented below:

INTERACTIVE READ-ALOUD

Reading aloud is a key to effective instruction across grade levels. In *interactive read-aloud*, you read to *and discuss* with students a large range of high-quality fiction and nonfiction texts. By reading texts aloud, you provide the opportunity for students to notice literary elements, build vocabulary and background knowledge, and expand their comprehension of texts that may be too difficult for many of them to process entirely on their own.

The term *interactive* characterizes the quality of the learning: as you read, you are, in effect, having a brief conversation with students around the ideas in the text. This conversation before, during, and after reading the text supports their understanding.

SHARED/MODELED READING

In *modeled/shared reading*, the entire group either follows along as you read aloud (sometimes making comments about your problem-solving as you go) or reads a text together. The print is large so all can view it. You support the reading and engage the students in processing it.

MODELED/SHARED/INTERACTIVE WRITING

In *modeled/shared writing*, you demonstrate writing for the group or act as their scribe as you guide them in composing a common text related to an experience, a piece of literature, or a subject in the curriculum. Modeled/shared writing is a chance to let students in on the problem solving that writers do relative to genre, word choice, organization, punctuation, spelling, etc. *Interactive writing*, in which children participate intensively by "sharing the pen" with the teacher at key points in the text, is an important activity for children in grades K and one and is also helpful in small-group work in later grades (see McCarrier, Pinnell, and Fountas 1999).

POETRY SHARING/RESPONSE

In *poetry sharing/response*, you or the students read and discuss poetry. Sometimes they select poems to read or they memorize and recite a special favorite. The focus is on talking about what appeals to individuals about poems, what students notice about the writing or what the poem makes them think about.

READERS' THEATER/PROCESS DRAMA

In *readers' theater and process drama*, students assume roles based on problems or issues they have encountered in their content area study or literature. In readers' theater, two or more students read a text or piece of text aloud, usually taking roles as the characters or narrator. The piece is first selected and practiced and then performed. Process drama is less about performance and more about assuming identities and roles over time. It usually involves reading and research and may involve writing, but the emphasis is on living through a vicarious experience that helps students understand the world and themselves at a new level.

CHORAL READING/READERS' THEATER

Choral reading is the rehearsed recitation of written language, either prose or poetry. It may grow from shared reading of texts as students read particular parts in unison or solo and work to use their voices to show their interpretations. In readers' theater, students use a script to perform roles from a text. The goal is for readers to interpret the text with their voices.

INTERACTIVE VOCABULARY

In *interactive vocabulary* students study word meanings. A short, focused lesson helps students solve the meaning of new words or associate words by their meanings. You may make a chart for students for reference as they read or write.

INTERACTIVE EDIT

In an *interactive edit*, you focus briefly on the conventions of language (capitalization, punctuation, grammar, spelling, word choice) by asking students to consider a few sentences that require editing. They try editing on their own and then the group shares the final edit.

HANDWRITING

Handwriting is a quick lesson on any aspect of handwriting, followed by focused practice.

CURRENT EVENTS

Current events is a way of helping students build interest in the world about them. A brief discussion of current events every day or every week creates the habit of noticing issues relative to the environment or science or politics. Students can prepare brief presentations on current events, and you can also provide guidelines for talking and writing about them.

TEST READING AND WRITING

In *test reading and writing*, you acquaint your students with the "genre" of tests, because tests often require them to use language in tricky and unexpected ways. You lead quick, lively practice sessions in which you help the students solve representative test items and support their work with demonstration and conversation. For an entire chapter on test reading and writing, see *Guiding Readers and Writers: Teaching for Comprehension, Genre, and Content Literacy.*

WORD STUDY

Word study is the systematic process whereby you help students learn the rules and principles of phonics and spelling. You present a minilesson on any spelling pattern, rule, or concept that will help students understand a specific spelling principle, and then have the students apply the principle (often by manipulating magnetic letters or letter tiles). The word study system described in detail in Pinnell and Fountas (1999, 2004) involves five days of planned activity for developing a set of spelling strategies. In a minilesson exploring a particular principle on day 1, students are guided to select six to ten words that exemplify an important principle and the same number from their words-to-learn list in their writing folders. On day one, they write their words on a study card and then make them with magnetic letters. On day two, they use "look, say, cover, write, check," an established word-study technique. Day three is a buddy check; after a practice test, students highlight parts of words that they do not know accurately and study them. On day four, students make connections between the words they are studying and many other words; the connections may involve a visual pattern, may be meaning-related, or may relate to letter-sound relationships. On day five, there is a test that is checked by the teacher.

Learning Across Contexts

Components of the language/word study block work together to help students understand how written language works. In interactive edit, modeled/shared writing, interactive vocabulary, handwriting, and word study, they look closely at the details of written language by studying words and word parts. Word study connections, as well as vocabulary, contribute to reading comprehension. Interactive read-aloud, modeled/shared reading, poetry sharing/response, readers theater and process drama, choral reading, and test reading and writing (as genre study) contribute overall to students' ability to process and understand continuous texts.

Reading Workshop

The reading workshop block is a laboratory in which students engage in the kind of reading that real readers do. They learn how to work together as a community as they think, talk, read, and write about topics that interest them. They take responsibility for their own growth in reading. During reading workshop, students are engaged in one of three activities, described below.

PRIMARY GRADES

The reading workshop for grades K and one is largely devoted to small-group (guided reading) and independent work and requires about ninety minutes of time. For a description of guided reading, see the next section. Children may engage in quiet reading, writing, or word study at their desks or work in literacy centers while you work with children in small guided reading groups using leveled texts.

INTERMEDIATE GRADES/MIDDLE SCHOOL

By grade two, most children are reading silently and can sustain reading and writing for longer periods of time. You can gradually transition to a full reading workshop structure that requires about sixty minutes and includes the following:

■ *Book Talk/Minilesson.* The reading workshop block begins with a whole-group meeting during which you:

❖ Give a brief "book talk"—introduce a new book or point out books you think students will find interesting. Students may jot down interesting titles on their Books to Read list in their reader's notebook.

❖ Present a minilesson on some aspect of reading that most students need to work on.

■ *Independent Reading.* Following the book talk and minilesson, students read independently and silently for about forty to fifty minutes, usually texts they've selected themselves. (Later in this chapter you will read about guided reading and literature discussion, which are also options for this time.) They also write in their reader's notebooks once a week. During any given week students write one thoughtful letter to you, which you answer. (You can manage this by responding to one fourth of the class each day, Monday through Thursday.) If you have an unusually large class, you may want to respond every two weeks to each reader. The questions and comments you pose in this written interaction prompt students to think more deeply about texts. You may also consider other forms of writing about reading that enable students to share their thinking, such as notes, a sketch, a focused paragraph, a book review, or a literary essay. (See Fountas and Pinnell 2006.) While the students are reading and/or writing, you confer with individuals, supporting their understanding, stretching their thinking, and making observations that will guide your teaching.

■ *Sharing and Evaluation.* At the end of the reading workshop block, you and your students meet again to revisit the minilesson, share insights and experiences, or call attention to specific points from the written responses. Students might "turn and talk" to share their thinking in pairs or triads, or each may have a turn to comment. The goal is to reinforce and extend students' thinking. This meeting is brief—every student won't share his or her thinking every day—but it is a way to reinforce and extend.

Maintaining the proper classroom atmosphere during independent reading is important. Students read silently without talking to one another. The only sounds are whispered conferences between teacher and individual students or the low voices of students working in small groups for guided reading or literature discussion with the teacher. The idea is to provide a time for sustained, engaged reading every day (or four out of the five days, devoting one day to a workshop for reading, writing, discussing, and performing poetry).

GUIDED READING

Guided reading is the heart of the literacy process. While students are reading independently and silently or working at centers, you can pull together a small group for guided reading. Guided reading is small-group instruction designed to expand each student's ability to process a text with understanding and fluency. Guided Reading groups are homogenous. The students in the group are at a similar stage in their development of reading and have similar needs. With teacher support, they read about the same level of text with accuracy and understanding. These kinds of groupings are flexible and change often, making them different from traditional reading groups. Guided reading groups are ongoing as you introduce texts that gradually increase the challenge to students. At the middle school level, you may want to conduct guided reading lessons with the children who are not performing at grade level.

You select a text that offers the group of students opportunities for problem solving and new learning. The text should be one that will be accessible, *with teacher support*. The gradient of increasing difficulty, discussed further in Chapter 2, helps you select the appropriate leveled texts. The selection is always made with the particular readers in mind, however.

As indicated in Figure 3–2, guided reading lessons have a consistent structure: (1) the teacher introduces the text (or a unified part of it); (2) students read the text, sometimes with teacher support and interaction; (3) teacher and students revisit the text after reading to discuss the meaning; (4) specific processing strategies are taught; (5) the meaning of the text is extended through writing, drawing, and discussion or other means [optional]; and (6) word work takes place [optional]. Guided reading with upper elementary/middle school students needs variety. It must include both fiction and nonfiction texts, some that are long and some that are short (see Figure 3–3). Indeed, one of the goals of guided reading is to broaden students' repertoires as readers.

Structure of Guided Reading

❖ Introducing the Text
❖ Reading the Text
❖ Discussing and Revisiting the Text
❖ Teaching for Processing Strategies
❖ Extending the Meaning [optional]
❖ Word Work [optional]

Figure 3–2. Structure of Guided Reading

Variety of Texts in Guided Reading

❖ Realistic Fiction
❖ Historical Fiction
❖ Fantasy and Science Fiction
❖ Traditional Literature—Folktales, fables, Myths, Legends
❖ Biography
❖ Informational Books

Figure 3–3. Variety of Texts in Guided Reading

Your text introduction supports students' comprehension and problem solving as they each read the text independently. You may introduce an entire text (a longer chapter book, for example), and assign students a unified part of it, or you may introduce one section at a time and have students read and discuss each section over consecutive days. You will also often use "short reads" (short stories) for guided reading lessons.

While the students are reading, you may want to sample some oral reading so that you can monitor individual processing. This is not necessary in every lesson. For the most part, students beyond kindergarten or grade one should be reading a text silently. Simply ask the individual to begin reading aloud for a short time at your signal. You can also prompt problem solving or draw attention to some aspect of the text that will help a student increase his reading powers. You can demonstrate effective reading strategies and prompt students to use those you have already taught them. These brief interactions give you a great deal of information:

- Whether the text level is appropriate.
- What aspects of the text students are reading fluently.
- Which aspects of processing students need further instruction in.
- Whether the group's next selection should be more difficult, easier, or at about the same level.
- Whether to revise group membership.
- How well each reader is understanding the text.

After reading, you revisit the text with students to discuss what they have understood and to deepen comprehension. They may talk about characters and why they do what they do or may discuss the plot and why it was exciting, interesting, or scary. They may offer opinions or make hypotheses and return to the text to cite evidence. You will also want to do some specific teaching based on your observations of students' reading behaviors over time. These teaching points provide explicit instruction that will expand students' reading ability at the word or text level.

You may want to extend the meaning of some texts through additional discussion or writing. Occasionally, you may use a graphic organizer to help students connect or compare ideas and concepts. If students need to develop stronger control of letters, sounds, and words, at the end of the guided reading lesson you may want to introduce very explicit word work geared specifically to what they need to know. You might use magnetic letters or a dry-erase whiteboard to explore words and how they are related structurally (endings, beginnings, middle parts, letter clusters, syllables) (see Pinnell & Fountas 1999).

LITERATURE STUDY

At the intermediate and middle school level, literature study groups (book clubs) may also meet while the rest of the class is involved in independent, silent reading. In contrast to guided reading, literature study is intended to involve students in mixed, or heterogeneous groups. Groups are brought together to engage in extended discussion of an age-appropriate text. Literature study is variously called *book club, literature circle, literature discussion group,* or *response group.* Whatever the name, the purpose is to enable readers to develop a deeper understanding of the texts they read. Literature study helps students become aware of the writer's craft in structuring and organizing a text as well as in using language.

There are several ways to organize book clubs. Literature study may be structured around the texts you use for interactive read-aloud; or students may select a text they want to discuss, set a time for discussion, and then read it during independent and home reading. You may select a text and assign it to a group; or you may give a brief book talk on a number of choices, ask students to sign up for their first, second, and third choices, and configure the groups based on these lists.

You'll want to set up assigned reading/writing tasks as well as meeting times. After that your initial role is to facilitate literature discussion groups and teach students effective routines for interaction and in-depth discussion. Over time, you will become more of an observer as students learn how to facilitate the group for themselves. You want the students to talk to one another, not just answer your questions; your role is to "lift" the discussion by modeling thoughtful responses and helping students get to the significant, worthwhile issues in high-quality texts. There may also be written responses or a culminating project (see Fountas and Pinnell 2001, 2006).

Text difficulty should not be a factor in keeping students from discussing a book of their choice. Even if a text is too hard for a student to read independently, she can still understand and discuss it after listening to it on tape or hearing it read by the teacher, a parent, or a buddy.

Managing Interrelationships Within the Reading Workshop

The three components of reading workshop are interconnected. What students learn as readers in one context informs their reading in another context. Sometimes one moves into another. A literary text used for guided reading may become the text for an in-depth literature discussion. Students who have read a certain text in independent reading (and responded to it in their notebooks) may sign up to discuss it as a work of literature. Even if students are reading a different text in each of the three settings, there will be related concepts and intertextual connections. Students in literature study who are exploring flashback as a literary device may offer examples from books in their independent reading. Students who encounter an author in guided reading may be prompted to remember a text that they discussed during literature study.

Since intermediate and middle school students are reading at least thirty minutes every day

in reading workshop and thirty minutes each evening for homework, *and* they are reading texts they can read with ease and fluency, they are expected to get through a lot of material. On average, students complete about one chapter book or several shorter books in a week. Students can keep more than one book going at a time, although you will want to minimize the number of books being read. They will always be reading an independent book and may be reading a text in either guided reading or literature study. When you are planning to begin work with a group of students in guided reading or in a book club, let them know they should finish up their independent book as home reading.

Writing Workshop

The structure for writing workshop is similar to that for reading workshop. For both primary and intermediate grades, the structure consists of:

1. A brief minilesson on any aspect of the writing process, management of the workshop, skills, and strategies or craft;
2. Independent writing during which you confer with individuals; and
3. A short sharing period in which you meet with the large group to share progress, reinforce the principle of the minilesson, and evaluate the session.

It is helpful to use "mentor texts" that you have read aloud to help students understand the writer's craft. By the intermediate and middle school level, students will be familiar with many writers and you may want to provide a brief "writer's talk," to help them develop insights into the way professional writers work. You may take a "status of the class" to find out the progress each student is making on his writing piece(s).

While most students are writing independently, you bring together small, temporary groups of writers who need a focused look at particular skills and strategies or aspects of craft. This approach allows you, very efficiently, to focus on what one group needs without wasting the time of others. The particular groupings will be based on your observations of students *while they are writing* and your evaluation of their written drafts.

Investigations are inquiry projects at the intermediate and middle school level that allow students to explore topics in depth. Both reading and writing are involved; students usually work individually but may work in pairs or small groups from time to time. Investigations are a way to integrate content areas; students may be researching subjects related to science, social studies, or any other area—even literature. You provide guidelines, a structure, and a timeline for projects; you also provide instruction and meet with individuals and groups as needed. Projects involve reading and writing informational texts and utilizing technology.

The Role of Text

Across all of their instructional contexts, texts play a critical and foundational role in expanding your students power to:

- Learn new ways of using language.
- Express ideas through discussion.
- Acquire new concepts and vocabulary.
- Get to know a variety of authors.
- Explore different genres.

Through the texts they hear read aloud, students have access to language and ideas that are usually more complex than those in the texts they read for themselves, and engaging in rich discussions helps them extend their understanding.

Students also need to engage with texts that they can process independently. A large amount of independent reading is essential for creating skilled, strategic readers. And finally, to constantly expand their abilities, they need the challenge of taking on more difficult texts and, with teacher support, processing them with deeper understanding. In the next chapter, we describe a variety of texts needed to support this learning.

Suggestions for Professional Development: Evaluating Text Reading Opportunities

1. Invite colleagues to come to a meeting with an estimate of the amount and variety of reading students do across instructional contexts over a month's time.

2. Divide into grade-level groups to compare notes and share perspectives. Do some brainstorming to come up with ideas for increasing the amount of engagement with texts (include interactive read aloud).

3. Have participants look across daily and weekly schedules to see where reading is occurring.

4. Set some goals for yearly engagement with texts (amount of reading) for the year.

5. Schedule a follow-up meeting later in the year to reflect on whether students have increased the amount of reading they have accomplished.

CHAPTER FOUR

THE TEXT BASE FOR AN EFFECTIVE LANGUAGE AND LITERACY PROGRAM

An effective literacy program rests on a foundation of good materials, and those materials are books: that is, books to be used by the knowledgeable teacher and books to be selected by students. Classroom libraries that brim with books foster a multitude of learning opportunities through picture books, novels, and short stories that include a range of literature and content. Libraries should include a variety of fiction and informational books, poetry, and children's magazines. They should include informational books, historical fiction, realistic fiction, biography, autobiography, memoirs, folktales and fairy tales, fantasy, and science fiction. Books organized in baskets by author, topic, genre, series, award label, and inclusive of a range of difficulty levels provide a rich text base for independent reading.

If we are serious about high literacy achievement, then we must be certain that our classroom materials offer the richest learning opportunities possible. That goal leads us back to books. Books are a one-time expense and the staple of a literate life. They are less costly than many of the commercial literacy "kits" or sets of materials we typically find on the market that quickly become outdated. Teachers can use and adapt books in multiple ways. Books are always available to the learner and do not require additional equipment or mechanical maintenance. Moreover, the enjoyment that children derive from exploring books sets the stage for a lifetime love of reading

Our goal is to help teachers develop and use a set of "leveled" books, books that have been analyzed in terms of how they support and challenge young readers as they learn how to read increasingly challenging texts and that have been organized in a gradient of difficulty. They are an important component of the materials teachers need to support literacy learning across instructional contexts.

The Classroom Collection of Books

The classroom resources support all the activities defined as components of the language and literacy framework. You will want a broad and varied collection of books that:

1. Expand students' literary experiences through interactive read-aloud and literature discussion.
2. Support investigations and inquiry in a variety of content areas.
3. Support independent reading.
4. Support guided reading instruction.

Only the fourth category will be "leveled" for the teacher's use in guided reading lessons. A rich classroom collection will include beautifully illustrated picture books, many kinds of novels, informational books, magazines and journals, newspapers, and other kinds of reading material that are not leveled for students' use in independent reading.

Books to Expand Students' Text Experience Through Interactive Read-Aloud and Literature Discussion

It is essential to have a good variety of books to read to students. High-quality picture books can usually be finished in a single setting. The illustrations offer further opportunity for students to interpret the texts and add to the enjoyment. Select picture books from the wide range that are available and appropriate for children at your grade level. Using picture books, you can:

- Build background and literary knowledge.

- Model the range of possibilities in the craft and process of writing.

- Explore language and vocabulary.

- Provide information on a topic.

- Introduce and develop understanding of a variety of genres (such as biography or question/answer books).

- Increase students' knowledge of an author's or illustrator's style.

- Build up a group of texts students can compare with one another and with the texts they encounter in guided and independent reading.

- Build a set of "mentor texts" to use in minilessons.

Many picture books are available in paperback, but you should also have lots of hardbound editions. Covered with clear plastic (which you can order through library supply catalogs), these volumes will last for many years. Properly and accessibly displayed, picture books invite students to read. If you can, store these books on shelves so that the covers face out, making it easier for students to find and revisit them (see Figures 4–1 and 4–2). Also, students can flip through a number of titles kept in a basket, looking at the covers easily, without having to pull out each one from a shelf.

Picture books are needed at all grade levels. A great many sophisticated picture books, in a variety of genres, are appropriate for intermediate and middle grades. Think of picture books as short stories with beautiful art. They can be read in a single sitting and offer rich meaning through the words and art.

You will also want to read some carefully selected chapter books. Texts that offer rich opportunities for discussion and follow-up will extend students' ability to understand and read longer texts. It's best to vary the experiences and explore as many different texts as possible. You will also want to read poetry aloud and have students read poetry for themselves. Poetry and prose texts can also form the basis for shared reading, choral reading, and readers' theater.

Books to Expand Students' Literary Experiences Through Independent Reading

All students need the opportunity to select their own books and build their tastes as readers. Reading aloud, independent reading, and litera-

Figure 4-1   Picture Books Displayed in a Classroom

Figure 4–2. Picture Books Displayed in a Classroom

ture study offer the chance to experience a wide range and large quantity of texts. Students need to learn how to:

- Select books.

- Vary their reading repertoire.

- Compare books.

- Discover the kinds of books they like.

- Consciously work to expand their tastes.

- Get to know a range of authors, illustrators, and genres.

- Talk with others about books.

As we discussed earlier, book talks are very brief introductions, like short commercials that whet the readers' appetites. Through book talks you raise students' interest in high-quality books. As with the picture books, make books available to students in a variety of ways. After they learn how, students can also give book talks.

As shown in Figure 4–3, you can organize books in tubs or baskets labeled by author, topic, or category:

- Series books.

- Biographies, historical fiction, science fiction, or other genres.

- Books by certain authors or illustrators.

- Short stories.

- Books about a specific topic (the human body, the Holocaust, space).

- Caldecott or Newbery Medal, social studies or other honor books (*Amelia Bedelia, Little House*).

Students will be interested in books because the books are written by their favorite authors or because they like adventure stories, not because they want to read a "level T" book. Students may notice the letter labels you place on the front or back cover or write inside the cover of a book for your reference. You can explain to the students that they need not pay attention to these letters as they are for you, not them. Explain that they help you think about how to help them become better readers.

You can also make a rack of "book recommendations," inviting students to make selections and including some of your own (see Figure 4–4). However you go about it, displaying books invites students to examine them and place them on their Books to Read list for future reading.

Books to Support Investigation and Inquiry

You will want to have a wide variety of books that help students expand their understanding of specific content areas. We have mentioned that many beautifully illustrated picture books provide information in interesting ways.

Reference books on various topics should also be part of the classroom collection. These books are not always intended to be read from beginning to end; rather, readers look up the information they need. Informational texts to support inquiry can be placed in the center in which they will be used. For example, books on the human body or rocks can be located in the science area. Topics that are included in the required curriculum may be clustered together and labeled. Even if students can't read everything in these informational texts, you can help them find the information they need; they can wrestle with a small section in an attempt to answer a particular question. You will want to have resources such as dictionaries, encyclopedias, and thesauruses handy as well.

Have a good supply of magazines as part of the classroom collection. Excellent resources such as *Cobblestone* ("The History Magazine for Young People"), *Cricket* magazine, *Kids Discover, Dragonfly, Ranger Rick, Muse Magazine,* and *Stone Soup* do not go out of date quickly. You can save these magazines and make them available throughout the year.

The Role of Leveled Books

Leveled books have an important role, particularly in guided reading. Being aware of book levels can also help you support and inform students' independent reading selections.

Books to Support Independent Reading

In the primary grades, children often reread books they have previously read. They may have individual book boxes that contain both familiar and new books that you know will be easy for them. You may also establish "browsing boxes" and assign children to read books from them as an independent activity during the reading workshop. Browsing boxes contain a narrow range of levels in both familiar and new (but easier) texts. They are usually identified by color, or you may list the names of children on a label fastened to the box or basket.

Older students also select their own books for independent reading based on their interests. They are also expected to monitor and make judgments about books that are appropriate for them at a point in time. For example, some teachers have students keep reading lists—lists of books they have completed. For each book on the list they indicate whether it was E (easy), JR (just right), or D (difficult). (See Fountas and Pinnell 2001.) This act requires that they think about their own reading and learn to make good choices. In your reading minilessons and conferences, you teach them how to make these judgments and keep their lists. Remember, this judgment should be broad and general. You wouldn't want to narrow a student's choices in independent reading to a particular level.

Although children do not use levels to select their independent books, the gradient is a useful tool for you as a teacher.

Figure 4–3. Books in Baskets by Authors, Topics, and Categories

Figure 4–4. Rack of Book Recommendations

It is extremely important that students' independent reading be within their control. They should be able to read these texts with ease and fluency so that they can concentrate on their responses and interpretations. Only by successfully processing texts they understand can they build reading power. Over time, because they are participating in guided reading and spending a great deal of time reading independently and reflecting on texts they can control, they will gradually increase the level of texts they can process successfully. You should expect the level of independent reading to move up as the guided reading lessons help students improve their processing powers.

Books to Support Guided Reading Lessons

The primary use for a leveled book collection is to support your instruction in guided reading. Knowing the gradient of difficulty will help you select texts that are just right for your students. You still need to analyze the text with the particular group of readers in mind, but having a ballpark level helps streamline the process. Your introduction to the text fine-tunes the selection.

Successful instruction in guided reading helps students expand their systems of strategic actions by applying them to increasingly challenging texts (Fountas and Pinnell 2006). Selecting the right book goes a long way in assuring that the instruction is helpful to students. In addition, the gradient of text is a way to track their progress. By recording text reading levels at regular intervals, you keep track of progress over time. (And as we explain in Chapter 9, you can identify benchmarks that provide a record of reading progress over several years of school.)

If you have knowledge of levels of difficulty, you can guide student choice as they learn to select "just right" books for themselves. If a student is reading and understanding a level L book, and rates it as "just right" on a reading list, the text you select for her guided reading group should be at least level L or M. If a student is struggling with a text that you know is an L, you can guide him toward choices below that level. On occasion, you may want to organize a basket of books for one or two readers who are having difficulty finding books that they can read. The point is not to make the student aware of the "level" but to narrow the choice so they can be successful in selecting texts. You need not label the baskets, but show it to the students who will benefit from it.

Value of a Leveled Book Set

A leveled collection is a group of books organized and labeled from easiest to hardest in terms of readability. Build your leveled book set over time as you acquire more books, and more copies of those books, at various levels. This collection is quite economical because you will never have to replace it (as you would if you adopt a new textbook). Rather, the collection grows gradually but steadily, as you add titles to the levels you need most. The leveled book set assists you as a teacher by:

- Making it easier to select appropriate books to use with groups in guided reading.

- Helping you assess and record students' progress over time.

- Providing a set of good reading materials that does not need to be replaced but can simply be expanded over time.

- Helping you guide individuals when they select books for independent reading.

- Providing ways to match books to readers so that the reading they do at home will be successful.

- Providing a "ladder" that students can use to gradually increase their reading abilities.

Home Reading

Home reading emerges from children's experiences in guided and independent reading at school. When you send a book home with a child, you want to be sure that parents understand its purpose. If you want children to read books for themselves at home, you must be sure the books are well within their control. You want to avoid at all costs making reading a struggle for parent and child at home. In that situation, reading becomes a negative, unpleasant experience, and both parent and child may avoid it in the future. When you understand levels and guide choices, you make it possible for children to read each book easily and enjoy the experience as

a result. Typically, at the primary level, teachers send home books that children have previously read at school. Resealable plastic freezer bags or cloth bags with the child's name facilitate the task of sending books home for reading. At the intermediate and middle levels, students take home books of their own choice that they can read independently.

Summary

The books in the classroom library are not organized by level; however, a leveled set of books for reading instruction is essential. Your knowledge and skill in using books underlies the success of your literacy program. Some books will expand children's knowledge of literature; others will support their knowledge in content areas; still others are critical to expanding their reading strategies and skills (still essential for intermediate and middle level students even though they have learned the basic processes).

Suggestions for Professional Development: Examining the Text Resources

Many different kinds of books are needed for a complete literacy program. Take one classroom in your school and consider the collection of books as a whole. You might work on your own classroom, or a group of colleagues might select a well-provisioned classroom as a laboratory

1. Think about the four categories of books mentioned in this chapter:
   - Books to expand children's literary experiences.
   - Books to support research and inquiry.
   - Books for independent reading.
   - Leveled books to support children's reading development.

2. Together, sort books into these four categories, discussing their use:
   - Which books offer rich literary experiences and should be reserved to read aloud to students or for literature discussion?
   - Which books are useful for reference or for learning content or for browsing in centers of interest?
   - Which books are useful for guided reading lessons at the appropriate level?
   - Which books would be good to place in browsing baskets for children to choose for independent reading?
   - Which books will be especially appealing to students at the appropriate grade level?

3. You may also want to think about:
   - What is the balance between genres in the books that support literary experiences (for example, biography, poetry, fantasy, realistic fiction)?
   - Could you add some baskets of journals or magazines to the collection?

4. Chances are, some books fit well into two or more categories, especially when you think about the diversity of the students in the class. Talk about how you would use books in flexible ways.

CHAPTER FIVE

THINKING ABOUT THE READABILITY OF TEXTS

A leveled book collection is an extensive set of books organized by level of difficulty—from very easy books appropriate for emergent readers to longer, complex books for advanced readers in the middle school. The book levels represent categories into which books are sorted. Placing a book within a level means considering a "cluster" of complex characteristics—many different aspects of the text that support and challenge readers. A level is only an approximation and some variability is expected within it. It is a teacher's tool for selecting texts for instruction, not a child's label. The individual levels are described in detail in Chapter 2.

In this chapter we discuss the various factors related to difficulty in texts. We explore a range of ways others have looked at text difficulty.

Book Levels

When we say that books are organized according to "level," we mean that they have been categorized according to characteristics that are related to the supports and challenges in the text for readers. We look at books in relation to readers and the reading process. Even for beginners it is more helpful to have a book that has a simple language structure rather than a book that has one- or two-word phrases or labels. For beginners, leveled books that support reading should have an increasing number of high-frequency words, natural sounding language, and familiar content.

A gradient of difficulty refers to "levels" designated by alphabet letters A–Z. The level is only an approximation of difficulty, because each child responds to a book differently. Each succeeding alphabet letter indicates increasing difficulty. So, books in a set are always "leveled" in relation to each other. Level B is a little bit harder than level A, and so on. In our leveling system, the gradient—the steps in difficulty—are finer at the earlier levels than at the later levels. We believe that smaller steps are needed at first. Differences in text, such as one line or three lines of print, can make a big difference for a young reader; on the other hand, the layout of print is not as much a factor for more experienced readers who can handle longer texts organized into chapters. Additionally, at more advanced levels, there is more variety in genre and format and more sophistication in language and content.

Text Readability

Text accessibility or "readability" has been a topic for discussion over many years of reading instruction. Many of us became frustrated with published reading programs because the materials were either too difficult for or inaccessible to many of our students. Most of the students' reading was done in literature anthologies and content area textbooks, and all students read the same texts.

Students are able to expand their power to process increasingly more complex texts because you help them anticipate content and format, introduce and demonstrate reading strategies, tell them about reading, support and prompt them as they engage in the process, and encourage them to extend their understanding of texts after reading.

Excellent teaching begins with matching books to readers, intentionally selecting books that will be accessible to the readers *with your help*. Not all of the texts you use in your classroom will be matched to readers. There will be grade level textbooks and other materials that all students need to read to satisfy the demands of the curriculum, and you can find ways to make these materials accessible (books on tape, reading aloud to students, shared reading, for example). But every day, students should read two kinds of accessible texts: (1) texts that they can read independently for extended periods of time and (2) texts that offer challenge and can be read with teacher support, giving the individual the opportunity to learn how to read better. The more we understand about texts and what makes them accessible to students, the better choices we can make in matching books to readers, and the more productive independent and guided reading will be.

A number of terms are used to describe the relationship between text difficulty and readers—*manageability, readability, accessibility*. Accessibility means that a given reader:

■ Can process the text well, using knowledge of what makes sense, sounds right, and looks right—simultaneously—in a smoothly operating system.

■ Reads most of the time at a good rate with phrasing, appropriate stress, pausing, and intonation (that is, in oral reading, putting words together in groups or phrases so the reading sounds like language).

■ Knows or rapidly solves most of the words and reads with a high level of accuracy.

■ Can interpret the full meaning of the text.

When these three characteristics (see Figure 5–1) are true relative to the reading of a text, the text is just about the right level of difficulty for the student to read independently.

We like the idea of a *considerate* text (Armbruster 1984; Armbruster and Anderson 1981, 1985), which is one that assists readers by the author's clear organization of the information. To us, a considerate text means that the writer signals when something—time, setting, topic, perspective—is about to change. Organization of the text is made clear, often through key words like *first, next, most important,* or by headings and subheadings. The voices of characters are clear; dialogue is either assigned or easy to attribute to the right speaker. Difficult or technical words are contextualized and sometimes defined within the text. If one feature of the text is challenging, other features are made easier.

A text may be considerate and yet too hard for a given reader, but given an appropriate level, considerate texts are very helpful in working with students. Considerate texts are excellent for guided reading because the "bones are showing"; that is, the organization is not too hard to discern. Students easily see some of these helpful text features and learn more about them as they read, thus acquiring a foundation for reading texts that are less considerate. When texts are inconsiderate, it's up to us to expose the "bones" to support effective processing.

Accessibility has sometimes been called readability, a relational term that means, How easy is it for this reader (or these readers, or readers at a certain grade level or age level) to read this book? Another term that we like very much is manageability, which refers to the individual's ability to read

Characteristics of Reading That Indicate an Accessible Text
1. Smooth processing.
2. Good rate, with phrasing and intonation.
3. Rapid word recognition and word solving.

Figure 5–1. Characteristics of Reading That Indicate an Accessible Text

the print, use the organizational features or structure, and construct meaning from a given text.

Researchers who study the readability or manageability of texts have identified a range of factors that seem to relate to the challenges that texts offer readers and have created tools, usually called *readability formulas,* by which to rate these factors. These formulas may be mathematical or may be checklists; generally, they focus on only a few of the many factors related to text difficulty.

Readability Formulas

There are many readability formulas, and we will highlight a few of them here. Each provides some useful information. Ideally, perhaps, we should apply a variety of different techniques to any one text, thereby building up a fuller picture of the supports and challenges; however, there's usually not enough time for that and some of the formulas are not as useful as others. Most provide options for using software to determine the level.

Lexiles

According to the developer, the Lexile Framework® for Reading is designed to be a measure of both text difficulty and a reader's ability level. The scale ranges from 200L for beginning readers to above 1700L for difficult texts. The student score means that the individual can be matched to texts. The tool uses two predictors of text difficulty: semantic difficulty, which is measured by word frequency and complexity, and syntactic complexity, which is measured by sentence length. KA text will be split into 125-word slices, which are compared to a database taken from a variety of sources and genres. Words in each sentence are counted and put into the equation. A statistical model is used to determine the Lexile measure for the entire text. Once a student's Lexile score is known, teachers can look for other books that are at the same level, with the expectation of about 75 percent comprehension. Lexiles are used to set goals, monitor reading progress, coordinate texts across the curriculum, and communicate to parents the kinds of texts that children should be reading. The publisher and manager of the Lexile Framework cautions that students should not always be encouraged to move to a higher level with each new book, but can build confidence at the same level. More than 450 publishers assign Lexiles to their titles; many newspapers and magazine articles also have these levels. Grade level equivalents are published for the levels. We have not found a strong correlation between these levels and our system as this system does not address all of the factors we use in analyzing texts. (See Chapter 9.)

Fry Readability Graph

One of the simplest and easiest-to-use formulas was developed by Edward Fry (1977). The formula analyzes sentence and word length. Choosing three 100-word passages from a text, you count the total number of sentences and the total number of syllables in each passage. Then you plot these numbers on Fry's graph (see Figure 5–2) and average the three scores to get an estimate of readability.

Cloze Procedure

A cloze procedure gives you another view of how accessible a text is to a reader. Type a 275-word passage from a text that students have not read. Skip the first sentence and then, at random, delete one of the first five words in the second sentence. Continue deleting every fifth word until you have marked out 50 words. Be sure the entire last sentence is complete. (You can vary the difficulty level by deleting every tenth word.) The result will look like the example in Figure 5–3. (The answers to this example are included at the end of this chapter.)

If you try completing this cloze procedure yourself, you'll see that you bring a great deal of knowledge to guessing the deleted words. You depend heavily on the sentence context as well as meaning of the whole text and, perhaps, the lan-

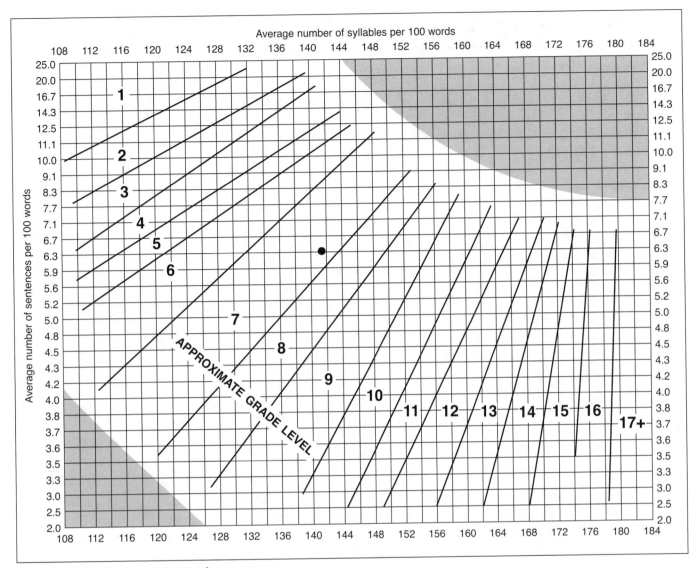

Figure 5–2. Fry Readability Graph

guage or writing style. How many words did you guess precisely, and how many times did you guess a word with the same meaning?

The cloze procedure has been criticized because it is a contrived task that deprives the reader of information. The reading process can break down, and you do not get a true picture of what the reader can do. (It does not tell you anything about the reader's ability to decode the missing words using visual patterns, letters, and sounds, for example.) If you need to know just how readers are using context, though, it provides some useful information.

Limitation of Formulas

Any formula or procedure provides only a very rough estimate of the readability of a text. Using a readability procedure to assess a text and match it to a reader's level (by grade) will not assure comprehension. At best, it provides another piece of information to consider. General limitations of readability procedures include the following:

■ Vocabulary difficulty will most likely be measured only one way—word length, defined by number of syllables. It makes sense that there is a relationship between the difficulty of a

Example of a Cloze Assessment[2]

"All right!" Grandma said. "_____ else are we going _____ get these walnuts chopped _____?"

She gave Josh a _____ of walnuts and a _____ of wood for breaking _____ nuts into smaller pieces. _____ was a tradition: whenever _____ made stolen the youngest _____ always got to smash _____ the walnuts. Josh took _____ wood and started pounding _____ a madman, as if _____ wanted to pulverize each _____ right down to dust.

_____ we finished making the _____ Grandma put it in _____ big bowl, covered it _____ a towel, and put _____ on the stove. It _____ take an hour for _____ dough to rise. Teddy, _____, and Cyn dragged Grandma _____ the living room and _____ her back onto the _____. Brad climbed onto her _____.

"Story! Story!" they yelled. "_____ us a story, Grandma."

"_____ right, all right," Grandma _____. "Cliff, Nate, you boys _____ over here. Don't tell _____ you're too old for _____ of your grandma's stories _____ I know you're not! _____ ever tell you about _____ first time I went _____ a vacation? You know _____ didn't get a vacation _____ I was forty-one years _____!"

How come?" I asked.

"_____ couldn't afford it when _____ was younger. We had _____ spend every cent we _____ on rent and food."

"_____ you poor, Grandma?" Cyn _____.

"I don't know," she _____. She stopped and seemed _____ think about it. "Maybe _____ little. Being poor is _____ to be ashamed of. _____ had food, we had _____, we had beds to _____ in. We just didn't _____ anything left over for _____ and such. But on _____ forty-first birthday my brother _____ took me out to _____, to the desert.

2 Fletcher 1995, 18.

Figure 5–3. Example of a Cloze Assessment

text and the number of multisyllable words, but there are many other factors related to vocabulary difficulty. For example, there are any number of difficult one-syllable words: think of *casque, eke, feign, hoist, mauve, orb, quirt, stoat, stob, svelte, thwart,* or *vie* for a start. Even a short word like *bow* has an array of meanings and two pronunciations.

■ Sentence difficulty is not accurately measured by its length; often, short sentences require readers to make more inferences in order to construct meaning.

■ The difficulty of reading material is directly related to the reader's background knowledge, which is not figured into the formula.

■ There is no attention to content, graphic and text features, organization of ideas, genre, print layout, and a variety of other features.

A number of researchers have concluded that readability formulas must be either replaced by or supplemented with qualitative information (Anderson and Armbruster 1984; Beck, McKeown, Gromoll 1989).

Features That Influence Readability

The research on readability has revealed some key features that are related to text difficulty.

Language

The language of a text includes the words, sentences, and syntactic structure.

VOCABULARY

The words in the text reflect the difficulty of the topic and/or the sophistication of the writing style. It might seem that the simpler the words, the easier the text, but it's not quite that cut-and-dried. The level of word sophistication must be appropriate to

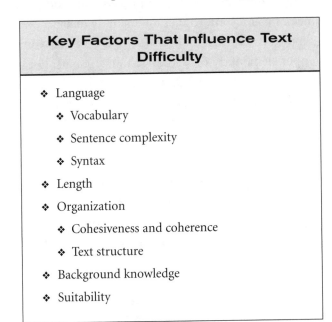

Key Factors That Influence Text Difficulty

- ❖ Language
  - ❖ Vocabulary
  - ❖ Sentence complexity
  - ❖ Syntax
- ❖ Length
- ❖ Organization
  - ❖ Cohesiveness and coherence
  - ❖ Text structure
- ❖ Background knowledge
- ❖ Suitability

Figure 5–4. Key Factors That Influence Text Difficulty

the conceptual underpinnings of the text if what is said is to be coherent. For example, in a book about space or in a novel with a mysterious moonlit setting, the word *orb* could be replaced by *sphere* without changing the meaning, but replacing it with *ball* would alter the style and therefore the meaning as well. Merely simplifying words does not necessarily make a text easier to understand (Beck, McCaslin, and McKeown 1980).

SENTENCE COMPLEXITY

In general, although vocabulary has a more direct relationship to difficulty, texts with long complex sentences are harder than texts with simple sentences. Again, however, the situation is not cut-and-dried. Sentence length alone accounts for only a small part of the difficulty (Davidson, Wilson, and Herman 1985). Artificially short sentences, which are sometimes used in textbooks to bring down the readability level, sound choppy and may change the meaning or make it harder for readers to construct meaning. For example, take this passage, from Cushman's *The Midwife's Apprentice* (1995):

> She had failed. Strange sensations tickled her throat, but she did not cry, for she did not know how, and a heavy weight sat in her chest, but she did not moan or wail, for she had never learned to give voice to what was inside her. She knew only to run away. (page 70)

The combination of the long sentence sandwiched between two short ones carries the feeling of emotion and the meaning of the text. But suppose Cushman had instead written:

> She had failed. Her throat tickled. She did not cry. She did not know how. There was a heavy weight on her chest. She did not moan.

The flow of the text simply isn't the same. What would readers learn or feel from reading such a chopped up text? When we are working with authentic texts, we need to look at sentence complexity within the whole.

Conversely, some writers use shorter sentences for effect and embed a great deal of complex meaning within them.

That Golz should be one of them too. That Golz should be in such obvious communication with the fascists. Golz that he had known for nearly twenty years. Golz who had captured the gold train that winter with Lucacz in Siberia. Golz who had fought against Kolchak, and in Poland. In the Caucasus. In China, and here since the first October. But he *had* been close to Tukachevsky. To Voroshilov, yes, too. But to Tukachevsky. And to who else? Here to Karkov of course. And to Lucacz. But all the Hungarians had been intriguers. He hated Gall. Golz hated Gall. Remember that. Make a note of that. Golz has always hated Gall. But he favors Putz. Remember that. And Duval is his chief of staff. See what stems from that. You've heard him say Copic's a fool. That is definitive. That exists. And now this dispatch from the fascist lines. Only by pruning out of these rotten branches can the tree remain healthy and grow. The rot must become apparent for it is destroyed. But Golz of all men. That Golz should be one of the traitors. He knew that you could trust no one. No one. Ever. Not your wife. Not your brother. Not your oldest comrade. No one. Ever.[3]

Total words, including reference: 230
213 words in the passage
39 "sentences"
5.5 average words per sentence

---

[3] Hemingway, Ernest. 1940. *For Whom the Bell Tolls*. New York: Scribner. p. 421.

You may not agree with this great writer's use of punctuation; indeed, he breaks the rules for his own reasons. But in this paragraph from *For Whom the Bell Tolls* (Hemingway 1940), it is obvious that comprehension demands are much higher than the 5.5 words per "sentence" would indicate.

Syntax
The complexity of language is an important factor that is strongly related to the difficulty of a text. When the language is closer to oral language, it is easier. The more technical or literary the language, the more difficult the text is to read.

Length
The length of the text adds to the demands on the reader. Many readers, even adults, find an extremely long text intimidating. Meaning and memory must be sustained over many days or even weeks. The reader must consistently return to the text without letting too much time go by. In general, the longer the text, the more complex the plot, the longer the time span, and the more likely characters are to develop in complex ways. As with other factors, however, length alone cannot be used to judge difficulty; some short texts are packed with complex meaning and some longer ones simply recount one simple adventure after another. (For many of your upper elementary or middle school students, however, length will be a major consideration in choosing books.) With informational texts, the reader may select only sections to read.

Organization
The challenge of a text varies by the reader's ability to understand and use the underlying organizational structure. Some texts are well organized for readers and provide signal words that support the organization.

Cohesiveness and Coherence
Think about reading a text in which topics, events, or characters seem to jump out of nowhere or it's

hard to tell how one idea or section relates to another. Most writers work hard to put in the "bridges," or connecting passages, that help the reader understand how parts fit within the whole. In fiction, writers reveal characters by what they do, how they look, what they say or think, or what others think about them, and with these revelations they help the readers make hypotheses. A coherent text supports meaning and carries the reader along. Irrelevant details or jumps from topic to topic make it harder to discern the full text meaning.

TEXT STRUCTURE

A text's structure is the way information is organized and presented. A narrative structure, for example, typically opens with an event followed by a series of additional chronological events (although more complex texts may use flashbacks or flash-forwards). The events and the characters who move through them reveal an overall theme or themes. The setting (which may or may not be important to the plot) is revealed, as well as the central characters and problem. The story unfolds through a series of events as the problem is resolved.

Expository texts can have a variety of organizational structures (cause and effect, temporal sequence, comparison/contrast, description, problem/solution), as described in Fountas and Pinnell 2001. The reader's comprehension is supported when the organization of the text is presented clearly and "called out" by words, titles, and headings. One of the difficulties in reading expository texts is that readers must internalize so many different organizational patterns (Calfee and Chambliss 1988).

BACKGROUND KNOWLEDGE

Readers' background knowledge is strongly related to their ability to comprehend the text (Adams and Bruce 1982). What immediately comes to mind is vocabulary; however, the role of background knowledge goes far beyond words. Reading in various content areas provides the definitions a reader needs to understand the vocabulary and is also likely to promote expertise in the various expository organizational structures. Readers use not only their experiential knowledge and their content knowledge but their *knowledge of text*. The extent to which a text requires readers to use background knowledge is a factor in judging its difficulty:

- How are the demands of this text related to the typical funds of knowledge that students have at this age level (based on a typical curriculum)?

- How are the demands of this text related to the funds of knowledge these particular students have?

- How are the demands of this text related to the range of personal or literary experiences these students have?

Addressing these questions helps you, first, determine the approximate difficulty level of a text and then be more precise when you select and introduce it to students.

You can also look for the way the writer of a text makes information available to the reader. For example, are unfamiliar concepts described and illustrated or does the writer expect the reader to know them? How well are the concepts explained? Are the examples interesting and understandable? An expository text that is friendly in its use of technical concepts is more available to students; a friendly narrative text helps them understand nuances.

SUITABILITY

A text may be the right level of difficulty for your students and at the same time be unsuitable because of the theme, the topic, or the writing style. For example, the topic might be too sophisticated or mature. Or students may not find the topic or theme interesting (Anderson, Shirey,

Wilson, and Fielding 1986). On the other hand, if material is very interesting to students, they may overlook poor writing and/or may persevere in reading a text that is too difficult. The interesting material should be integral to the text, not a "gimmick" to attract students' attention. The quality of the writing also contributes to suitability. The text needs to "hang together" in a way that provides the needed information, creates interest, and keeps the reader moving.

Key Questions for Thinking About Readability

The two central questions to consider in any discussion of readability are:

- What does the reader bring to the text?
- What does the text require of the reader?

Readability procedures and formulas address the second question in a very limited way (Ruddell 1997). Cloze procedures include the reader but do not account for their attitudes and the way readers construct meaning. A qualitative look at texts provides more information. For example, the readability checklist developed by Irwin and Davis (1980) focuses on two concepts:

- *Understandability* refers to the way the writer has accounted for readers' background knowledge, the way concepts and ideas are developed, and the syntactic difficulty of sentences. Some texts offer more support to readers in terms of comprehension. To determine understandability, you would analyze the assumptions that the writer makes about the readers' prior knowledge, vocabulary, and experiences; you might also ask how links to that understanding are provided within the text. You would notice the degree to which definitions and examples are provided as well

as how explicitly important concepts and relationships (cause and effect, for example) are stated.

- *Learnability* refers to the way the text is organized to present ideas, engage the reader, and reinforce the readers' acquisition of knowledge. For example, there may be special features such as an index or chapter titles and headings that clearly show the reader how to recognize and find information. To determine learnability, you would analyze whether the text has a clear and simple organizational pattern, provides opportunities to encounter concepts several times (for example, in summaries or end-of-section questions), or appeals to students in its physical layout, illustrations, writing style, or concepts.

The Friendly Text Evaluation Scale (Singer 1992) was designed to be used in combination with readability formulas. The principle is similar to Irwin and Davis's readability checklist in that you are looking into the organization and structure of a text from the point of view of the reader, estimating what makes it "friendly" or "understandable." For example, to what extent is the reader acquainted with the purpose, sequence, and contents? Does one idea build logically on another? Are there signals to the reader as to what to expect (introductory paragraphs, for example)? A "friendly" text will define new terms in language that readers can understand and use examples, analogies, and metaphors that help readers understand new ideas and become interested in them. Sometimes, authors explicitly highlight important information or make explicit connections between ideas.

Another consideration in the evaluation of text difficulty is how authors treat issues related to race relations and how they portray minority groups. Here, you need to think about whether the text respects personal and cultural differences and portrays problems and issues in a way that provides insights for all ethnic, linguistic, and racial groups. Does it present ethnic characters in positive ways or patronize them?

Evaluating texts for readability is a complex process, so the challenge of creating a gradient of leveled texts should come as no surprise. There is nothing more intricate than the human brain. Throw literacy into the mix, and we realize that teaching reading is much more complex than rocket science. Written language requires a vast range of cognitive and affective actions to access and comprehend.

Reading the Internet

Chances are your students are searching the Internet for materials to support them in their content area studies. While this resource is unprecedented and wonderful, it nevertheless presents an additional challenge to readers. What is readable and suitable in this context? You can apply the same criteria to assess the appropriateness of Web materials as you would apply to any other kind of text. In Figure 5–5 we list some questions that you may want to ask about texts, including Internet, novels, factual texts, articles, and others.

Questions to Ask About Texts

1. What concepts, background information, or vocabulary are needed to understand this text?

2. To what extent does the text provide readers with definitions and examples to help them understand concepts?

3. Is there a sufficient number of examples to help students understand concepts?

4. Are important relationships (for example, cause and effect) explicitly stated or do readers need to infer them?

5. Are concepts summarized or does the text require readers to select the important information and remember it?

6. Do paragraphs, chapters, and sections have clear summaries of main ideas?

7. What is the level of sentence complexity? Are there embedded clauses?

8. Is the organizational pattern simple, straightforward, and clear?

9. To what extent do the titles, headings, and subheadings help readers find information?

10. Is the writing style appealing and interesting?

11. Does the text include illustrations? How helpful are these illustrations?

12. Are graphic features (maps, charts, cutaways, graphs, etc.) helpful in terms of understanding information?

13. Does the text present positive images of a variety of social, linguistic, ethnic, and cultural groups?

14. To what extent does the text offer readers the opportunity to infer meaning?

15. To what extent does the text offer readers the opportunity to add to their own knowledge?

16. Are there opportunities to analyze the text's structure?

17. Is this a text that requires readers to be critical?

18. To what extent is the text interesting and appealing to these readers?

19. What are the strengths and weaknesses of this text in terms of helping these readers gain information and expand their reading abilities?

Figure 5–5. Questions to Ask About Texts

Readability: The Essential First Step in Effective Reading Instruction

Whatever your students read, your ability to analyze texts for a broad range of qualities is very important in your success as a teacher of reading. The important thing is that you learn to "size up" a text's appropriateness and the benefits it offers your students.

Over the last years, we have observed teachers and students as they participate in guided and independent reading. We have analyzed numerous selections in terms of how successful students were in:

■ Reading the specific text with ease, fluency, phrasing, and understanding.

■ Learning more about the reading process.

We have had the privilege of working with highly skilled teachers who reflect continually on their work. Our conversations with them have centered on the nature of the texts students read, behaviors indicating successful processing, students' needs in terms of comprehending strategies, and teaching procedures. When we meet together to reflect on guided reading lessons and watch them over and over on videotape, one thing is crystal clear: *the teaching can be effective only if the text is right.*

We have seen competent teachers and competent students struggle if the text is too hard. The learning process breaks down; the atmosphere is tense. The teacher doesn't know what to attend to because there are so many problems. Concepts are not available no matter how much you discuss them; words are hard and often mispronounced (without understanding). Students read slowly, word by word. Meaning is lost.

The "too easy" picture is not as difficult to contemplate; after all, the students are gaining experience as fluent readers. But if the text is too easy, you are not accomplishing your goal as a teacher. Students whiz through it; there's not much to discuss and no problems to untangle (and therefore no attendant learning). Students may be bored.

Either way, no matter how good a teacher you are, if the text is not right, the picture is negative. Of course, we know that matching texts to readers does not in itself equal good instruction. You can have an appropriate text and still miss many opportunities to help students take on new learning. All of us work continually on helping our students develop an effective reading process through text introductions, effective instructional interactions, and postreading discussions. But starting with the right text goes a long way. That is why readability (or manageability, if you prefer that term) is so important. Simply recognizing read-

---

Answers to Cloze Exercise, Figure 5–3

How	the	the	me	I	clothes
to	like	Brad	one	to	sleep
up	he	into	because	had	have
pile	walnut	pushed	I	Were	vacations
block	When	couch	the	asked	my
the	dough	lap	on	said	Paul
that	a	Tell	I	to	Arizona
Grandma	with	All	until	a	
kid	it	said	old	nothing	
up	would	come	we	We	

ability is an important step toward the complex analysis required to understand and work with the texts that our students read.

Summary

Research on the readability and manageability of texts shows that text characteristics should be considered when matching books to readers. We can measure the readability of texts in a number of ways, but no one formula or method will do the job precisely. We need to look at a wide range of factors and keep the readers in mind.

Suggestions for Professional Development: Considering Readability

1. Explore readability with colleagues in your school. You can invite teachers from grades 2–3, 4–5, or 6–8 to this meeting, but if you want to grasp the big picture, make it K–5 or 5–8.

2. An important concept to keep coming back to in this meeting is that at each grade level, teachers are *reading aloud* to students texts they cannot read independently but are able to comprehend. This "lift" is critical to developing the reader's ability to take on more difficult texts over time.

3. Collect three or four texts from every grade level. You can use the basal reading system if you have one, or you can have teachers select texts that students are likely to read and that they consider appropriate for "average" students at some point in the year.

4. Explore readability formulas:
   - If you have not already done so, have each participant take the sample cloze test in this chapter and then compare results with one another and with the "answers" (on page 48). What thinking processes did you engage in to predict the words?
   - Ask several teachers to perform a cloze procedure using one of the texts. It is not necessary to collect a great deal of data. You will generate a really interesting conversation from only three or four examples.
   - Apply the Fry readability formula to at least one text at every grade level. Look at the general trends. Then look at the texts to determine the range of factors that seem to be related to difficulty. Almost all formulas will be less reliable at levels A–I.
   - Think about the texts in relation to the understandability and learnability factors listed on the Irwin and Davis readability checklist.
   - Finally, consider the texts in the light of Figure 5–5, Questions to Ask About Texts. Come up with a list of principles for examining texts for purchase in your school district.

CHAPTER SIX

TEXT FACTORS RELATED TO ACCESSIBILITY

Have you ever as an adult reread a book you'd read in junior high or high school? For example, perhaps you read *Middlemarch* in your high school senior English class. Your teacher may have attempted to increase your understanding through lecture or discussion, or presented his own interpretation of the book. But the nuances of this work of literature might be clearer after much more "life experience." You would recognize Dorothea's passionate commitment to intellectual ideas, unusual for a woman of her times. While your reading as a high school senior may have been excellent, the text probably was more accessible to you as a mature adult.

That's the essence of text difficulty. Readers apply everything they know, at a point in time, to their understanding of a text. Text accessibility is always related to the individual reader's particular background. Not every reader will take away the same meaning or level of understanding. But if we can select texts that have good potential for reader understanding, and if we can support readers' processing, we will be able to enrich their reading experiences. The process starts with "leveling" texts so that we know the supports and challenges we have to work with.

When we seek to determine readability, manageability, or the level of a text, we are matching characteristics with aspects of the reading process. We are exploring this essential and critical question: *What does this text demand of the reader?* Don't be intimidated or overwhelmed with the number of factors there are to examine. Your examination will heighten your awareness of a text's demands on the students you teach. Reading a text is complicated; so is looking at the level of difficulty. As teachers, it helps us to know that as we look at texts, we are really thinking about readers. What knowledge and strategies will they need in order to be able to read this text with understanding? What are the opportunities to learn? Leveling books sets us up for thinking about our instruction.

When we assign levels to books, we are looking at readability or accessibility across a broad range of text characteristics. The process requires reading the book and then analyzing it in several different ways that together represent the complex set of supports and challenges in the text. You can make your analyses more reliable by checking them with fellow teachers. You will find that you and your colleagues have excellent insight into the underlying difficulties of text. When you have read and discussed several books at a level, you will have a good sense of the composite of characteristics that make it more difficult or easier than the books at another level.

Text Factors Related to Accessibility

Genre

The origin of the word *genre* is the French word meaning type. Genre refers to a classification system for categories of fiction and nonfiction that have similar characteristics. (For more specific information about genres, refer to Chapter 23 of Fountas and Pinnell, *Guiding Readers and Writers.*)

Factors in Looking at the Supports and Challenges in Written Texts

FACTOR	DEFINITION	FEATURES TO EXAMINE
Genre and Forms	The "genre" is the type of text and refers to a system by which fiction and nonfiction texts are classified. "Form" is the format in which a genre may be presented. Each form and genre have characteristic features.	❖ Each genre and form have characteristic features. ❖ Fiction genres: traditional literature, fantasy, science fiction, realistic fiction, historical fiction. ❖ Nonfiction genres: informational texts, biography, autobiography, memoir. ❖ Forms: picture books, plays, chapter books, short stories, diaries and logs, photo essays.
Text Structure	The "structure" is the way the text is organized and presented. It may be *narrative*, as in most fiction and biographical texts. Factual texts are organized categorically or topically and may have sections with headings. Writers of factual texts use several underlying structural patterns to provide information to readers. The most important are: *description, chronological sequence, compare/contrast, cause/effect*, and *problem/solution*. The presence of these structures, especially in combination, can increase the challenge for readers.	❖ Fiction: narration, development of plot; information given in heads; how characters are revealed; relevance of setting; use of literary devices such as flashbacks or changes in perspective; chapters that continue or chapters that stand alone. ❖ Nonfiction: enumeration, established sequence, temporal sequence; description, compare/contrast, cause/effect, problem/solution; combination of structures. Structures are signaled by words that indicate patterns; for example, first, second; while, yet; because, since, thus; conclude, the evidence is; furthermore.
Content	The "content" refers to the subject matter of the text—the concepts that are important to understand. In fiction, content may be related to the setting or to the kinds of problems characters have. In factual texts, content refers to the topic of focus. Content is considered in relation to the prior experience of readers.	❖ Information on cover, and in chapter titles. ❖ Topics. ❖ Background knowledge required. ❖ Information in graphics, titles, heads. ❖ Concepts related to science and technology.
Themes and Ideas	The "themes and ideas" are the big ideas that are communicated by the text. A text may have multiple themes or a main theme and several supporting themes or ideas.	❖ Sophistication of themes (from simple everyday problems to issues requiring maturity). ❖ Complexity of ideas (from obvious to subtle and difficult to understand).
Language and Literary Features	Written language is qualitatively different from spoken language. Fiction writers use dialogue, figurative language, and other kinds of literary structures such as character, setting, and plot. Factual writers use description and technical language. In hybrid texts you may find a wide range of literary language.	❖ Perspective. ❖ Language structure and quality. ❖ Word choice. ❖ Literary devices. ❖ Figurative language. ❖ Dialogue—assigned (specifying character) or unassigned.

Figure 6–1.   Factors in Looking at the Supports and Challenges in Written Texts

Factors in Looking at the Supports and Challenges in Written Texts (continued)

FACTOR	DEFINITION	FEATURES TO EXAMINE
Sentence Complexity	Meaning is mapped out onto the syntax of language. Texts with simpler, more natural sentences are easier to process. Sentences with embedded and conjoined clauses make a text more difficult.	❖ Length of sentences. ❖ Sentence style. ❖ Embedded clauses.
Vocabulary	"Vocabulary" refers to the meaning of the words and is part of our oral language. The more the words are accessible to readers in terms of meaning, the easier a text will be. The individuals' *reading and writing vocabularies* refer to words that they understand and can also read or write.	❖ Complex layers of meaning (as in metaphor). ❖ Content/technical words. ❖ Words particular to written rather than oral language.
Words	"Words" refer to recognizing and solving the printed words in the text. The challenge in a text partly depends on the number and the difficulty of the words that the reader must solve by recognizing them or decoding them. Having a great many of the same high frequency words makes a text more accessible to readers.	❖ High frequency words. ❖ Multisyllable words.
Illustrations	The "illustrations" include drawings, paintings or photographs that accompany the text and add meaning and enjoyment. In factual texts, illustrations also include graphics that provide a great deal of information that readers must integrate with the text. Illustrations are an integral part of a high quality text. Increasingly, fiction texts are including a range of graphics.	❖ Illustrations—placement and relation to text. ❖ Graphic features such as diagrams, tables, graphs, drawings, illustrations and maps with legends.
Book and Print Features	The "book and print features" are the physical aspects of the text—what readers cope with in terms of length, size, and layout. Book and print features also include tools like the table of contents, glossary, pronunciation guides, indices, and sidebars.	❖ Length of text, length of chapters. ❖ Punctuation. ❖ Print size, style, and spacing (between words and lines). ❖ Layout of print and illustrations, including format: columns, margins, white space, shading, sidebars, insets, bulleted and numbered lists. Also includes placement of phrases and line breaks, sentences that end on a page, or carry over to the next. ❖ Organizational tools (such as indexes and glossaries).

Figure 6–1.   Factors in Looking at the Supports and Challenges in Written Texts (Continued)

FICTION

- Traditional literature includes stories that have been handed down orally through the ages. These stories have no known author; they include folk and fairy tales, myths, legends, and epics.

- Fantasy includes stories that have fantastic or otherworldly elements; these stories are similar to traditional literature but have a known author. They are constructed so that the events, however fantastic, seem believable within the world depicted. Sometimes fantasy is highly complex.

- Science fiction is fantasy that incorporates technology or scientific information. Some stories seek to provide a glimpse of the future or some time in the distant past. Others open up completely imaginary worlds.

- Realistic fiction includes stories that are true to life because they portray characters or events that could really exist in the here and now. Many stories reveal the human condition or probe social issues.

- Historical fiction includes stories that are realistic but take place at some time in the past. Stories are concerned with universal human problems and sometimes help readers understand the past or present.

NONFICTION

- A biography is the story of a real person's life. Biographies may be authentic, or they may be fictionalized to create greater interest for readers. The degree to which a biography is fictionalized alters its authenticity.

- An autobiography is the story a person writes about his or her own life.

- A memoir is autobiographical writing that focuses on a particular event that had great impact on an individual. A memoir may focus on another person, a place, an event, or action period.

- Information books focus on a science or social sciences discipline or on recreation—history, geography, sociology, or the physical sciences. The reader derives content knowledge from informational texts.

Text Structure

Text structure refers to the way information is organized and presented. A narrative is typically chronological, although flashbacks or flashforwards may be used. Characters interact throughout a series of events related to an overall theme or themes. Lower-level texts have simple plots; plots become more complex as you move up the gradient of difficulty. Expository texts employ a variety of organizational structures: cause and effect, temporal sequence, comparison/contrast, description, problem/solution or question/answer. These structures are often signaled by particular words, phrases, and headings. Structure aids coherence. Most writers work hard to show how parts fit within the whole, how one idea connects with another. A coherent text leads the reader to meaning.

Text structure is related to genre. For example, most fiction texts have a narrative structure. But nonfiction texts, for example, biography and history, may also be organized in "story" format.

Content

A text is easier when it is close to the students' own experience. That's one reason narrative texts are the easiest for students to use in beginning reading.

Informational texts are more difficult because they usually provide information about something that the reader doesn't know. When looking at texts, think about what kind of background experiences your students will bring to the reading.

In learning to read, familiar content supports children's learning about print. As students move through the grades, however, they learn to take more information from the print and match it to their own funds of knowledge. They know enough about the print to use it as a tool for learning. If the content is too far from students' own background knowledge, simply decoding the words will not make the text understandable.

Themes and Ideas

Themes and ideas are the underlying central messages of the text—what it is really about, for example:

■ Lies can get you in trouble.

■ We need to appreciate people for who they really are.

■ Hard work is needed for success.

Texts may have multiple themes. Themes for younger children are usually straightforward and easy to access—friends, family, love of animals, or school challenges. As texts grow in complexity, so does the sophistication of the theme or major idea—the horrors of war, struggles for survival, or prejudice and discrimination. Through exploration of a wide range of themes, upper elementary and middle school students broaden their perspectives and learn about life.

Language and Literary Features

Clarity of language is important whatever the genre. The sophistication of the language and the literary features, including the complexity of characterizations and plots, affect the readability of a text. Early texts are generally simple narratives with a beginning, middle, and an end. Higher-level texts have literary devices such as flashbacks or stories within stories. They also include idiom, dialect, literary language and poetic devices such as metaphor, simile, and onomatopoeia. The key here is that metaphor should contribute to and enhance understanding rather than confuse the reader. The ability to manage the literary features of texts is built through experience.

Sentence Complexity

A sentence's complexity has to do with its syntax; the way words are put together to form phrases and clauses. Shorter sentences usually have a single subject and predicate. Longer sentences may have compound or complex subjects and predicates, with many embedded clauses.

Vocabulary

Knowing the meaning of the words in a text is basic to understanding. The more words a text contains that are within readers' oral vocabularies, the more accessible it is. But as they learn new content, they also acquire new categories for words. Vocabulary involves making connections among words to form networks of understanding. Sophisticated readers understand that the context of the sentence, the paragraph, and the whole text make a difference in understanding the vocabulary. Words not only have multiple meanings, but they also have connotative meanings within the context. All of us constantly develop new vocabulary throughout our lives.

Words

The challenges in terms of word-solving are a key factor in text difficulty. Some words are easier to recognize or take apart. Students need to use a range of strategies and texts that have large numbers of unfamiliar words pose greater challenges. Inclusion of multisyllable words requires readers to take them apart while maintaining a focus on meaning.

Illustrations

In narrative texts, illustrations help the reader form images of the setting and characters. They enhance the mood of the story, prompt emotional responses, and help the reader comprehend the meaning in a deeper way. In informational texts, illustrations (photographs, drawings, diagrams, maps, cross-sections) help students understand the concepts and ideas being discussed. Illustrations that are clearly related to the information in the text and that are themselves easy to understand assist the reader. Graphic features that are clearly labeled and explained through legends and keys are easier for readers to process and understand.

Book and Print Features

Book and print features are the physical aspects of the text. The way a text is laid out—font size, margins, spacing between words and lines, placement of phrases and sentences, headings and subheadings—can support the reader or make a text harder. If the features of a text work together to support the reader in constructing meaning, the text is more accessible.

LENGTH

In general, the longer the text, the more demanding it is. Chapters can be long or short. However, see the caveats relative to length discussed in the Chapter 5.

PRINT AND LAYOUT

The size and clarity of the print contribute to ease in reading. Ample space between words and between lines helps make the text friendly to the reader because it is easier to search for and pick up information. Print features such as italics, boldface, or a larger type size are used to signal meaning.

The placement of print in space is a factor in helping readers find information. How the text appears on the page can make the text more "reader friendly." For example, look at the page from *Henry and Mudge and the Best Day of All* (Rylant 1997) shown in Figure 6–2. Even though the sentences are quite long, the layout helps the reader process the print. All sentences start at the left-hand margin rather than being run together. In contrast, when a new sentence continues in the middle of the line,

Henry and Henry's parents and Henry's big dog Mudge sat quietly in the backyard and closed their eyes. They listened to the birds. They rested.

Figure 6–2. *Page from* Henry and Mudge and the Best Day of All

the layout is slightly harder. A sentence that carries over to a new page introduces even more difficulty.

Paragraphs break up text into groups of ideas. Paragraphed text can be continuous and unbroken, or it can be organized into chapters, sections, or columns. For longer texts, the use of headings at logical breaks helps the reader gather and summarize meaning. The degree to which organizational aids are clearly laid out, meaningful, and available contributes to text manageability. The text may also have supports such as a glossary or index that allow the readers to access information quickly.

PUNCTUATION

Punctuation is used to signal the meaning being delivered by the words and phrases as well as the relationship between ideas. As readers encounter longer and more complex sentences, punctuation helps them identify the units of meaning. More difficult texts require more sophisticated uses of punctuation. Simpler texts contain periods, commas, question marks, quotation marks, and exclamation marks; as the gradient increases, readers encounter semicolons, dashes, ellipses, quotes within quotes, and the like.

TOOLS

Many books, particularly informational texts, provide readers' "tools." These tools include table of contents, section or chapter headings, main headings and subheadings, footnotes, references, index, glossary, and pronunciation guides. Tools assist the reader in understanding the text.

Dealing with a Complex Set of Text Characteristics

It is obvious that analyzing texts to determine level of difficulty is a complex task. Even more apparent, reading involves complex processing. The challenges and supports in a text may lie in any combination of these features. The features also represent opportunities to learn. The first step in making learning possible is to analyze what makes a text accessible to your students. Then you can design your teaching to bring together the readers and text.

Suggestions for Professional Development: Analyzing Text Characteristics

1. Get together with a group of colleagues. Ask each person to come to the meeting with a text he or she knows *very well* and has read several times.

2. Go through the text factors in Figure 6–1 one at a time. Have each person address the factor through a few minutes of analysis and then share with the group.

3. After the "rounds," have the group talk about what they have learned about text factors.

4. Discuss ways the analysis and sharing will impact your teaching of students.

CHAPTER SEVEN

Putting Text Analysis into Action

Every text demands that readers:

- Use strategic actions to recognize and solve words.

- Orchestrate different sources of information in comprehending the text.

- Use the punctuation and sentence structure to identify phrase units.

- Monitor their reading to be sure it makes sense, looks right, and sounds right—and correct themselves when necessary to gain accurate meaning.

- Recognize important elements of narrative (setting, plot, characters, perspective) and use them to anticipate, analyze, and understand the text.

- Recognize important informational or expository structures (compare/contrast, description, cause/effect, temporal sequence, problem/solution) and use them to anticipate, analyze, and understand the text.

- Sustain attention and memory over periods of time, from a few minutes to several hours.

- Activate and use background knowledge and make personal and text connections.

- Revise their ideas as they take new ideas and information from the text.

- Recognize elements of the writer's craft.

- Think critically about the text, making judgments as to accuracy and quality.

The reading process is *not* a collection of discrete strategic actions that you use *one at a time*. You don't use some strategic actions on lower-level texts and others on higher-level texts. So, even though harder texts demand more of the reader, the requirements pertain to the depth and sophistication of strategies rather than to additional strategies. For example, in a simple, easy chapter book like *Henry and Mudge: The First Book* (Rylant 1990), readers are required to use background knowledge—relative to pets, family, dog collars—that most children have. It also requires readers to infer that Henry is lonely and afraid to walk to school alone, feelings most children understand. Nevertheless, the strategic actions required are the same as those required by highly sophisticated texts like *Number the Stars* (Lowry 1989), a story about the Holocaust.

Our goal in using a gradient of text is to provide a graduated "ladder" that leads to growth in the full range of strategic actions as students meet the demands of increasingly difficult and more complex texts. In this chapter, we will illustrate the analysis of texts at several levels to help you understand the complex characteristics that contribute to a level.

Thinking About Texts in Terms of Teaching

As teachers we recognize that readers orchestrate the full range of strategic actions every time they read a high-quality text. Teachers' guides sometimes suggest that you can use a particular text or group of texts, to "teach inferencing" or to "teach

On Saturday, Willy helped me wash the tub.

What a mess!

Figure 7–1. Willy the Helper

visualizing." It is simply not true that a text requires a single strategy or is the "best" text for teaching a certain kind of thinking. Of course, we come across texts that support deeper thinking than others, but all texts require readers to use a variety of strategic actions simultaneously. Complex strategies cannot be taught in one (or even ten!) lessons. Readers must use them again and again as an integrated system that they bring to many different texts. They need to use them together, not one at a time. Some strategic actions will need to be introduced explicitly; others the students will discover and apply for themselves. Further, just because a reader can verbalize a strategy such as "inferring" does not necessarily mean he has gained the full meaning of a text or can draw inferences from other texts.

Our job as teachers is, while keeping the reading process in mind, to see the potential in each text and decide what to call to students' attention. We have identified twelve broad, interrelated cate-

gories of strategic actions for processing texts and expanding meaning (see Chapter 2; also see Fountas and Pinnell 2001, 2006). We always keep these systems of strategic actions in mind as we look at texts and what they demand of readers.

Text analysis reveals the supports and challenges offered in a text. We then think, *What do my students need to know how to do in order to read this text with fluency, understanding, and—we should not forget—enjoyment!* After all, we want students to read voluntarily, and that will not happen if the experience is painful or boring day after day.

Our introductions to texts are derived from our analysis of the text characteristics. In the introduction, we "unlock" the text by providing the support students need to use the twelve systems of "in-the-head" strategic actions in an orchestrated way. We may demonstrate our own thinking to help students understand what they will need to do or how they'll need to think as they read the text. We may touch on one or several aspects of the text; we may bring one or several strategic actions to conscious attention. The challenge here is simultaneously to:

- Provide the information and support students need to read *this* text successfully.

- Enable students to improve their reading ability by using strategic actions successfully.

Text analysis is basic to meeting those challenges. Below are some examples (from easier to harder) that illustrate the process of text analysis, what we call "thinking through a text." This kind of thinking will help you use the text effectively with your students.

Realistic Fiction, Level D

Willy the Helper is the simple story (realistic fiction) about a family dog is told from the point of view of a little girl who talks about how her dog "helps" in many ways (see Figure 7–2).

The text is short—only eight pages of print and seventy-nine words. Print is in a large, clear font with ample, but not too much, space between words and between lines. Every page has a clear and engaging picture and about three lines of print, consistently placed on the page. Basic punctuation is evident—period, comma, question mark, and exclamation mark.

Illustrations are quite important in *Willy the Helper* and inference is required. The reader must gather information from the illustrations to grasp the central idea: Willy doesn't really help at all. In fact Willy gets into mischief on every page. Reading the text literally indicates that Willy helps all the time; the reader would miss the point. The contrast between the message in the print and the information in the picture creates humor. In addition, the reader really should infer that the little girl really loves Willy and doesn't mind the mischief.

On the last page, the writer asks a question: "On Saturday, Willy didn't help at all. Do you know

why?" Here, we should understand that the question is directed toward the reader, who is invited to go beyond the text to speculate about the answer. It is truly hard to predict the ending, since most readers will assume Willy is male. But on the last page, you see that Willy has a litter of puppies and you can predict that a lot more mischief is going to occur.

The vocabulary and content will probably be accessible to most first graders, although some may need some help on concepts like *garage*. The book is organized around the days of the week, so knowing that sequence (and then realizing the organizational pattern) will be very helpful to the reader. There are a few contractions. The basic theme has to do with family life and relationships, also accessible to children. (We note that it is important to include within your guided reading and read aloud collections stories about many different kinds of families.)

All of the factors we have discussed would figure into your thinking about introducing *Willy the Helper* and teaching the group of children who are reading it. What you select to emphasize will depend on:

- What children know how to do as readers and can do independently (and will therefore not need your teaching support).

- What children will be able to solve on their own.

- What information children will need to read the text with understanding, accuracy, and fluency.

- Your teaching goals for this particular group of children.

Realistic Fiction, Level J

Henry and Mudge: The First Book is a wonderful first experience in reading chapter books. The seven chapters, each averaging about eight pages, are tied together by the themes of home, family, and pets (see Figure 7–3).

Text Analysis of: *Willy the Helper,* by Catherine Peters (Level D)

FACTOR	FEATURES
Genre and Forms	❖ Realistic fiction.
Text Structure	❖ Episodic structure. ❖ Past tense—days of the week.
Content	❖ Familiar setting. ❖ Chores. ❖ Parts of house.
Themes and Ideas	❖ Home/pet. ❖ Helping family. ❖ Messes. ❖ Tolerance.
Language and Literary Features	❖ Repetition. ❖ Humor/Irony. ❖ Conversational tone. ❖ Twist in plot. ❖ Literary voice. ❖ Surprise.
Sentence Complexity	❖ Simple sentences. ❖ Sentences beginning with a phrase
Vocabulary	❖ A few content words. ❖ Days of the week. ❖ Household items/chores.
Words	❖ High frequency: *on, what, but, me, the.* ❖ Contractions.
Illustrations	❖ Support and extend meaning.
Book and Print Features *Length*	❖ 79 words. ❖ 8 pages.
Print & Layout	❖ Large, clear font. ❖ Good space between words and lines. ❖ 3 lines per page. ❖ Consistent placement.
Punctuation	❖ Period. ❖ Comma. ❖ Question mark. ❖ Exclamation mark.

Figure 7–2. Text Analysis of Willy the Helper *by Catherine Peters (Level D)*

Text Analysis: *Henry and Mudge: The First Book,* by Cynthia Rylant (Level J)

FACTOR	FEATURES
Genre and Forms	❖ Realistic fiction. ❖ A story about a boy and his pet that is fiction but could be real.
Text Structure	❖ Narrative.
Content	❖ Familiar, everyday experiences—eating, sleeping, playing, school. ❖ Setting is home and neighborhood; not critical to understanding the story. ❖ Story about a boy and a dog. ❖ Dealing with everyday problems. ❖ Exploration of feelings such as loneliness, fear. ❖ Chapter titles support context. ❖ Chapters stand alone but are related by sequence and theme.
Themes and Ideas	❖ Friendship, family relationships.
Language and Literary Features	❖ Chapters alternate perspective—first chapter is told from Henry's perspective, second from Mudge's, and so on. ❖ Some use of literary phrases.
Sentence Complexity	❖ Mostly simple sentences joined by *and.* ❖ Some embedded clauses. ❖ Dialogue is assigned to characters.
Vocabulary	❖ Generally simple, familiar words.
Words	❖ Only a few three-syllable words. ❖ Many easy frequently encountered words.
Illustrations	❖ Pictures of characters extend the meaning and evoke feelings. ❖ Pictures of characters reveal personality, are appealing. ❖ Pictures have some simple symbolism (for example, Mudge's collection of collars from small to huge).
Book and Print Features *Length*	 ❖ 40 pages; average of 8 pages per chapter. ❖ Over 250 words; 117 words in first chapter.
Print & Layout	❖ Medium font (14- to 16-point). ❖ Clear, simple print; no italics, bold, or all capitals.
Punctuation	❖ Full range of punctuation except for semicolons and dashes. ❖ Dialogue clearly marked and separated by a phrase identifying the speaker.
Tools	❖ Table of contents. ❖ Chapter titles.

Figure 7–3. *Text Analysis,* Henry and Mudge: The First Book, *by Cynthia Rylant (Level J)*

The story, which focuses on the young boy Henry and his large dog Mudge, is a simple third-person narrative with one episode per chapter; the text is organized chronologically. The content will be familiar to young students. Even if they do not have pets, most are familiar with some of the problems and issues related to having them. Henry and Mudge's everyday problems offer many opportunities for readers to empathize with the characters. For example, Henry is scared of walking to school alone. When he walks alone, he thinks about tornadoes, dogs that bite, bullies, and ghosts. He walks fast and never looks behind him. When Mudge is with him, however, he thinks about rain, rocks, vanilla ice cream, and good dreams. He likes walking to school!

The chapters are narrated alternately by Henry and Mudge, but the change is signaled by the appropriate name's being used in the chapter titles (Henry, Mudge, Henry, Mudge). The setting, which is not critical to understanding the story, is the home and neighborhood.

The language of this book is straightforward; it includes many easy frequently encountered words and no technical language. The writer has used very few words of more than two syllables. Most of the sentences are simple, and there are only a few embedded clauses. Dialogue is assigned to characters with words like *said, cried,* and *thought.* The font is clear, the print size large (a 14- or 16-point font). The layout supports young readers who are just beginning to read longer pages of print. As mentioned earlier, new sentences always start at the left margin and there is plenty of space between lines (see Figure 4–2). There is an illustration on every page and lots of white space. The pictures evoke feelings and add meaning to the story. There is some symbolism: on one page, the illustrator shows seven of Mudge's collars, each bigger than the one before.

In introducing this text, you would want readers to understand Henry and Mudge and their special relationship. The whole book is really about how Henry feels about Mudge and Mudge feels about Henry. Becoming aware of this strong relationship in the first few chapters helps students understand how Henry feels when Mudge gets lost later in the book. You might point out chapter titles and help students realize how titles sometimes help you think what the chapter might be about.

Traditional Literature, Level K

Let's think about the text characteristics of a more difficult book in a different genre. *The Pancake* is a traditional cumulative tale that will be familiar to many children as *The Gingerbread Boy* (see Figure 7–4). The story is presented as one long continuous narrative with no chapter divisions. The plot unfolds chronologically. Episodes are highly predictable; events and language are repetitive.

The theme, or "moral," of the story could be "don't boast" or "don't be too cocky." Other possible themes include "people working together" or "watch out for tricky foxes." The same basic ideas are repeated page after page. Told in third-person narrative, the tale features "flat" characters (i.e., they do not have complex motives). Readers can empathize with the "seven hungry children," who are mentioned several times. The language of the text is rhythmic; the writer has repeated the same adjectives and verbs in pairs (for example, *swelled and rose, thick and tempting*). The language is representative of traditional tales:

> "Please, mother," they cried,
> "let us eat the pancake right away!
> We are so hungry."
> "Wait, my dear ones,"
> said the woman.
> "Before we eat,
> I must flip the pancake over
> and cook it on the other side."
> (p. 8)

At the same time, the long, complex sentences provide some challenge, and there are interesting

Text Analysis, *The Pancake*, by Anita Lobel (Level K)

FACTOR	FEATURES
Genre and Forms	❖ Traditional literature. ❖ Folktale about a pancake who comes to life and rolls away from the other characters, only to be tricked and eaten by a fox.
Text Structure	❖ Narrative.
Content	❖ Familiar story to many children.
Themes and Ideas	❖ Traditional tale with some moral lessons—"Don't be too cocky!" or "People should work together."
Language and Literary Features	❖ Repeated use of the same adjectives and adverbs in pairs. ❖ Rhythmic language that moves the story along. ❖ Repetition of phrases. ❖ Characters are "flat," in that they do not change or develop (The Pancake is eaten rather than learning a lesson. The lesson is for the readers.) ❖ Little interpretation of characters' motives other than children being hungry. ❖ Personality of the Pancake dominates. ❖ Cumulative tale. ❖ Episodes follow in sequence with repeated events. ❖ Straightforward revelation of plot in temporal sequence. ❖ One long, continuous narrative; no chapter divisions. ❖ Third-person narrative; no chapter divisions.
Sentence Complexity	❖ Long, complex sentences.
Vocabulary	❖ Interesting adjectives (*splendid, tempting, soggy, stupid*). ❖ Use of the unusual verb *shall*.
Words	❖ Words with letter clusters. ❖ Many easy frequently encountered words. ❖ Mostly one- and two-syllable words. ❖ A few three-syllable words and compound words (*mouth-watering, delicious, wonderful*).
Illustrations	❖ Show engaging characters. ❖ Closely follow text.
Book and Print Features	
Length	❖ 47 pages. ❖ About 11–14 lines on text pages and about 5–6 lines on picture pages.
Print & Layout	❖ Medium font (14- to 16-point). ❖ Clear spaces between words and between lines.
Punctuation	❖ Full range of punctuation except for semicolons and dashes. ❖ Long sentences with phrases separated by commas. ❖ Dialogue separated by a phrase identifying the speaker; standard punctuation.

Figure 7–4. Text Analysis, The Pancake, *by Anita Lobel (Level K)*

adjectives that many children might not have read before, such as *splendid* and *tempting*. There are a few three-syllable words and several compound words, along with many frequently encountered words.

The text is forty-seven pages long, with between eleven and fourteen lines of text on each page. The layout is consistent, alternating full pages of print with pages showing an illustration and a half-page of print. Illustrations appear on every spread and are closely related to the text on that spread. The font is medium-size (14- or 16-point) and there are clear spaces between words and between lines. Dialogue is assigned, and a full range of punctuation is used except for semicolons and dashes. A challenge to young readers might be the longer "lists" of actions that are joined by and set off by commas.

Introducing *The Pancake*, you would certainly remind children of *The Gingerbread Man* if they are familiar with that story. You would want to highlight some of the difficult words by using them in conversation; your conversation can also give children a feel for the language of the story. If they have heard folktales read aloud, they will have expectations for this kind of story. You may also want to draw attention to and/or demonstrate the way you read a long sentence, pausing at each comma to show what this mark of punctuation means.

Biography, Level Q

A Pocketful of Goobers: A Story About George Washington Carver (Mitchell 1986) is a well written biography of the famous scientist who found over three hundred uses for peanuts (see Figure 7–5). It is a third-person narrative, beginning with Carver's early life and continuing through his old age. While the text is clear and readable, readers need some background information (how Carver persisted in spite of the shadow of slavery and endemic racism, for example) in

order to understand it. The author takes a few liberties in ascribing feelings and dialogue to Carver, but the circumstances described speak for themselves.

The theme of the biography is the subject's triumph over the odds against him (societal factors). There are some abstract ideas within the text that might require discussion. For example, Carver is told that he should learn all he can so that someday he can "give back" to his people.

Sentence structure is for the most part simple; a full range of punctuation is used. While most concepts are explained within the text, one section deals with Carver's scientific experiments; the language here includes more-technical words (*technician* and *substance*, for example). There are also some more-difficult words related to his profession (*university* and *dean*, for example).

The text is sixty-four pages long and has five chapters with between five and eight pages each. The font is 12 point and easy to read. There are many words in italics or all capitals for emphasis. Illustrations are soft black-and-white charcoal drawings; most are full-page. The text is made more interesting by the inclusion of an illustration every three or four pages. Chapters begin with a full half-page of white space. Two informational tools are provided: an author's note in the front and a list of more facts about Carver in the back.

In introducing the book, you will want to ask students what they already know and then enrich their knowledge. Establishing the setting is important, but it's not necessary to present a long lesson on slavery or Carver's time period; students will learn more as they read and discuss this text. Students will be interested in the significance of the title (*goober* was an African word for *peanut*). Many adults have heard peanuts called "goober peas" but do not know that the word has African origins. You may also want to "unlock" some of the scientific words and help students with some strategies to recognize word parts.

Text Analysis, *Pocketful of Goobers,* by Barbara Mitchell (Level Q)

FACTOR	FEATURES
Genre and Forms	❖ Biography. ❖ Authentic biography of George Washington Carver, a botanist and chemist who was born to a slave family in southern United States and went on to make important scientific discoveries; covers his life from 1864 to 1943.
Text Structure	❖ Nonfiction text—biography. ❖ Presented in narrative form. ❖ Organized in straightforward temporal sequence. ❖ Most concepts elaborated to help the reader.
Content	❖ Background knowledge provided in the author's note (examples—*goober* is African word for *peanut*; information on slavery). ❖ Some background knowledge required to understand the significance of George's experiments.
Themes and Ideas	❖ Persistence in overcoming society's wrongs. ❖ Value of education. ❖ Contributions of a brilliant man who was ignored and ridiculed because of race but kept on learning. ❖ Traditional tale with some moral lessons—"Don't be too cocky!" or "People should work together." ❖ Some abstract ideas (example: learning all he could and then "giving back" to his people).
Language and Literary Features	❖ Well-written biography. ❖ Organized in straightforward temporal sequence.
Sentence Complexity	❖ Long, complex sentences. ❖ Most sentences have only one or two embedded clauses.
Vocabulary	❖ Requires background information (for example, *Ku Klux Klan, university, dean, technician,* and *substance*).
Words	❖ Most of the three- and four-syllable words are related to George's scientific experiments and his profession.
Illustrations	❖ Soft, black-and-white charcoal drawings. ❖ Mostly full-page drawings. ❖ Approximately one illustration every 3–4 pages.
Book and Print Features *Length* *Print & Layout* *Punctuation* *Tools* *Punctuation*	❖ 64 pages; 5 chapters—range from 5 to 8 pages each. ❖ Easy-to-read font—approximately 12-point. ❖ Words in italics and all capitals for emphasis. ❖ Full range of punctuation. ❖ Table of contents. ❖ Chapter headings. ❖ Full range of punctuation.

Figure 7–5. Text Analysis, A Pocketful of Goobers, *by Barbara Mitchell (Level Q)*

Historical Fiction, Level S

The Witch of Fourth Street and Other Stories (Levoy 1974) is a wonderful collection of nine interconnected short stories (see Figure 7–6). Each story has its own plot and contributes to the overall plot of the collection. The settings are important, because readers are expected to understand the influence of places that are distant in space and time. Stories are presented as third-person narratives. Each is told from the point of view of one main character—a different one in every story. Some of these narrators are present in some of the other stories, however, and are revealed more fully as we discover how others see them.

The stories are full of complex ideas, presented both implicitly and explicitly. Understanding the text requires inference and analysis. For example, in one story a character dies, but the event is implied metaphorically rather than specifically stated:

Until the breeze fell to a murmur of voices, and the great wings softly let him down; down to the very edge of Moscow, to the very street, to the very house, to the very room, to the very bed that was waiting for him. The curtains fell over him like warm blankets; the murmur of voices fell over him like the voices of his mother and father. And he slept and sighed *ah ah haha humm kremph,* but very gently, very, very gently.

And the children of Second Avenue in New York city never saw Samuel Moscowitz from Moscow again. (pp. 109/110)

There are multiple themes: the Holocaust and immigration figure strongly as the characters' stories are told. The text has complex sentences but the language is mostly straightforward. A challenge to the reader is dealing with some dialect, as well as some words that are from languages other than English. There are also some onomatopoetic words, and the author uses metaphor frequently. Vocabulary specific to the setting (*bambino, hand*

organ, macushla, elevated train line, highballing, goulash) may require some discussion either before or after reading the stories. Most of the words are one or two syllables; any multisyllable words are generally easy to solve.

The whole book is 110 pages; each story is about fifteen pages. The length and challenge of these stories is just about right for a single lesson; however, you will want students to read the entire text, because the interconnections among the stories offer the opportunity to build a more sophisticated understanding of text structure and enable readers to synthesize the whole meaning.

The print is presented in a clear font, but it is small (about 10-point). There is clear spacing and varied print style—italics and capital letters are used for emphasis, for example. Sentences are organized into paragraphs and carried over between pages. The text contains nine black-and-white line drawings, one per story, that enhance readers' knowledge of the setting and help them interpret the text. The pages on which a story begins have a half-page of white space above the title. The text contains the full range of punctuation for complex sentences, including dashes and ellipses.

Informational Text, Level U

Insects (Bird and Short 1999) is an informational text full of beautiful photographs, drawings, and charts (see Figure 7–7).

The print and graphics present a great deal of information about insects—for example, the different kinds of insects, the parts of their bodies, what they eat. Information is presented in a straightforward way, with many details; it is organized into categories.

Readers are required to acquire and integrate information from both the print and the graphics, many of which require interpretation. Readers will also need to understand the way information is organized into categories and subcategories. Overall, *Insects* presents three layers of headings—section, main heading, and subheadings. Each

FACTOR	FEATURES
Genre and Forms	❖ Historical fiction short stories. ❖ Stories of New York's East side, where many immigrants lived in the early 1900s.
Text Structure	❖ Narrative—series of short stories that intertwine to create a larger story. ❖ Well-developed story structure.
Content	❖ Unfamiliar content to most students. ❖ Requires background information (examples: Holocaust, immigration). ❖ Setting is important to understanding the text.
Themes and Ideas	❖ Multiple and interrelated themes, both concrete and abstract (examples: immigration, stereotypes, discrimination, Holocaust, courage).
Language and Literary Features	❖ Mostly straightforward language. ❖ Dialect (examples: *gee-up, give 'em up, neither, huh*). ❖ Onomatopoetic words (example: *clikety-clik*). ❖ Use of simile or metaphor (example: *She held her penny tightly in her fingers as if it were about to fly from a bird from its nest.*) ❖ Third-person narrative. ❖ Each story told from point of view of a main character. ❖ Stories reveal more about each main character from another's point of view. ❖ Complex plot (overall theme and subplots).
Sentence Complexity	❖ Many sentences with embedded clauses.
Vocabulary	❖ Words from language other than English (examples: *humn kremph, macushla, matzo*). ❖ Dialect. ❖ Many frequently encountered words. ❖ Vocabulary specific to the setting (examples: *highballing; goulash*). ❖ Some words from language other than English.
Words	❖ Mostly one- or two-syllable words. ❖ Some multisyllable words that are easy to solve.
Illustrations	❖ Nine illustrations. ❖ Black-and-white line drawings. ❖ Illustrations enhance interpretation of the text.
Book and Print Features *Length* *Print & Layout* *Punctuation* *Tools*	 ❖ 110 pages; 9 stories, each about 15 pages. ❖ About 250 words per page. ❖ Small, clear font (about 10-point). ❖ Clear spacing. ❖ Varied print style—use of italics and all capitals for emphasis. ❖ Full range of punctuation ❖ Chapter titles. ❖ Table of contents

Figure 7–6. Text Analysis, The Witch of Fourth Street *by Myron Levoy (Level S)*

Text Analysis, *Insects,* by Bettina Bird and Joan Short (Level U)

FACTOR	FEATURES
Genre and Forms	❖ Informational. ❖ Informational text about insects, including those that undergo no change, those that partially change, and those that undergo a complete metamorphosis. Provides information about their bodies, their life histories, their behavior, and their ability to survive.
Text Structure	❖ Content unfamiliar to most upper elementary students. ❖ Expository.
Content	❖ Information organized into categories with major ideas and subcategories. ❖ Highly technical subject matter.
Themes and Ideas	❖ Complex ideas supported with details and illustrations. ❖ Complex ideas supported with tools such as glossary.
Language and Literary Features	❖ Concrete information. ❖ Straightforward presentation of information. ❖ Provides many details. ❖ Requires integration of information from text and graphics.
Sentence Complexity	❖ Generally simple sentences with few embedded clauses.
Vocabulary	❖ Many technical words related to subject matter.
Words	❖ Many multisyllable words. ❖ Words require complex analysis. ❖ Many frequently encountered words.
Illustrations	❖ Many diagrams, charts, and photographs that provide important information.
Book and Print Features *Length*	 ❖ 45 pages of text and additional pages for the index, life histories, and pronunciation guide. ❖ 4 sections, each with 2–3 subsections and further sub-subsections.
Print & Layout	❖ Print in a variety of sizes related to main ideas and subcategories. ❖ Size of print is clue to categorically organized information.
Punctuation	❖ Simple punctuation.
Tools	❖ Table of contents. ❖ Headings, subheadings. ❖ Pronunciation guide.

Figure 7–7.   Text Analysis, Insects, *by Bettina Bird and Joan Short (Level U)*

heading signals that more details are being provided about the particular categories and subcategories. (A sample page layout is provided in Figure 7–8.)

The sentences in the text are generally simple, with few embedded clauses and simple punctuation, but the words are highly technical and related to the subject matter. There are many multisyllable words that will not be familiar to students and that they will find difficult to pronounce. It would be a good idea to show them how to look at these longer words and recognize some root words or word parts. Students will not need to be able to say aloud perfectly every single word in this text. You would not want readers to be blocked from reading and understanding the ideas in the text as they struggle to pronounce words like *stribulating, tracheae,* and *ovipositor.* After all, as adults, we read many words in texts even when we are unsure of the exact pronunciation. The goal is to help students see how these scientific words are connected to the subject matter. For example, *metamorphosis* may be understood by learning:

> *morph = form or shape*
> *meta = change or alteration*
> *osis = state or condition*

A *metamorphosis,* therefore, is the state of changing in form.

An index, species life history, and punctuation guide are provided to help readers. These tools are complex because of the subject matter. Presumably,

---

Mouth Parts

An insect's mouth is simply a hole in the lower part of the head. A flap called a *labrum,* or lip, is attached to the top of the mouth opening. Around the mouth opening are several mouth parts which vary in shape from species to species according to the way the insect feeds.

Insects that bite and chew their food (such as grasshoppers) have two pairs of jaws. The front pair (*mandibles*) often have sharp teeth and are used for biting, tearing and chewing. The second pair (*maxillae*) are behind the mandibles. The maxillae hold the food that is in the insect's mouth and push it down the insect's throat. Both pairs of jaws move in a sideways fashion.

Insects that live on fluids like nectar and plant sap have a long tube for sucking. The sucking tube is usually called a *proboscis.* The butterfly's proboscis coils up under the insect's head when it is not feeding.

Insects that pierce plants to suck sap (such as cicadas), or the skin of animals or humans to suck blood (such as mosquitoes), have sharp, needle-like spikes called *stylets* as part of the sucking tube. The stylets help to pierce the food source.

THE THORAX

The thorax is the part of an insect's body between the head and the abdomen. An insect's legs and wings are joined to segments of the thorax. Muscles that control the movements of the legs and wings are attached to the inner walls of these segments.

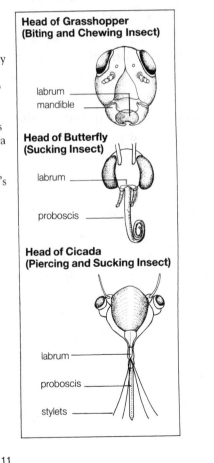

11

Figure 7–8.   Page from Insects *by Bettina Bird and Joan Short*

students reading at this level will already be familiar with these tools rather than learning to use them for the first time; nevertheless, you may want to point them out and practice using them within the context of this text.

Insects is forty-eight pages long. It is divided into four sections, each with several subsections. The print size varies with the level or hierarchy of the idea; in other words, it is related to the nature of the information being presented. Print is also included in many of the graphics in the form of labels and legends. This text would not need to be read from beginning to end, but it bears a great deal of close examination, because you can find so much information of different kinds on different parts of each page. You may want to show students how they can generate different questions and then find places in the text that answer precisely what they want to know.

Every page has both print and illustrations. The layout is attractive and invites the reader to scan for information. You will want to point out how some information is provided in the graphics and print connected to them; this information is important and part of what you need to read to find out about insects.

Summary

The more complex texts are, the greater their demands on readers, and that's good: reading them offers a chance for learning. The trick is to guide students to texts they can read successfully with the help of your text introduction and teaching. In this way, you "up the ante," asking students to expand their reading powers by applying their processing strategies in new ways.

Whether we are guiding students' choices for independent reading (in school or at home) or introducing books in guided reading, detailed knowledge of the texts and their accessibility is an indispensable tool for us as teachers. But, as you continue to work with texts—analyzing them, talking about them, and observing students as they read them—you will develop a mental framework for detecting text factors that offer chances to learn and/or will cause confusion for students. Your understanding of the characteristics will help you level new texts and teach more effectively with texts you select for readers.

Suggestions for Professional Development: Analyzing Texts

1. Work with your grade-level colleagues to analyze a few texts in depth. You might select one fiction text, one biography, and one informational text that you have used with students. Ask everyone to read these three books before the meeting.

2. In pairs, using the blank form in Figure 7–10, examine each of the texts. Write notes in the appropriate boxes.

3. Compare your analyses with those of others in the group. Then discuss each text, asking:

   ■ What does this text demand of the reader in terms of comprehension? In terms of word solving?

   ■ What aspects of the text will support the reader? What aspects will be a challenge?

   ■ What can this text teach typical students in your school about reading?

   ■ What would you want to "unlock" in a book introduction so that these typical students will have some background when they encounter the problem while reading independently? What will you want to leave for them to discover on their own?

   ■ For which students in your classes would this text be "just right"? Identify one of these students by name and share his or her characteristics as a reader with your colleagues.

4. Make a combined list of the characteristics— what they know and can do, as well as what

they need to know—of readers who would find this text just right (with support, they could read the text in a way that exhibits smooth processing at a good rate, with phrasing, intonation, word recognition, and rapid word solving).

When you complete these activities, you will have engaged in a thorough analysis of the three texts and will have done the kind of thinking that results in a good introduction and successful teaching in guided reading. Your notes are a good resource for you as you plan your introduction.

Text Analysis of: _____	
FACTOR	FEATURES
Genre and Forms	
Text Structure	
Content	
Themes and Ideas	
Language and Literary Features	
Sentence Complexity	
Vocabulary	
Words	
Illustrations or Art	
Book and Print Features Length Print & Layout Punctuation Tools	

Figure 7–9.   Text Analysis Form

CHAPTER EIGHT

CREATING AND USING A HIGH-QUALITY LEVELED BOOK COLLECTION

For readers of all ages, two principles relative to guided reading lessons consistently stand out:

- To expand the ability to read with ease, successful problem solving, and understanding, readers must work on texts that are within their control but that include a few challenges.

- To teach skillfully in guided reading lessons, teachers must select texts that are within the readers' control, presenting only a few challenges in terms of word solving, concepts and ideas, and language.

At first glance, it may appear that these two points are the same, just stated in slightly different language. They do speak to the same issue, but one has to do with learning, the other with teaching. Appropriate text selection is so important that the point is worth making in both contexts.

Good readers use "working systems" that make it possible for them to engage in moment-to-moment problem solving and learn more about the process of reading simply by doing it (Clay 2001). As we read, we meet challenges to word solving or understanding; we apply strategies with ease and fluency to solve problems and learn more from doing so. If the text is too hard, the whole process breaks down, and comprehension is lost. The struggling reader is not performing effectively and cannot learn more; it is therefore of paramount importance for students to read texts effectively every day. Text selection is basic to that learning.

For most elementary students, reading independently is not a sufficient means by which to expand their abilities; they require teaching. In lessons and individual conversation, teachers make a difference in student learning by interacting in ways that support efficient processing of appropriate texts. If the text is too easy, students do not have enough opportunities to learn; if it is too hard, no amount of good teaching will "work." Good text selection is a necessary but not sufficient factor in the success of a reading program.

Creating a Leveled Collection

You may create a leveled collection simply by gathering a large number of books and working with your colleagues to discuss the characteristics of the texts (see Chapter 2). Using your experiences in teaching reading, you will find that by discussing the supports and challenges, you can place a variety of books along a continuum of difficulty. Of course, your beginning categorizations should be tested as you work with children in independent and guided reading over a period of time. Gradually, categories will become more stable.

Many groups of teachers have worked with their book collections over several years, periodically coming together to discuss the books, revise levels, and add new books. They have used running records or other coded observations of reading behavior with children of varying levels to assess text difficulty. As you read and analyze the books with your colleagues, you will discover that you are talking about more than the texts. You will be talking about the students and their reading behavior. You will be getting to know the books and getting to know the readers.

Another way to create a leveled collection is to begin with a set of books that have already been analyzed and organized along a gradient of difficulty and then to add to the collection. The set should be one that you have found reliable in the past. If you select a collection from a particular publisher, it should be one that you have used with children over time and with which you are familiar. We suggest that you begin with the book list we have developed (Fountas and Pinnell 2006, or available at *www.fountasandpinnellleveledbooks.com*), but we advise you to go beyond it in developing your own knowledge and skill. As always, you are considering difficulty based on your experience with children, so don't hesitate to occasionally "relevel" texts that, in your judgment, present particular challenges or are easy for the students you teach. Then, as you acquire them, add new books from many different publishers to the levels. Selecting a few books on each level that typify the range of characteristics for that level will give you something to use in comparison with new texts. Soon, you will have a rich and varied collection.

In creating our leveled book list, we engaged in a process that involved working with teams of teachers over many years:

1 We discussed the way texts support readers in the development of a reading process. We explored the use of texts with readers and observed their behaviors with running records and other coded records of reading behavior.

2. We worked with many teams of teachers to gather a collection of books that were appropriate for use in guided reading, K–8. We considered teachers' descriptions of the ways in which they used the books, and we observed guided reading lessons. We examined records

of individual children reading many of these books and reflected on their reading in relation to their literacy performance in other areas.

3. For this beginning collection of books, we looked at the characteristics of texts in relation to what we know about children's development of a reading process.

4. With various teams of teachers, we grouped books with similar characteristics and placed them along a continuum according to their level of complexity.

5. We described the specific characteristics of texts at each level.

6. We worked with many teachers to field-test the book collection with guided reading groups. As we learned more about the books, we revised the levels as needed.

7. We added new books to the collection by carefully analyzing the composite of text characteristics and estimating their appropriate levels and then inviting teachers to use the books and reading records to assess text difficulty. Again, we revised our levels accordingly.

8. We expanded the book list to include thousands of other published books based on their similarity to books that exemplified the levels.

Many of the books on our list have been field-tested; others are in the process of field-testing. Levels are continually revised as they are used over time with varying groups of students and as we receive feedback from teachers. Your input (see Appendix 1/website) is welcomed; the list is ever expanding and changing based on wide experience with the books and readers.

Gradient Versus Grade Level

In considering *gradient* and *grade level*, we are thinking about two different but related hierarchies. *Grade level* refers to the traditional organizational strata for students in elementary and middle schools. In most parts of the United States, students enter a grade; spend nine-and-a-half months learning according to the established curriculum; and, given satisfactory performance, move on to the next higher grade. The term also refers to the *expected performance* or *standard of performance* (in this case performance in reading) for the grade level. We do have grade-level expectations; if a student is performing significantly below those levels, then extra instruction is required.

Gradient, on the other hand, is defined as a slope of increasing and decreasing steps along a continuum. In a text gradient the books are placed in categories that are more narrowly and specifically defined than *grade level.* The characteristics at a level, taken together, generally represent text difficulty as indicated by the supports and challenges to the reader. *In general,* if a student can read and understand (with appropriate support) one or two books at a level, then most of the others will be accessible to him (again, within structured support). If the texts are quite easy for the reader, then the next level on the gradient may be appropriate for instruction.

The point of the gradient is to think about continuous progress along it. The idea is for the students to read books in an instructional context at the appropriate level and to be working always on expanding the variety of texts read within the level or moving to the next instructional level. Grade level is somewhat incidental to this day-to-day process. *Good teaching begins where the readers are and takes them forward.* If the teacher begins beyond where the students are able to be successful, there is "no point of contact." Since readers in any grade have different levels of development, a variety of books at different text levels will be required for effective teaching.

We have attempted to create a universal gradient of difficulty in our leveled book list, one that combines many different kinds of books that may be used as a foundation for reading instruction. Encountering variety makes the reader flexible. A variety of excellent texts makes it easier for you to create a supportive sequence for any particular group of readers. The books on our list are leveled based on multiple factors that are related to children's literacy learning over time.

Grade Level Equivalents

As shown in Figure 2–1, the book levels in our collection correspond in an approximate way to grade levels. The range within the arrows are approximate goals for the grade. As you are well aware, placement in a grade does not mean that a student reads at that level.

Notice that no rigid division between grade levels exists. Also, grade levels may vary according to school district or geographic region. Matching texts to readers is more important than precise definitions of grade levels. As children become more sophisticated in processing texts, many of them can read books well beyond their present grade levels; the key is their understanding and ability to learn from text. As we move up in our text gradient we need broader levels, with many more books, and more-varied so other factors will enter into the process. Some students may need to spend more time reading at a particular level to build experience and fluency even when they are reading with high accuracy.

While it may seem paradoxical to lay the gradient alongside grade-level expectations, that is exactly what we need to do when we think of our teaching and the changes we expect in students over time. We select books for daily teaching against a background of expected grade-level performance and progress over time. This juxtaposition helps us know which students need extra help of what particular kind.

Different publishers have based their materials on different book features, but they do not necessarily use the same set of book characteristics. Some use controlled vocabulary, for example; others use phonics elements; still others use stages of reading development. In this book list, we have

Book Grade-Level Equivalence Chart[1]

	GRADE	CLASSROOM LEVEL[2]	BASAL LEVEL	READING RECOVERY
Emergent	Kindergarten	A	Readiness	1
	Grade One	B		2
Early	Kindergarten Grade One			2
	Kindergarten Grade One	C	PP1	3 & 4
	Grade One	D	PP2	5 & 6
	Grade One	E	PP3	7 & 8
	Grade One	F	Primer	9 & 10
	Grade One	G		11 & 12
Transitional	Grade One Grade Two	H	Grade One	13 & 14
	Grade One Grade Two	I		15, 16, 17
	Grade Two	J	Grade Two	18, 19, 20
	Grade Two	K		
	Grade Two Grade Three	L		
	Grade Two Grade Three	M		
Self-extending	Grade Three	N	Grade Three	
	Grade Three Grade Four	O		
	Grade Three Grade Four	P		
	Grade Four	Q	Grade Four	
	Grade Four Grade Five	R		
Advanced	Grade Four	S		
	Grade Four	T	Grade Five	
	Grade Five	U		
	Grade Five Grade Six	V		
	Grade Five Grade Six	W	Grade Six	
	Grade Six Grade Seven	X		
	Grades Seven, Eight	Y	Grade Eight	
	Grades Seven, Eight	Z		

[1] All levels and equivalencies are approximations and are subject to revision.
[2] Source: Fountas and Pinnell 1996.

Figure 8–1.   Book Grade-Level Equivalence Chart

attempted to create a universal gradient that incorporates a variety of complex factors related to readability.

Our list includes books from hundreds of different publishers. You will find that many publishers have devised number or letter systems of their own, but they are probably different from the gradient discussed here. Many publishers have started to use the Fountas and Pinnell levels in their catalogues and have referenced *Guided Reading: Good First Teaching for All Children* (Fountas and Pinnell 1996) or our books on levels as the source for the levels for new books, but this does not mean that we have reviewed them. You can check our website or book list to determine if we have leveled them. We have provided this list for the convenience of teachers, but you can always use the book to help you do your own labeling as well.

Basal Levels

Figure 8–1 indicates an approximate correspondence between the levels in our book list and basal reader levels. We have used the terminology of older basal systems that may still be in use. Instead of using the words "preprimer" and "primer," the newer basal systems may simply refer to grade level: early, middle, and late.

Many schools use basal systems. Using this book list does not require discarding all of your present reading materials. Stories appropriate for guided reading may be selected from basal anthologies, for example, and leveled for your use. You might get together with colleagues at your grade level or across grade levels and talk about the characteristics of the stories in your basal or anthology, comparing them to the books we have leveled. Chances are you have used the stories or selections many times with children, which is an advantage! Pencil in approximate guided reading levels in the table of contents and consider using them in a different sequence with small groups of students at different points in time.

Think of the anthologies as a text resource. You may encounter some stories that you will not choose for guided reading but that you can read aloud to students or use for shared reading. If you want the entire class to experience a particular selection that might be related to curriculum themes, you can read selections aloud. You can also do shared reading with some students, use the selection for guided reading with others, and have a third group of children read it on their own. Some stories, currently used at one grade level, might be more appropriate for another grade level. Advanced readers in second grade, for example, might enjoy reading appropriate selections from the third-grade basal. After you pencil in a level in the table of contents, try the stories with groups, and meet again with colleagues to refine and solidify your judgments of the levels of the stories.

Guided Reading Systems

Many guided reading systems are organized by stages or phases in the acquisition of reading. In the far left column of the equivalence chart, you will notice broad descriptors that correspond to our chart in Figure 1–1, Characteristics of Readers, discussed in Chapter 1. We are not advocating a stage theory of reading; as noted earlier, these broad categories help in using reading behaviors as a guide for matching books to readers. No one child precisely fits a category, but it helps to have clusters of characteristics in mind. We also caution against overuse of checklists, which can limit our thinking. We may check characteristics on a list but possess varying understandings of the checklist phrases. We may rely on the checklist instead of our much more important observations of students' reading.

Many publishers' guided reading systems offer somewhat different categories and labels for phases of reading. We encourage you to examine publishers' materials critically, looking at children's behaviors as examples to guide your decision-making process.

Reading Recovery Levels

A finely leveled collection of books is used in the Reading Recovery tutorial program for first graders (Clay 1993b). The last column on the equivalence chart provides approximate correlations between classroom levels and the levels used in Reading Recovery. These correlations will be helpful to classroom teachers in working with children who are also receiving Reading Recovery services. Consultation between the classroom teacher and the Reading Recovery teacher is important in this process.

Reading Recovery is a one-to-one tutorial program for young children (grade one in the U.S.) who are having extreme difficulty in learning to read and write (see Clay 1993a; Fountas and Pinnell 1996, Chapter 15). The children are generally confused about aspects of reading and are lagging behind others. Books recommended for use in Reading Recovery are organized into a very fine gradient, labeled from 1 to 20. Small steps are very important; the goal is accelerated progress. In the U.S., these levels are appropriate from about the beginning of grade one to the beginning of grade two. Using careful diagnostic information collected every day, the teacher selects one book for one particular child, introduces the book, and supports the child's reading.

Instruction in Reading Recovery is different from instruction in a classroom where students are taught in groups. In creating our gradient of text for the classroom, we returned to the books themselves. We thought about them in relation to classroom reading instruction, necessary to accommodate the small range of differences within groups of children, allowing for slightly more variability within a level as the gradient progresses.

Some variability within a text level is needed to accommodate the differences among children within groups. There are some books that we would use in the classroom that we would not recommend for use in Reading Recovery. Our gradient of text also incorporates books at much higher levels and more sophisticated demands than needed for a first-grade tutorial.

How the Gradient Supports Teaching and Learning

Organizing books and other texts along a gradient of difficulty provides essential support for teaching in several ways:

- The leveled collection supports the selection of books for guided reading. In addition, knowing how the characteristics of a text relate to its difficulty helps you introduce books to students. The introduction makes the text more accessible to students, thus mediating the difficulty level for the group you are working with.

- When you are helping children choose books for independent reading, the level of the books on the gradient will not be obvious. There will simply be good books, well displayed, from which all students choose. In minilessons, you will be teaching students how to examine texts to decide whether they are "easy," "just right," or "challenging." They will read a variety of texts, not just books at their "level." It's extremely helpful, however, if you have the level in mind as you help students make their selections. You will also want to give book talks that draw students' attention to good books in the range of levels needed by your group.

- You will use the leveled collections to help students who are struggling in their reading make good choices for their independent reading in school and at home. Knowing levels will help you check whether students are looking within the appropriate range of books.

- You may want to create some baskets of appropriate books for particular literature study groups. That does not mean you should limit students to the levels they can read. If you want them (or they choose) to discuss books that are too difficult for them to read independently, you can find another way to make the texts accessible (books on tape or buddy reading).

The Leveled Collection

A good leveled collection is made up of texts you select for instruction and organize yourself in containers. A great deal of learning takes place in the process. The gradient supports your text selection and allows you to fit the program to the students rather than pull them through a fixed sequence of texts or make them read materials that are too difficult.

Level is not the only factor to consider as you create your collection. Quality and variety are essential within each level. You will find variety in format and variety in genre.

Variety in Format

The earlier levels of the text gradient introduce children to early print concepts in the beginning stages of reading. For more skilled readers (levels J and up), the leveled collection includes a wider range of text genres. Essentially four kinds of books are included, with varieties within each.

SHORT TEXTS

Many of the texts are short stories or short informational texts with a variety of art. If you select carefully, you can find topics and subjects that are interesting and amusing for students in all grade levels from K to the upper levels.

More complex short texts for older readers provide an opportunity to expand vocabulary, interpret stories, and analyze illustrations and their contributions to the expression of meaning. A short text is a piece of simpler to more complex reading that can usually be completed in a single sitting and be the basis for discussion and analysis.

The students take what they learn how to do on short texts to longer texts they read.

The reading levels for more complex short texts range from about M or N all the way to adult. They have a wide range of themes that provoke much thought and discussion.

EASY CHAPTER BOOKS

Many of the first chapter books are simple narratives organized into short chapters and sections. These beginning chapter books may be much easier than many of the more complex picture books students read. They contain many easy frequently encountered words and simple sentences. The themes and settings are close to students' own experiences. Characters are memorable and do not change much during the story. There are many "series" books in this category. These books are quite helpful in that readers are required to sustain reading over longer stretches of text and to remember information over several days. Many of these are useful in helping readers transition to longer chapter books.

CHAPTER BOOKS

A wide variety of longer, more complex chapter books are included in the gradient. Most books range from about 100 pages to about 300 pages and have complex plots; there are often subplots. Characters develop in response to the events in the story. Readers are required to sustain reading over one to two weeks, and there is much opportunity for discussion at various points. The authors of these books use complex literary language, and themes are increasingly mature as the gradient rises.

SHORT STORY COLLECTIONS

We include numerous short story collections in our leveled list and they are marked for your convenience. They address different cultures and themes. Short stories are excellent texts for guided reading purposes.

Variety in Genre

Our book list includes a variety of fiction and non-fiction. Lower-level narratives are mostly realistic fiction that focuses on themes close to the lives of children. Short texts are likely to include traditional tales, fantasy, and realistic stories. As you move up the gradient, there is more opportunity for students to experience other worlds vicariously. Settings may be distant in time or space, requiring readers to imagine other cultures and technologies.

Informational books present complex ideas and may use technical language that is more difficult for students. Biographies have a structure similar to narratives, but some of them incorporate the additional difficulty of understanding concepts related to historical times. In general, the informational books within any given level are shorter than the narrative texts. Students need to understand specific concepts related to the content and become familiar with the organizational structures typical of informational texts.

The Demands of Texts on Readers

Every text demands that the reader use a combination of strategic actions to solve words and construct meaning. *At every level of this gradient,* texts demand that readers:

- Recognize easy, frequently encountered words quickly and automatically.

- Use multiple sources of information in an integrated way while reading for meaning.

- Process the text at a good pace, with phrasing, slowing down to problem-solve and speeding up again.

- Read silently when reading independently (at about levels H/I and above).

- Use a range of strategies to problem-solve new words, particularly multisyllable words.

- Correct errors that result in loss of meaning.

- Make inferences to understand what is implied but not stated.

- Work to understand characters.

- Recognize important elements of setting.

- Predict and analyze the plot.

- Sustain attention to meaning and interpretation over several days of reading.

- Bring background knowledge to bear in understanding concepts and topics.

- Predict events, outcomes, and problem resolutions while reading sections of text.

- Determine the perspective from which narrative texts are told.

- Understand the organizational structures used to present information.

- Revise interpretations as new information becomes available.

- Recognize relevant aspects of the writer's craft.

- Think critically about the concepts and ideas in the text.

This long list is only a sampling of what readers do during the act of processing text with understanding. Readers meet the demands of texts by simultaneously engaging in these strategies. Reading texts that are easy makes fewer demands on the processing system.

As a teacher you select books from a level on the gradient that is just challenging enough to require processing strategies such as those listed above, and your readers go into action. As they read more, they problem-solve and gain power, and the texts at that particular level become easier, making fewer demands. Then you select books from a level that is just a bit more challenging, and the readers again use this complex constellation of strategic actions. Teachers use the gradient of text as a ladder to help readers learn how to apply their strategies to increasingly more demanding texts.

Balancing Readability and Theme

Because our gradient is based on a range of characteristics rather than a single dimension, you may find a wider range of easier-to-harder texts at the upper levels. There are good reasons to place books with mature themes and subtle messages at the higher levels even though the text may be easy to read. First, the ideas may be very demanding. Second, the circumstances may be hard to understand without a certain degree of life experience. In *The Midwife's Apprentice* (Cushman), for example, a young girl who has been deserted is found by a midwife and eventually takes on the profession herself.

A High-Quality Collection of Genres at All Levels

You will want both your classroom leveled collection and the school leveled collection to be of high quality, supporting students' learning and adding to their reading enjoyment. It is important to include a wide variety of topics, themes, and genres so that you can find books that will interest students as well as expand their reading power. Some suggestions for creating a high-quality collection were described in Figure 2–5.

- You will want to include both fiction and nonfiction, and we advise searching for as many shorter texts as you can find. Collections of short stories are very useful for guided reading.

- Purchase texts from a number of publishers. Buy single titles so you can consider each book separately. Sometimes buying in "sets" may seem economical, but you want to avoid acquiring a great number of books written to the same formula, some high-quality titles mixed with lower-quality ones, or a number of books that neither you nor your students enjoy.

- Select books by authors and topics that are popular with students, and be sure that your collection reflects the diversity of our multicultural society: include a variety of African American, Asian, Latino, and Native American, as well as Caucasian authors.

- Series books like the Matt Christopher or Amber Brown books are always appealing; once students have read one or two in guided reading, they may choose to read more for independent reading (in school or at home).

- High-quality illustrations and interesting graphic features engage students' interest and have the additional value of helping them learn to search for information in many different sources.

Finally, look at the general quality of texts. Students deserve to read books that are put together with care using high quality materials. They should have good bindings, professional layout, and striking illustrations.

Summary

The leveled book collection is vital to your guided reading lessons. This collection will include multiple copies of books at all levels appropriate for the students in your class. It is not necessary to have a lot of books at the extreme low and high levels for your group; you can borrow books from the school bookroom if you have one. You can organize your multiple copies of leveled books into a teacher's collection that is not accessible to students. In the photograph in Figure 4–1, notice the collection of multiple copies of books the teacher keeps on special shelves for use in guided reading lessons.

You will use these titles for your guided reading lessons, introducing particular students to particular books that will support their development as readers. This collection is also helpful in giving students limited choices for their independent reading.

You might create a specially selected basket or box of books for a particular group of readers in your classroom library, choices you think will interest them and that are within the range of levels they can read with fluency and comprehension.

Suggestions for Professional Development: Examining Books in Relation to Readers

If possible, work in cross-grade-level groups to examine texts. Every teacher needs a thorough knowledge of the characteristics and demands of texts in levels A through at least W. (Third-grade teachers, for example, will almost certainly have children reading at level J or even lower; at the same time, these teachers need to have a vision of where their students are going, of the demands of the texts they will be likely to read in fourth, fifth, and sixth grades.)

1. Prepare for the meeting by collecting several titles at each level, A through X or Y. (Tailor the specific levels to the interests of your group; however, be sure to go beyond the specific grade-level designations. You'll be using this collection of titles to explore texts in the next three chapters, so it is worth spending a little time on it.) As a resource, use classroom collections, your school's book collection, and the library. You may want to visit a local public library to get more titles. Many libraries now have substantial collections of series books, etc. Finally, you can take your group to visit a local children's bookstore to examine titles.

2. Place the books in piles or tubs by level and make them easily accessible to participants.

3. Spend some time examining the books and talking about them informally with one another. Ask everyone to sample books from at least three levels. Since most of the books will be from your school, chances are several teachers in the group will know them well. For unfamiliar books, you'll find that teachers can tell quite lot about a book from reading material on the front and back of the book, sampling one or two chapters, and looking at the illustrations.

4. Now do a few comparisons to help you think about the demands of texts on readers and how those demands shift over time. Depending on the interests of your group, select two texts at least two levels apart for comparison. For example, you compare:

   ■ A level B book with a level E book.
   ■ A level J book with a level L book.
   ■ A level M book with a level O book.
   ■ A level P book with a level R book.

5. In pairs, perhaps using the chart of text characteristics presented in Figure 6–1, discuss:

   ■ What do readers have to know and do to read text 1 (the lower-level book)?
   ■ What *different* demands does text 2 (the higher-level book) present to readers?

6. *Alternative A.* If you have time, choose still another book two levels higher than text 2. Ask again: Compared to text 2, what *different* demands does text 3 present to readers? This alternative will help the group begin to see the gradient and the leveled book collection as a long continuum.

7. *Alternative B.* If you have time, choose another text at the text 2 level, asking: Compared to text 2a, what *different* demands does text 2b present to readers? Repeat the process with still another book at that level. This alternative will help the group see the variation within a level that allows students to develop flexibility.

8. Bring participants back to a general discussion. Ask pairs to share some of their discoveries and provide examples from specific texts.

9. Summarize by making a two-column chart of new insights about texts and implications for teachers.

CHAPTER NINE

FINDING THE RIGHT BOOKS FOR READERS

Matching books to readers is the foundation for helping students build and expand reading strategies across the grades. Often in the past we have tried to match readers to books. We assigned reading and assumed all students could accomplish it with understanding and fluency. We handed "grade level" books to students in a particular grade and demanded they "get through" them, a process that may have been possible but was often tedious and even painful for some. Of course, our goal is to raise the reading levels of every student by keeping a close eye on standards; however, we also recognize how reading skills develop. Every day, students must read material that will allow them to use and expand the strategies they currently control. You don't get better by struggling through material you do not understand; you *do* get better by meeting challenges successfully.

There are many ways to think about matching books to readers, and all have value. For example, when selecting books for interactive read aloud and literature study, we pay careful attention to subject matter, writing style, age-level interest, and language use. We want books that appeal to students and expand their knowledge of a variety of texts. The content and literary quality of books is of primary importance, and the themes and concepts should be age appropriate; however, we are not necessarily concerned with students' ability to process them independently. We may make these books available by reading them aloud or providing them on tape. The goal is for the students to comprehend the language and ideas; to notice the writer's craft and to discuss the books with others.

When selecting books for independent and guided reading, we also consider content, themes, and ideas, but we add another requirement. The book must be matched to the readers' current strengths. Successful independent reading means that the individual can process the text with ease, fluency, and understanding using her current strategies and skills. Successful performance in guided reading means that, *with teaching and support,* the student can read the text at the level with ease, fluency, and understanding, expanding his current strategies in the process. To match books to readers we need to analyze the supports and demands of texts carefully in relation to what we know about individual readers.

The Gradient in Relation to Processing Text

When we discuss matching books to readers, we sometimes use terms like *easy, just right,* and *difficult* or *challenging.* The question is always whether the text is appropriate for individual readers, so these designations are relative and vary with the level of teacher support required.

The most powerful tool for observing and analyzing the reading behavior of children in grades K–2 is the running record, which was developed by Marie Clay (2002). The entire observation survey consists of six tasks that are derived from Clay's theory of how young children become literate. The observation survey includes Letter Identification, Hearing and Recording Sounds in Words, Concepts about Print, Word Reading, Writing Vocabulary, and Text Reading (in which the observer takes a running record). The running record enables the observer to make a detailed analysis of a child's reading, noting significant behaviors such as substitutions, omissions, repeats, and hesitations. To take a running record, you do not need anything but a blank form because you simply use check marks to represent the words. Much of the child's processing is indicated by overt behaviors, so you can formulate well-based hypotheses about the strategic actions that may be going on in the head. You can extend your knowledge through conversing with the child about the text just read.

As children begin to read much longer texts, for example at about level K and above, running records are less practical because the lines are much longer and it is harder to follow the text. Also, children's reading behaviors are less overt, and you need a wider variety of information. We recommend moving to a "conference protocol," which involves silent reading, writing, oral conversation, and analysis of a section of text that the student reads aloud and the teacher codes on a photocopy.

In the next section, we discuss the observation of reading behaviors. The principles are the same from grades K–6. Through close observation of oral reading, you can note significant error behaviors that provide a window on processing. Added information from conversation and writing will help you probe the depth of understanding that the reader has constructed.

An "easy" text is one that the reader can independently process with accuracy and fluency, appropriate phrasing, and excellent understanding. Reading easy texts is effortless; word solving requires very little attention. As adults, most texts are easy for us, and we enjoy reading them for relaxation and escape. The same is true for your students; those who like to read will select a range of texts from easy to harder, depending on their purposes for reading. It is beneficial for your students to read easy texts frequently, because they will build fluency and increase their enjoyment.

Reading a "hard" text is quite different from reading an easy text. Here the reader is forced to attend very closely to the print and to employ a range of word-solving strategies. The reader may have to untangle sentence structure that is unfamiliar or difficult or may reread to capture nuances of plot or follow the organizational patterns. If the concepts are quite challenging, the reader may have to seek additional information by consulting references or asking someone for help. If the text is too hard, the process begins to break down. The reading is slow, choppy, word by word. Readers become frustrated and cease to enjoy the process. Those who read difficult texts day after day embed ineffective strategies into the routine they habitually bring to reading. They *expect* reading to be slow and tedious. They *expect* not to understand most or all of what they read.

In independent reading, a "just right" text is one a reader can process easily, but for reading instruction, a "just right" text for a particular individual is one that provides a context for building a more effective reading process. The just-right text provides a small amount of challenge so that the readers will engage in some kind of problem solving while reading, thus expanding their ability. Selecting the right texts for readers depends not only on their current development but on the level of instructional support you plan to give them.

Using the Gradient to Match Books to Readers

A gradient of text is an invaluable tool in supporting reading instruction. In Chapter 2 we defined a gradient of text as a varied collection organized into approximate levels of difficulty. Texts that increase demands in terms of concept, theme, vocabulary, length, and so on, are more difficult. Observing reading behavior while noting the level of the book is essential for matching books to readers.

Using Running Records or Records of Reading Behavior to Assess Children's Reading

The best way to determine an appropriate reading level for a child is to observe reading behavior. Select leveled books (for example, benchmark books) to get started. We strongly encourage you to learn to take a running record or record of reading behavior because they are the most powerful and objective tool you can find. A general guide is that the child must be reading a text at about 90 to 94 percent accuracy, with evidence of successful processing, to determine an instructional level. Take a record on the entire text if a book has less than 200 words. If there are more than 200 words, you will usually want to take the running record on between 150 and 200 words of text to get a sufficient sampling of the child's processing at that level. You will want to continue to have the child read texts at increasingly difficult or easier levels until you determine the instructional level. This will be a "readable" text, one that will be just right for "learning how to read."

Using Running Records with Book Levels

Decisions about using the gradient of text are based on careful observation of children. While benchmark books are used to help in initial placement, continuous running records or records of reading behavior are also used to capture progress over time. Take these running records on any book that the child has read in the guided reading group. They are an effective tool for assessing what children can do in reading without teacher support. This ongoing process of taking running records on "seen" text (a text that has been read before) differs from using benchmark books to take a running record on unseen text for the purpose of periodic interval assessment. Here are some general guidelines for using running records as part of guided reading instruction.

- Find a time to take two or three running records or close observations of reading behavior per day on a systematic basis. It might be just at the beginning of the day while children are independently engaged in reading or writing. It might be at the beginning or end of the group's reading lesson. You will be taking 10 to 15 records in a week.

- Take more frequent records on children who are having difficulty or are lagging behind and less frequent records on high-progress readers. The number of observations may vary from one per week to one per month or even to one per quarter on a given student. The assessment folder, though, will contain a sufficient number of observations to document every student's reading behaviors over time. This collection of running records or other observations serves as a resource as you make ongoing decisions about grouping and regrouping students for instruction and about text selection.

- Observe reading behavior on a book that has been introduced and that the student has read only once, preferably the day before (seen text). Keeping a list of children with a schedule for taking records will help you standardize your procedures.

- Sit beside the child, recording the precise reading behavior. Place your form on a clipboard.

- Afterward, calculate the accuracy rate and the self-correction rate. Self-corrections do not count as errors, but the self-correction rate indicates what ratio of the total number of errors were self-corrected.

- Analyze the errors and self-corrections. This qualitative look at the child's reading behavior can give you important insights. For example, a child might read a selection with high accuracy but the errors may indicate that he is neglecting important sources of information, such as letter-sound relationships and not noticing errors. This analysis is quite helpful in making teaching moves as well as in deciding whether a text is appropriate. (For further information, see Clay 1993b; Fountas and Pinnell 1996; *fountasandpinnellleveledbooks.com*).

■ Write a brief comment about the child's fluency and phrasing to indicate whether the reading was choppy or smooth, fast or laborious, well-phrased or read in a robotic way. This information can help you decide whether the text was too easy, too hard, or just right and can guide teaching emphases.

■ Periodically, reflect on the reading behaviors of a group of children, comparing their responses to books and their reading behaviors. Use this reflection as a basis for deciding the kind of texts to select for the group and whether to choose more difficult texts.

These running records will prove to be an invaluable resource when making decisions such as moving children from one group to another, deciding when to change the book level for instructing a particular group, or considering a suggestion to change a text level in the collection.

Documenting Change

To document your students' reading development, you may use systematic assessments like those described in *Guiding Readers and Writers, Teaching Comprehension, Genre, and Content Literacy* (Fountas and Pinnell 2001), in which students read silently as well as orally and then discuss the reading and write about the text. This information will allow you to evaluate the student's accuracy, rate, fluency, and comprehension of the text at that level. You may also want to use the benchmark book system we have developed for kindergarten through grade 8 (Pinnell and Fountas 2006).

The gradient is also a way to document your students' reading progress over time. As they read books in guided reading lessons, you will note how successfully they process them. At regular inter-

vals, you can record students' reading levels (see the example in Figure 9–1). A blank form is included in Appendix 2. These records can be passed along from year to year in the school or even to other schools in the district.

Look at the record of Catherine's reading progress shown in Figure 9–1. The titles and levels read are listed along the top. (A clear dot on the graph indicates reading above 90 percent accuracy; a filled-in dot means accuracy was below 90 percent.) Catherine began reading at level A in kindergarten and made quick progress through the primary grades. As she read more sophisticated texts, Catherine also encountered greater variety and read for a longer time within each level. She was assessed reading a variety of fiction and nonfiction texts. In fourth grade, she read at level P for quite a while but then moved rapidly over the next several levels. She finished her elementary years reading at level W. Catherine's reading development was smooth, and each teacher was able to build on her previous success.

Using Benchmark Books

A benchmark book is a reliable exemplar selected for each level on the gradient that you can use to determine a reader's level and to measure progress over time. The following chapters contain examples of prototype fiction and nonfiction for levels J through Z on the gradient.

To create a set of benchmark books, you need to identify some very reliable books at each level of the gradient. After you have used the gradient of text for a while, you will begin to notice that a particular text at a given level is almost always just right for students who are reading well at that level. That text is "stable" in that the results do not vary widely from reading to reading.

After identifying several stable fiction and nonfiction books at each level, try them out with a range of students (not necessarily matched to level). Sample their oral reading, have conversations with them, perhaps ask them to do a little

Record of Book Reading Progress

Student's Name: Benjamin Eldridge   **School:** Madison Elementary

Record book reading progress three or four times per year, as agreed upon with your school faculty. Note dates in bottom row. Put an open circle ○ at the child's instructional level on each date indicated. A filled in circle ● indicates student is having some difficulty at the level. Mark the level ○* if additional teaching is also being provided by specialists. Give the year and descriptions of additional reading services on back.

Teacher	Wasson				Haseltine				Spack				Yates				Kieley				Harris			
Book Level	K	K	K	K	1	1	1	1	2	2	2	2	3	3	3	3	4	4	4	4	5	5	5	5
Z (7-8)																								
Y																								
X																								
W (6+)																								
V																								
U																								○
T (5)																					●	●		
S																			○	○				
R																	●	●						
Q (4)															○	○								
P														○										
O																								
N (3)													○											
M											○	○												
L										○														
K																								
J (2)									○															
I																								
H							○	○																
G																								
F						○																		
E																								
D					○																			
C (1)																								
B		○	○																					
A	○																							
Date			3/8	5/4	10/1	1/5	3/8	5/21	10/4	1/7	3/6	5/18	10/3	1/8	3/9	5/30	10/6	1/10	3/6	5/22	10/8	1/12	3/12	5/15

Figure 9–1. Record of Book Reading Progress

writing about what they've read. Then look at the texts again, asking:

- Are the results consistent across different readers?

- Are these books too difficult for students who are not yet reading at this level?

- Are these books quite easy for students who are reading above this level?

Consider factors such as accuracy, comprehension, and fluency as you work with the texts. Remember that successful reading means much more than simply reading the right words.

Over time, you will build up a collection of reliable texts that you can use to:

- Assess and group students at the beginning of the year (and assess new students whenever they enter your classroom).

- Help you make decisions about your reading group configurations.

- Systematically document reading progress over time.

It's best to select the set of benchmark books in collaboration with the other teachers in your school or district. When everyone is involved, you are all more committed to using the gradient and better understanding the supports and challenges in the texts.

Creating a Benchmark Book Set

To create a benchmark book set, you first need to work with a large variety of books at each of the levels. It helps for a group of teachers to collaborate on this process. You get to know the books at a level very well, and you get to know the variety within a level.

1. Have the teachers select five books each that they consider to be reliable at a level. Compare the selections and reach consensus on about five books to try out with individual readers. Use your experience from informal observation as well as your systematic running records or reading records which offer more objective information because while the child was reading you were observing in a very neutral way. You were not teaching or actively supporting the reading, so you can be sure that the child was processing the text independently.

2. Try out the five books for each level by taking reading records on a group of children, all of whom are reading well but still finding some challenge in books on the particular level.

3. Meet again with the group, compare the observations, and select the three most reliable benchmarks for each level.

4. Continue to work with the benchmarks over time. You may find that as you use them with children, some will prove to be less reliable and you will need to make substitutions. This system works best if teachers engage in a continual dialogue.

Introductions for Benchmark Books

To make the benchmark assessment systematic, you will want to create short, standardized introductions for each benchmark book. Remember, you will be working with children individually for this assessment. Introductions consist of two or three sentences that focus on the main idea of the book and use some of the language, which might include the names of characters, specific or technical vocabulary, or other unusual language. Glue or tape the introduction to the front cover of the book so that you can read it aloud to the child before he or she reads it. Include the book's level and, for levels A to J, the number of running words (to help with running records). Two examples are shown in Figures 9–2 and 9–3. For longer texts, select passages of 200–300 words and type them on a sheet to be duplicated.

Introductions for the Benchmark Book *At the Zoo* **(Peters)**

At the Zoo
written by Catherine Peters

Level B
RW 54
E 4

In this book a little girl tells a story about all of the animals at the zoo. On each page she says that she likes the animal and the animal likes her.

Figure 9–2.   Introductions for the Benchmark Book At the Zoo

---

Introductions for the Benchmark Book *The Hole in Harry's Pocket* **(Bloksberg)**

The Hole in Harry's Pocket
written by Robin Bloksberg

Level I
RW 279
E 27

This story is about a little boy whose mother gives him some money to go to the store to buy some milk. He puts the money in his pocket along with his toys and then he has a big problem when he gets to the store.

Figure 9–3.   Introductions for the Benchmark Book The Hole in Harry's Pocket

Using the Benchmark System

A group of colleagues who were working together in an elementary school created an efficient way to use the benchmark system. A description of their process follows.

Preparing the Benchmark Books for Assessment

We selected books and wrote an introduction for each. We typed the introduction to be read to the student, as well as the title, level, number of words, and number of errors a reader can make before the score goes below 90 percent accuracy. We duplicated the material onto sticky-backed paper, and then stuck them onto the outside front cover of each book (see Figure 9–4). You can purchase label printing software and sheets of labels at office supply stores.

We placed a collection of the benchmark books, one at each level, in a two-gallon resealable plastic bag to create a set for each primary teacher and a similar set for each intermediate teacher with sections of text typed and duplicated. Each teacher used the benchmark bag several times over the year to measure students' reading progress. Several other benchmark books were identified on each level to serve as a resource so that teachers would have alternatives if they needed them.

Using the Benchmark Books to Determine Instructional Level

Benchmark books are used to place students in initial instructional groups and to document their reading progress over time. When assessing instructional level at the beginning of the year, you will want to read the introduction aloud and then the student reads the story silently. At lower levels the child does not read the text beforehand, so you should expect it to be more difficult than if read once before. If the child reads the text at about 90 percent accuracy or above with good processing, it is a good instructional level for the child. If it is read below 90 percent accuracy, it was probably too difficult. At higher levels, the student will hear the

Level E

RW = 120

E = 12

Peaches the Pig
By Kana Rilry

Peaches is the name of a little pig.
She wanted to play, so she kept
asking other animals to play with
her. Read to find out what
happened.

by Kana Riley   Illustrated by Ellen Childers

Figure 9–4.   Peaches the Pig

introduction and then read the text once silently before reading it aloud. Apply the same accuracy principle to determine whether the level is a match, but also consider the students' oral and written responses. You will want to try an easier benchmark text. The goal is to find a "just right" level for each child.

Creating Conference Protocols

You can create conference protocols for any level of text, but they are especially useful at levels J–Z. After you have selected some benchmark texts, you

may want to create conference protocols to systematize your assessment further. A conference protocol is a standardized procedure that may be used with any text to assess what students can read without support (see Figure 9–5).

You first select a text and then provide a very brief introduction—one or two sentences delivered in a standard way. You then ask the student to read the text silently and write a response guided by a prompt. If you are working at levels A–G, omit silent reading and writing. Afterward the student reads the response aloud and discusses it with you

CONFERENCE PROTOCOL:
Level N (Nonfiction)

Frogs by Michael Tyler

TEXT INTRODUCTION
This is a book about frogs. The three sections that you are going to read will tell you about the size, shape, and color of different kinds of frogs. You will also learn about the differences between frogs and toads.

INSTRUCTIONS
Silently read pages 5–15. Be sure to read all of the captions that go with the pictures. After you have finished, write a paragraph comparing frogs and toads. Use information from the book to help you do this. When we meet again, I will ask you to talk with me about what you wrote and to share your thinking about what you read. As we talk about this book, I may also have a few questions to ask you. [When the student returns, have her/him read the response aloud and discuss it. Prompt the child to share his/her thinking further.]

DISCUSSION QUESTIONS [ANSWERS]
[Accept reasonable answers that the student accurately supports with evidence from the text.]

T1. How are tree frogs' feet different from those of frogs that live on the ground?
[They have sticky disks on them to help them hold on to trees.]

T2. Tell two things you learned about frogs.
[Frogs have smooth skin, leap, need to live near a source of moisture, vary in size 5/8" – 12", and have eyes and nostrils on top of the head so they can see and breathe while under water, etc.]

BT3. Why is life harder for frogs that live in the desert?
[It is dry in the desert and frogs need moisture to live. They have to dig into the ground to stay moist.]

BT4. What is something that helps frogs to protect themselves in their environment?
[Their colors help them blend into their environment so they will be protected.]

T5. What are two different ways that frogs can swim?
[Frogs can kick with their strong back legs or use dog-paddle style.]

BT6. An animal leaps up next to you. It has smooth skin. It is green in color. Is it a frog or a toad? [It is a frog.]

Figure 9–5.   Conference Protocol: Level N (Nonfiction)

on the basis of questions you create. In the example in Figure 9–5, note that some of the questions require the student to go beyond the text (BT) and others ask the reader to provide information from the text (T). Finally you use a typed passage (100 to 200 words) from the silently read text and code the student's reading behaviors (substitutions, insertions, deletions, repeats, and long pauses) as he or she reads the passage aloud. Use the coding system presented in Figure 9–6 (or one you devise) to record significant behaviors.

Also indicate the starting and ending time so that you can calculate the rate (words per minute) for the reading. (A general guide for rate of reading is provided on page 492 of *Guiding Readers and Writers*. You can also use the rubric for assessing fluency on page 491.)

Using the Gradient to Group Students

Assessment systems like those described above, in conjunction with your daily observations, provide

Coding Reading Behaviors

Behavior	Code shown with error
Accurate reading	✓ ✓ ✓ ✓ ✓ ✓ ✓ ✓ ✓ The giant's heavily loaded cart rumbled to a halt.
Substitution	✓ ✓ **heavy** ✓ ✓ ✓ ✓ ✓ ✓ The giant's heavily loaded cart rumbled to a halt.
Self-correction	✓ ✓ **heavy|SC** ✓ ✓ ✓ ✓ ✓ ✓ The giant's heavily loaded cart rumbled to a halt.
Repetition	✓ ✓ ↶ ✓ **R** ✓ ✓ ✓ ✓ ✓ ✓ The giant's heavily loaded cart rumbled to a halt.
Repetition with self-correction	✓ ✓ **heavy| R |SC** ✓ ✓ ✓ ✓ ✓ ✓ The giant's heavily loaded cart rumbled to a halt.
Omission	✓ ✓ —— ✓ ✓ ✓ ✓ ✓ ✓ The giant's heavily loaded cart rumbled to a halt.
Insertion	✓ ✓ ✓ ✓ **woo** ✓ ✓ ✓ ✓ ✓ The giant's heavily loaded cart rumbled to a halt.
Long pause	✓ ✓ ✓ **#** ✓ ✓ ✓ ✓ ✓ ✓ The giant's heavily loaded cart rumbled to a halt.
Told	✓ ✓ ———— ✓ ✓ ✓ ✓ ✓ ✓ The giant's heavily|**T** loaded cart rumbled to a halt.

Figure 9–6. Coding Reading Behaviors

valuable information for forming groups for guided reading at the start of the school year.

For one thing, you'll have identified the level of text each student can read with instructional support and can form groups based on these levels.

Your assessment may reveal other needs, however. For example, some students may:

- Need help in reading the social studies or science textbook.
- Become familiar with the structure of a certain genre.
- Need more help in summarizing and thinking about texts.
- Need to learn how to skim and scan a text.

- Need to learn to read more fluently.

- Need to read with more expression.

- Need to attend to characterization.

- Need to recognize aspects of a writer's style.

In this case, you may want to pull together a temporary group of students needing work in the same area, select a text level that is accessible to them all, and focus on that aspect of processing.

Using the Gradient to Support Independent Reading

In grades 2–6, students begin to keep records of their reading (see the example in Figure 9–7), and engage in reflection and self-assessment. Texts are longer and students are reading fewer titles. In addition, texts make greater demands on the reader. The terms *easy, just right*, and *difficult* are also used by students as they describe books in independent reading within the reading workshop. *Easy* means the same thing in both guided and independent reading: the individual can read the text without effort and understands it easily. In independent reading, *just right* refers to books with only a few challenges that students can read successfully *without teacher support*. The student evaluates the text herself, marking it *just right* on her reading list if the reading was successful and informative.

The term *difficult* as used by students to evaluate their independent reading means they found it too hard. Students may select a text for independent reading that

is beyond their present reading level but be so motivated to read it that they try it. They may struggle with too many words but may have to reread some of the material, do some research, or ask for some help. We encourage students to avoid books that are too difficult for them, though sometimes they may be interested enough in a book to try it.

Although you may put out "browsing boxes" for younger students that help them read books at an easy range of levels, we do not recommend organizing students' independent reading around leveled texts; it's more important for your students to learn to use a range of criteria for selecting books for themselves. You don't want readers to

Reading List

Select a book to read. Enter the title and author on your reading list. When you have completed it, write the genre, and the date. If you abandoned it, write an (A) and the date you abandoned it in the date column. Note whether the book was easy (E), just right (JR) or a difficult (D) book for you.

#	Title	Author	Genre	Date Completed	E JR,D
	The Littles and the Big Blizzard	John Peterson	F	9/7	E
	Stay away from Simon	Carol Carrick	HF	9/26	JR
	An Angel for Solomon Singer	Cynthia Rylant	HF	10/2	E
	The Hundred Penny Box	Sharon Bell Mathis	RF	10/6	E
	Double Fudge	Judy Blume	RF	10/15	JR
	Harry Potter and the Chamber of Secrets	JK Rowling	F	11/1	D
	The Boys Return	Phyllis Reynolds Naylor	RF	11/6	JR
	The Vile Village	Lemony Snicket	F	11/17	JR
	The Reptile Room	Lemony Snicket	F	11/23	JR
	Hatchet	Gary Paulsen	RF	12/1	JR
	Iditarod Dream	Ted Wood	I	12/3	E
	Harry Potter and the Sorcerer Stone	JK Rowling	F	12/8	JR/D
	Titanic	Victoria Sherrow	I	12/17	E

Figure 9–7. Sam's Reading List

see themselves as limited to a level. Of course, they do have to consider the difficulty of a text. You'll want them to read *just right* books most of the time, *easy* books some of the time, and occasionally tackle a *difficult* text. You'll want them to vary the genre and range of authors.

Sam's reading list in his reader's notebook (Figure 9–7) shows all the books he's read so far this year. He has designated each book as E (easy), JR (just right), or D (difficult). We want readers to be aware of the "matches" they are making for themselves, and these three levels provide enough discrimination for students to realize that they change as readers over time. Books that were difficult before may now seem easy, so this documentation system helps them realize their growth as readers. The list also helps you as a teacher monitor students' behavior so that you can guide their choices when necessary:

- Are they consistently reading easy books rather than challenging themselves with just right books?

- Are they consistently selecting books that are too hard? (In this case, they may be abandoning too many books.)

- Are they reading a wide variety of genres?

Poor readers have a tendency either to make "safe" choices (always going for short and very easy books) *or* to choose books that are much too difficult just to pretend to be one of the group. These students lack confidence and do not really know themselves as readers. You'll want to guide them through a wide range of reading, including:

- Shorter and longer texts.

- Picture books, easy chapter books, short story collections, and longer chapter books.

- Award-winning books.

- Series books.

- Different genres.

- Different topics.

- Different authors and illustrators.

- Different cultures and books that show the diversity of Earth's people.

This variety will build breadth in their reading.

In the reading workshop for grades 2–6, you will be providing minilessons on how to select books and how to tell if a book is just right. You want students to become skilled at selecting books for themselves. If they consistently choose books that are too hard, they may be making their way through them but not gaining full meaning.

In independent reading, the concept of *just right* is both similar to and different from the way we use it in guided reading. The term is similar in the two instructional settings in that the text is mostly under the students' control and offers challenges that can be met successfully. The difference is that in guided reading, successful processing is taking place with strong and skillful teacher support, so that the *just right* text is probably a little more difficult than the same student can read independently. In guided reading, that is the case for both primary and intermediate students. For independent reading, the student must process the text alone; a *just right* text is one that the student can read smoothly with understanding.

In your collection of books for independent reading, you can pencil the level unobtrusively inside a book's front or back cover. This designation is a quick reference (for you alone) if you need to help readers make selections. We recognize that many students will be aware of the level, but you can explain that the levels are not for them, but for you to use in selecting books that will help you teach them how to read better. Knowing the levels of text is helpful for you as a teacher in several ways:

- You can use your knowledge of levels to be sure that you build a classroom library that offers the appropriate range of books from which your students can choose.

- For struggling students, you can make a basket of books holding a varied collection at levels you know they can read and suggest that they choose from those texts.

- You can notice and compare the levels students are choosing to read for independent reading and the levels you are choosing for them in guided reading.

- You can guide readers toward easier or harder books, according to their needs.

Summary

The gradient of text *is a teacher's tool* rather than something you want your students to pay attention to as an important aspect of their reading development. They will be aware that texts vary in the demands they make on readers, and you will explicitly teach them how to select texts based on the amount of challenge as well as interest and other factors. The gradient supports your decisions relative to guided reading, assessment, grouping for instruction, and guiding students' independent reading. It is a "ladder" by which to recognize your students' progress; more important, it will help you match books to readers so that you can ensure that they make consistent reading progress.

Suggestions for Professional Development: Creating a Set of Benchmark Books

After you have created a gradient of text and worked with it for a while, set up a meeting to create your own set of benchmark books. Work with colleagues at grades 3, 4, and 5, or involve teachers at every grade level in your school. These benchmarks will provide a picture of the path of progress.

1. Have each teacher bring several well-known texts to a discussion of why these texts might be good benchmarks.

2. Select five potential benchmarks at each level and identify passages of about 250 words to be used in benchmark assessment. Try to select passages for which comprehension depends on reading other parts of the text.

3. Have teachers at appropriate grade levels try these assessments with their students using an informal reading inventory or miscue analysis (see Chapter 28 in *Guiding Readers and Writers*). Have students read passages until the material becomes too hard.

4. Look at the results of your inventories. Ask:
   - Did the books clearly discriminate among readers, showing some books they could read and others beyond their ability?
   - What are the specific characteristics of texts that add to their level of difficulty?
   - What are the specific characteristics of the texts that support readers?
   - Did the selected passages of the text present any problems for readers? Do you need to select other passages?
   - Which texts were stable at each level in that students who can read other books at that level can also read these texts at 90 to 95 percent accuracy and with understanding?

5. Assemble again to discuss and revise the set of benchmark books.

6. Revise the set over time, trying out new benchmark texts.

7. Assemble packets of benchmark texts that can be used as assessment packets by everyone in the school.

CHAPTER TEN

USING LEVELED BOOKS IN GUIDED READING

It is essential for students to read successfully, and that can of course be achieved with easy books; but fueling reading power requires successful problem solving. Your students need to learn how to read a wide range of books with different organizational patterns, writing styles, topics, and themes. By using the gradient, you can identify a collection of books that is within the range of the students in your class. Within that range, there will be one or two levels of texts appropriate for each student. If he reads books at those levels with the support of your teaching, he will strengthen his processing strategies. From the collection of books at those levels, you select texts for each student that will offer learning opportunities.

In this chapter we describe the use of the text gradient to select books for the groups you have formed. We also discuss the components of guided reading with emphasis on text factors.

Using the Gradient to Help in the Selection of Texts

A gradient of text is not a precise sequence in which children read books in a specific order. In fact, children who are making rapid progress will not even read books on every level; they may skip levels. The goal in guided reading is to select and introduce texts that are "just right" for readers at a point in time and to continue to select books at that level until the processing is going very well. You can take advantage of the breadth of each level if you decide that children need to read at about the same level of difficulty for some time, building fluency and effective strategies. But, if children are finding books very easy and there is no opportunity for the readers to learn something new about processing text, you should move them to another level. (Children will sometimes change very quickly, making leaps in learning, so that you skip a level or read only a few books on a level. Remember that they need to understand and think about the ideas in the texts rather than just read accurately.) It is important to provide strong teaching and variety at every level to enable the children to develop and change over time.

Making decisions about changing the text level requires continuous, careful observation of children. The observation can be informal (notes and records) or more systematic (using running records or conference protocols). When an individual child is processing well on a level and has had enough experience with those texts, go up a step. The child may need to change groups, or the entire group may be ready to move forward. Select a book from the next (or even higher) level, introduce it, and observe children's reading. Sampling oral reading from individuals will give you immediate feedback. If necessary, simply move back and select another book from a lower level and, again, observe behavior carefully. Remember that text characteristics and opportunities to solve problems are as important as the level in selecting a book.

The Guided Reading Lesson

Your support and teaching takes place within all the elements of the lesson. Let's look at how each guided reading lesson element supports the reader's development.

Text Introduction

Through an introduction, you prepare readers for the way the text "works"—that is, you talk about how it is organized and provide important background information they will need in order to understand it. You may introduce vocabulary or difficult language structures. You might point out a few words or something unusual or new in the print layout. You leave work for readers to do but provide just enough support to enable them to take on a more difficult text than they can read on their own. Through the introduction, you mediate the difficulty of the text. For a very challenging text for a particular group of students, you may provide a rich introduction; for one that is almost within a group's independent reading power, your introduction can be brief and "lean."

In the next sections, we discuss guided reading introductions in two texts: *Willy the Helper* (Peters, Level D) and *A Pocketful of Goobers* (Mitchell, Level Q). Both of these texts were discussed in Chapter 7 in connection with text analysis.

INTRODUCTION TO WILLY THE HELPER (LEVEL D)

In Chapter 7 we presented an analysis of a level D text, *Willy the Helper*. Figure 10–1 is a transcript of one teacher's introduction of this text to young students. Keep in mind that every introduction is different. Your decisions depend on your own analysis of the text and the information that will be easy or difficult for your students to access. Also, students' own contributions to the introduction shape the conversation.

As in most text introductions, Jann Osgood, the teacher, began by introducing the title, author, and setting. Since a great deal of information is provided in the illustrations (see the Chapter 7 analysis), it is important for the readers to notice details. On the cover, along with the title, there is a picture of Willy holding the newspaper. This picture does not appear anywhere in the text but it foreshadows the major theme—that Willy doesn't really help at all but is a lovable dog who makes messes! If Sam had not noticed the torn paper, Jann might have pointed it out to the children. It is important that, throughout this text, children notice the discrepancy between the information in the text and that in the pictures. Appreciation of the humor and true understanding of the text depend on it. Jann alerts them to this text demand by "thinking aloud" about the question: "Is Willy really a good helper?"

Throughout this introduction, Jann used language and vocabulary words from the text in a conversational way. It is important for beginning readers to hear the words and phrases that they will be reading. Do not be afraid that you are "giving too much away." What you want to happen is that they will be processing the print, but that recency and familiarity will enable them to process a more difficult text with efficiency.

The teacher also drew attention to known words and had children locate them. For example, on page 2, the text says

> On Monday, Willy helped me
> fold the clothes.
> What a mess!

Jann had the children quickly find the word *on*, which they know. This word signals a fairly complex sentence structure (beginning with a prepositional phrase), so close monitoring of the word is important. In addition, she helped the children notice that

Introduction to *Willy the Helper* (Peters, Level D)

MRS. O: In this book a little girl is going to be talking about her dog. The title is *Willy the Helper*. It's by Catherine Peters. [**Introduces the title, author, and setting.**] What do you notice about the cover of the book? [**Invites prediction.**]

KYLA: He's got a collar with his name.

DEVON: I got a dog, too.

SAM: He tore up the paper.

MRS. O: You're good at noticing things. [**Affirms the value of noticing details in the picture and thinking about them.**] I wonder if Willy is going to be a good helper. [**Demonstrates questioning the text (conflict between text and pictures).**] It's Monday and the girl is saying that Willy is helping to fold the clothes. [**Alerts children to the significance of sequence—days of the week.**]

DEVON: What's her name?

MRS. O: I'm not sure what her name is. Maybe we'll find out. Take a close look at the picture. [**Draws attention to the pictures and invites thinking.**] Do you think Willy is helping to fold the clothes? [**Uses language from the text.**]

SAM: No! He's just rolling around in them.

DEVON: He's on the bed and he's not supposed to do that.

MRS. O: Quickly find the word *on*. [**Draws attention to a known word that signals a difficult sentence structure.**] That's a word you know. That's what is happening on Monday. On the next page, we'll find out what is happening on... [**Draws attention to the sequential days of the week and checks to be sure children know and can use this information.**]

CHILDREN: Tuesday!

MRS. O: Turn the page. What's happening on Tuesday, Jennifer? [**Invites a previously silent child to participate.**]

JENNIFER: He's getting paint on her. Oooh, her mom's gonna be mad.

MRS. O: That's right. I don't think Willy is doing a very good job helping her paint the fence, do you? [**Demonstrates thinking critically about the text.**] In fact, I'm thinking that every day the

girl is going to say Willy is helping. But what is Willy really doing? [**Demonstrates making predictions.**]

DEVON: Making a mess.

MRS. O: That's just what the little girl says—"What a mess!" You say that and make your voice sound excited. [**Has children practice reading with phasing. Draws attention to language.**]

CHILDREN: What a mess!

MRS. O: Now look at the next page. They are cleaning the garage where they keep the car and all kinds of other things. Do you ever help clean the garage or another part of the house? [**Invites children to make connections to their own lives.**]

SAM: I clean my room.

JENNIFER: I clean too. I help my mom.

DEVON: He's spilling the paint again.

MRS. O: What do you expect to see at the beginning of the word clean? [**Draws attention to letter-sound relationships and makes connection to word study.**]

SAM: *c* and *l*.

MRS. O: We've been learning about letter clusters, haven't we? Clean starts with the letter cluster cl. Find it quickly. (Children locate the word.) Turn the page. Willy is helping her water the garden. And she always says...

CHILDREN: What a mess!

MRS. O: You'll see on the next page that Willy is helping her wash the tub, and then turn to the next page-Sunday. Something different is going to happen on Sunday. Don't turn the page! On Sunday, Willy didn't help the little girl at all. Why do you think? Can you guess? [**Foreshadows the surprise ending without giving it away.**]

SAM: Maybe he ran away?

JENNIFER: He's asleep?

MRS. O: Well, the little girl is going to ask you why. Find the word but. That says, "But why?" And you get to guess and there will be a big surprise. Turn back to the front and begin reading.

Figure 10–1.   Introduction to Willy the Helper

the text pattern moves from week to week, and checks on their understanding by saying, "On the next page, we'll find out what is happening on...." The fact that children enthusiastically finished her sentence provides evidence that they were picking up on the pattern of the text and can use background knowledge as a support for reading it. Knowing the sequence of the days of the week may seem to be very basic information, but for the first grader, it represents important content knowledge. Using prior knowledge will be increasingly important for these students. Upper-level texts require an immense amount of background knowledge, but from the beginning, these readers must learn to automatically access what they already know.

You'll notice that by page 2, Jann noticed that Jennifer had not yet participated, so she invited her into the conversation. Then, she did some thinking aloud again about the central theme of the text—that Willy is not really helping. The teacher's behavior illustrates something quite important about the text introduction. You are not trying to drag it out of the students by questioning, although you do want to hear their opinions and ideas. In this introduction, Jann was actively demonstrating how to think about a text. She was putting ideas into students' heads by demonstrating how to think critically about the text and also how to make predictions.

If you wonder aloud, asking questions and entering into conversation about a text, students will naturally begin to do so themselves. They will understand that they have roles and responsibilities during the text introduction—for example, accessing prior knowledge and anticipating the text. These are cognitive actions in which we as readers automatically engage without conscious attention. For the young reader, teacher support is important. Many children seem to think that reading is just "doing the words." They need the teacher's prompting to do the active thinking that is necessary.

Across the text, Jann prompted children to attend to details in the pictures. She also, on page 4/5, had children practice the language, "What a mess!" In doing so, Jann was simultaneously helping readers become familiar with the language syntax and supporting their ability to read with fluency and phrasing.

In the text introduction, Jann also helped the children attend to the details of print. For example, she drew attention to the exclamation point at the end of "What a mess!" She also pointed out the letter cluster *cl*, in *clean*, which she linked to her phonics/word study minilessons.

She explained a new vocabulary word, *garage*, because many of her students live in apartment buildings without individual garages such as the one depicted in the text. Moving on through the text, she made sure that students are continuously noticing the information in the text and remembering the language pattern "What a mess!" Finally, without giving away the surprise ending, she foreshadowed it. She invited children to think why Willy might not have been a "helper" on Sunday and helped them realize that in the end, the girl directly addresses the readers, asking them to guess. Actually, Willy has a litter of puppies, so we now know that she is female.

In this text introduction, Jann successfully untangled the text for her students, but she accomplished something even more important. Her goal is not simply to help them read this text. It is to help them do the kind of thinking that good readers do. She prompted them to notice details in pictures, make predictions, use prior knowledge of content, use their understanding of language structure, notice aspects of print, and anticipate the ending. Even on this simple text, the demands are high. With Jann's support, these students engaged in the kind of thinking that proficient readers do.

INTRODUCTION TO A POCKETFUL OF GOOBERS (LEVEL Q)

In this introduction Carol described the title, setting, and genre and also provided the background information students needed to be aware of George

---

Introduction to *A Pocketful of Goobers: A Story about George Washington Carver* (Mitchell, Level Q)

MRS. B: This book is about George's life. It's called a... [**Reminds students of genre name and characteristics.**]

EVAN: Autobiography. No, biography.

MRS. B: Well, both of those are stories about people's lives, but there's one big difference. In an autobiography, the person writes the story about his or her own life. In a biography, somebody else writes the story about the person. Which one do you think this is?

ALL STUDENTS: It's a biography.

MRS. B: Yes, this is a biography because somebody else, Barbara Mitchell, wrote it about George Washington Carver.

ANDREW: I've read a biography about Abraham Lincoln before. It was good.

JANINE: I've read one on Helen Keller and Louisa May Alcott.

MRS. B: That's great. I bet you learned a lot about those people. George was an African American boy who was born to a slave woman. His mother was killed, but someone else raised George. [**Recognizes connections students are making; provides summary of the text.**] He was very smart; he found a way to go to school and study agriculture. That's how he learned how to be a scientist and help people with their farming. [**Pauses, conversationally, to invite student comment.**]

EVAN: Didn't this happen a long time ago?

JANINE: It must have, because his mother was a slave, remember?

MRS. B: Yes. George was born just when slavery was ending, in the 1860s. That was almost a hundred and fifty years ago. He was born in Missouri. [**Responds to student questions, encouraging more.**]

KRISTEN: The South was where all the slaves were.

MRS. B: The South did have the most slaves, but there were slaves all over the country. [**Elaborates information about the context.**]

ANDREW: They ended it with the Civil War.

MRS. B: That's right Andrew. After the war, slavery was abolished, but many black people were still treated unfairly. When you read, you'll see that even though George wasn't a slave, he still wasn't always treated well, and he still didn't have all the rights that white people had. Do you think this made it hard for him to go to school and to get a good job? [**Probes for personal response.**]

EVAN: Yeah. He couldn't go to lots of schools.

KRISTEN: And I bet people always teased him and stuff and called him mean names.

MRS. B: That was hard, but he never gave up. [**Prompts for inference.**]

MRS. B: It was important for George Washington Carver to help people farm better.

JANINE: Because back then that's the way everybody got their food. There weren't all the grocery stores like we have.

EVAN: It was how people made their money, by selling their crops.

KRISTEN: Yeah, Like on *Little House on the Prairie*, when the crops died, they became poor.

MRS. B: In this book you're going to learn more about George's childhood and school. [**Further defines the focus of the text.**] There is an important note from the author at the beginning of the book that gives you some background information. Be sure to read that carefully. [**Draws attention to text feature.**]

Read the first two chapters, up to page 25, and as you finish each chapter, write one or two sentences telling what you think was important about the way George lived his life. Stop after Chapter 2 so we can discuss what you've learned so far. [**Provides direction to readers.**]

Figure 10–2.   Introduction to A Pocketful of Goobers

Washington Carver's significance as a figure in history. She probed students' knowledge and added to it; she also made connections to what they have learned about how words work. As we found in Chapter 7, the book has quite a few technical words; Carol knew that calling attention to word roots and endings would remind her students to use what they know to figure out these words.

She also recognized the connections students have been making to other texts of the same genre and invited them to raise questions and make comments. She encouraged them to respond personally to the text as well as to make some inferences. Finally, she pointed out an important feature of the text—the note from the author—and asked them to read the first two chapters and write about what they had read. Students began reading with a clear idea of what this text will be about, how it is organized, and the kinds of words they would likely meet.

Reading the Text

Most of the time, your students are processing the text silently while you confer with other readers or meet with another group. We suggest that they remain together at the table rather than moving to their desks, thus providing the least amount of interruption. As students read, you occasionally ask some of them to read aloud softly so you can observe their behavior. Sampling their reading like this gives you a good idea of how well you "matched" the text to the readers and how effective your introduction was in mediating the text for them. You may also talk briefly with students, providing extra support or prompting them to use effective strategies you've already taught them. If you have to do too much "telling," either the text was too hard or your introduction was too scanty.

After Reading the Text

After reading, you discuss the meaning of the text with the students; you have the opportunity to clear up misconceptions and encourage students to think more deeply about their reading by providing evidence for their thinking. If students are reading longer chapter books over several days, this ongoing discussion serves as a support for their continued reading. You also teach specific processing strategies that will help students be more effective readers.

Teaching Decisions in Guided Reading

Teaching decisions in guided reading are based on your assessment of students' strengths and needs, a process that is supported by the use of a gradient of text. Decision making must also rest on a thorough analysis of the supports and challenges in the particular text to be read. In the next chapters, we present a more detailed analysis of the features of text at each level.

Suggestions for Professional Development: Analyzing and Introducing Texts

Continue exploring leveled texts and introductions with colleagues in your school. We encourage working with cross-grade-level groups. Use collections of books at levels A through V or W.

1. Before the meeting, ask grade-level colleagues to select (from books you have provided) and read a book at the level. (If you have a very small group, you might want to have everyone read *Willy the Helper* and *A Pocketful of Goobers*.) All participants can consider both books and develop knowledge of a continuum of progress in the process.

2. Have participants read the demands of text for *Willy the Helper* and *A Pocketful of Goobers* (Chapter 7). Ask participants (in small groups)

to create a list for the books they have selected. What does this text call for the readers to do?

3. Then have them read the introductions in this chapter. They can discuss:
   - How did the teacher support students in using effective reading strategies?
   - What did students contribute to the introduction?
   - How did the introduction help students learn more about the reading process?

4. Have them plan an introduction to the text they have selected. Ask some group members to use the plan to introduce the text to their students. (This assumes that some teachers have a group for whom the text is appropriate.)

5. Plan a follow-up meeting for those teachers to share their experiences in introducing a text to a group of students.

CHAPTER ELEVEN

UNDERSTANDING LEVELS OF TEXT: A TO I

When we think about levels of texts, we are always exploring combinations of characteristics. Not every characteristic typical of a level applies to every text categorized at that level. A certain factor makes one text challenging; something else presents a challenge in a different text. Thinking about levels in this complex way may seem difficult, but it helps us in our teaching. We want students to experience different combinations of demands so that they expand their reading powers.

It is also true that some characteristics are extremely important in differentiating texts at earlier levels, while others become more important later on. For example, greater print variety (italics, all capitals, boldface) or more-sophisticated punctuation (dashes, parentheses, ellipses) may provide challenges in texts for the levels that third or fourth graders read but are no longer a factor once students have become accustomed to them. Length is an important factor in general at most lower levels; however, as students grow more sophisticated, they will encounter difficulties in both long and very short texts. Factors such as technical vocabulary, idea sophistication, theme maturity, and sentence complexity are important in the assessment at all levels.

This chapter begins with descriptions of texts generally considered appropriate for students in grades K and 1. Elementary school is a time of transition. You may have students in grades two or even grade three who are reading at this level, and you will need to select texts that are appropriate to their development of a reading process.

Level Descriptions

Our goal is to give you a good idea of the cluster of characteristics readers will encounter at each level. These descriptions cannot be exhaustive; rather, they are inventories that will help you understand the level and that you can use to categorize texts for yourself.

For each level, we discuss important characteristics that contribute to the difficulty of the text as well as those that support readers. Then we present several examples. We also discuss some of the important new demands that texts at this level make of readers. These are the important general parameters:

- All books are identified by genre, form, and content.

- Relevant specialized background information is indicated.

- Font size can vary from a large and easy-to-read font to medium or small, placing greater visual processing demands on readers.

- For each example, we indicate the number of pages and the approximate length of chapters; these factors affect the length of the text and the amount of time the reader is required to sustain reading.

- When relevant, we indicate vocabulary demands, as well as the extent to which multi-syllable and technical words are used.

- When relevant, we comment on the language complexity and/or the literary language included in the text.

■ The text structure is referred to as simple and straightforward or more complex.

As we said, not every book at a level will have all the attributes listed here. A book may be difficult and short, or easy and long. It is also important to remember that the way a text is introduced will influence how difficult or easy it is for the reader to process. As a teacher you are constantly balancing the text level and the amount of support you provide to readers. You may decide to provide a high level of support as you move readers to a new level, or a lean introduction at a level the readers are now processing well.

These characteristics are meant to be heuristic in that they will help you think about texts and what they require of readers. The precise demands on your students will be individually determined but will be affected by:

■ The ongoing experiences with literature and content areas that students have in your school.

■ The way you introduce texts to students and converse with them as they read them.

Levels A Through I

Previously, we described changes in the reading process over time. These broad descriptions do not represent discrete stages; rather, they give us a general road map of the development of a reading process. We have matched reader descriptions with approximate grade levels and gradient levels, but we have also indicated overlap. We do not designate certain book levels for readers at any one grade level. No matter where you teach, you will undoubtedly have a range of readers at every grade level.

This road map gives us a vision of development of reading across grades so that:

■ We can be concerned about and give extra help to students who are lagging behind. These are the students who will find it most difficult to profit from whole-class instruction and who will likely not do as much successful reading as the others.

■ We can guide advanced students to books that challenge them in a variety of ways. This may not mean simply moving up the gradient as far as they can read with accuracy. Many of these students can "decode" just about anything. Instead, we want to pay attention to the topics, genres, and themes that interest them and are appropriate. We want to create more varied opportunities for them.

Profound changes in processing take place as a learner progresses from level A to I, from the very beginning of the development of a reading process to silent reading of much longer texts.

Level A

Text Characteristics

Level A books are the very easiest texts for beginning readers. They have sentences (rather than single words or phrases) because knowledge of language structure is a powerful source of information for young children as they begin to read. Level A books have predictable language patterns and very easy high frequency words that are used over and over within a text. They have one line of print. There may be a few books on the list that have been leveled as "A" that depart from this descriptor because teachers thought they were so accessible to children, but be cautious in using them. Print is presented in a very plain, clear font that is as large as possible without distorting the reader's view of the line of text. There are clear spaces between words (usually two to three spaces rather than one). Text characteristics are listed on the next page.

Text Characteristics: Level A

GENRE AND FORMS

Genre:
- Realistic fiction
- Simple animal fantasy
- Some simple factual texts

Forms
- Picture books

TEXT STRUCTURE

- Focused on a single idea
- Some texts with very simple stories implied by pictures

CONTENT

- Familiar, easy content—family, play, pets, school
- All concepts supported by pictures

THEMES AND IDEAS

- Very familiar themes and ideas

LANGUAGE AND LITERARY FEATURES

- Repeating language patterns (simple 3–7 words on each page)
- Mostly nameless "flat" characters
- Very familiar settings close to children's experience

SENTENCE COMPLEXITY

- Short, predictable sentences that are close to oral language
- Simple sentences (no embedded phrases or clauses)
- Subject preceding verb in most sentences

VOCABULARY

- Almost all vocabulary familiar to children and likely to be used in their oral language
- Word meanings illustrated by pictures

WORDS

- Mostly 1 syllable words with very easy and predictable letter/sound relationships
- Repeated use of a few easy high frequency words
- Some simple plurals
- Some words with –s and –ing

ILLUSTRATIONS

- Illustrations that match print very closely
- Clear illustrations that fully support meaning
- Very simple illustrations with little distracting detail
- Illustration to support each page of text

BOOK AND PRINT FEATURES

Length
- Very short, usually 8 pages of print
- One line of text on each page

Print and Layout
- Print clearly separated from pictures
- Print in large plain font
- Ample space between words
- Consistent placement of print

Punctuation
- Period only punctuation in most texts

Tools
- NA

Examples

BALLOON RIDE [A] (SEE FIGURE 11–1)

Animal fantasy; 16 pages; 32 words; print on every other page; one line of print per page; repeating pattern ("I see the ___.") with one word changing on each page; print consistently on left page on white; opportunity to distinguish *band, barn, boat*; challenging content with some labels; clear picture clues; first person narrative; story of rabbits adventures in a balloon carried in pictures.

ME [A] (SEE FIGURE 11–2)

Informational format; 16 pages; 24 words; print on every other page; one line of print per page; repeating pattern ("I am ___.") with one word changing on each page; print consistently on left page with no picture; clear picture clues for each word; told in first person; not a narrative although the last page shows the girl sleeping as if it is the end of a day.

Other Descriptions at Level A

MY CAT [A]

Informational format (not narrative); fantasy because of illustrations showing cat jumping on two legs, chasing a butterfly, and smiling; eight pages; 28 words; print at bottom of every page; one line of print per page; repeating pattern ("My cat can ___.") with one word changing on each page; told in first person; clear picture clues for words for each word.

SO MANY THINGS TO DO [A]

Informational format; eight pages; 21 words; print at bottom of each page; one line of print per page; two illustrations on each page; repeating pattern ("We can ___.") with one word changing on each page; clear picture clues for each word; complexity in illustrations in that activity is shown twice (for example, riding on a sled and riding on a bike).

Figure 11–1. Balloon Ride *(Level A)*

Figure 11–2. Me *(Level A)*

DAD [A]

Informational text; 16 pages; 24 words; print on every other page; one line of print per page; repeating pattern ("I am ___.") with one word changing on each page; print consistently on left page with no picture; clear picture clues for each sentence; not a narrative although the last page shows Dad sleeping as if tired.

WINGS [A]

Informational text; eight pages; 24 words; print at bottom of every page; one line of print per page; repeating pattern ("A ___ has wings." with one word changing on each page; some challenging content words (*dragonfly, bat*); clear picture clues for all content words; simple index with pictures on last page.

Level B

Text Characteristics

Level B books are very similar to A except that they add the challenge of two lines of text. Like level A, texts focus on a single idea or have a simple story line. There is a direct correspondence between the text and the pictures, and children can easily relate the topics to their personal experience. Content words are supported by pictures and there are usually repeating language patterns. The language, while not exactly duplicating oral language, includes naturally occurring syntactic structures. Print is regular, clear, and easy to see and there is a full range of simple punctuation, including period, question mark, exclamation mark, and some commas. There is ample space between words so that children can point and read. Text characteristics are listed below:

Examples

SALLY'S NEW SHOES (SEE FIGURE 11–3)

Realistic fiction; 58 words; 16 pages; print on left page; two lines of print per page; each page a two-line sentence; sentences with prepositional phrases; repeating pattern ("I'm going to _____ in my new shoes."); contraction; pattern changes at end with one sentence carried over to next page and ellipses; clear picture support; opportunity to predict ending (that she won't swim in her new shoes).

LOOK AT ME [B] (SEE FIGURE 11–4)

Informational format; 48 words; 16 pages; two lines of print per page; each line a sentence; print on left page and picture on right until last page; repeating pattern ("Look at me. I am _____.", with one word change per print page; clear picture support; -ing words; familiar content (activities at school).

Text Characteristics: Level B

GENRES/FORMS

Genres
- Realistic fiction
- Simple animal fantasy
- Some simple factual texts

Forms
- Picture books

TEXT STRUCTURE
- Focused on a single idea
- Some texts with very simple stories implied by pictures

CONTENT
- Familiar, easy content—family, play, pets, school
- All concepts supported by pictures

THEMES AND IDEAS
- Familiar themes and ideas

LANGUAGE AND LITERARY FEATURES
- Repeating language patterns (simple 3-7 words on each page)
- Mostly nameless "flat" characters
- Familiar settings close to children's experience

SENTENCE COMPLEXITY
- Short, predictable sentences that are close to oral language
- Mostly simple sentences (no embedded phrases or clauses)
- Subject preceding verb in most sentences

VOCABULARY
- Almost all vocabulary familiar to children and likely to be used in their oral language
- Word meanings illustrated by pictures

WORDS
- Mostly one syllable words with easy, predictable letter/sound relationships
- Repeated use of a few easy high frequency words
- Simple plurals
- Some words with –s and –ing

ILLUSTRATIONS
- Illustrations that match print very closely
- Clear illustrations that fully support meaning
- Very simple illustrations with little distracting detail
- Illustration to support each page of text

BOOK AND PRINT FEATURES

Length
- Very short, usually 8 pages of print
- Two lines of text on each page

Print and Layout
- Print clearly separated from pictures
- Print in large plain font
- Consistent placement of print
- Ample space between words and lines
- Sentences turn over one line
- Line breaks match ends of phrases and sentences

Punctuation
- Period only punctuation in most texts

Tools
- NA

Figure 11–3. Sally's New Shoes *(Level B)*

Figure 11–4. Look at Me *(Level B)*

Other Descriptions at Level B

CAT AND MOUSE [B]

Realistic fiction; 75 words; 16 pages; two lines of print on each page; each line a simple sentence; repeating pattern ("Mouse ran over the ____. Cat ran over the ___."); pattern change on last page ("under the door."); clear picture clues for each event; sequence of events with cat chasing mouse and mouse finally getting away.

HOT DAY AT THE ZOO [B]

Fantasy; 16 pages; two lines of print on a page; print on left page with white background; each line a simple sentence; repeating pattern ("The [animal] has a hat. It is [color].") with two words changing on each page; meaningful connection between the animal, the type of hat, and the color; pattern change on last page with summary statement (implication that on a hot day the animals wear hats).

CLIMBING [B]

Informational format; 48 words; two lines of print on a page; print on left page with white background; two-line sentence on each print page; repeating pattern ("She is up on the _____.") with one word changing each page layout; challenge in the word *bunk* instead of *bed*; topics familiar, connecting by being things you can "get up on"; clear picture support.

BEFORE I GO TO SCHOOL [B]

Informational format; 71 words; two lines of print on a page; print on left page with yellow background; two-line sentence on each print page; introductory dependent clause; repeating pattern ("Before I go to school I ____ my ____.") with two words changing on each page; clear picture support; timeline shown at bottom of print pages with small picture indicating each activity in sequence of events; pattern changes on last two pages; very challenging last page.

Level C

Text Characteristics

Books at level C have simple story lines and topics that are familiar to children. They tend to be longer than level B books but still have only a few (two to six) lines of text on a page. At this level more of the story is carried by the text, but pictures are still very important in supporting meaning and there is a direct correspondence between text and pictures. Print appears on both left and right pages but it is still clearly separated from text. Print may appear at a variety of places on the page. Sentence structure is very simple. Oral language structures are used and often repeated, and phrasing is often supported by print placement. There is a full range of punctuation, with quotation marks included.

Patterns and repetition are used in some books; others support prediction through natural language and meaning. There is more variation in language

---

Text Characteristics: Level C

GENRES/FORMS	SENTENCE COMPLEXITY	ILLUSTRATIONS
Genres	❖ Simple, predictable sentence structure but patterns vary	❖ Illustrations that match print very closely
❖ Realistic fiction	❖ Many sentences with prepositional phrases and adjectives	❖ Very simple Illustrations with little distracting detail
❖ Simple animal fantasy	❖ Subject preceding verb in most sentences	❖ More meaning carried in the text
❖ Some simple factual texts		❖ Illustrations on every page or every other page
Forms	**VOCABULARY**	
❖ Picture books	❖ Almost all vocabulary familiar to children and likely to be used in their oral language	**BOOK AND PRINT FEATURES**
TEXT STRUCTURE	❖ Some variation in words used to assign dialogue (mostly *said*)	*Length*
❖ Focused on a single idea or series of related ideas	❖ Word meanings illustrated by pictures	❖ Very short, usually 8 pages of print
❖ Story lines with very few episodes	❖ Almost all vocabulary familiar to children and likely to be used in their oral language	❖ One to five lines of text on each page
CONTENT	**WORDS**	*Print and Layout*
❖ Familiar, easy content—family, play, pets, school	❖ Mostly 1 syllable words	❖ Print clearly separated from pictures
❖ All concepts supported by pictures	❖ Same words used in different language structures	❖ Print in large plain font
THEMES AND IDEAS	❖ Some simple contractions and possessives (words with apostrophes)	❖ Some words in bold for emphasis
❖ Very familiar themes and ideas	❖ Many words with easy, predictable letter/sound relationships	❖ Ample space between words and lines
LANGUAGE AND LITERARY FEATURES	❖ Greater range of easy high frequency words	❖ Sentences turn lines
❖ Repeating language patterns	❖ Some words with –s and –ing	❖ Line breaks match ends of phrases and sentences
❖ Simple dialogue (assigned by said in most texts)	❖ Simple plurals	*Punctuation*
❖ Amusing one-dimensional characters		❖ Periods, commas, quotation marks, exclamation point and question marks
❖ Familiar settings close to children's experience		❖ Ellipses in some texts to create expectation
		Tools
		❖ NA

patterns, requiring children to attend closely to print at some points. Sentences are a little longer but the syntax is simple and easy to control; there are more words than in level B texts. There are many easily decodable words as well as many easy high frequency words, with a few multisyllable words. Text characteristics are listed on the previous page.

Examples

THE BIG KICK [C] (SEE FIGURE 11–5)
Realistic fiction; 16 pages; 67 words; varies from two to four lines on a page; no repeating patterns; simple dialogue (assigned to speakers) with two characters; print layout supports phrasing; some words in bold; familiar topics; simple story; many easy high frequency words; clear picture support.

MAKING A HOUSE [C] (SEE FIGURE 11–6)
Informational text; 16 pages; 89 words; varies from one to three lines on a page; repeating pattern ("A _____ is a tool.") on first line but second line variable; pattern change on last page; logical sequence of events from planning to building a house and then moving in; challenging content (*house plan*; *drill*; *saw*); clear picture support.

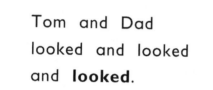

Figure 11–5.   The Big Kick *(Level C)*

Figure 11–6.   Making a House *(Level C)*

Other Descriptions at Level C

ACROSS THE SEASONS [C]

Informational text; 16 pages; 75 words; varies from two to five lines on a page; no repeating patterns; pages alternate content that is logically linked (putting on swimsuits followed by "It's a hot day for swimming."); clear picture support; many easy high frequency words; familiar topics.

BOATS [C]

Informational text; 24 pages; 100 words; two lines of print per page, except for last page which has three; one sentence on each line of print except page 21, which is challenging because one sentence begins in the middle of a line; challenging content (names of boats and names of bodies of water); repeating pattern ("A [name of boat] is a boat. It can work on a [body of water].)"; table of contents; glossary; references; Internet sites; index.

THE BEST PLACE [C]

Realistic fiction with informational format and fanciful pictures; eight pages; 77 words; two lines of print per page; two sentences per page, except for the words "no" and "yes" as short answers; question/answer format; simple dialogue on one page in the form of character's thoughts; logical reasoning as character tries one solution after another for a home for the snake, finally deciding that "by the pond" is best.

THE TROLLEY RIDE [C]

Fantasy; 16 pages; 87 words; one line of print per page except for pages 14 and 15; repeating pattern ("A [animal] got on the trolley. then the trolley zoomed off.") until the last page; circular sequence of events with animals getting on the trolley until finally a monster gets on and the animals get off one by one.

Level D

Text Characteristics

Stories are slightly more complex but still very easy for children to understand. Concepts are familiar within children's experience. The illustrations are supportive, but more attention to the print is required. Most texts have clear print; spacing is obvious. Most texts range from two to six lines of print per page and have more words than the previous levels. Sentences are generally a little longer than level C, but are not complex. There is a full range of punctuation; words encountered in previous texts are used many times. The vocabulary contains more inflectional endings—*ing, ed, s*—so that children have an opportunity to notice the variations in word structure. Text characteristics are listed on the next page.

Examples

THE MIRROR [D] (SEE FIGURE 11–7)

Realistic fiction in the style of a traditional tale; eight pages; 112 words; five lines of print; more words on a line (up to six); split dialogue; traditional illustrations that provide high support; five characters, with different characters speaking on each page; challenging words (*young, old, woman, mirror, shouted. laughed*); predictable story; requires reader to understand point of view (that every person who looks at the mirror thinks it is a picture of him/herself); amusing story.

BATTERIES [D] (SEE FIGURE 11–8)

Informational text; 16 pages; 105 words; three to four lines of print on a page; print every other page with small close-up inset (picture of enlarged battery); same technical concept throughout but new machine; repeating pattern ("Look at their [machine]."), followed by explanation of what the battery does; vocabulary—labels for machines;

Text Characteristics: Level D

GENRES/FORMS

Genres
- Realistic fiction
- Simple animal fantasy
- Some simple factual texts

Forms
- Picture books

TEXT STRUCTURE

- Focused on a single idea or series of related ideas
- Story lines with more episodes (usually repetitive in nature)

CONTENT

- Familiar, easy content—family, play, pets, school
- Most concepts supported by pictures

THEMES AND IDEAS

- Familiar themes and ideas

LANGUAGE AND LITERARY FEATURES

- More complex repeating language patterns
- Simple sequence of events (often repeated) needed to understand story
- Simple dialogue included and assigned to speaker
- Variety in assignment to speaker (other than *said*)
- Simple dialogue and some split dialogue
- Simple sequence of events (often repeated) needed to understand story
- Amusing or engaging one-dimensional characters
- Familiar settings close to children's experience

SENTENCE COMPLEXITY

- Some longer sentences (some with 6+ words)
- Many sentences with prepositional phrases and adjectives
- Some sentences that are questions
- A few sentences beginning with phrases

VOCABULARY

- Almost all vocabulary familiar to children and likely to be used in their oral language
- A few labels that require explanation or teaching
- Variation in words used to assign dialogue
- Word meanings illustrated by pictures

WORDS

- Mostly 1-2 syllable words
- Many easily decodable words—growing range
- Some words with inflectional endings (*–ing*)
- Many high frequency words
- Simple plurals
- Mostly simple spelling patterns
- Some words used in different language structures (*said Mom; Mom said*)
- Some words with *–s* and *–ing*

ILLUSTRATIONS

- Highly supportive illustrations
- More details in the illustrations
- Variety in layout of illustrations
- Illustrations on every page or every other page

BOOK AND PRINT FEATURES

Length
- Very short, usually 8 pages of print
- Mostly 2-5 lines of print per page (but variable)

Print and Layout
- Print clearly separated from pictures
- Print in large plain font
- Some words in bold for emphasis
- Sentences begin on left
- Many texts with layout supporting phrasing
- Some limited variation in print placement
- Text layout easy to follow with both larger and smaller print
- Ample space between words and lines
- Line breaks match ends of phrases and sentences

Punctuation
- Periods, commas, quotation marks, exclamation point in most texts
- Ellipses in some texts to create expectation

Tools
- NA

---

logical sequence of related ideas with "sum up" page at the end; some new content to learn for many young children.

Other Descriptions at Level D

TOM IS BRAVE [D]

Realistic fiction; 16 pages; 57 words; simple dialogue and split dialogue; one to four lines of print per page; varied placement of print; no repeating patterns; everyday topics familiar to most; highly supportive pictures; sequence of events, ending with Tom's being proud of the bandage on his leg.

GREEDY CAT IS HUNGRY [D]

Realistic fiction; 12 pages; 103 words; split dialogue; two to four lines of print per page; longer sentences (up to nine words) with dependent clauses; seven characters; repeating pattern ("No!" said ____. "You're a greedy cat!"); vocabulary—family names like *uncle*; highly supportive pictures; spelling of relevant words in magnetic letters on fridge; predictable plot with satisfying conclusion.

HOW MANY LEGS [D]

Informational text; 16 pages; 104 words; two to four lines of print per page; sentences up to 10 words with embedded dependent clauses; animal names and number concepts; clear and supportive illustrations; insets—small drawings on the print page; series of related ideas, each time showing an animal, the number of legs, and what that animal uses the legs to do; interesting ending showing a snake and inviting inference as to how a snake gets around.

Figure 11–7. The Mirror *(Level D)*

> Look! They have a car.
> Their car uses a battery.
> The battery makes it go.

Figure 11–8. Batteries *(Level D)*

APPLE TREES [D]

Informational text; 24 pages; 62 words; two lines of print per page; one sentence (about seven words) on each page; repeating pattern ("In [season], apple trees have..."); pattern change on last page; series of related ideas (that apple trees have leaves and fruit and that seasons make a difference); some new content to learn for many young children; table of contents; glossary; references; Internet sites; index.

Level E
Text Characteristics

The amount of text is gradually increasing; most stories have three to eight lines of text per page and text placement varies. Stories are more complex. Repeating patterns appear less frequently; when they are used, they vary within the text. The ideas in stories are more subtle and may require a greater degree of interpretation. Illustrations strongly support the story but are busier several ideas; the text carries the story line. Problem solving is needed to figure out new words and to relate the illustrations and text.

The reading vocabulary requires skill in word analysis; words are longer and have inflectional endings. Texts at level E build on and extend children's vocabulary of frequently used words. Taking words apart will help children problem-solve. A full variety of punctuation is evident. Some concepts may be less familiar to children. Texts may look easy (having only one line or few words) but the ideas require more control of aspects of print. Specific text characteristics are listed below.

Text Characteristics: Level E

Genres/Forms

Genres
- Realistic fiction
- Simple animal fantasy
- Some simple factual texts
- Some very simple retellings of traditional tales

Forms
- Picture books
- Simple plays

Text Structure

Fiction
- Focused on a single idea or series of related ideas
- Narrative texts with clear beginning, series of events, and ending

Nonfiction
- Series of related ideas around one topic in informational text

Content
- Familiar content that extends beyond home, neighborhood, and school
- Most concepts supported by pictures

Themes and Ideas
- Themes related to typical experiences of children
- Concrete, easy to understand ideas
- Many light, humorous stories, typical of childhood experiences

Language and Literary Features
- Both simple and split dialogue, speaker usually assigned
- Some longer stretches of dialogue
- More literary stories and language
- Simple sequence of events (often repeated) needed to understand story
- Amusing or engaging one-dimensional characters
- Familiar settings close to children's experience

Sentence Complexity
- Some longer sentences (some with 10+ words)
- Some complex sentences with variety in order of clauses
- Sentences with prepositional phrases and adjectives
- Some sentences that are questions
- Use of commas to set words apart (addressee in dialogue, qualifiers, etc.)
- Some sentences with verb preceding subject

Vocabulary
- Almost all vocabulary familiar to children and likely to be used in their oral language
- Variation of use of words to assign dialogue in some texts (said, cried, shouted)
- A few labels that require explanation or teaching
- Word meanings illustrated by pictures

Words
- Mostly 1-2 syllable words
- Some 3 syllable words
- Mostly words with easy, predictable letter/sound relationships and spelling patterns
- Some words with inflectional endings (–ing)
- Many high frequency words
- Simple plurals and possessives
- Easy contractions
- Simple letter-sound relationships in most words
- Variety of easy spelling patterns
- Some words used in different language (said Mom; Mom said)

Illustrations
- More details in the Illustrations
- Variety in layout of illustrations
- Most pages with illustrations and print
- Illustrations complex with multiple ideas
- Illustrations on every page or every other page

Book and Print Features

Length
- Short, 8-16 pages of print
- Most texts 2-7 lines per page

Print and Layout
- Print in most texts separated from pictures
- Print in large, plain font
- Some words in bold for emphasis
- Sentences beginning on the left in most texts
- Many texts with layout supporting phrasing
- Varied placement of print
- Wide variety of print styles and text layout
- Ample space between words and between lines
- Sentences carrying over 2-3 lines and some over 2 pages
- Line breaks match ends of phrases and sentences

Punctuation
- Periods, commas, quotation marks, exclamation points, question marks, and ellipses

Tools
- NA

Examples

BABY BEAR GOES FISHING [E]
(SEE FIGURE 11–9)

Fantasy—personified animal family; 16 pages; 112 words; two to six lines of print per page; variation in print placement; some words in bold to supporting emphasis; print placement supportive of phrasing; simple and split dialogue; information in illustrations to infer characters' motives and feelings; simple plot with several episodes, ending with Baby Bear saying he isn't too little to fish.

BIG ROCKS, LITTLE ROCKS [E]
(SEE FIGURE 11–10)

Informational text; 16 pages; 180 words; two to three lines of print per page; no repeating patterns; some sentences beginning in middle of a line; related ideas but change of topic on each page; supportive illustrations—photographs inset of page with print; sentences beginning with *these*, *this*, *here* —talking directly to reader; some technical language (*print, volcano, layers*); some content new to most young children.

"I'm going fishing,"
said Father Bear.

"I like fishing, too,"
said Baby Bear.
"I will go with you
and help you."

Figure 11–9. Baby Bear Goes Fishing *(Level E)*

This big rock is made
of layers of rock. The oldest rock is
down at the bottom.

This big rock was made from fire.
It came out of a volcano.

Figure 11–10. Big Rocks, Little Rocks *(Level E)*

Other Descriptions at Level E

KATIE'S CATERPILLAR [E]

Realistic fiction; 16 pages; 149 words; three to six lines of print per page; no repeating patterns; some long sentences (up to 13 words); longer pieces of dialogue; simple and split dialogue; some words in bold to support emphasis; print layout supportive of phrasing; simple plot with several episodes; problem stated but requires some inference (that Katie doesn't like school because she didn't get to look after the fish; solution of plot (that Katie will take care of the caterpillar and so is willing to go back to school) requires further inference; portrayal of understanding family/friend relationship; not clear whether Joe and Katie are siblings or friends.

MRS. WISHY-WASHY [E]

Fantasy—talking animals; 16 pages; 102 words; two lines of print on most pages; repeating patterns in beginning and ending pages ("Oh, lovely mud" and "In went the ____."; literary language structure; onomatopoetic words (*wishy-washy*); variation in sentence length; simple dialogue within longer sentences; predictable story, with animals getting dirty, then being washed; invites inference at the end when animals again say, "Oh, lovely mud!"

MAKING A CATERPILLAR [E]

Informational text; 16 pages; 115 words; one to six lines of print plus illustration on each page; one heading in bold signaling a new section; no repeating patterns but some sentences structured in parallel form; familiar vocabulary for most young children; new content for some young children; highly supportive pictures (placed by each direction); "how to" sequence of actions, requiring reader to follow and understand directions.

BABY ANIMALS [E]

Informational text; 16 pages; 109 words; four to five lines of print on each page; told in rhyme, with one verse on each page; new animal every two pages; no repeating patterns; some personification on two pages (animal is narrator) but ideas and photographs authentic; vocabulary—names of animals and some babies; new content and/or vocabulary for some young children; summary on last page.

Level F

Text Characteristics

Texts are slightly longer than level E; the print is necessarily somewhat smaller. There are usually between three and eight lines of text per page. Pictures continue to support reading although the text carries more of the meaning. Literary language is mixed with typical oral language structures, but the syntax of the text largely reflects patterns peculiar to written language. The variety of frequently used words continues to expand. Story lines include more episodes (actions or events), which follow one another chronologically, and some characters are more fully developed. The text has a distinct beginning, middle, and end. Dialogue has appeared at earlier levels, but at this level there is greater variety in the way it is signaled and presented. Punctuation supports phrasing and meaning. There are many more opportunities for word analysis. A summary of text characteristics is presented on the next page.

Examples

THE LION AND THE RABBIT [F] (SEE FIGURE 11–11)

Traditional fable (Aesop)—animal fantasy; 16 pages; 99 words; one to six lines of print per page; no repeating patterns but some sentences with parallel structure; some long sequences of dialogue; split dialogue; some words in bold to support emphasis; print layout that supports phrasing; some literary language; sequential plot, ending with the lion coming back to get the rabbit, which is now gone; invites inferring the "lesson" (that if you are always chasing something bigger, you may end up with nothing).

Text Characteristics: Level F

GENRES/FORMS

Genres
- Realistic fiction
- Simple animal fantasy
- Some simple factual texts
- Some very simple retellings of traditional tales

Forms
- Picture books
- Simple plays

TEXT STRUCTURE

Fiction
- Focused on a single idea or series of related ideas
- Narrative texts with beginning, series of events, and ending

Nonfiction
- Series of ideas around one topic in informational texts

CONTENT
- Familiar content that expands beyond home, neighborhood and school
- Concepts accessible through text and illustrations

THEMES AND IDEAS
- Themes related to typical experiences of children
- Concrete, easy to understand ideas
- Many light, humorous stories, typical of childhood experiences

LANGUAGE AND LITERARY FEATURES
- Both simple and split dialogue, speaker usually assigned
- Some longer stretches of dialogue
- More literary stories and language
- Simple sequence of events (often repeated) needed to understand story
- Amusing or engaging one-dimensional characters
- Familiar settings close to children's experience

SENTENCE COMPLEXITY
- Some long sentences (10+ words) with prepositional phrases, adjectives, and clauses
- Some complex sentences with variety in order of clauses
- Some question and answer text patterns or formats
- Use of commas to set words apart (addressee in dialogue, qualifiers, etc.)
- Some compound sentences conjoined by *and*
- Variation in placement of subject, verb, adjectives, adverbs

VOCABULARY
- Most vocabulary words familiar to children and likely to be used in their oral language
- Variation in use of words to assign dialogue in some texts (*said, cried, shouted*)
- A few labels that require explanation or teaching

WORDS
- Mostly 1-2 syllable words
- Some 3 syllable words
- Mostly words with easy predictable letter/sound relationships and spelling patterns
- Many words with inflectional endings
- Many high frequency words
- Plurals, contractions, and possessives
- Some complex letter-sound relationships in words
- Variety of easy spelling patterns
- Some words used in different language structures (*said Mom; Mom said*)

ILLUSTRATIONS
- Some illustrations complex with many ideas included
- Illustrations supportive of the text but not carrying important aspects of meaning
- Illustrations on every page or every other page
- Variety in layout of illustrations

BOOK AND PRINT FEATURES

Length
- Short, 8-16 pages of print
- Most texts 3-8 lines of print per page

Print and Layout
- Print in most texts clearly separated from pictures
- Sentences carrying over 2-3 lines and some over 2 pages
- Some short sentences, starting middle of a line
- Longer sentences starting on left margin
- Variable placement of print
- Ample space between words and lines
- Print in large, plain font
- Some words in bold or larger font for emphasis

Punctuation
- Periods, commas, quotation marks, exclamation points, question marks, dashes, and ellipses in most texts

Tools
- NA

GOING TO THE DENTIST [F] (SEE FIGURE 11–12)
Informational text; 24 pages; 122 words; three to five lines on a page; some compound sentences; vocabulary related to the topic (*cavities, decayed, filling*); new vocabulary/content for many young children; series of related ideas with new content on each page; table of contents; glossary; index; references; internet sites.

Other Descriptions at Level F
COOKIE'S WEEK [F]
Realistic fiction—antics of a cat; 28 pages; 84 words; one line of text on most pages; text integrated with pictures; predictable text—organized around days of the week; sentences not continuous in layout—many sentences beginning on one page continuing below or on the next, with use of

The lion looked up.
"Here comes a big deer,"
he said.
"I'll go and get the deer.
This rabbit is too little."

And he let the rabbit go.

Figure 11–11. The Lion and the Rabbit *(Level F)*

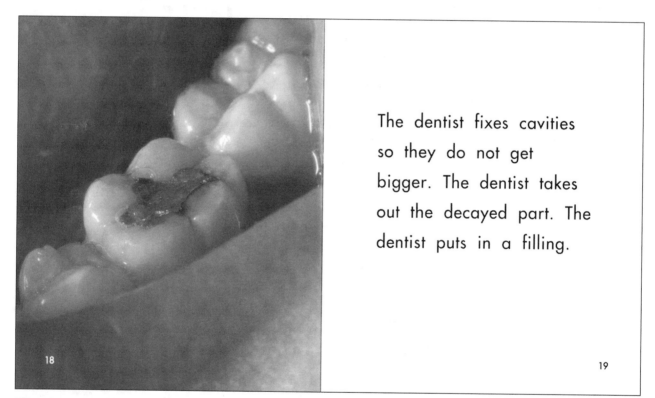

The dentist fixes cavities
so they do not get
bigger. The dentist takes
out the decayed part. The
dentist puts in a filling.

Figure 11–12. Going to the Dentist *(Level F)*

ellipses; repeated phrases ("On [day], Cookie…" and "went everywhere"); requires following simple plot, ending with prediction about whether Cookie will rest tomorrow (Sunday).

THE HUNGRY GIANT [F]
Fantasy; 16 pages; 183 words; one to six lines of print per page; print placement variable; simple and split dialogue, embedded in longer sentences; repeated phrase ("…or I'll hit you with my bommy-knocker" and "so the people ran and ran"); some words in larger print to support expression; episodic plot that builds to the conclusion; invites prediction (that the beehive is full of bees and will get even with the giant); invites character discussion (that people were smart and that the giant was greedy).

OAK TREES [F]

Informational text; 24 pages; 132 words; three to four lines of print per page; vocabulary—technical words related to parts of trees (*branches, bark, leaves, buds, lobes, rounded*); no repeating phrases; new content for most young children; related ideas but new content each page; table of contents; glossary; references; Internet sites; index.

WHERE DID ALL THE WATER GO? [F]

Informational text; 16 pages; 139 words; two to four lines of print per page; some difficult language structures ("are made of" and "down comes the rain"); new content for most young children; abstract ideas although explained in clear language and simple vocabulary; some key words in bold; some print white on gray; invites rethinking the concept on last page.

Level G

Text Characteristics

Books at level G contain more challenging ideas and vocabulary. Most books still have between three and eight lines of text per page, but the sentences

---

Text Characteristics: Level G

GENRES/FORMS

Genres
- Realistic fiction
- Simple animal fantasy
- Some simple factual texts
- A variety of informational texts on easy topics
- Traditional literature (mostly folk tales)

Forms
- Picture books
- Plays

TEXT STRUCTURE
- Focused on a single idea or series of related ideas
- Narrative texts straightforward structure (beginning, series of episodes, ending) but more episodes included
- Some unusual formats, such as letters or questions followed by answers
- Underlying text structures—description, compare/contrast
- Some longer texts with repeating longer and more complex patterns
- Informational texts largely focused on one category of information
- Some texts with sequential information

CONTENT
- Accessible content that expands beyond home, neighborhood and school
- Concepts accessible through text and illustrations

THEMES AND IDEAS
- Themes related to typical experiences of children
- Concrete, easy to understand ideas
- Many light, humorous stories, typical of childhood experiences

LANGUAGE AND LITERARY FEATURES
- Variety in presentation of dialogue—simple with pronouns, split, direct, with some longer stretches of dialogue
- More literary stories and language
- Simple sequence of events (often repeated) needed to understand story
- Amusing or engaging one-dimensional characters
- Some texts with settings that are not typical of most children's experience

SENTENCE COMPLEXITY
- Some long sentences (10+ words) with prepositional phrases, adjectives, and clauses
- Sentences with clauses and embedded phrases, some introductory
- Some complex sentences with variety in order of clauses, phrases, subject, verb and object.
- Some simple questions in fiction
- Some question and answer formats for nonfiction

VOCABULARY
- Most vocabulary words familiar to children and likely to be used in their oral language
- A few labels that require explanation or teaching
- Some content-specific words introduced and explained and illustrated in the text
- Variation of use of words to assign dialogue in some text (*said, cried, shouted*)

WORDS
- Mostly 1-2 syllable words
- Some 3 syllable words
- Many high frequency words
- Easy contractions
- Many words with inflectional endings
- Plurals, contractions, and possessives
- Some complex letter-sound relationships in words
- Wide variety of easy spelling patterns
- Some words used in different language structure (*said Mom; Mom said*)

ILLUSTRATIONS
- Some illustrations complex with many ideas
- Illustrations playing a role in mood and tone (artistic quality)
- Illustrations support and extend meaning
- Illustrations on every page or every other page in most texts
- Variety in layout of illustrations
- Some simple graphics (illustrations with labels)
- One kind of graphic on a page

BOOK AND PRINT FEATURES

Length
- Short, 8-16 pages of print
- Most texts 3-8 lines of print per page

Print and Layout
- Print in most texts clearly separated from pictures
- Sentences carrying over 2-3 lines and some over 2 pages
- Some short sentences, starting middle of a line
- Longer sentences starting on left margin
- Variable placement of print
- Ample space between words and lines
- Print in large, plain font
- Some words in bold or larger font for emphasis

Punctuation
- Periods, commas, quotation marks, exclamation points, question marks, dashes, and ellipses in some texts

Tools
- NA

---

are longer. As at level F, literary language, structures, and concepts are integrated with natural language. A greater range of content extends children's experiences. The reading vocabulary continues to expand; new vocabulary is introduced. Stories have more events; occasionally repetition is built into the episodic structure to support reading. Text characteristics for level G are listed on the previous page.

Examples

SUMMER AT COVE LAKE [G] (SEE FIGURE 11–13)
Realistic fiction; 16 pages; 288 words; personal narrative told in letter format as a young girl writes to Mom and Dad about here visit to the lake; four to five word letter on every other page; includes salutation, body, closing, and P.S. on each letter; day by day episodes, with each letter starting with "Today"; illustrations supportive—paintings; new format for many young children; invites prediction

at end (that the girl will return next summer); invites inferring characters' feelings.

EARTH AND MOON [G] (SEE FIGURE 11–14)
Informational text; 16 pages; 250 words; three to seven lines of print on a page; question/answer format; photographs illustrating content; some long sentences (for example one with 13 words over three lines); some sentences with lists divided by commas; new content for many young children; use of compare/contrast (earth and moon); index.

Other Descriptions at Level G

PACO'S GARDEN [G]
Realistic fiction; 12 pages; 118 words; one to four lines of print on a page; print at the bottom of each page; some complex sentences with introductory independent clauses and items in a series; series of adjectives divided by commas

Figure 11–13.   Summer at Cove Lake *(Level G)*

Why is the sky black on the moon?

The sky on the moon is black
because there is no air
on the moon.

12

There is no air on the moon,
and there is no water.
The moon has no wind
and no clouds.

13

Figure 11–14. Earth and Moon *(Level G)*

before nouns; step-by-step "how to do it" for planting a garden; inset picture of seed packet with label on each page; simple dialogue; invites insight into characters' feelings (when woodchuck ate the garden); invites prediction at end (with picture of the new garden surrounded by a fence but no words); nonfiction note at the end—information on woodchuck; pictures of author and illustrator on the back.

GREEDY CAT [G]

Realistic fiction with elements of fantasy; 16 pages; 166 words; one to six lines of print on a page; variable placement of print; vocabulary—food names (*sticky buns)*; three different repeating patterns; predictable story with seven episodes; invites prediction of ending (when Mom buys pepper); illustrations support the text and add humor.

GLASS [G]

Informational text; 14 pages; 112 words; two to five lines of print per page; variable placement of print; some print in white on top of illustrations; photographs—often a series on a page that add meaning; invites noticing and discussing details in pictures; new content for most young children; invites inquiry (noticing many things that are made of glass).

WASHING THE DOG [G]

Informational text; eight pages; 94 words; two to four lines of print per page; some long complex sentences with introductory dependent clauses and lists separated by commas (for example, one with 21 words); print consistently at bottom of page; signal words such as *first, next, then, finally;* directions for the sequence.

Level H

Text Characteristics

Level H is very similar to G, but the language and vocabulary are even more complex, the stories longer and more literary, and there is less repetition in the episodic structure. Readers will meet dialogue in many texts. Characters are straightforwardly drawn and easy to understand, but have greater dimension than at previous levels. Text characteristics for level H are listed below.

Examples

THE SLEEPOVER [H] (SEE FIGURE 11–15)

Text is realistic fiction but personified picture of cat's antics makes illustrations fantasy; 12 pages; 297 words; four to seven lines of print per page; text and illustrations on every page; text arranged in paragraphs; text wraps around, with new sentences started after final punctuation; long sentences (for example, 26 words; sentences with embedded dependent and independent clauses,

---

Text Characteristics: Level H

GENRES/FORMS

Genres
- Realistic fiction
- Simple animal fantasy
- Informational texts
- Traditional literature (mostly folk tales)

Forms
- Picture books
- Plays

TEXT STRUCTURE

Fiction
- Narrative texts organized in predictable ways (beginning, series of repeated episodes, ending)
- More episodes and less repetition in them

Nonfiction
- Clearly organized into categories
- Underlying structures used and presented clearly—description, compare/ contrast, temporal sequence, problem/solution
- Largely focused on one category of information

CONTENT

- Accessible content that expands beyond home, neighborhood and school
- Concepts accessible through text and illustrations

THEMES AND IDEAS

- Mostly accessible themes and ideas
- Greater variety in themes, going beyond everyday events
- Many light, humorous stories, typical of childhood experiences

LANGUAGE AND LITERARY FEATURES

- Some stretches of descriptive language
- Use of dialogue for drama
- Full variety in presentation of dialogue (simple, simple using pronouns, split, direct)
- Almost all dialogue assigned to speaker
- More episodes that provide related information across time
- Amusing or engaging one-dimensional characters
- Some texts with settings that are not typical of children's experience

SENTENCE COMPLEXITY

- Some long sentences (10+ words) with prepositional phrases, adjectives, and clauses
- Variation in placement of subject, verb, adjectives, adverbs
- Some complex sentences with variety in order of clauses, phrases, subject, verb and object.
- Some simple questions in fiction
- Some question and answer formats for nonfiction

VOCABULARY

- Most vocabulary words known by children through oral language or reading
- A few content-specific words introduced and explained and illustrated in the text
- Wide variety in words used to assign dialogue to speaker

WORDS

- Mostly 1-2 syllable words
- Some 3 syllable words
- Multisyllable words that are generally easy to take apart
- Wide range of high frequency words
- Many words with inflectional endings
- Plurals, contractions, and possessives
- Some complex letter-sound relationships in words
- Some complex spelling patterns
- Some easy compound words

ILLUSTRATIONS

Fiction
- Illustrations complex with many ideas
- Illustrations playing a role in mood and tone (artistic quality)
- Illustrations support and extend meaning
- Word reading not supported by illustrations
- Illustrations on every page or every other page in most texts

Nonfiction
- Some simple graphics (illustrations with labels)
- One kind of graphic on a page

BOOK AND PRINT FEATURES

Length
- Short, 8-16 pages of print
- Most texts 3-8 lines of print per page

Print and Layout
- Print in most texts clearly separated from pictures
- Print in large, plain font
- Some texts in smaller font size
- Words in bold and italics—important to meaning and stress
- Italics indicating unspoken thought
- Some short sentences, starting middle of a line
- Longer sentences starting on left margin
- Variable placement of print
- Ample space between words and lines
- Sentences carrying over 2-3 lines and some over 2 pages

Punctuation
- Periods, commas, quotation marks, exclamation points, question marks, dashes, and ellipses

Tools
- NA

"Glen is my friend who has bunnies,"
Max said. "But I didn't ask Glen. He
always hides my glasses. Then he tells me
that his rabbits took them!"

6

"Did you invite Stan, then?"
"Not Stan," said Max. "He likes to
build with blocks like I do. But he never
wants to play soccer."

7

Figure 11–15. The Sleepover *(Level H)*

come with dialogue; split dialogue; some unassigned dialogue; illustrations support and extend meaning; some words in all caps to support expression; invites prediction as to who the guest really is (turns out to be Grandpa).

UNDER A MICROSCOPE [H] (SEE FIGURE 11–16)

Informational text; 16 pages; 254 words; two to five lines of print per page; smaller font; phrases with several adjectives before a noun; some sentences with dependent clauses; words related to sizes (*tiny, long, bigger*); connected ideas across the text with new items each page; builds concept of making larger; abstract idea but illustrated over and over; new content for many young children; index.

Other Descriptions at Level H

HOLE IN HARRY'S POCKET [H]

Realistic fiction; 16 pages; 250+ words; two to four lines of print on each page; split dialogue, all assigned; high picture support but some difficult words not illustrated; some complex sentences with dependent clauses; full range of punctuation, including dashes; sentences wrap around with new sentences starting after final punctuation; predictable story with child going to the store and then retracing steps; demands that the reader remember details (items in Harry's pocket and that he forgot the milk).

BEN'S TOOTH [H]

Realistic fiction; 16 pages; 197 words; two to seven lines of print per page; split dialogue; full range of punctuation, including ellipses; most of story carried in dialogue; some words in bold to support stress on words; some words in italics to represent Ben's thoughts; use of contractions; invites use of background knowledge (knowing that "tooth fairy" will come as well as that it's

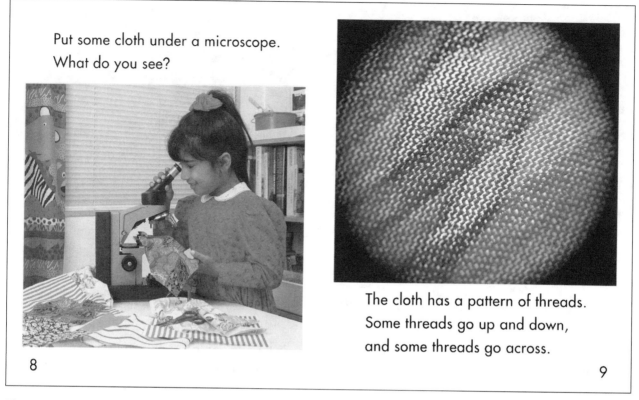

Put some cloth under a microscope.
What do you see?

8

The cloth has a pattern of threads.
Some threads go up and down,
and some threads go across.

9

Figure 11–16. Under a Microscope *(Level H)*

Mom); invites inferring of character's thinking (why Mom laughed).

Fun with Plaster [H]

Informational text; 16 pages; 150 words; two to six lines of print per page; bold headings for five sections indicating categories of information; some key words in bold; photographs with labels on specific items; some step-by-step directions (temporal sequence); some description; poses questions for the reader to answer using illustrations (answers in the back); concepts explained clearly; some new content but highly accessible; vocabulary related to topic (*casts, crimes, sets*); table of contents; glossary; index; suggested activity.

The Earthworm [H]

Informational text; 12 pages; 157 words; two to four lines of print per page; smaller spaces between words; technical vocabulary (*damp, skin, diet, sad-*

dle; sac; gizzard); new content for most young children; several lists of nouns, set off by commas; supportive illustrations—combination of drawings and photographs; some complex sentences with dependent clauses; new content on each page related to the central topic; information on author and illustrator at the end.

Level I

Text Characteristics

At level I there are a variety of texts in several genres. Story structure is more complex; episodes are elaborated in more detail and themes are varied and sophisticated. Illustrations provide low to moderate support, extend the texts, and assist children in interpretation. Readers are asked to understand different points of view. Texts offer many opportunities to discuss new ideas.

Texts are generally longer than the previous level, with more sentences per page. Specialized, unusual, and challenging vocabulary is evident. Texts include a large number of words that by now will be familiar to most children; problem solving will be needed only for unfamiliar words. Characters are memorable. There are many possibilities for comparison with other texts, those previously read and those children have heard read aloud. Text characteristics are listed below.

Examples
A Good Knee for a Cat [I] (See Figure 11–17)
Realistic fiction; 16 pages; 205 words; eight to twelve

Text Characteristics: Level I

Genres/Forms

Genres
- Realistic fiction
- Simple animal fantasy
- Informational texts
- Traditional literature (mostly folk tales)

Forms
- Picture books
- Plays

Text Structure

Fiction
- Narratives with more elaborated episodes
- Little repetition of similar episodes

Nonfiction
- Texts with categorical information
- Underlying structures—description, compare/ contrast, temporal sequence, problem/solution
- Largely focused on one category of information

Content
- Some new content that children typically would not know
- Concepts accessible through text and illustrations

Themes and Ideas
- Themes accessible given typical experiences of children
- Some ideas new to most children
- A few abstract ideas but highly supported by text and illustrations
- Many light, humorous stories, typical of childhood experiences

Language and Literary Features
- Variety of dialogue—may be between more than two characters in many texts
- Language characteristic of traditional literature in some texts
- May have more than one point of view within one text
- Amusing or engaging one-dimensional characters
- Description of character traits
- Some texts with settings that are not typical of children's experience

Sentence Complexity
- Some long sentences (10+ words) with prepositional phrases, adjectives, and clauses
- Many compound sentences
- Many sentences with embedded clauses and phrases
- Sentences with nouns, verbs, adjectives, and adverbs in series, divided by commas
- Use of commas to set words apart (addressee in dialogue, qualifiers, etc.)
- Variation in placement of subject, verb, adjectives, adverbs
- Questions in dialogue (fiction) and questions and answers (nonfiction)

Vocabulary
- Most vocabulary words known by children through oral language or reading
- A few content-specific words introduced and explained in the text
- Content words illustrated
- Wide variety of words to assign dialogue (*said, cried, shouted, thought, whispered*) and adverbs describing the dialogue (*quietly, loudly*)

Words
- Many 2-3 syllable words
- Multisyllable words that are generally easy to take apart
- Wide range of high frequency words
- Many words with inflectional endings
- Plurals, contractions, and possessives
- Some complex letter-sound relationships in words
- Some complex spelling patterns
- Some easy compound words

Illustrations

Fiction
- Illustrations that support interpretation, enhance enjoyment, set mood but are not necessary for understanding
- Illustrations on every page or every other page in most texts
- Some whole pages of print

Nonfiction
- Some simple graphics (illustrations with labels)
- One or two kinds of graphics on a page

Book and Print Features

Length
- Short, 8-16 pages of print
- Most texts 3-8 lines of print per page
- Some easy illustrated chapter books of 40-60 pages

Print and Layout
- Print in most texts clearly separated from pictures
- Print in large, plain font
- Some texts in smaller font size
- Some words in bold or larger font for emphasis
- Italics indicating unspoken thought
- Some short sentences, starting middle of a line
- Longer sentences starting on left margin
- Variable placement of print
- Ample space between words and lines
- Variety in layout, reflecting different genres
- Sentences carrying over 2-3 lines and some over 2 pages

Punctuation
- Periods, commas, quotation marks, exclamation points, question marks, dashes, and ellipses in most texts

Tools
- Some texts with a table of contents
- Some texts with a simple glossary

The old cat slept on a chair,
but it was not as good as a knee.
There was no kind hand
to stroke him.

"Here's Aunt Maria and Anna!"
said Juan.
He went out to meet them.
Juan pushed Anna's wheelchair
along the path and into the house.
"How about some coffee?" said Mom.
"Show Anna your room, Blanca."

6

7

Figure 11–17. A Good Knee for a Cat *(Level I)*

lines of print per page; paragraphing indicated by space; sentences starting on the left; split dialogue; long pieces of dialogue; most of story carried by dialogue; six characters, four with dialogue; some compound sentences; story builds to arrival of Anna; invites prediction that the cat will like Anna's lap; invites discussion of characters' feelings (why Anna likes the cat).

GRANDPARENTS ARE GREAT [I] (SEE FIGURE 11–18)

Informational text; 11 pages; 151 words; one to five lines of print per page; photographs illustrating diversity; wrap-around text with new sentences starting after final punctuation; new vocabulary (for example *volunteers*) explained in the text; new information every page but clearly explained in the text; prompts thinking about personal connections.

Other Descriptions at Level I

CAT'S SURPRISE PARTY [I]

Fantasy—personification of animals; 12 pages; 376 words; print inset in white box in pictures or at bottom of pages; four to nine lines of print on a page; paragraphing; wrap-around text with new sentences starting after final punctuation; variable length of sentences; predictable plot (animals buying *their* favorite foods but neglecting Cat); easy-to-follow plot (each animal preparing to go to the party); opportunity to derive theme (that friendship is important); supportive illustration on last page (food in front of each animal).

THE PRINCESS, THE MUD PIES, AND THE DRAGON [I]

Traditional tale; 15 pages; 250+ words; long sentences; literary language ("there lived a dragon");

Mr. Jackson has ten grandchildren and two great-grandchildren. Most of them live far away. Mr. Jackson stays in touch with them by e-mail. He sends them letters, jokes, and photos.

Many grandparents still go to a job away from home every day. Some work in offices. Others work in stores. Darrell loves to visit his grandmother at her job. She teaches children how to ride horses.

8

9

Figure 11–18. Grandparents are Great *(Level I)*

print and pictures on every page; requires background knowledge (that fire will melt metal); requires inference (that dragon was so frightened by noise he wouldn't come back); invites prediction (that mud pies would frighten a dragon).

ANIMAL GROUPS [I]
Informational text; 16 pages; 265 words; print in various places on the page; two kinds of print—ongoing descriptive text and very specific facts (in blue); labeled photographs (blue for photographs; components labeled red with arrows), several on a page; headings in bold for each section; requires considering questions and searching for answers; technical vocabulary—*mammals, reptiles, amphibians, salamander, thorax, abdomen*); knowledge of all technical vocabulary not required for understanding; ends with question prompting recall of information from the text.

COMMUNITY JOBS [I]
Informational text; 16 pages; 207 words; three to five lines of print per page; supports large concept of community helpers; change of subject every one or two pages; supportive photographs on every page; requires background knowledge (work with and without pay); vocabulary related to employment—*goods, pay, packages*; summary on last page through photographs.

Summary: Level A to I

In this chapter, we have examined text characteristics for levels A through I. Typically this span is applicable to your teaching of children in kindergarten and grade one; but there are many second and even third graders who are reading at these levels. The continuum is not different for inexperienced or struggling readers, except that they may be reading texts below grade level. If the texts are well-matched to the readers, we will be expecting effective processing in terms of comprehending, fluency, and word-solving. Readers should be able to read with phrasing and fluency and should be able to discuss the texts after reading. It is by behaving like proficient readers (with teacher support) at each level that readers get better. They use the gradient as a ladder of support.

Suggestions for Professional Development: Analyzing the Demands of Texts A to I

Begin to explore leveled texts with colleagues in your school. We suggest that you work in cross-grade-level groups. You may want to work only with teachers from K and grade one, but consider involving a much more diverse group of professionals.

When teachers work together to study leveled texts, they learn a great deal about what is demanded of readers. Teachers of young children can learn much about what will be expected of children later as they read harder texts. And, teachers of older students can learn from looking at how texts are structured to support beginners.

Create a collection of books from levels A to I.

1. Before the meeting, divide into four groups or pairs and assign a level to each. Distribute the books you have collected and ask the group members to read the three or four texts they have been given. (If you have a very small group, have the whole group do one level at a time.)

2. Have each group create a list: What does this text call for readers to do? Brainstorm a list of demands, looking at the books you have read. Consider the ten characteristics: genre/form, text structure, content, themes/ideas, language and literary features, sentence complexity, vocabulary, words, illustrations, and book and print features.

3. Bring the entire group together and compare the grids. Ask:
   - What variety is there within levels in what texts call on readers to do?
   - What variety is there across levels in what texts call on readers to do?
   - What significant changes do you notice from level A through level I? If you like, you can record these statements on a chart with two columns, one labeled *From* and the other labeled *To*.

4. Complete the discussion by asking the group to make some concluding statements about texts at levels A through I. This range of difficulty, in general, represents the distance from beginning to read to processing texts with whole pages of print (beginning second grade).

CHAPTER TWELVE

UNDERSTANDING LEVELS OF TEXT: J TO M

In this chapter, we continue the level-by-level descriptions of text features, always remembering that the important goal is to find appropriate reading material for individual students—instructional level for the texts that they will read with your support and easier texts that they can read independently. Levels of text correlate with grade levels and help us to build a collective vision for students' progress. It also lets us know which students need more intensive instruction and daily extra help. But daily reading of a wide variety of appropriate texts is the single best way to increase comprehending and fluency—far better for older students than rereading or "practicing" the same text over and over, especially if it was difficult the first time. All voracious readers process a large quantity of texts, including many easy ones.

Since almost all texts from J to Z have more than 250 words, we will no longer address that feature, but length remains an element in the challenge offered by the text. Even if the words, content, and sentence structure are easy, a longer text with many words on each page requires stamina on the part of the reader because of the memory load and the need to sustain interest. So here we will comment on book length and sometimes the density of the text in terms of number of lines, paragraphs, or number of chapters or sections.

Levels J Through M

At level J through M, readers have made the transition to mostly silent reading. They have learned to process texts smoothly, and many operations have become automatic. They can orchestrate several different kinds of information as they engage in reading continuous text; while they enjoy and take meaning from illustrations, they do not need to rely on them. They are just beginning to notice and interpret the graphic features of informational texts. Levels H through M are appropriate for most second graders, but many third- and even fourth-grade teachers have transitional readers in their classrooms.

If you are working with transitional readers in the intermediate grades, your goal will be to engage them daily in reading a large amount of continuous text and to increase their variety in reading, including learning much more about how informational texts are organized. When introducing new genres to these readers, you want to be sure that the material is within their ability to process successfully. By providing daily reading that is instructional, you can increase their ability to apply strategic actions to harder texts.

Level J

Text Characteristics

Level J includes a variety of short informational texts on familiar topics, as well as easy narratives. The longer narratives have short chapters that may or may not have titles. Characters are usually well presented but don't show a great deal of change or development, since plots are relatively simple and texts are not long. Only one or two characters are generally featured. Most texts contain dialogue, which is usually assigned to the speaker by signal words like *said, cried,* and *answered.* Print is in a larger font, with clear spaces between words and lines. There are illustrations on most pages. Sentences usually return to the left margin to start. Informational texts focus on topics that are familiar to second graders.

Some books offer a large amount of print with easy words and language; others offer challenge in that they present new information or use literary language. Texts have many frequently encountered words, as well as some technical words and unfamiliar words. Technical words are explained within the text, and there are clear illustrations to help the reader. A list of text characteristics is presented below.

Text Characteristics: Level J

GENRES/FORMS

Genres
- Realistic fiction
- Simple animal fantasy
- Informational texts
- Traditional literature (mostly folk tales)
- Some simple biographies

Forms
- Picture books
- Plays

TEXT STRUCTURE

Fiction
- Narratives with more elaborated episodes
- Little repetition of similar episodes

Nonfiction
- Texts with categorical information
- Underlying structures—description, compare/contrast, temporal sequence, problem solution
- Largely focused on one category of information

CONTENT

- Some content new for most children
- New content accessible through text and illustrations

THEMES AND IDEAS

- Themes accessible given typical experiences of children
- Some ideas new to most children
- A few abstract ideas but highly supported by text and illustrations
- Many light, humorous stories, typical of childhood experiences

LANGUAGE AND LITERARY FEATURES

- Variety of dialogue—may be between more than two characters in many texts
- Language characteristic of traditional literature in some texts
- May have more than one point of view within one text
- Amusing or engaging one-dimensional characters
- Description of character traits
- Some texts with settings that are not typical of children's experience

SENTENCE COMPLEXITY

- Longer (10+ words) more complex sentences (prepositional phrases, introductory clauses, lists of nouns, verbs, or adjectives)
- Many compound sentences
- Many sentences with embedded clauses and phrases
- Variation in placement of subject, verb, adjectives, adverbs
- Occasional use of parenthetical material embedded in sentences
- Questions in dialogue (fiction) and questions and answers (nonfiction)

VOCABULARY

- Most vocabulary words known by children through oral language or reading
- Some new vocabulary and content-specific words introduced and explained and illustrated in the text
- Content words illustrated
- Wide variety of words to assign dialogue (*said, cried, shouted, thought, whispered*) and adverbs describing the dialogue (*quietly, loudly*)

WORDS

- Many 2-3 syllable words
- Multisyllable words that are generally easy to take apart
- Wide range of high frequency words
- Many words with inflectional endings
- Plurals, contractions, and possessives
- Many words with complex letter-sound relationships
- Some complex spelling patterns
- Many compound words

ILLUSTRATIONS

Fiction
- Illustrations that support interpretation, enhance enjoyment, set mood but are not necessary for understanding
- Illustrations on every page or every other page in most texts
- Some whole pages of print
- Some picture books that have illustrations on every page

Nonfiction
- Some simple graphics (illustrations with labels)
- More than one kind of graphic on a page

BOOK AND PRINT FEATURES

Length
- Shorter (most approximately 24-36 pages of print) texts on single topics (usually nonfiction)
- Chapter books (most approximately 40-75 pages of print)
- Many lines of print on a page (3-12)

Print and Layout
- Print in most texts clearly separated from pictures
- Print in large, plain font
- Some texts in smaller font size
- Words in bold and italics—important to meaning and stress
- Italics indicating unspoken thought
- Some short sentences, starting middle of a line
- Longer sentences starting on left margin
- Ample space between lines
- Variable placement of print
- Variety in layout, reflecting different genres
- Sentences turn over 2–3 lines and some over 2 pages

Punctuation
- Periods, commas, quotation marks, exclamation point, question marks, dashes and ellipses

Tools
- Chapter titles in some books
- Some texts with a table of contents
- Some texts with headings in bold to show sections
- Some texts with a glossary

Examples

HENRY AND MUDGE: THE FIRST BOOK [J]
(SEE FIGURE 12–1)

Realistic fiction—series book; 40 pages; illustrations and print on every page; easy layout with all sentences starting on the left margin; double-spaced type; seven chapters with alternating titles (*Henry, Mudge, Henry, Mudge,* etc.) that suggest the focus of the chapter; layout that supports phrasing; many high frequency words; simple plot with one episode per chapter; familiar topics (home, family, pets); dialogue with pronouns; split dialogue; opportunity to infer Henry's feelings; point of tension when Mudge is lost and then found.

RACHEL CARSON [J] (SEE FIGURE 12–2)

Biography; 12 pages; text and pictures on every page; one paragraph on every page; double-spaced type; exposition of the character and what she accomplished on opening pages and chronological order of her life after that; clear and explicit explanation of her accomplishments and character; opportunity to understand an abstract "gift" to the world; probably children's first information about Rachel since she wrote adult books.

Other Descriptions at Level J

MR. PUTTER AND TABBY WALK THE DOG

Realistic fiction—series book and beginning chapter book; 39 pages; three chapters; full range of punctuation, including parentheses; all dialogue assigned; split dialogue with pronouns; words in italics for emphasis; figurative use of words (*dream* and *nightmare*); straightforward plot; problem revealed in the first two chapters (that Mr. Putter and his cat Tabby

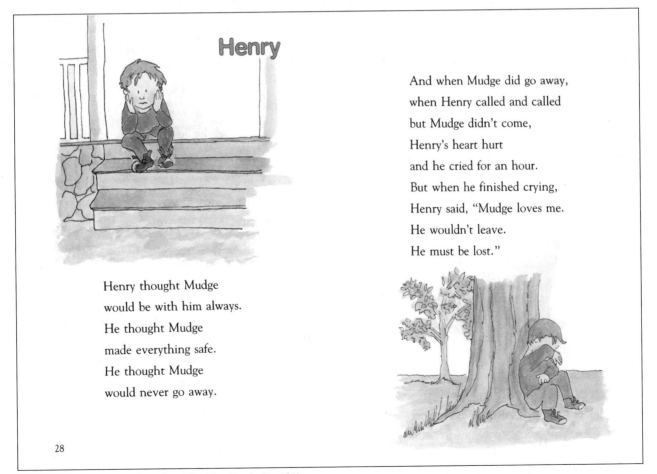

Henry thought Mudge
would be with him always.
He thought Mudge
made everything safe.
He thought Mudge
would never go away.

And when Mudge did go away,
when Henry called and called
but Mudge didn't come,
Henry's heart hurt
and he cried for an hour.
But when he finished crying,
Henry said, "Mudge loves me.
He wouldn't leave.
He must be lost."

28

Figure 12–1. Henry and Mudge: The First Book (*Level J*)

Rachel Carson wrote books about the things she learned. Few people knew as much about the sea as she did.

She also wrote about how people were hurting nature. Planes were spraying the land to kill bugs. But the spray was killing many birds and animals too. Her books made people see that the spray was not safe.

10

11

Figure 12–2. Rachel Carson *(Level J)*

had to walk Zeke the dog, who was very badly behaved); problem resolved in the third chapter; familiar content (neighbors and pets).

MOUSE TALES [J]

Fantasy—beginning chapter book; 64 pages; seven chapters; assigned dialogue; sentences start at left margin; supportive illustrations on every page; short tales about the same animal characters; each chapter a complete story; easy-to-follow narrative; readers required to understand characters and their traits.

THE BIRD LADY [J]

Informational text—focused on an individual's work, Sylvia Durrant; 16 pages; seven sections, each with a different category of information; table of contents, glossary, and index; busy illustrations with a great deal of additional information, including,

photographs of Sylvia and birds, inset pictures with sentences in smaller font, Sylvia's records on birds, lists, relationships of birds to habitats, questions and answers; samples of many genres of informational texts; content clearly explained and accessible.

SEEDS [J]

Informational text; 24 pages (no chapters, a short informational paragraph about a different aspect of seeds on each page); no paragraphing but text wraps around so that new sentences start within lines after final punctuation; glossary, Internet sites, index, word lists; clear illustrations—close-up photographs of flowers and seeds; a few technical words (names of flowers, *seeds, soil, nature*); new meaning for familiar words like *hairs*; mostly one- and two-syllable words; familiar content for most younger children but difficult for some.

Level K

Text Characteristics

At level K, chapter books are simple but are slightly longer, presenting more text to read (see Figures 6–3 and 6–4). Chapters are short; most pages have illustrations but they are less important to students' understanding of the meaning of the text. As with level J, stories have multiple episodes related to a single plot, but there will be more to remember. Texts feature only one or two characters, and there is little development. There is generally dialogue, sometimes unassigned (without identifying words like said).

Text Characteristics: Level K

GENRES/FORMS

Genres
- Realistic fiction
- Simple animal fantasy
- Informational texts
- Traditional literature (mostly folk tales)
- Some simple biographies

Forms
- Picture books
- Plays
- Illustrated chapter books
- Series books

TEXT STRUCTURE

Fiction
- Simple, straightforward plots
- Many episodes
- Chapters connected by character or broad theme
- Chapters usually connected to a longer plot
- Some beginning chapter books with short chapters

Nonfiction
- Variety in nonfiction formats (question/answer; paragraphs; boxes; legends; call-outs)
- Underlying structures—description, compare/ contrast, temporal sequence, problem/solution, cause/effect
- Variety in organization and topic

CONTENT

- Some texts with settings outside children's typical experience
- Some texts with plots and situations outside typical experience
- New content requiring prior knowledge to understand in some informational texts
- New content accessible through text and illustrations

THEMES AND IDEAS

- Themes accessible given typical experiences of children
- Texts with universal themes illustrating important human issues and attributes (friendship, courage)
- Some ideas new to most children
- A few abstract ideas, supported by the text but with less illustration support
- Many light, humorous stories, typical of childhood experiences

LANGUAGE AND LITERARY FEATURES

- Wide range of dialogue, with some unassigned to speaker
- Some figurative language (metaphor, simile)
- More complex plots with numerous episodes and time passing
- May have more than one point of view within one text
- Character attributes described
- Some complex and memorable characters
- Some texts with settings that are not typical of children's experience
- Setting important to understanding the plot in some texts

SENTENCE COMPLEXITY

- Longer (15+ words), more complex sentences (prepositional phrases, introductory clauses, lists of nouns, verbs, or adjectives)
- Variety in sentence length and complexity
- Many complex sentences with clauses
- Variation in placement of subject, verb, adjectives, adverbs
- Wide variety of words to assign dialogue, with verbs and adverbs essential to meaning
- Questions in dialogue (fiction) and questions and answers to impart content (nonfiction)

VOCABULARY

- New vocabulary words introduced and explained and/or illustrated in the text
- Wide variety of words to assign dialogue, with verbs and adverbs essential to meaning
- Some content specific words, all defined and illustrated in the text
- Some longer descriptive words—adjectives and adverbs

WORDS

- Many 2-3 syllable words
- Multisyllable words that are challenging to take apart
- Many words with inflectional endings
- Plurals, contractions, and possessives
- Many words with complex letter-sound relationships
- Some complex spelling patterns
- Many compound words

ILLUSTRATIONS

Fiction
- Some illustrations that support interpretation, enhance enjoyment, set mood but are not necessary for understanding
- Some long stretches of text without Illustrations
- Some picture books that have illustrations on every page
- Some texts with illustrations that are essential to interpretation

Nonfiction
- Variety in the layout of print in nonfiction texts (question/answer; paragraphs; boxes; legends; call-outs)
- Combination of graphics providing information that matches and extends the text
- In most texts, graphics that are clearly explained (simple diagrams, illustrations with labels, maps, charts)

BOOK AND PRINT FEATURES

Length
- Shorter (most approximately 24-48 pages of print) texts on single topics (usually nonfiction)
- Chapter books (60-100 pages of print)
- Many lines of print on a page (3-15; more for fiction)

Print and Layout
- Print and font size varied with some longer texts in small fonts
- Some words in bold or larger font for emphasis or to signal importance
- Some words in bold or italics to signal specific meaning
- Print and illustrations integrated in many texts
- Ample space between lines
- Variety in color and background of print
- Usually friendly layout in chapter books, with sentences starting on the left

Punctuation
- Periods, commas, quotation marks, exclamation point, question marks, dashes and ellipses

Tools
- Table of contents, a few headings, simple glossary, chapter titles, authors' notes

In most level K texts, the layout is still very friendly to the reader with clear spaces between lines. The print is in a large, clear font, and there are clear spaces between words and between lines. Illustrations include interesting artwork that enhances meaning. Some stories are based on concepts that are distant in space and time, and readers will be using the text as a way to expand their understanding of cultures beyond their experiences. Readers will encounter greater variety in writing styles. Informational texts are like Level J in that they use some technical language that is clearly explained within the text. They also include supportive illustrations. Topics tend to be concrete—animals, plants, and other phenomena that will be familiar to students. Generally, informational texts are shorter but difficult, because different concepts are presented on each page or in each section. A summary of text characteristics is presented on the preceding page.

Examples

FROG AND TOAD ARE FRIENDS [K] (SEE FIGURE 12–3)

Fantasy—series book and beginning chapter book; 64 pages; five chapters, about 12 pages each; split dialogue and some long sequences of dialogue; some complete pages of text with no pictures; double-spaced type; friendly layout with most sentences starting on the left; five complete stories about the characters of frog and toad, with new problem and resolution each chapter; familiar topics (getting letters, going swimming, friends); one story within a chapter; opportunity to infer characters' feelings and describe their traits (helpful, kind).

Then Toad began to bang his head against the wall.

"Why are you banging your head against the wall?" asked Frog.

"I hope that if I bang my head against the wall hard enough, it will help me to think of a story," said Toad.

24

"I am feeling much better now, Toad," said Frog. "I do not think I need a story anymore."

"Then you get out of bed and let me get into it," said Toad, "because now I feel terrible."

Frog said, "Would you like me to tell you a story, Toad?"

"Yes," said Toad, "if you know one."

25

Figure 12–3. Frog and Toad are Friends (Level K)

CACTUSES [K] (SEE FIGURE 12–4)

Informational text; 12 pages; photographs showing many varieties of cactuses; highly focused on the topic, with each page providing information in another category; no sections or headings; provides basic information in a clear way; some technical vocabulary (*ribs, stems, desert roots, waxy, spines*); uses compare/contrast; ends with a question requiring reader to compare and contrast.

Other Text Descriptions at Level K

KEEP THE LIGHTS BURNING, ABBIE [K]

Biographical text—true historical account; 40 pages; some whole pages of text; double-spaced type; some difficult names; no paragraphing; many whole pages of print; assigned dialogue, with some long stretches to talk; vocabulary related to ocean and lighthouse; requires reader to imagine life in a former time; background knowledge of the historical functions of the lighthouse and its keeper are needed (how it operated and why it was so important to keep it lighted). It is unusual to have historical fiction at this level, but this text is very accessible.

SOIL [K]

Informational text; 24 pages; three sections, each with a different category of information; table of contents and glossary; mostly simple sentences that start on the left; signal words indicating time passing (*over time, then, after thousands of years, after a long time*); descriptions of breakdown of materials into soil; technical vocabulary (nutrients, rot, roots); explicit central theme (that all living things need soil) to make the topic relevant; photographs with inset drawings that have legends illustrating processes.

Most cactuses have thick stems.
These stems help them live in the desert.
When it rains, cactuses can store a lot of water in their stems.

Many cactuses have ribs on their stems.
These ribs help them live in the desert.
They shade the cactus from the sun and help keep the plant cool.

6

7

Figure 12–4. Cactuses *(Level K)*

Supermarket [K]

Informational text; 24 pages; four sections, each with a different category of information; no section headings or paragraphs; opportunity to become more analytical and learn precise labels for a familiar place; vocabulary related to the supermarket (*aisle, department, butcher, weighs, checkout, cashier, scanner*); mostly simple sentences; table of contents; glossary; references; Internet sites; index.

Level L

Text Characteristics

Chapter books at level L are longer with more sophisticated plots. Characters are likely to develop and change in response to the events in the story; one or two characters are featured. Vocabulary includes more multisyllable words that present challenges in terms of new labels for familiar concepts. These longer texts have many easy and harder frequently encountered words. There are illustrations on most pages, but there are some whole pages of print. A major change at level L is that the layout is more difficult. For most texts, sentences end in the middle of lines and continue from one line to the next. The font is generally smaller, and there is more print on the next page.

Informational books present some new concepts that students can connect with their own background knowledge; the number of new concepts presented is limited, but as in level K, even shorter informational texts are difficult because a different concept is presented on each page or in each section. Simple biographies, told in temporal sequence, tell the stories of past times. Text characteristics are summarized on the next page.

Examples

Horrible Harry in Room 2B [L] (See Figure 12–5)

Realistic fiction—series book; 56 pages; five chapters, each with a different adventure of a group of second grade friends; school setting; a mischievous boy as a central character; first person narrative, told by Harry's friend Doug; black and white drawings (full page and half page), about 5 per chapter; some words in italics for emphasis; some unassigned dialogue; some longer strings of dialogue; paragraphing throughout, mostly short; 1.5 spaces between lines; sentences flow onto the next page; familiar topic and setting; content very accessible; chapters connected to each other as incident after incident reveals Harry's character and the nature of the boys' friendship; some complexities of plot

Baking Bread [L] (See Figure 12–6)

Informational text; 16 pages; two sections; table of contents, glossary, and index; section headings; key words in bold; vocabulary related to content (*bakeries, recipe, flour, grains, preheat, batter*); photographs and drawings; illustrations on every page; includes description, an illustrate list of ingredients, and step-by-step directions; content accessible.

Other Text Descriptions at Level L

Pinky and Rex and the Spelling Bee [L]

Realistic fiction; series book; 40 pages; six short chapters; less space between lines than earlier levels; full print pages (about 25 percent of the book); assigned dialogue; sentences starting in the middle of lines; everyday experiences; themes relate to friendship and problems at school; somewhat complex issues and feelings depicted.

Looking at Insects [L]

Informational text/science; 21 pages (nine sections of two pages each); glossary, index; colored illustrations, diagrams and photographs; question-answer format in each section, with answers at the back of the book; some technical vocabulary; mostly simple straightforward sentences, and many stand-alone phrases in answer section with picture support.

Text Characteristics: Level L

GENRES/FORMS

Genres
- Realistic fiction
- Simple fantasy
- Informational texts
- Traditional literature
- Biography

Forms
- Picture books
- Plays
- Illustrated chapter books
- Series books
- Special type: simple mysteries

TEXT STRUCTURE

Fiction
- Simple plot structures
- Narrative structure including chapters with multiple episodes related to a single plot
- Plots with detailed episodes

Nonfiction
- Underlying structures—description, compare/contrast, temporal sequence, problem/solution, cause/effect
- Variety in organization and topic

Content
- Some technical content that is challenging and not typically known
- Content requiring prior knowledge to understand in many informational texts
- New content accessible through text and illustrations

THEMES AND IDEAS

- Themes accessible given typical experiences of children
- Texts with universal themes illustrating important human issues and attributes (friendship, courage)
- Some ideas new to most children
- A few abstract ideas, supported by the text but with less illustration support
- Many light, humorous stories, typical of childhood experiences

LANGUAGE AND LITERARY FEATURES

- Various perspectives revealed through dialogue
- Plots with numerous episodes, building toward problem resolution
- Various ways of showing characters' attributes—description, dialogue, thoughts, others' perspectives on them
- Figurative language and descriptive language
- Setting descriptions sometimes important to plot
- Multiple characters to understand
- Some complex and memorable characters
- Wide variety in showing dialogue, both assigned and unassigned
- Setting important to understanding the plot in some texts

SENTENCE COMPLEXITY

- Longer (15+) more complex sentences (prepositional phrases, introductory clauses, lists of nouns, verbs, or adjectives)
- Variety in sentence length and complexity
- Sentences with nouns, verbs, or adjectives in series, divided by commas
- Questions in dialogue (fiction) and questions and answers (nonfiction)

VOCABULARY

- New vocabulary words introduced and explained and illustrated in informational texts
- New vocabulary in fiction texts largely unexplained
- Wide variety of words to assign dialogue, with verbs and adverbs essential to meaning
- Some longer descriptive words—adjectives and adverbs

WORDS

- Many 2-3 syllable words
- Some words with more than 3 syllables
- Many plurals, contractions, and compound words
- Words with suffixes

ILLUSTRATIONS

Fiction
- Some illustrations that support interpretation, enhance enjoyment, set mood but are not necessary for understanding
- Some long stretches of text without illustrations
- Some picture books that have illustrations on every page

Nonfiction
- Combination of graphics providing information that matches and extends the text
- In most texts, graphics that are clearly explained (simple diagrams, illustrations with labels, maps, charts)

BOOK AND PRINT FEATURES

Length
- Shorter (most approximately 24-48 pages of print) texts on single topics (usually nonfiction)
- Chapter books (60-100 pages of print)
- Many lines of print on a page (5-24; more for fiction)

Print and Layout
- Font size signaling importance or level of information
- Some words in bold or larger font for emphasis or to signal importance
- Variety in color and background of print Some complex sentences with variety in order of clauses, phrases, subject, verb and object.
- Print and illustrations integrated in many texts
- Ample space between lines
- Variety in the layout of print in nonfiction texts (question/answer; paragraphs; boxes; legends; call-outs)
- Usually friendly layout in chapter books, with sentences starting on the left
- More difficult layout, with denser format
- Some sentences continuing over several lines or to the next page

Punctuation
- Periods, commas, quotation marks, exclamation point, question marks, dashes and ellipses

Tools
- Table of contents, a few headings, simple glossary, chapter titles, author's notes

CAM JANSEN AND THE MYSTERY OF THE HAUNTED HOUSE [L]

Realistic fiction—series book; mystery; 58 pages; eight chapters; chapters numbered rather than titled; black and white drawings (full and half page), about three per chapter; many whole pages of print; paragraphing throughout; both assigned and unassigned dialogue; some short sequences of unassigned dialogue; problem or "mystery" revealed in the first three chapters; Cam (short for camera), the sleuth's thinking revealed explicitly through her recording of details in her photographic memory; some words in italics for emphasis; main characters Cam and Eric; characters "flat" and unchanging; easy, straightforward plot.

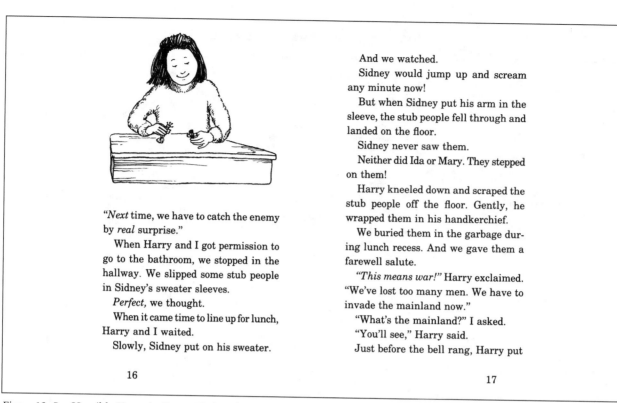

"*Next* time, we have to catch the enemy by *real* surprise."

When Harry and I got permission to go to the bathroom, we stopped in the hallway. We slipped some stub people in Sidney's sweater sleeves.

Perfect, we thought.

When it came time to line up for lunch, Harry and I waited.

Slowly, Sidney put on his sweater.

16

And we watched.

Sidney would jump up and scream any minute now!

But when Sidney put his arm in the sleeve, the stub people fell through and landed on the floor.

Sidney never saw them.

Neither did Ida or Mary. They stepped on them!

Harry kneeled down and scraped the stub people off the floor. Gently, he wrapped them in his handkerchief.

We buried them in the garbage during lunch recess. And we gave them a farewell salute.

"*This means war!*" Harry exclaimed. "We've lost too many men. We have to invade the mainland now."

"What's the mainland?" I asked.

"You'll see," Harry said.

Just before the bell rang, Harry put

17

Figure 12–5. Horrible Harry in Room 2B *(Level L)*

Step 2 Ask an adult to **preheat** the oven to 350 degrees. Then the oven will be hot and ready when you need to use it.

Step 3 Ask the adult to melt the butter in a pan on the stove. Set the melted butter aside to cool.

Step 4 Peel the bananas and put them in a large bowl. Mash them up.

Step 5 Put the flour, sugar, salt, baking powder, and baking soda together in another bowl. Mix these dry things.

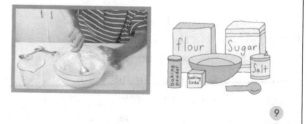

8

9

Figure 12–6. Baking Bread *(Level L)*

FUN WITH MAGNETS [L]

Informational text; 24 pages; 10 sections with headings; table of contents, glossary, index, and test questions at the end; photographs and text on every page; legends for photographs in smaller font than body; key words in bold; focused on the concept of magnetism, with each section having new content; uses description and compare/contrast; has directions for experimentation; somewhat abstract idea explained in clear language with supportive diagrams; new content for many second graders.

Level M

Text Characteristics

A change at level M is that texts have many whole pages of print without illustrations. Illustrations are usually black-and-white drawings or photographs and are scattered throughout the text; they extend the meaning and enhance enjoyment. Chapters are longer. Most texts have a great deal of text in smaller print with narrower word spacing. Vocabulary is greatly expanded, including many multisyllable words and technical words.

Topics of informational texts are widely varied, from subjects that are familiar to students to new topics they are expected to study and learn. Sections of informational texts may provide different information but there is elaboration to help the reader. Most technical terms are explained and illustrated within the text. Real biographies, structured as simple narratives, require readers to think about historical concepts. Text characteristics for level M are summarized on the next page.

Examples

WHAT'S COOKING, JENNY ARCHER? [M]
(SEE FIGURE 12–7)
Realistic fiction—series book; 69 pages; 12 chapters; full page black and white drawings, about one per chapter; words in italics to indicate what Jenny is writing; inclusion of dialogue from a TV show Jenny watches (integrated with what jenny is thinking); Mostly assigned dialogue; straightforward plot, with the main character starting a "lunch" business, but ending up short of money; content mostly familiar (school, friends, food); all characters backdrop for Jenny; characters mostly "flat," although Jenny does learn a lesson from her mistakes.

CREATURES OF THE NIGHT [M] (SEE FIGURE 12–8)
Informational text; 16 pages; 11 short sections with headings; inset photographs with legends in different font; labels for parts of animals' bodies; directions for experimentation on last page; content loosely tied together by the theme (night creatures); many new and difficult concepts on each page.

Other Text Descriptions at Level M

MATT CHRISTOPHER: MAN OUT AT FIRST [A PEACH STREET MUDDERS STORY] [M]
Realistic fiction/sports story—series book; 60 pages; 10 short chapters; no table of contents; medium font; ten black-and-white illustrations; simple narrative sequence; familiar experiences, one or two episodes in each chapter; descriptions of sports; fast moving; mostly one- and two-syllable words; some technical language; larger number of characters to remember and follow in action.

MOLLY'S PILGRIM [M]
Realistic fiction; 41 pages; no chapter divisions; words in italics that show a teasing verse; other words in italics show non-English words; larger than usual font; paragraphing throughout; variable sentence length; black and white drawings (half- and full page) about every three pages; requires some background knowledge of immigration; requires inference to understand central theme (that there are modern Pilgrims); told as first person narrative that has the quality of a memoir.

Caves [M]

Informational text; 24 pages; six sections, two, three or four pages per section; glossary and index; easy-to-read font; supportive illustrations, with legends, on every page; cutaway diagram of cave formation; different information in each chapter; some unfamiliar concepts; technical words related to aspects of caves (for example, *stalactites*); quite a few multisyllable words.

Measuring Tools [M]

Informational text; 16 pages; five sections with

Text Characteristics: Level M

Genres/Forms

Genres
- Realistic fiction
- Simple fantasy
- Informational texts
- Biography
- Traditional literature

Forms
- Picture books
- Plays
- Illustrated chapter books
- Series books
- Special types: mysteries

Text Structure

Fiction
- Simple plot structures
- Narrative structure including chapters with multiple episodes related to a single plot
- Plots with detailed episodes

Nonfiction
- Underlying structures—description, compare/contrast, temporal sequence, problem/solution, cause/effect
- Variety in organization and topic

Content

- Some content that is challenging and not typically known
- Content requiring prior knowledge to understand in most informational texts
- Most of content carried by the print rather than pictures
- Content supported and/or extended by illustrations in most informational texts

Themes and Ideas

- Some abstract themes requiring inferential thinking to derive
- Texts with universal themes illustrating important human issues and attributes (friendship, courage)
- Some texts with deeper meaning—still familiar to most readers
- A few abstract ideas, supported by the text
- Many light, humorous stories, typical of childhood experiences

Language and Literary Features

- Various perspectives revealed through dialogue
- Wide variety in showing dialogue, both assigned and unassigned
- Figurative language and descriptive language
- Plots with numerous episodes, building toward problem resolution
- Various ways of showing characters' attributes—description, dialogue, thoughts, others' perspectives on them
- Multiple characters to understand and notice how they develop and change over time
- Some complex and memorable characters
- Setting descriptions sometimes important to plot
- Setting important to understanding the plot in some texts

Sentence Complexity

- Longer (15+), more complex sentences (prepositional phrases, introductory clauses, lists of nouns, verbs, or adjectives)
- Variety in sentence length, with some very long and complex sentences
- Sentences with nouns, verbs, or adjectives in series, divided by commas
- Sentences with parenthetical material
- Questions in dialogue (fiction) and questions and answers (nonfiction)

Vocabulary

- New vocabulary introduced and explained and illustrated in the text
- New vocabulary in fiction texts largely unexplained
- Wide variety of words to assign dialogue
- Some longer descriptive words—adjectives and adverbs
- Some complex content-specific words, all defined and illustrated in the text

Words

- Many 2-3 syllable words
- Some words with more than 3 syllables
- Many plurals, contractions, and compound words
- Words with suffixes

Illustrations

Fiction
- Many fiction books with only a few illustrations
- Most illustrations in fiction black and white
- Some long stretches of text without Illustrations
- Some picture books that have illustrations on every page

Nonfiction
- Combination of graphics providing information that matches and extends the text
- In most texts, graphics that are clearly explained
- Variety of graphics (diagrams, labels, cutaways, maps)
- More than one kind of graphic on a page

Book and Print Features

Length
- Shorter (most approximately 24-48 pages of print) texts on single topics (usually nonfiction)
- Chapter books (60-100 pages of print)
- Many lines of print on a page (5-24; more for fiction)

Print and Layout
- Print and font size varied with some longer texts in small fonts
- Font size signaling importance or level of information
- Use of words in italics, bold, or all capitals to indicate level of importance or signal other meaning
- Variety in print and background color
- Print and illustrations integrated in many texts
- Ample space between lines
- Variety in the layout of print in nonfiction texts (question/answer; paragraphs; boxes; legends; call-outs) in the same text
- Captions under pictures that provide important information to supplement the body of the text
- Usually friendly layout in chapter books, with sentences starting on the left
- More difficult layout, with denser format
- Some sentences continuing over several lines or to the next page

Punctuation
- Full range of punctuation, including dashes and ellipses

Tools
- Table of contents, a few headings, simple glossary, chapter titles, author's notes

"I can't eat clams," said Beth. "I'm allergic to them."

"Can you eat shrimp salad?" asked Jenny.

Beth shook her head. "I'm allergic to shrimp, too."

Jenny began to worry. What if Clifford and April couldn't eat clams or shrimp either?

"I like shrimp," Wilson said.

"Okay," Jenny said. "You can have the shrimp salad lunch."

"Yay!" Wilson pulled his money out of his pocket and gave it back to Jenny.

"Do you want a deviled ham and sweet pickle sandwich?" she asked Beth.

"Like you had yesterday?" said Beth. "Sure. That was good."

"Okay." Jenny handed her a bag.

Someone will like clam dip and mushrooms, Jenny told herself. Wilson is just too young for such a classy sandwich.

*   *   *

31

Figure 12–7. What's Cooking, Jenny Archer *(Level M)*

headings; table of contents, glossary, and index; photographs with labels; technical vocabulary (*ruler, measure, scale, expanded meaning of tool*); problem posed to the reader on each page, prompting the reader to choose from different tools; answers in sentences under pictures that provide further information (different font and color).

Summary: Levels J to M

Readers of texts at levels J through M are growing in their ability to process longer, more complex narrative texts over several days as opposed to the short, straightforward texts (which can often be read in twenty or thirty minutes) at lower levels. Literary elements such as characters, setting, and plot become more important in understanding the stories. Instead of stories with only one or two episodes, these longer texts, some with several chapters, show characters changing and developing through their experiences. Readers are increasingly required to think about how characters feel and their motivations for doing what they do.

Books, especially at levels J and K, have many frequently encountered words; in general you will not see many three- and four-syllable words or many technical or specialized words. Layout may be very friendly, with sentences beginning on the left, a

Night flights

Nocturnal animals also use the cover of night to travel. For some animals, nighttime provides perfect cover from predators. This sugar glider uses the cover of darkness for protection as it glides from tree to tree.

Some migratory birds, such as the curlew, fly during the night. Scientists think this is because the air is cooler and the wind is calmer, which makes it easier to fly.

Never-ending darkness

There are some places where it is always dark—the depths of the oceans, beneath the surface of the Earth, in caves, and at the Poles during the long winter season.

Many of the animals that spend time in these places have developed the same kinds of features found in nocturnal animals.

Worms use their sense of touch to find their way through the soil.

fishing rod

Some dolphins can locate sound across long distances.

Angler fish have a built-in fishing rod which lights up to attract prey.

14

15

Figure 12–8.   Creatures of the Night *(Level M)*

large, clear font, and plenty of space between lines; but it gradually becomes more sophisticated by level M. Just about all of the texts at these levels, however, are parsimonious about the amount of text on any one page; in many texts there are half-page illustrations on every page or every other page.

Most children reading at level J and up have been reading silently most of the time. This transformation usually begins soon after they no longer need the finger to guide their reading, which happens around level C or D. Children usually read orally through several more levels. Reading then becomes "whisper" reading, and you will find some children spontaneously switching to silent reading around levels I or J. The switch is an important one. While there are reasons to read aloud (reading stories and books

to children and adults, reading scripts of various kinds, reading poetry for the pleasure of the sound, and so on), reading is, generally a silent activity. As children grow in fluent processing, they read very softly and begin to read parts without voicing the words.

Suggestions for Professional Development: Analyzing the Demands of Text J to M

Continue exploring leveled texts with colleagues in your school. Again, we suggest that you work in cross-grade-level groups. Use a collection of books at levels J through X that you gathered for your Chapter 5 professional development discussions. This time, focus on levels J, K, L, and M. If you need more titles at these levels, collect them. You will need at least three titles per level. Try to include one nonfiction book for each level.

1. Before the meeting, divide into four groups or pairs and assign a level to each. Distribute the books you have collected and ask the group members to read the three or four texts they have been given. (If you have a very small group, have the whole group do one level at a time.)

2. Have each group create a list: What does this text call for readers to do? If you completed the professional development suggestions at the end of Chapters 4 and 5, you have analyzed texts and also become familiar with the kinds of changes in text demands along the gradient. Now, simply brainstorm a list of demands, looking at the books you have read.

Consider the ten characteristics: genre/form, text structure, content, themes/ideas, language and literary features, sentence complexity, vocabulary, words, illustrations, and book and print features.

3. Bring the entire group together and compare the grids. Ask:
   - What variety is there within levels in what texts call on readers to do?
   - What variety is there across levels in what texts call on readers to do?
   - What significant changes do you notice from level J through level M? If you like, you can record these statements on a chart with two columns, one labeled *From* and the other labeled *To*.

4. Complete the discussion by asking the group to make some concluding statements about texts at levels J through M.

CHAPTER THIRTEEN

UNDERSTANDING LEVELS OF TEXT: N TO S

In this chapter, we extend the level-by-level examinations of texts to look at levels N through S on the gradient. As readers build their processing systems by reading a variety of increasingly difficult texts, they expand their abilities to meet more complex demands. We call these readers self-extending, because they have developed a system for expanding their system of strategic actions by encountering and solving the problems of complex and varied texts. In other words, they learn more about reading by reading every day; however, that does not mean that instruction is unnecessary. These readers need demonstration, teaching, and carefully selected texts to support their learning.

Children have been building this self-extending system since the early grades, and, by the time they begin reading their first chapter books, the foundation of the system is in place. There is much room to grow, however.

Successful reading of texts at levels N through S on the gradient, which are appropriate for most readers in grades 3 and 4, requires largely unconscious orchestration of in-the-head actions. Readers concentrate primarily on the deeper meaning. Self-extending readers can sustain silent reading over longer periods of time as well as through longer texts. Their oral reading is fluent at these levels, and their phrasing identifies units of meaning. It is important to help readers maintain fluency as they move on to longer, more complex texts.

Students are rapidly developing their tastes as readers, and learning more about themselves and their world through reading. They are learning rapid and sophisticated ways of taking words apart, although they will benefit from further word study.

In grades 3 and 4, there is great change in how and what students read. The variety in students' reading increases dramatically. They are introduced to new genres as well as to topics, themes, and settings that are not within their personal experiences. The challenge for these readers will be to delve deeply into their reading, thinking about aspects of texts such as character, plot, and theme. The texts at these levels are much richer than earlier stories and provide opportunity for discussion. These learners need to spend more time reading more books and a variety of texts in order to increase their flexibility.

Level N

Text Characteristics

Level N includes longer texts organized in a variety of ways. Topics of informational texts and settings for narrative texts go well beyond readers' personal experience. Chapter books present memorable characters that are well developed and change over time. They also offer an opportunity to feel empathy for characters and to experience suspense. Characters are revealed through what they say, think, and do, as well as through what others say about them.

Informational texts require much more content knowledge. There are many technical words, but these are usually explained within the text. Biographies are longer and focus on subjects that are less well known to students. They are expected to learn about these subjects through reading. Below is a summary of text characteristics.

Examples

AMBER BROWN WANTS EXTRA CREDIT [N]
(SEE FIGURE 13–1)

Realistic fiction—series book; 120 pages; 17 chapters; 1.5 spaced type; black and white half-page

---

Text Characteristics: Level N

GENRES/FORMS

Genres
- Realistic fiction
- Simple fantasy
- Informational texts
- Traditional literature
- Biography
- Historical fiction
- Special types: mysteries

Forms
- Picture books
- Plays
- Illustrated chapter books
- Series books

TEXT STRUCTURE

Fiction
- Narrative structure including chapters with multiple episodes related to a single plot
- Plots with detailed episodes

Nonfiction
- Underlying structures—description, compare/contrast, temporal sequence, problem/solution, cause/effect
- Variety in organization and topic
- Some texts with several topics, organized categorically

CONTENT

- Topics that go well beyond readers' personal experiences
- Content requiring prior knowledge to understand in most informational texts
- Most of content carried by the print rather than pictures
- Content supported and/or extended by illustrations in most informational texts
- Content requiring the reader to take on perspectives from diverse cultures and bring cultural knowledge to understanding

THEMES AND IDEAS

- Texts with deeper meanings applicable to important human problems and social issues
- Many abstract themes requiring inferential thinking to derive
- Many light, humorous stories, typical of childhood experiences

LANGUAGE AND LITERARY FEATURES

- Wide variety in showing dialogue, both assigned and unassigned
- Descriptive and figurative language that is important to understanding the plot
- Details that are important to understanding the plot
- Some suspense characteristic of plots
- Multiple characters to understand
- Characters and perspectives revealed by what they say, think, and do and what others say/think about them
- Memorable characters that change and develop over time
- Factors related to character change explicit and obvious
- Setting important to understanding the plot in some texts

SENTENCE COMPLEXITY

- Longer (15+), more complex sentences (prepositional phrases, introductory clauses, lists of nouns, verbs, or adjectives)
- Variety in sentence length, with some very long and complex sentences
- Sentences with nouns, verbs, or adjectives in series, divided by commas
- Sentences with parenthetical material
- Questions in dialogue (fiction)
- Questions and answers to impart content (nonfiction)

VOCABULARY

- Many complex content specific words in nonfiction, mostly defined in text or illustrations
- New vocabulary in fiction texts largely unexplained
- Some longer descriptive words—adjectives and adverbs
- Some words used figuratively
- Words with connotative meanings that are essential to understanding the text

WORDS

- Many words with 3+ syllables
- Some words divided (hyphenated) across lines
- Many plurals, contractions, and compound words
- Some multisyllable proper nouns that are difficult to decode
- Words with suffixes
- Some words with simple prefixes

ILLUSTRATIONS

Fiction
- Many fiction books with only a few illustrations
- Most illustrations in fiction black and white
- Some long stretches of text without Illustrations
- Some picture books that have illustrations on every page

Nonfiction
- Combination of graphics providing information that matches and extends the text
- In most texts, graphics that are clearly explained
- Variety of graphics (diagrams, labels, cutaways, maps)

BOOK AND PRINT FEATURES

Length
- Shorter (most approximately 24-48 pages of print) texts on single topics (usually nonfiction)
- Chapter books (80-150 pages of print)
- Many lines of print on a page (5-24; more for fiction)

Print and Layout
- Variety in color and background of print
- Print and font size varied with some longer texts in small fonts
- Font size signaling importance or level of information
- Use of words in italics, bold, or all capitals to indicate level of importance or signal other meaning
- Print and illustrations integrated in many texts
- Ample space between lines
- Variety in the layout of print in nonfiction texts (question/answer; paragraphs; boxes; legends; call-outs) in the same text
- Captions under pictures that provide important information
- More difficult layout, with denser format
- Some sentences continuing over several lines or to the next page

Punctuation
- Full range of punctuation, including dashes and ellipses

Tools
- Readers' tools—table of contents, a few headings, glossary, chapter titles, author's notes

was a boy friend . . . . but I said he was a boyfriend because I didn't want to kiss Fredrich Allen.

I do miss him.

He would understand why I don't want my mother to go out with Max, why I miss my father.

My dad used to take Justin and me to baseball games. He took us fishing. He took us to see the gory horror movies that my mother hates.

"Amber," my mother says softly.

"Yes?" I get nervous sometimes when my mother speaks very softly. . . . It's like she wants me to listen very carefully . . . . usually to something I don't want to hear.

"Amber . . . . remember yesterday when you said that you would be willing to meet Max? . . . Well, he's going to take us out to dinner tonight." She refills my glass of milk and then looks at me.

30

I have to figure out what I want to say, so I sit quietly for a minute.

"Mom . . . . . I said sometime . . . not immediately. . . . I have homework to do today. . . . . I have to think about it. . . . How about over Christmas vacation?"

"Amber." She shakes her head. "This is the beginning of October. We're not waiting until the end of December."

"My homework," I plead, knowing that she knows how important it is that I get it done.

She stares at me. "Do it now. You have all day to finish it . . . . and you know it better be done well. Max won't be here until around six o'clock. That gives you a lot of time. Now, Amber, you promised that you'd meet Max. I'll even use up two of the Amberino Certificates on this."

I stand up.

I know it's no use to argue.

31

Figure 13–1. Amber Brown Wants Extra Credit *(Level N)*

drawings, about one per chapter; first person narrative told in present tense; some unusual punctuation such as dots indicating pauses and thoughts inserted parenthetically in sentences or presented in italics; first person narrative; some words in all caps for emphasis; main character with a distinctive voice and features; more complex and serious problems (for example, Amber is angry because she misses her dad and her mother has a boyfriend); large amounts of dialogue revealing characters (Amber and friends); some sentence fragments for interest; detailed description of the communication between Amber and her mother; use of sarcasm and humor; characters change and develop over time.

WEATHER WATCH [N] (SEE FIGURE 13–2)
Informational text; 24 pages; no sections or headings; extra large font, with long lines stretching across the page and/or narrow columns; great variety in place ment of print; photographs ; some key words in bold; insets with labeled drawings that provide additional information; maps and charts; heavy content load, with many different place names and climates and new content on every page; technical vocabulary (*temperature; liquid, mercury, electrical, hurricane, vapor,* etc.); many three and four syllable words;

Other Text Descriptions at Level N

SHOESHINE GIRL [N]
Realistic fiction; 84 pages; 11 chapters; a few black-and-white drawings; straightforward narrative structure; character development; fiction featuring problems related to growing up; requires readers to empathize with characters and infer motivations.

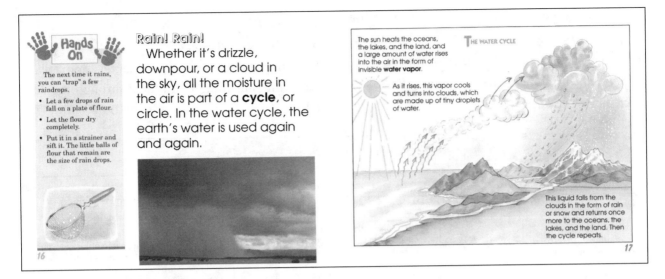

Figure 13–2. Weather Watch *(Level N)*

MY NAME IS MARIA ISABEL [N]

Realistic fiction about an immigrant in a new school; 57 pages (ten chapters, six or seven pages per chapter); medium font; a few black-and-white drawings; a few Spanish words; requires understanding traditions of a cultural group.

HELEN KELLER: COURAGE IN THE DARK [N]

Biography; 47 pages; five chapters; told chronologically as a straightforward narrative; Braille alphabet included at end; illustrations on almost every page; large, easy-to-read font; sentence structure generally simple; two- and three-syllable words but few technical words.

UNUSUAL SPIDERS [N]

Informational text; 16 pages; five sections with headings and some sub-headings; table of contents and glossary; photographs with labels; summary charts and diagrams with a great deal of information; some change of print color to capture attention; vocabulary related to content (names of spiders, *burrow, liquid, poisonous, venom*, place names); challenging new content in each section but concepts build on one another across the text.

Level O

Text Characteristics

A range of challenges are presented in chapter books at level O. Books have multiple characters who are revealed through what they say, think, and do or through what others say about them. Characters encounter everyday experiences; some must deal with serious problems such as war or death.

This level includes a wide variety of genres, including realistic fiction, historical fiction, biography, science fiction, humor, and traditional literature. Most chapter books have between fifty and two hundred pages. Texts have only a few illustrations, and they are usually black-and-white drawings or photographs.

Informational texts have a wide range of graphics. Technical words are usually illustrated or defined with the texts. Readers' tools such as table of contents and section headings indicate the categories of content. Many details are presented relative to major topics.

Vocabulary is sophisticated and varied. There are many multisyllable words. Frequently encountered words, both easy and more difficult, are used; most words will be within readers' decoding control.

Readers are expected to form new meanings for known words. Highly complex sentences require a full range of punctuation, which is important to accessing the meaning of the text. A list of text characteristics is presented below.

Examples

ALDO PEANUT BUTTER [O] (SEE FIGURE 13–3)

Realistic fiction; 113 pages; 10 chapters; some black and white illustrations scattered through the text; table of contents and information about the

---

Text Characteristics: Level O

GENRES/FORMS

Genres
- Realistic fiction
- Simple fantasy
- Informational texts
- Traditional literature
- Biography
- Historical fiction
- Mysteries

Forms
- Picture books
- Plays
- Illustrated chapter books
- Chapter books
- Series books
- Chapter books with sequels
- Short stories

TEXT STRUCTURE

Fiction
- Narrative structure including chapters with multiple episodes related to a single plot
- Plots with detailed episodes

Nonfiction
- Underlying structures—description, compare/contrast, temporal sequence, problem/solution, cause/effect
- Variety in organization and topic
- Some texts with several topics, organized categorically

CONTENT

- Topics that go well beyond readers' personal experiences
- Content requiring prior knowledge to understand in most informational texts
- Most of content carried by the print rather than pictures
- Content supported and/or extended by illustrations in most informational texts
- Content requiring the reader to take on perspectives from diverse cultures and bring cultural knowledge to understanding

THEMES AND IDEAS

- Some more challenging themes such as war and the environment
- Texts with deeper meanings applicable to important human problems and social issues
- A few abstract ideas, supported by the text
- Many light, humorous stories, typical of childhood experiences

LANGUAGE AND LITERARY FEATURES

- Wide variety in showing dialogue, both assigned and unassigned
- Descriptive and figurative language that is important to understanding the plot
- Details important to understanding the plot
- Some suspense characteristic of plots
- Multiple characters to understand
- Characters revealed by what they say, think, and do and what others say/think about them
- Memorable characters, with good and bad traits, that change and develop over time
- Factors related to character change explicit and obvious
- Setting important to understanding the plot in some texts

SENTENCE COMPLEXITY

- Longer (15+), more complex sentences (prepositional phrases, introductory clauses, lists of nouns, verbs, or adjectives)
- Variety in sentence length, with some very long and complex sentences
- Sentences with nouns, verbs, or adjectives in series, divided by commas
- Sentences with parenthetical material
- Questions in dialogue (fiction) and questions and answers (nonfiction)

VOCABULARY

- Many complex content specific words in nonfiction, mostly defined in text or illustrations
- New vocabulary in fiction texts largely unexplained
- Some longer descriptive words—adjectives and adverbs
- Some words used figuratively
- Words with connotative meanings that are essential to understanding the text

WORDS

- Many words with 3+ syllables
- Some words divided (hyphenated) across lines and across pages
- Many plurals, contractions, and compound words
- Some multisyllable proper nouns that are difficult to decode
- Words with suffixes
- Some words with simple prefixes

ILLUSTRATIONS

Fiction
- Many fiction books with only a few illustrations
- Most illustrations in fiction black and white
- Some long stretches of text without Illustrations
- Some picture books that have illustrations on every page

Nonfiction
- Combination of graphics providing information that matches and extends the text
- In most texts, graphics that are clearly explained
- Variety of graphics (diagrams, labels, cutaways, maps)

BOOK AND PRINT FEATURES

Length
- Shorter (most approximately 24-48 pages of print) texts on single topics (usually nonfiction)
- Chapter books (80-150 pages of print)
- Many lines of print on a page (5-24; more for fiction)

Print and Layout
- Print and font size varied with some longer texts in small fonts
- Font size signaling importance or level of information
- Use of words in italics, bold, or all capitals to indicate level of importance or signal other meaning
- Variety in print color and background color
- Variety in the layout of print in nonfiction texts (question/answer; paragraphs; boxes; legends; call-outs) in the same text
- Print and illustrations integrated in many texts
- Ample space between lines
- Usually friendly layout in chapter books, with sentences starting on the left
- More difficult layout, with denser format
- Some sentences continuing over several lines or to the next page
- Captions under pictures that provide important information

Punctuation
- Full range of punctuation, including dashes and ellipsis

Tools
- Readers' tools—table of contents, a few headings, glossary, pronunciation guides, chapter titles, author's notes, simple index

author; problem described in first two pages when Aldo gets five dogs for his birthday and keeps two, naming them Peanut and Butter; straightforward plot (children staying alone for the week, messing up the house, and then facing parents' coming home); familiar content (home, pets, siblings).

LOOK WHAT CAME FROM RUSSIA [O]
(SEE FIGURE 13–4)

Informational text; 32 pages; 13 short sections with headings; categories of information (for example, food, space, sports); many challenging Russian names and words; photographs and drawings; maps; technical vocabulary (*caviar, blintzes, Zakuski, valenki*); labels on pictures; includes a recipe for kissel; English and Russian expressions with pronunciation guide; references; Internet sources; glossary and index; picture and information about the author at the end.

Other Text Descriptions at Level O

HENRY AND THE PAPER ROUTE [O]

Realistic fiction—series about one family; 192 pages; six chapters; black and white drawings (some very dated) at the beginning of each chapter and randomly spaced throughout; paragraphing throughout; very few long sentences; familiar content (home, neighborhood, pets), some dated material (for example typewriters and carbon paper, may cause confusion); plot revealed over all chapters as Henry solves problems related to getting a paper route; although requires taking Henry's perspective on Beezus and Ramona.

BEEZUS AND RAMONA [O]

Realistic fiction—series about one family; 159 pages; six chapters; mostly one-, and two-syllable words; everyday experiences; many frequently

---

Aldo put Peabody down on the ground. "You have a very nice house," he said politely. "If people come to look at it, they aren't going to care about your grass."

"Of course they are going to care. It's the very first thing they'll see, and first impressions are very important."

"Well, Peabody did not do it," said Aldo. "He never did a thing like this before, so it doesn't make any sense that, out of the blue, he would do it now."

"Then it must have been your dogs," asserted Mrs. Crosby.

"None of my pets did this," said Aldo, looking at his neighbor. Although he was angry at her for blaming the Sossi pets for this mess in the yard, he also began to feel sorry for her. She looked as if she was about to start crying. He wondered how it felt to live all alone. Maybe she was scared in the night, like his sisters.

"I know they didn't do it," Aldo repeated. "But if you wait until I walk my dogs and feed them some breakfast, I'll come try and fix up this mess for you."

"All right," said Mrs. Crosby. "But hurry. The first real estate agent is bringing a couple here to see the house at ten o'clock."

Aldo walked back to his house with Peabody at his heels. "You'll never believe what's bothering Mrs. Crosby," he told his sisters as he opened up a can of food for the cat.

"Do you think it's possible that Peabody did it?" asked Karen after she heard about their neighbor's complaint.

"Of course not," shouted Aldo. It was bad enough that Mrs. Crosby was suspicious of Peabody. How could his own sister say a thing like that?

"Could Peanut or Butter have done it?" asked Elaine.

"That's a stupid question," said Aldo. "You know they are always on their leashes. How could either of them dig up Mrs. Crosby's lawn?"

As he waited for Elaine to come up with a solution to his question, Aldo came up with the answer himself. He remembered that, the night before, Peanut had broken loose from him and had run off

Figure 13–3. Aldo Peanut Butter (*Level O*)

Figure 13–4. Look What Came from Russia *(Level O)*

encountered words and some three-syllable words; some black-and-white drawings; complex sentences with commas, dashes, embedded clauses; requires readers to look at various perspectives of characters in the same family and neighborhood.

MIEKO AND THE FIFTH TREASURE [O]
Realistic fiction; 79 pages; 11 chapters; small font; illustrated with calligraphy; assigned dialogue; complex sentences with commas, dashes, embedded clauses; requires understanding traditions of a cultural group; mature theme of war and the atomic bomb and results.

HAIRY LITTLE CRITTERS [O]
Informational text; 31 pages; eight sections; table of contents, index, and information about the author; varied font; some technical words (for example, *marsupials, rodents, crepuscular, spinifex*) with no help in pronunciation; photographs on every page; information on many different topics linked by the theme indicated in the title; calls for synthesis of information.

THE HISTORY OF MACHINES [O]
Informational text; 24 pages; 10 sections, each presenting a different category of machines, with simple and complex examples; table of contents and glossary; section headings; photographs and drawings, some labeled; some cutaway diagrams; requires accessing background knowledge of simple machines and making connections; some new content for most readers at this level.

Level P

Text Characteristics
Level P includes a wide variety of fiction and non-fiction. Informational texts and biographies present complex ideas on many different topics that may be unfamiliar. Technical language is evident. Fiction texts include novels with longer chapters. Characters are concerned with issues related to growing up, family relationships, and the problems of preadolescence.

In comparison to previous levels, in general, level P texts are longer, have more complex ideas and language, and use a more sophisticated vocabulary. They include more detailed descriptions of setting. More interpretation is required to understand themes at several levels. Many texts are long (over 100 pages), requiring readers to sustain interest and attention over several days. At this level, length becomes less important than the structural complexity, theme sophistication, and

Text Characteristics: Level P

GENRES/FORMS

Genres
- Realistic fiction
- Simple fantasy
- Informational texts
- Traditional literature
- Biography (less well known subjects)
- Historical fiction
- Genre combination (hybrids)
- Mysteries

Forms
- Picture books
- Plays
- Chapter books
- Series books
- Chapter books with sequels
- Short stories

TEXT STRUCTURE

Fiction
- Narrative structure including chapters with multiple episodes related to a single plot
- Plots with detailed episodes

Nonfiction
- Underlying structures—description, compare/contrast, temporal sequence, problem/solution, cause/effect
- Variety in organization and topic
- Some texts with several topics, organized categorically

CONTENT

- Topics that go well beyond readers' personal experiences
- Most of content carried by the print rather than pictures
- Content supported and/or extended by illustrations in most informational texts
- Content requiring the reader to take on diverse perspectives (race, language, culture)

THEMES AND IDEAS

- Some more challenging themes such as war and the environment
- Texts with deeper meanings applicable to important human problems and social issues
- Ideas and themes requiring taking the perspective not familiar to the reader
- Ideas and themes requiring understanding of cultural diversity

LANGUAGE AND LITERARY FEATURES

- Wide variety in showing dialogue, both assigned and unassigned
- Descriptive language providing details important to understanding the plot
- Extensive use of figurative language that is important to understanding the plot
- Some suspense characteristic of plots
- Multiple characters to understand
- Characters revealed by what they say, think, and do and what others say/think about them
- Memorable characters, with both good and bad traits, that change and develop over time
- Factors related to character change explicit and obvious
- Settings distant in time and space from students' experiences
- Some more complex fantasy elements

SENTENCE COMPLEXITY

- Longer (some 15+) complex sentence structures including dialogue and many embedded clauses and phrases
- Sentences with nouns, verbs, or adjectives in series, divided by commas
- Sentences with parenthetical material
- Questions in dialogue (fiction)
- Questions and answers to impart content (nonfiction)

VOCABULARY

- Many new vocabulary words that depend on readers' tools such as glossaries
- Many new vocabulary words that readers must derive from context
- Some complex content-specific words, mostly defined in text, illustrations, or glossary
- Many longer descriptive words—adjectives and adverbs
- Some words used figuratively—metaphor, simile, idiom
- Words with connotative meanings that are essential to understanding the text

WORDS

- Many words with 3+ syllables
- Many complex multisyllable words that are challenging to take apart
- Many plurals, contractions, and compound words
- Many multisyllable proper nouns that are difficult to decode
- Words with suffixes
- Some words with simple prefixes

ILLUSTRATIONS

Fiction
- Many books with only a few or no illustrations
- Most illustrations in fiction black and white
- Typically have long stretches of text without illustrations
- Some picture books that have illustrations on every page

Nonfiction
- Full range of graphics providing information that matches and extends the text
- Some texts with graphics that are complex and not fully explained
- Some texts with graphics that have scales or legends important to understanding

BOOK AND PRINT FEATURES

Length
- Shorter (most approximately 24-48 pages of print) texts on single topics (usually nonfiction)
- Chapter books (most approximately 60-150 pages of print)
- Many lines of print on a page (5-30; more for fiction)

Print and Layout
- Large variation among print styles and font size (related to genre)
- Use of bold, larger font, or italics for emphasis or to indicate importance or level of information
- Variety in print color and background color
- Print and illustrations integrated in most texts, with print wrapping around pictures
- Varied space between lines, with some texts having dense print
- Variety in layout of nonfiction formats (question/answer; paragraphs; boxes; legends; call-outs)
- More difficult layout of informational text, with denser format
- Some sentences continuing over several lines or to the next page
- Captions under pictures that provide important information

Punctuation
- Full range of punctuation as needed for complex sentences

Tools
- Full range of readers' tools (table of contents, glossary, headings/subheadings, call-outs, pronunciation guides, index, references)

---

necessary background experience. Above is a list of text characteristics for level P.

Examples

HARRY'S MAD [P] (SEE FIGURE 13–5)

Fantasy; 123 pages; 15 chapters; several half-page black and white drawings scattered through the text; reality turned into fantasy with the arrival of a highly sophisticated, educated and articulate parrot who changes a family's life; some highly sophisticated language as Madison, the parrot, informs Harry about history and literature that he has

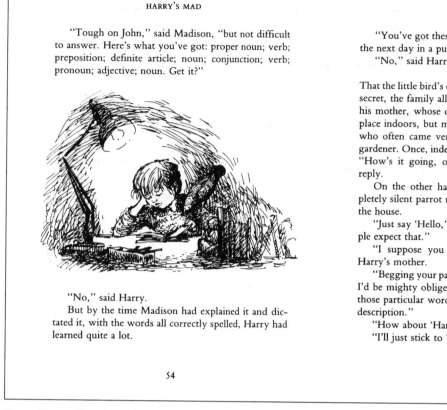

Figure 13–5. Harry's Mad *(Level P)*

learned; constant play on words using multiple meanings of *mad*; some strings of unassigned dialogue; some long speeches by the parrot; multisyllable words with affixes (some created, for example, *pre-Madison*); use of humor, sometimes subtle; requires inferring how and why Mad made such a difference in the family's life as well as what happened when he was stolen.

INCREDIBLE PLACES [P] (SEE FIGURE 13–6)

Informational text with some aspects of fiction; 32 pages; four sections, each on a different place (Florida, Africa, Italy, and Turkey); information about a specific, unusual place within each geographic area; many difficult place names; many three-, four-, and five-syllable words; many technical words (names of animals, *carnivores, ecosystem, gondola, barges,* some non-English words; ques-

tions inserted through speech bubble of a talking crocodile adds a fantastic element; narrative inserted in one section with story of two Seminole boys; one large foldout map with pictures of animals on it; inclusion of some history in several sections; sections not related except through the theme of "incredible places" and so may be read separately.

Other Text Descriptions at Level P

YANG THE YOUNGEST AND HIS TERRIBLE EAR [P]

Realistic fiction—series book; 134 pages; eight chapters; one whole-page or two half-page black-and-white illustrations per chapter; every title page illustrated with symbolic articles; first-person narrative; a great deal of dialogue; straightforward plot; centered on familiar themes and concepts related to the relationships and expectations of

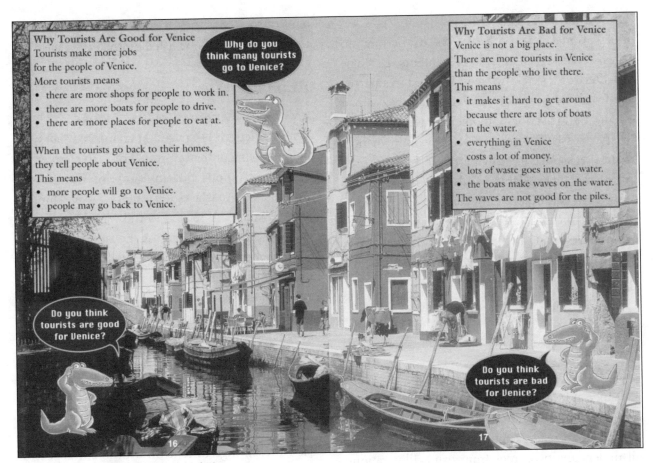

Figure 13–6. Incredible Places *(Level P)*

family members and friends; characters learn and change; comparison of cultures; requires seeing things from different perspectives.

SHOEBAG [P]

Fantasy; 136 pages; 22 short chapters; information about the author; single spaced type; requires accepting the unusual idea that a roach can turn into a person; mostly accessible vocabulary with some figurative language; many long and complex sentences, some a paragraph long; large amount of dialogue, mostly assigned; some dialogue between characters who are hidden, requiring the reader to understand complex situation; many unique uses of language to describe roach culture; highly exaggerated characters who seem to be stereotypic versions of themselves (for example, Pretty Soft, who must always be looking in a mirror and the princi-

pal who always says he is a "pal"); explores different perspectives and larger themes such as language and cultural differences, change, beauty, prejudice, perspectives, and being yourself.

MAPS AND CODES [P]

Informational text; 31 pages; four sections; presentation of many different types of maps; information about maps (purposes, how they are made; purpose of keys and legends and the meaning of "scale," codes and signals, semaphore, Braille, how to make a secret code); includes a short story related to map making; varied font sizes but easy to read; technical words related to subject matter; many illustrations, maps, diagrams, and directions (for example, how to read Braille); writing style conversational; a great deal of content; presents complex and elaborate meanings of the word "code."

PENGUINS OF THE GALAPAGOS [P]

Informational text with aspects of fiction; 46 pages; seven sections; table of contents, glossary, and afterword; single-spaced type; told in a narrative from the point of view of a family (with a marine biologist for a mother) traveling to the Galápagos Islands; much descriptive information about the islands; friendly narrative format; some three- and four-syllable words, but definition of most new vocabulary provided within the text; complex concepts (scientific information, history) explained through the family's conversation; opportunity to take on new information and learn about distant places.

Level Q

Text Characteristics

A change at level Q is that most narrative texts will have very few illustrations. The cover illustrations contribute to readers' anticipation, but just about all understanding comes from print. Illustrations in informational books at this level carry a great deal of meaning and require interpretation.

Chapter books at level Q employ a complex sentence structure and more difficult vocabulary, with themes that will engage third or fourth graders. Themes require interpretation; characters are memorable and develop over time. Children's literature selections offer sophisticated humor, complex plots, and interesting ideas that will be a good foundation for group discussion. In addition, illustrations and their relationships to the text can be analyzed. All texts contain difficult words, some from languages other than English, for readers to solve.

Thoughts and perspectives of characters are revealed in a variety of ways—through dialogue and from the viewpoint of other characters. Books are generally quite long, requiring the reader to sustain interest and meaning over many days. Some books have more mature themes, focusing on problems of society as they affect children. Text characteristics for level Q are listed on the next page.

Examples

ANASTASIA KRUPNIK [Q] (SEE FIGURE 13–7)

Realistic fiction; 114 pages; 11 chapters; small symbolic drawing at the beginning of each chapter; no other illustrations but insertion of lists in two columns by Anastasia ("Things I Love, Things I Hate") which are related to the way the character changes and develops across the story; preadolescent reaction to issues such as choices in religion, pregnancy, boy-girl relationships. puberty, old age and death; some dated material (for example, *mimeographed*); some profanity and figurative language and sophisticated vocabulary (for example, *solitude, mercurial, humungus*—some made-up words) mostly explained within the text;

OCEAN LIFE [Q] (SEE FIGURE 13–8)

Informational text; 32 pages; 12 short sections, each presenting content on a different aspect of ocean life; table of contents, glossary, index, and credits and notes; drawings and text on every page; several drawings on each page spread with insets and additional information in different fonts, sometimes interesting and esoteric facts from history; technical vocabulary (animal names; *lava; kraken; masts, rigging, sediment, navigation*); mostly description with some directions for experiments and time sequences; challenge in the variety of information presented; challenge in the new category of information presented in each section.

Other Text Descriptions at Level Q

DEAR MR. HENSHAW [Q]

Realistic fiction; 134 pages; unique format—a series of letters and journal entries ranging from three sentences to ten pages); dialogue between characters recounted, and also presented in the form of letters; moves from simple language in beginning of

Text Characteristics: Level Q

GENRES/FORMS

Genres
- Realistic fiction
- More complex fantasy
- Informational texts
- Traditional literature
- Biography, memoir, autobiography
- Historical fiction
- Genre combination (hybrids)
- Mysteries

Forms
- Picture books
- Plays
- Chapter books
- Series books
- Chapter books with sequels
- Short stories
- Diaries and logs

TEXT STRUCTURE

Fiction
- Narrative structure including chapters with multiple episodes related to a single plot
- Plots with detailed episodes

Nonfiction
- Underlying structures—description, compare/contrast, temporal sequence, problem/solution, cause/effect
- Variety in organization and topic
- Some texts with several topics, organized categorically

CONTENT

- Topics that go well beyond readers' personal experiences
- Most of content carried by the print rather than pictures
- Content supported and/or extended by illustrations in most informational texts
- Content requiring the reader to take on diverse perspectives (race, language, culture)
- Fiction—settings requiring knowledge of content (history, geography, etc.)

THEMES AND IDEAS

- Some more challenging themes such as war and the environment
- Complex ideas on many different topics requiring real or vicarious experiences (through reading)
- Texts with deeper meanings applicable to important human problems and social issues

LANGUAGE AND LITERARY FEATURES

- Descriptive language providing details important to understanding the plot
- Extensive use of figurative language that is important to understanding the plot
- Some suspense characteristic of plots
- Multiple characters revealed by what they say, think, and do and what others say/think about them
- Memorable characters, with both good and bad traits, that change and develop over time
- Factors related to character change explicit and obvious
- Settings distant in time and space from students' experiences
- Some more complex fantasy elements
- Some complex narratives that are highly literary

SENTENCE COMPLEXITY

- Longer (some 15+) complex sentence structures including dialogue and many embedded clauses and phrases
- Sentences with nouns, verbs, or adjectives in series, divided by commas
- Sentences with parenthetical material
- Questions in dialogue (fiction)
- Questions and answers to impart content (nonfiction)

VOCABULARY

- Many new vocabulary words that depend on using readers' tools such as glossaries
- Many new vocabulary words that readers must derive from context
- Some complex content-specific words, mostly defined in text, illustrations, or glossary
- Many longer descriptive words—adjectives and adverbs
- Some words used figuratively—metaphor, simile, idiom
- Words with connotative meanings essential to understanding the text

WORDS

- Many words with 3+ syllables
- Many plurals, contractions, and compound words
- Many words with affixes (prefixes and suffixes multisyllable proper nouns that are difficult to decode)
- Many technical words that are difficult to decode
- Words with affixes (prefixes and suffixes)
- Words that are seldom used in oral language and are difficult to decode

ILLUSTRATIONS

Fiction
- Many books with only a few or no illustrations
- Most illustrations in fiction black and white
- Typically have long stretches of text without illustrations
- Some picture books that have illustrations on every page

Nonfiction
- Full range of graphics providing information that matches and extends the text
- Some texts with graphics that are complex and not fully explained
- Some texts with graphics that have scales or legends important to understanding

BOOK AND PRINT FEATURES

Length
- Shorter (most approximately 24-48 pages of print) texts on single topics (usually nonfiction)
- Chapter books (most approximately 60-150 pages of print)
- Many lines of print on a page (5-30; more for fiction)

Print and Layout
- Large variation among print styles and font size (related to genre)
- Use of bold, larger font, or italics for emphasis or to indicate importance or level of information
- Variety in print color and background color
- Print and illustrations integrated in most texts, with print wrapping around pictures
- Varied space between lines, with some texts having dense print
- Variety in layout of nonfiction formats (question/answer; paragraphs; boxes; legends; call-outs)
- More difficult layout of informational text, with denser format
- Some sentences continuing over several lines or to the next page
- Captions under pictures that provide important information

Punctuation
- Full range of punctuation as needed for complex sentences

Tools
- Full range of readers' tools (table of contents, glossary, headings/subheadings, call-outs, pronunciation guides, index, references)

---

book to complex sentences at the end; no technical language; centers on family problems, growing up, and school issues; requires readers to infer characters' feelings and motivations, as well as how and why they change.

BUNNICULA [Q]

Fantasy; 98 pages; nine chapters; told from the point of view of Harold the dog; mysterious tale of two animals' theory about a vampire bunny who sucks the juice out of vegetables; sophisticated

book was called *Bittersweet*; and it said, inside, "To someone special: Anastasia."

Sometimes, when no one was in the room, Anastasia took *Bittersweet* down from the shelf, just to look at that page. Looking at it made her feel awed, unique, and proud.

Awed, unique, and *proud* were three words that she had written on page seven of her green notebook. She kept lists of her favorite words; she kept important private information; and she kept things that she thought might be the beginnings of poems, in her green notebook. No one had ever looked inside the green notebook except Anastasia.

On page one, the green notebook said, "My name is Anastasia Krupnik. This is the year that I am ten."

On page two, it said, "These are the most important things that happened the year that I was ten:"

So far, there were only two things on the list. One was, "I got a small pink wart." And the other was, "My teacher's name is Mrs. Westvessel."

Mrs. Westvessel wore stockings with seams up the back, and shoes that laced on the sides. Sometimes, while she sat at her desk, she unlaced her shoes when she thought no one was watching, and rubbed her feet against each other. Under the stockings, on the tops of her toes, were tiny round things like small doughnuts.

Anastasia described the toe doughnuts to her mother, and her mother nodded and explained that those were called corn pads.

4

Anastasia wrote "corn pads" on page twenty-seven of her notebook.

Mrs. Westvessel also had interesting brown spots on the backs of her hands, very large and lop-sided bosoms, and a faint gray mustache.

"I think Mrs. Westvessel is probably over one hundred years old," Anastasia told her parents at dinner. "Probably about one hundred and twenty."

"Nobody lives to be one hundred and twenty," said her mother as she poured some mushroom gravy over Anastasia's meat loaf. "Unless they're in Tibet."

Her father wrinkled his forehead. "Perhaps Mrs. Westvessel is a mutant," he said.

"Yes," agreed Anastasia. "Mrs. Westvessel is a mutant, I believe."

Later she wrote "mutant" on page twenty-seven, under "corn pads." Anastasia was a very good speller; she sounded out the syllables of "mutant" correctly on the first try.

Anastasia didn't like Mrs. Westvessel very much. That made her feel funny, because she had always liked — sometimes even loved — her teachers before.

So she wrote in her green notebook, "Why don't I like Mrs. Westvessel?" and began to make a list of reasons. Making lists of reasons was sometimes a good way to figure things out.

"Reason one:" wrote Anastasia, "Because she isn't a good teacher."

But then she crossed out reason one, because it was a lie. Anastasia wasn't crazy about telling lies, even to

5

Figure 13–7. Anastasia Krupnik *(Level Q)*

vocabulary since Harold is highly educated (for example, *sauntered casually, obscure, regarded, disregarding; emanated*); requires understanding the perspective of animals who try to communicate danger to the humans; conflict between Harold and Chester the cat; many adult sayings such as "be in touch with yourself" and "we've never really communicated"; sophisticated and subtle humor.

AMAZING SPIDERS [Q]

Informational text; 31 pages; 11 sections; many small pieces of information organized under phrases and all related to a big idea; page layout like a "web," organizing different bits of information; interesting facts presented in conversational language; some entries require background knowl-

edge (for example, that the tarantella dance relates to the tarantula spider); only a few technical words; pronunciation guide provided for technical words; table of contents and index.

KAYAKING [Q]

Informational text; 48 pages; five chapters with additional information in the ending sections in the form of a photo diagram, scales of river difficulty, and a diagram; photographs with labels; table of contents, glossary references, Internet sites, and index; key words in bold; single-spaced type; extra facts in bold at the bottom of pages; technical vocabulary (*portaging, buoyant; bladders; sinews; capsize; collapsible; fiberglass*) ; use of compare/contrast (canoe and kayak); chronological sequence used to describe history.

Figure 13–8. Ocean Life *(Level Q)*

Level R

Text Characteristics

Books in Level R, both fiction and nonfiction, represent a range of topics and settings. Fiction texts have settings that are distant from students' own lives. In general, these texts extend the skills needed for level Q over a wider variety of texts. Some longer books may require a great deal of sustained interest. Vocabulary is sophisticated, requiring understanding of connotative meanings, and will challenge the reader.

Literary devices such as simile and metaphor require background knowledge, as do some of the technical aspects of texts. Informational books such as biography and autobiography extend readers' understanding and take them to places distant in time and space. Books at this level may deal with mature themes like family problems, war, and death. Readers are required to connect concepts and themes with political or historical events or environmental information. Specific text characteristics are listed on the next page.

Examples

Spider Boy [R] (See Figure 13–9)
Realistic fiction; 183 pages; 17 chapters and author's note with references; incorporates journal; familiar topics (moving, school, bullying; hobbies; family relationships; teasing); some unassigned dialogue; includes scientific information about spiders explained in a friendly way in the journal; requires reader to construct meaning from both the first person narrative in the journal and the third person narrative of the rest of the text; requires inference to understand why Bobby lies about himself and also to derive the symbolic meaning spiders have for him.

Text Characteristics: Level R

GENRES/FORMS

Genres
- Realistic fiction
- Complex fantasy
- Informational texts
- Traditional literature
- Biography, memoir, autobiography
- Historical fiction
- Genre combination (hybrids)

Forms
- Picture books
- Plays
- Chapter books
- Series books
- Chapter books with sequels
- Short stories
- Diaries and logs
- Mysteries

TEXT STRUCTURE

Fiction
- Narrative structure including chapters with multiple episodes related to a single plot
- Plots with detailed episodes
- Some short stories with plots that intertwine

Nonfiction
- Underlying structures—description, compare/contrast, temporal sequence, problem/solution, cause/effect
- Variety in organization and topic
- Some texts with several topics, organized categorically

CONTENT

- Topics that go well beyond readers' personal experiences
- Most of content carried by the print rather than pictures
- Content supported and/or extended by illustrations in most informational texts
- Content requiring the reader to take on diverse perspectives (race, language, culture)
- Fiction—settings requiring knowledge of content (history, geography, etc.)

THEMES AND IDEAS

- Some more challenging themes such as war and the environment
- Complex ideas on many different topics requiring real or vicarious experiences (through reading)
- Texts with deeper meanings applicable to important human problems and social issues

LANGUAGE AND LITERARY FEATURES

- Some texts requiring the understanding of connotative meaning of words
- Long stretches of descriptive language, important to understanding setting and characters
- Figurative language that is important to understanding the plot
- Complex plots, creating suspense and leading toward problem resolution
- Multiple characters revealed by what they say, think, and do and what others say/think about them
- Memorable characters, with both good and bad traits, that change and develop over time
- Settings distant in time and space from students' experiences
- Some more complex fantasy elements
- Some complex narratives that are highly literary

SENTENCE COMPLEXITY

- Longer (some 15+) complex sentence structures including dialogue and many embedded clauses and phrases
- Sentences with nouns, verbs, or adjectives in series, divided by commas
- Sentences with parenthetical material
- Questions in dialogue (fiction)
- Questions and answers to impart content (nonfiction)

VOCABULARY

- Many new vocabulary words that readers must derive from context or use glossaries or dictionaries
- Many complex content-specific words, mostly defined in text, illustrations, or glossary
- Many longer descriptive words—adjectives and adverbs
- Many words used figuratively—metaphor, simile, idiom
- Words with connotative meanings essential to understanding the text

WORDS

- Many words with 3+ syllables
- Many plurals, contractions, and compound words
- Many multisyllable proper nouns that are difficult to decode
- Many technical words that are difficult to decode
- Words that are seldom used in oral language and are difficult to decode
- Words with affixes (prefixes and suffixes)

ILLUSTRATIONS

Fiction
- Many books with only a few or no illustrations
- Most illustrations in fiction black and white
- Typically have long stretches of text without illustrations
- Some picture books that have illustrations on every page

Nonfiction
- Full range of graphics providing information that matches and extends the text
- Some texts with graphics that are complex and not fully explained
- Some texts with graphics that have scales or legends important to understanding

BOOK AND PRINT FEATURES

Length
- Shorter (most approximately 24-48 pages of print) texts on single topics (usually nonfiction)
- Chapter books (most approximately 60-150 pages of print)
- Many lines of print on a page (5-30; more for fiction)

Print and Layout
- Large variation among print styles and font size (related to genre)
- Use of bold, larger font, or italics for emphasis or to indicate importance or level of information
- Variety in print color and background color
- Print and illustrations integrated in most texts, with print wrapping around pictures
- Varied space between lines, with some texts having dense print
- Variety in layout of nonfiction formats (question/answer; paragraphs; boxes; legends; call-outs)
- More difficult layout of informational text, with denser format
- Some sentences continuing over several lines or to the next page
- Captions under pictures that provide important information

Punctuation
- Full range of punctuation as needed for complex sentences

Tools
- Full range of readers' tools (table of contents, glossary, headings/subheadings, call-outs, pronunciation guides, index, references)

LANDSLIDES [R] (SEE FIGURE 13–10)
Informational text; 18 pages; no section divisions or headings; photographs with full sentence legends providing additional information; diagrams illustrating the phenomenon; technical vocabulary (for example, *erosion, volcanoes, earthquakes, boulders, geologists, erupts*); includes a large amount of description; uses cause/effect (reasons for landslides and consequences of them).

> **Five**
>
> *September 28*
>
> *Spiders lie. Well, not exactly lie. But some spiders change what seems to be true by pretending to be something they're not. And isn't that what lying is all about?*
>
> *They do it through camouflage. Some spiders can change to look like the bark of a tree. This makes them invisible to birds and other predators.*
>
> *There is one spider that imitates an ant. Other ants don't get scared when the disguised spider comes near. When it gets close enough, it pounces.*
>
> *A certain kind of crab spider can make itself look like the stamen on the inside of a flower. A bee sees it, flies in and—WHAM! Supper time.*
>
> 44
>
> *Spiders lie, all right, but there's a good reason for it, the only reason animals do anything: Survival.*
>
> Lying was easy. Simple. You could tell people all sorts of fake stories about yourself, but if you told them with a straight face, well, people would believe you. Especially if you had just moved to town from another state, with no way for people to check whether or not you were telling the truth. This was maybe the only advantage to being the new kid in town.
>
> It amazed Bobby how easily everyone swallowed the tall tale about the spider silk farm. Afterward he felt funny about it, the same way he had felt after lying to Mike about all the amazing things Thelma had been doing. It was wrong, and he told himself he had to stop making up stuff like that.
>
> On Tuesday Miss Terbaldi talked to him after English class.
>
> "I've been wanting to welcome you to New Paltz," she told him. "You moved here from Illinois, right? What brought you here?"
>
> "Spiders," he said. Miss Terbaldi looked surprised.
>
> "What do you mean?"
>
> "My dad just took a job as director of the spider department at the Museum of Natural History in New York City. That museum has just
>
> 45

Figure 13–9. Spider Boy *(Level R)*

Other Text Descriptions at Level R

FIG PUDDING [R]

Realistic fiction about family relationships (each chapter focuses on a different family member); 136 pages (nine chapters, varying from four to thirty-five pages); variety of short and longer, more complex sentences; some stretches of unassigned dialogue; medium font; literary language; description.

SADAKO AND THE THOUSAND PAPER CRANES [R]

Informational text/history; 64 pages (nine chapters, five to seven pages each); prologue and epilogue; black-and-white illustrations add to mood; theme of war and death; requires background knowledge about history and health; evokes empathy with character; requires understanding of cultural traditions; genre, topic, and sophistication of the writing places new demands on readers.

MEASURING THE WEATHER [R]

Informational text; 32 pages; five sections; table of contents, glossary, and index; technical vocabulary (for example, *meteorologists, satellites, forecast, atmosphere, troposphere, climate, equator*); text and pictures on every page; photographs and drawings; insets with different kinds of information; diagrams illustrating technical names (such as parts of the atmosphere); graphs; uses scales (gradient of wind); uses sequence (directions for experiments and water cycle); uses cause and effect (climate on famine); uses compare/contrast (climates).

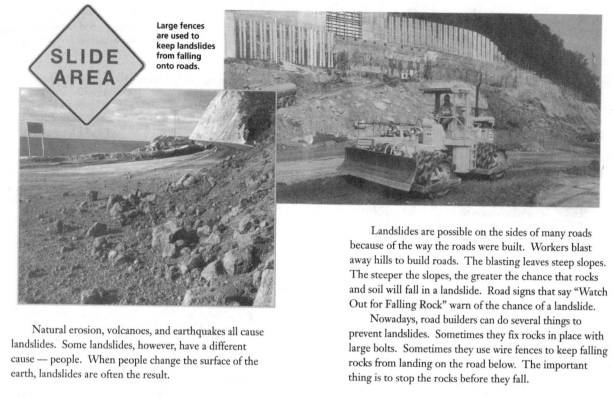

Large fences are used to keep landslides from falling onto roads.

SLIDE AREA

Natural erosion, volcanoes, and earthquakes all cause landslides. Some landslides, however, have a different cause — people. When people change the surface of the earth, landslides are often the result.

12

Landslides are possible on the sides of many roads because of the way the roads were built. Workers blast away hills to build roads. The blasting leaves steep slopes. The steeper the slopes, the greater the chance that rocks and soil will fall in a landslide. Road signs that say "Watch Out for Falling Rock" warn of the chance of a landslide.

Nowadays, road builders can do several things to prevent landslides. Sometimes they fix rocks in place with large bolts. Sometimes they use wire fences to keep falling rocks from landing on the road below. The important thing is to stop the rocks before they fall.

13

Figure 13–10. Landslides *(Level R)*

THE CHOCOLATE FLIER [R]

Informational text/history/biography about the Berlin Airlift, told in straightforward narrative (biography section on Gail Halverson); 47 pages (three sections of varied lengths); unfamiliar topic for most students; table of contents, glossary, index, and information about the author; tables in each section; small font; authentic photographs from World War II on every page; legends under photographs; insets present "did you know" facts; technical or content-related words in boldface and presented in glossary.

Level S

Text Characteristics

Texts at level S present complex ideas and information that will be a good foundation for group dis-

cussions. They reflect a wide variety of topics and cultures. At this level, words present many shadings of meaning that readers must construct from their interpretations of the text. Sentences and paragraphs are complex, requiring rapid and fluent reading with attention to meaning and automatic assimilation of punctuation.

Many works of historical fiction are included in this level of the gradient; students at this age tend to find historical events interesting. There are also many more biographies. Texts present settings that are far distant from students' own experiences. Literary selections offer opportunities for readers to make connections with previously read texts as well as with historical events. This category includes chapter books in many genres. Picture books present complex ideas and information that will be a good foundation for group discussions. Specific text characteristics are listed below:

Examples

Letters from Rifka [S] (See Figure 13–11)
Historical fiction; 148 pages; series of letters over one year of a 12-year-old girl's life; author's note at beginning and end; setting in the Ukraine, Poland, and the U.S. in 1919 and 1920, when Russians were conducting pogroms against Jewish people; first person narrative, but with dialogue included; full range of dialogue; perspective of a teenage girl who

---

Text Characteristics: Level S

GENRES/FORMS

Genres
- Realistic fiction
- More complex fantasy
- Informational texts
- Traditional literature
- Biography, memoir, autobiography
- Historical fiction
- Genre combination (hybrids)
- Mysteries

Forms
- Picture books
- Plays
- Chapter books
- Series books
- Chapter books with sequels
- Short stories
- Diaries and logs

TEXT STRUCTURE

Fiction
- Narrative structure including chapters with multiple episodes related to a single plot
- Plots with detailed episodes
- Some short stories with plots that intertwine

Nonfiction
- Underlying structures—description, compare/contrast, temporal sequence, problem/solution, cause/effect
- Variety in organization and topic
- Some texts with several topics, organized categorically

CONTENT

- Topics that go well beyond readers' personal experiences
- Most of content carried by the print rather than pictures
- Content supported and/or extended by illustrations in most informational texts
- Fiction—settings requiring knowledge of content (history, geography, etc.)
- Content particularly appealing to preadolescents
- Content requiring the reader to take on diverse perspectives (race, language, culture)

THEMES AND IDEAS

- Some more challenging themes such as war and the environment
- Complex ideas on many different topics requiring real or vicarious experiences (through reading)
- Texts with deeper meanings applicable to important human problems and social issues

LANGUAGE AND LITERARY FEATURES

- Long stretches of descriptive language, important to understanding setting and characters
- Complex plots, creating suspense and leading toward problem resolution
- Multiple characters revealed by what they say, think, and do and what others say/think about them
- Memorable characters, with both good and bad traits, that change and develop over time
- Settings distant in time and space from students' experiences
- Some more complex fantasy elements
- Some complex narratives that are highly literary

SENTENCE COMPLEXITY

- Longer (some 15+) complex sentence structures including dialogue and many embedded clauses and phrases
- Sentences with nouns, verbs, or adjectives in series, divided by commas
- Sentences with parenthetical material
- Questions in dialogue (fiction)
- Questions and answers to impart content (nonfiction)

VOCABULARY

- Many new vocabulary words that readers must derive from context or use glossaries or dictionaries
- Many highly technical words, mostly defined in text, illustrations, or glossary
- Many longer descriptive words—adjectives and adverbs
- Many words used figuratively—metaphor, simile, idiom
- Words with connotative meanings essential to understanding the text

WORDS

- Many words with 3+ syllables
- Many complex plurals, contractions, and compound words
- Many multisyllable proper nouns that are difficult to decode
- Many technical words that are difficult to decode
- Words that are seldom used in oral language and are difficult to decode
- Words with affixes (prefixes and suffixes)

ILLUSTRATIONS

Fiction
- Many books with only a few or no illustrations
- Most illustrations in fiction black and white
- Typically have long stretches of text without illustrations
- Some picture books that have illustrations on every page

Nonfiction
- Full range of graphics providing information that matches and extends the text
- Some texts with graphics that are complex and not fully explained
- Some texts with graphics that have scales or legends important to understanding

BOOK AND PRINT FEATURES

Length
- Shorter (most approximately 24-48 pages of print) texts on single topics (usually nonfiction)
- Chapter books (most approximately 60-150 pages of print)
- Many lines of print on a page (5-30; more for fiction)

Print and Layout
- Large variation among print styles and font size (related to genre)
- Use of bold, larger font, or italics for emphasis or to indicate importance or level of information
- Variety in print color and background color
- Print and illustrations integrated in most texts, with print wrapping around pictures
- Spaces between lines varies, with some texts having dense print
- Variety in layout of nonfiction formats (question/answer; paragraphs; boxes; legends; call-outs)
- More difficult layout of informational text, with denser format
- Many sentences continuing over several lines or to the next page
- Captions under pictures that provide important information

Punctuation
- Full range of punctuation
- Occasional use of less common punctuation (colon, semicolon)

Tools
- Full range of readers' tools (table of contents, glossary, headings/subheadings, call-outs, pronunciation guides, index, references)

has to use her gift for language and have courage to survive; difficulties such as fear of arrest; letters written in a book of poetry; symbolic poems by Pushkin included at the beginning of each chapter, with Rifka finally writing poetry herself; development of the central character as she struggles and develops through compassion for others; mature themes such as persecution, starvation, cholera, family separations.

ALICE'S DIARY: LIVING WITH DIABETES [S]
(SEE FIGURE 13–12)

Informational text—diary; 32 pages; table of contents, glossary, index, and information on the author and photographer; entries by date over six weeks in the life of a diabetic girl; scientific information about diabetes inserted in whole- and half-page boxes; some diagrams and charts; technical vocabulary (for example *dietitian, insulin, syringes, hyperglycemia, carbohydrates; glucose*); requires adjusting between narrative to expository throughout the text; friendly explanation of the disease through the narrative; allows reader to infer how to treat friends who are diabetic; allows reader to infer the theme (that diabetics must learn how to live with the disease).

Other Text Descriptons at Level S

THE STAR FISHER [S]

Historical fiction; 150 pages; 14 chapters; acknowledgments; italics to indicate characters speaking in Chinese; some archaic words; many multisyllable words; long, complex sentences with full range of punctuation; centers around friendship, prejudice, and persecution.

> ...And I shall know some savor of elation
> Amidst the cares, the woes, and the vexation...
> —*Pushkin*

July 29, 1920
Antwerp, Belgium

Dear Tovah,

Antwerp is a wonderful city. The people are so kind and generous, even the children.

I play with them in the park outside my room. Gizelle is the name of the girl who reminds me of Hannah. She really isn't like Hannah at all, now that I've come to know her. She is more practical and solid than Hannah. She brings her ball to the park and we play catch. I have learned many bouncing rhymes though I don't always understand what I am singing. The children laugh at my accent, but not in a cruel way.

It seems I have lived in Antwerp always. The old couple I board with, Marie and Gaston, are kind to me. They enjoy when I speak with them in Flemish. Gaston laughs and claps his hands when I tell him a story about my day. "Listen to her, Marie," he crows. "Is she not wonderful?"

I can hardly believe that it ever felt strange to me here. The bridges over the canals, the market at the Grunaplatz, the beautiful carriages and horses trotting along the streets, the cabarets and the hula dancers, they are all so familiar to me now. I wish Mama and Papa were here. The boys, too. And you, Tovah, and Hannah and Uncle Avrum and Bubbe Ruth, everyone, I wish you were all here. How I would love to share this wonderful city with you.

Not only are the people kind in Belgium, but the food is splendid. Sister Katrina and the lady from the HIAS have introduced me to so many new tastes. Almost always, I eat in the market. It costs very little, so I am saving Papa's money, and the food, Tovah, you wouldn't believe. There is a fruit called a banana, colored yellow like a June sun and curved. You peel the skin off and underneath is a white fruit so sweet and creamy, it makes even Frusileh's milk seem thin by comparison.

And ice cream! If the people in Berdichev could taste ice cream, they would give up eating everything else. In the afternoon, the ice cream man comes down King Street with a giant dog pulling his cart.

66
67

Figure 13–11.   Letters from Rifka (*Level S*)

CRY OF THE CROW [S]

Realistic fiction; 149 pages; 14 chapters; contrast in perspectives (farm family and scientific interest); detailed descriptions of crows and their behavior, but little technical vocabulary; onomatopoetic words representing crows' cries; some sophisticated vocabulary (for example, *bespoke; disperse, impish, fallow*); requires inference to understand the theme (parallel between the crow's freedom and growing up).

ENDURANCE: SHACKLETON'S ANTARCTIC EXPEDITION [S]

Informational text; 32 words; seven sections; table of contents, epilogue, timeline, glossary, index, and author's information; true story of begins dramatically with description of the plight of men on a ship stranded in Antarctica; historical account in chronological order; excerpts for diaries inserted in italics; maps and photographs; some bulleted lists; key words in bold; technical vocabulary (for example, *ballast, caulked, tiller, hull, sextant,* some archaic words); vivid description; requires readers to imagine hardship and analyze characters' determination and strength to survive; allows readers to consider qualities of leadership.

THE CROCODILIANS: REMINDERS OF THE AGE OF DINOSAURS [S]

Informational text; 64 pages; seven chapters; subheadings within chapters; table of contents, glossary, references, extensive index, and information about the author; technical vocabulary (for example, *reptiles, archosaurs, crocodilians, species, amphibians*);

WHAT IS DIABETES?

Having diabetes means there is too much glucose (a kind of sugar) in your blood.

If your blood glucose is too high, you:
- feel tired and thirsty
- need to go to the bathroom often
- lose weight.

If your blood glucose gets very high, you feel sick and cross and may throw up.

In the United States, the United Kingdom, Australia, and New Zealand, about 15 out of every 100,000 children get diabetes every year.

INSULIN

The pancreas is a gland behind your stomach that makes insulin. Insulin controls the level of glucose in your blood.

It does this by making sure that the glucose from the food you eat goes into your muscles and all the other parts of your body that need it. If your pancreas stops making insulin, glucose can't get out of your bloodstream to do its work. So it builds up there until you become sick.

DAILY TIMETABLE

7:55 A.M.	Test and shot
8:00 A.M.	Breakfast
10:40 A.M.	Snack
12:30 P.M.	Test and lunch
3:00 P.M.	Snack
5:50 P.M.	Test and shot
6:00 P.M.	Supper
8:45 P.M.	Test and snack
9:00 P.M.	Bed

Lyn, the diabetes educator, came to see me this afternoon. She talked about hypoglycemia and hyperglycemia. It's all kind of confusing.

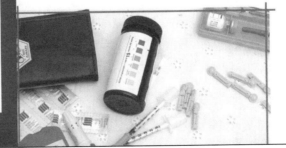

Figure 13–12. Alice's Diary *(Level S)*

charts and diagrams; time scale; maps; photographs to illustrate the content but many full pages of print; long, complex sentences (some 25 to 30 words long) that include technical concepts and vocabulary; large amount of information included in each section; uses description and compare/contrast (different kinds of crocodilians, their habitats and appearance); uses time sequence (crocodile laying eggs).

Summary: Levels N to S

The exemplars we have highlighted at levels N, O, P, Q, R, and S represent a wide variety of writing styles, genres, and formats. At these levels, length, as a characteristic, becomes less important. Many more informational books are included at these levels, demanding that readers access and use much more background knowledge than at previous levels.

Suggestions for Professional Development: Analyzing the Demands of Text N to S

Continue exploring leveled texts with colleagues in your school. Again, we suggest that you work in cross-grade-level groups. Use the collection of books at levels J through X that you gathered for your Chapter 5 professional development discussions. This time focus on levels N, O, P, Q, R, and S. If you need more titles at these levels, collect them. You will need at least three titles per level. Try to include one nonfiction book for each level.

1. Before the meeting, divide into six pairs and assign a level to each. Distribute the books you have collected and ask the members of each group to read the texts they have been given. (If you have a very small group, have the whole group do one level at a time and use only two titles at each level.)

2. Have each group create a list: What does this text call for readers to do? If you completed the professional development suggestions at the end of Chapters 4 and 5, you have analyzed texts and become familiar with the kinds of changes in text demands along the gradient. Now, simply brainstorm a list of demands, looking at the books you have read. Consider the ten characteristics: genre/form, text structure, content, themes/ideas, language and literary features, sentence complexity, vocabulary, words, illustrations, and book and print features.

3. Bring the entire group together and compare the grids. Ask:
   - What variety is there within levels in what texts call on readers to do?
   - What variety is there across levels in what texts call on readers to do?
   - What significant changes do you notice from level N through level S? If you like, you can record these statements on a chart with two columns, one labeled *From* and the other labeled *To*.

4. Complete the discussion by asking the group to make some concluding statements about texts at levels N through S.

CHAPTER FOURTEEN

UNDERSTANDING LEVELS OF TEXT: T TO Z

In this chapter we continue level-by-level descriptions for the most advanced levels. Remember that the variety of texts vastly increases at these levels. Here, you will find many texts that contain archaic language, for example, "he was very near with his money" (p. 125, *War Comes to Willy Freeman*, Collier & Collier 1983). You will find texts with dialect, sometimes archaic dialect, for example, "If tha'd ha' stayed another two-three weeks th' birds would ha' been nesting, and th' primroses all showing their little pink faces. Herondale's a gradely place i' springtime" from *The Wolves of Willoughby Chase* (Aiken 1962). This kind of language is quite challenging for readers. Writers of fantasy often seem to have created a language of their own to describe the cultural worlds in which their characters live, often requiring not only interpretation of terms within those words to taking perspectives far from reality. For example, in the Redwall series, you will often find language like this:

> The mousemaid stood over a stunned toad. It was an indescribably ugly specimen, completely covered in large wartlike growths. In one paw Mariel twirled her gullwhacker, while in the other she held a curious contrivance. It was a lantern on a small carrying frame, wonderfully made from thin-cut rock crystal. Inside the lantern half a dozen fat fireflies buzzed, giving off a pale golden light. (*Mariel of Redwall*, p. 229)

Even greater challenge is offered by texts demanding a depth of background knowledge. Historical fiction, for example, requires readers to access memory of information about the setting. When presenting a complex plot, with character development, it is impossible for writers to provide all of the information readers need in order to completely understand of the setting. On the other hand, knowledge of the setting may be all important in understanding characters' attitudes and decisions. For example, in *War Comes to Willy Freeman* (Collier & Collier 1983), Willy philosophizes that "some people was going to be more free that others" and "nobody was free all the way." Deep understanding of the meaning of these statements is related to the readers' knowledge of the historical legacy of slavery, socio-economic differences among people, and the necessary restrictions of community living.

Also at these advanced levels, you will find texts that explore very mature themes such as violence, death, sexuality and child abuse. In *War Comes to Willy Freeman*, a young African American girl witnesses the violent death of her father and her mother's death through abuse. As the author's note indicates, the offensive word *nigger* is used throughout, as it was during the 1700s. *The Egypt Game* (Snyder 1967) is an example of a text that is easier to read than might be expected at level X; however, content related to the Egyptian culture the children create, as well as two child murders and one attempted murder by a serial killer, make the text more challenging.

On the following pages are descriptions and examples of texts at levels T through Z. Levels X, Y, and Z have been combined.

Levels T through Z

As self-extending readers encounter a larger variety of texts and apply their processing skills to longer and more difficult texts, they greatly expand that they use to construct meaning from print. Most students in fifth and sixth grade fall into a category we call "advanced," in that they read quickly, paying attention to meaning almost all the time. They immediately and automatically recognize most of the words they read and rapidly apply a wide range of word-solving strategies. They are developing strategies for rapidly expanding their vocabularies.

These readers have the stamina to engage in large amounts of reading and to sustain the activity over days and weeks, quickly recalling what has been previously read. They can skim and scan for information or can lose themselves in books, identifying with the characters and experiencing the unfolding events along with them. By now, they have read a large number of texts and are building networks of understanding that help them recognize and appreciate the writer's craft. They are developing an understanding of aspects of literature such as figurative language and symbolism. Our goal for these advanced readers is to further broaden their experience with texts.

They need to become even more sophisticated in their ability to read all kinds of informational texts, thereby expanding their knowledge of content-area topics, and to integrate information from a range of graphic features. They tend to need much more experience looking at how informational texts are organized and using tools such as indexes, charts, pronunciation guides, glossaries, and headings and subheadings.

Their reading of narrative encompasses all genres; many readers will take on the more difficult works of fantasy that require suspending disbelief, entering into other worlds, engaging the imagination, interpreting actions, and noticing symbolism in the struggle between good and evil.

At the same time, they will be reading realistic fiction that grapples with serious social issues and provides the opportunity to understand perspectives very different from their own. These levels offer a way for students to explore their world through reading and to learn to analyze and criticize the texts they read.

Although this chapter explores sample texts at levels T through Z, we recognize that many books at levels X, Y, and Z are not appropriate for most elementary school students, even though they may be able to read them accurately. The topics of many texts at these levels are for use in a middle school setting or may be used with high school students. With fiction, the themes and topics may be uninteresting or too mature, or the writing styles and text structures so complex that they will not enjoy the reading. Even excellent texts may require more experience to truly understand them. Along the same lines, informational texts at levels X, Y, and Z may require so much background knowledge or be so dense that elementary students may have difficulty in sustaining their attention and understanding the topics. Nevertheless these levels complete the spectrum of students' reading development, and you will probably have some students for whom these texts are appropriate.

Level T

Text Characteristics

Selections at level T include a variety of genres and text structures. Chapter books are long, with few illustrations, and they require the reader to recognize character development as well as symbolism. All selections contain many sophisticated, multisyllable words that readers will need to analyze in terms of both literal and connotative meaning.

The range of books at level T incorporates fantasy, historical fiction, informational books, biographies, and realistic fiction. Readers need to know

Text Characteristics: Level T

GENRES/FORMS

Genres
- Realistic fiction
- Fantasy
- Some science fiction
- Informational texts
- Traditional literature, including myths and legends
- Biography, memoir, autobiography
- Historical fiction
- Genre combination (hybrids)
- Mysteries

Forms
- Picture books
- Plays
- Chapter books
- Series books
- Chapter books with sequels
- Short stories
- Diaries and logs

TEXT STRUCTURE

Fiction
- Narrative structure including chapters with multiple episodes related to a single plot
- Plots with detailed episodes
- Some short stories with plots that intertwine

Nonfiction
- Underlying structures—description, compare/contrast, temporal sequence, problem/solution, cause/effect
- Variety in organization and topic
- Some texts with several topics, organized categorically

CONTENT
- Topics that go well beyond readers' personal experiences
- Most of content carried by the print rather than pictures
- Content supported and/or extended by illustrations in most informational texts
- Content requiring the reader to take on diverse perspectives (race, language, culture)
- Fiction—settings requiring knowledge of content (history, geography, etc.)
- Content particularly appealing to preadolescents

THEMES AND IDEAS
- Many texts focusing on human problems related to war, hardship, economic classes
- Texts with deeper meanings applicable to important human problems and social issues
- Some themes presenting mature issues and the problems of society, for example racism
- Themes focusing on the problems of preadolescents
- Themes that evoke alternative interpretations

LANGUAGE AND LITERARY FEATURES
- Long stretches of descriptive language, important to understanding setting and characters
- Complex plots, creating suspense
- Multiple characters revealed by what they say, think, and do and what others say/think about them
- Memorable characters, with both good and bad traits, that change and develop over time
- Settings distant in time and space from students' experiences
- Many complex narratives that are highly literary
- Some more complex fantasy elements, some showing conflict between good and evil
- Some obvious symbolism in all types of fiction

SENTENCE COMPLEXITY
- Longer (some 20+) complex sentence structures including dialogue and many embedded clauses and phrases
- Sentences with nouns, verbs, or adjectives in series, divided by commas
- Sentences with parenthetical material
- Wide range of declarative, imperative, interrogative sentences
- Complex sentences –phrases, clauses, compound

VOCABULARY
- Many new vocabulary words that readers must derive from context or use glossaries or dictionaries
- Many highly technical words, mostly defined in text, illustrations, or glossary
- Many longer descriptive words—adjectives and adverbs
- Many words used figuratively—metaphor, simile, idiom
- Words with connotative meanings essential to understanding the text
- Words used in regional or historical dialects
- Some words from languages other than English

WORDS
- Many words with 3+ syllables
- Some easy compound words
- Many multisyllable proper nouns that are difficult to decode
- Many technical words that are difficult to decode
- Words that are seldom used in oral language and are difficult to decode
- Words with affixes (prefixes and suffixes)

ILLUSTRATIONS

Fiction
- Many books with only a few or no illustrations
- Most illustrations in fiction black and white
- Typically have long stretches of text without illustrations
- Some picture books that have illustrations on every page

Nonfiction
- Full range of graphics providing information that matches and extends the text
- Some texts with graphics that are complex and not fully explained
- Some texts with graphics that have scales or legends important to understanding

BOOK AND PRINT FEATURES

Length
- Shorter (most approximately 24-48 pages of print) texts on single topics (usually nonfiction)
- Chapter books (most approximately 100-200 pages of print)
- Many lines of print on a page (5-30; more for fiction)

Print and Layout
- Large variation among print styles and font size (related to genre)
- Use of bold, larger font, or italics for emphasis or to indicate importance or level of information
- Variety in print color and background color
- Print and illustrations integrated in most texts, with print wrapping around pictures
- Spaces between lines varies, with some texts having dense print
- Variety in layout of nonfiction formats (question/answer; paragraphs; boxes; legends; call-outs)
- More difficult layout of informational text, with denser format
- Many sentences continuing over several lines or to the next page
- Captions under pictures that provide important information

Punctuation
- Full range of punctuation
- Occasional use of less common punctuation (colon, semicolon)

Tools
- Full range of readers' tools (table of contents, glossary, headings/subheadings, call-outs, pronunciation guides, index, references)

more about political and historical events and about the problems of different cultural and racial groups. Themes include growing up, courage, survival, hardship, and prejudice. Text characteristics for level T are listed on the preceding page.

Examples

Nory Ryan's Song [T] (See Figure 14–1)

Historical fiction; 148 pages; 24 chapters; glossary of Irish words, author's note to reader, and author information; survival story; vocabulary—many Irish words, some specific words (*turf, dulse, limpets*); some sentences in italics representing singing or important thoughts; reference to Irish folk songs and legends; requires some background knowledge to understand circumstances at the time of the Potato Famine and they way people lived; requires inference to understand characters' different perspectives on going to America and their willingness to sacrifice themselves for others; story of courage; hint of romance.

Wild West Shows: Rough Riders and Sure Shots [T] (See Figure 14–2)

Informational text; 63 pages; seven chapters; references, glossary, index, and author information; historical account of Buffalo Bill and other "rough riders" that helped shape America's concept of the West; key words in bold red; told in chronological order; photographs with legends; technical vocabulary (for example, *legendary, billboard, heralds, vaquero, clay pigeon, vaudeville, Wild West*); requires background knowledge of concepts such as "Native

But even as she said it, I shook my head. I would never leave her. It was Patch who had to go to America, Patch who had to have that chance. "Will you, Sean Red . . . ," I began, and he knew what I was going to say.

Mrs. Mallon knew too. "How can we take someone so small?" she asked, but Sean held up his hand.

We looked at each other, the two of us, and I remembered walking to Patrick's Well together. How many times? I had danced with him at Maggie's wedding, making faces at Celia. *Dear Celia.* I remembered singing and sharing dulse with him. I remembered the cliffs.

Sean nodded. "You can trust him with me."

"Don't I know that?" I told myself I couldn't cry now, not until they were gone. I went to the side of Anna's house. Patch was there, bent over, humming to himself, piling one stone on top of another. I sat down next to him and touched his hair and his little shoulders, and his neck that was almost too thin to hold up his head. "Someone is waiting for you," I said.

He looked up at me with blue stone eyes. "And who is that, Nory?"

I could hardly talk. "It is your own Maggie," I said. "You will climb up on the cart with Mrs. Mallon. You will take your best stones and your coat. And a ship will be waiting for you in Galway."

"The *Emma Pearl*," he said dreamily. "And you, too, on the cart."

132

I shook my head. "I must stay here. I will find stones for you and send them someday."

He shook his head, beginning to sob, reaching out for me. I held him, his hair fine under my hands, his arms tight around me. He was the last one left.

I pried his fingers away. "You must go," I said, my voice hard. "Maggie is waiting, and there will be food."

"No." He pulled at my arm, at my skirt. "Let me stay."

"Maggie will be waiting at the port of New York for you. She will lift you up, hug you. She will be so happy to see you."

He was on the ground now, sobbing, his face buried in the earth. I pulled him up on his knees, looking into that little face. "You will find stones in America. You will build a house and tall buildings."

He shook his head hard.

I cupped his cheeks in my hands, kissed his tiny nose. "You will remember something, when you are an old man like Granda." I said it slowly, each word above the noise of his crying. "You will say that your own Nory sent you because she loved you. You will say that no one ever loved you more."

He shut his eyes over his tears, the lids swollen.

"Patcheen with the blue stone eyes," I said, and stopped. I could not cry. Not yet. I darted into the house, trying to think. An egg hard-boiled for one pocket, another for his hand, a pile of stones. And Anna grabbed up the old black coat to cover him.

133

Figure 14–1.   Nory Ryan's Song, *Level T*

Annie Oakley was not a westerner. Born Phoebe Anne Moses, she grew up in the woods of Ohio. She was famous for providing head-shot birds for local hotels to serve their guests. Unlike others at the time, Annie Oakley killed a bird by shooting it in the head. She did not scatter birdshot—the small pellets that fill the shell—through the edible portions of the bird, which reduced its value on a fancy menu.

By the 1880s, Annie Oakley and her husband Frank Butler were touring as sharpshooters with the Sells Circus. When the show closed in 1885, they found themselves abandoned in New Orleans, Louisiana, and hired on with Buffalo Bill, who was at first reluctant to hire a woman sharpshooter. He put Oakley on trial—and immediately hired her when he saw what she could do with a rifle and a shotgun. Butler withdrew from competition to promote his wife's career. Annie Oakley became the greatest of the Wild West stars, next to Buffalo Bill himself. The newspapers called her "America's Sweetheart." Sitting Bull dubbed her "Little Sure Shot."

Annie Oakley customarily had the second spot on the program. Some say it was to help the women in the audience get accustomed to the sound of gunfire before Buffalo Bill's marksmanship demonstrations later in the show.

24

Sharpshooter Annie Oakley earned her fame in Wild West shows.

Apparently, gunfire was less likely to offend if a woman did the shooting.

Annie Oakley was prim, proper, and barely 5 feet (1.5 m) tall. Almost childlike, she charmed audiences as she skipped onto the stage. But she impressed everyone with her marksmanship. She could shoot unlimited numbers of **clay pigeons**, 943 out of 1,000 glass balls, and 4,772 out of 5,000 targets with a rifle in nine hours. Her most famous trick was splitting a playing card

25

Figure 14–2. Wild West Shows: Rough Riders and Sure Shots, *Level T*

Americans," "Westward Movement," and entertainment with no television or movies; requires analytic thinking to understand the influence of Wild West Shows on Americans' thinking about the West.

Other Text Descriptions at Level T

SOUNDER [T]

Historical fiction; 116 pages (13 chapters, each about nine pages); small font; author's note; short sentences among long, complex sentences; symbols between sections of text to indicate passage of time or new episode; characters not named; some representation of southern dialect; requires background knowledge of historical events and issues; mature themes of racism, persecution, and death; symbolism (what Sounder represents to the family and the fact that characters have no names).

PREACHER'S BOY [T]

Historical fiction; 186 pages; 15 chapters; no pictures; many "sayings" (for example, "Chaos took charge and rumor reigned," "Land-o-Goshen," "breathing fire and brimstone" and "tarnation"); set in 1899-1900 in rural area of Vermont; most speech in dialect; some very short sentences for effect; some sophisticated vocabulary (for example, *turpitude, obscene, gawkers, covetousness*); some words used metaphorically (for example, *apocalypse*); first person narrative; readers required to understand the times; for example, reading *Tom Sawyer* is considered rebellious; moral issues explored by Robbie, the "preacher's boy" (for example, making fun of handicapped people); justification for war; conflicting views of evolution; alcoholism and child kidnapping.

SHARKS [T]

Informational text; 28 pages; no page numbers; no sections or headings; small font; double-spaced type; no glossary or index; full page dramatic photographs; technical vocabulary (for example, names of sharks, *buoyant, filter-feeder, plankton, denticles, tapetum lucidum, electroception*); some vocabulary explained in the text; pronunciation guides in parentheses for names of sharks and some scientific words; bulleted list within the text; thorough treatment of topic, covering many different kinds of sharks, their characteristics, behaviors, and habitats; requires readers to remember and categorize information.

INVENTORS [T]

Informational text; 93 pages; no table of contents; index; forewords; 12 sections, each on a different aspect of invention, with titles of sections not always giving a clue to the contents; busy pages with photographs, drawings and paintings, quotes in boxes); many dropped capitals at the beginning of new topics; words related to the concept of inventions (for example, *revolutionizes, extraordinary, reality, breakthrough, enterprising*); a whole range of technical vocabulary specific to inventions (for example, *dry-plate, ridership, steam-driven, transcontinental*); density of information (for example, many inventions typically mentioned in a single paragraph, with readers' background assumed); much background information required; a wide variety of content under the single theme of inventions; may be read in pieces, according to readers' interests but is generally organized in chronological order; provides a great deal of description.

Level U

Text Characteristics

Informational texts at level U cover a wide range of topics and present specific technical information. As with earlier levels, illustrations require interpretation and connection to text. Narrative texts are complex; there are plots and subplots. Texts typically have several different themes and many characters. Characters, too, are complex, with multiple dimensions to their personalities. Writers use symbolism, and themes are more abstract. Creative formats are also used (for example, short stories connected by common characters). Text characteristics for level U are listed on the next page.

Examples

WAR COMES TO WILLY FREEMAN [U]
(SEE FIGURE 14–3)

Historical fiction; 178 pages; 14 chapters; afterword regarding authentic basis for the book; set in Revolutionary War; fast-paced account of young African American girl who was freed with her mother and father on condition that her father would join the Americans in fighting; demands understanding of the complex rules regarding slavery in the 1700s; harsh language reflecting the attitudes of the times; conflicting feelings about the war since neither side promised much to African American slaves; includes violent death, cruelty and abuse; survival story.

GIANT PANDAS [U] (SEE FIGURE 14–4)

Informational text; 64 pages; nine sections; table of contents, introduction, glossary, references, and index; photographs, drawings, maps, diagrams, and charts; several different kinds of information in boxes with different colors and fonts; direct dialogue as the writer talks directly to the reader; technical vocabulary (for example, *bamboo, camouflage, carnivore, vocalizations, predators, migration, genetic testing, delayed implantation*); uses

Text Characteristics: Level U

GENRES/FORMS

Genres
- Realistic fiction
- Fantasy and science fiction
- Informational texts
- Traditional literature, including myths and legends
- Biography, memoir, autobiography
- Historical fiction
- Genre combination (hybrids)
- Mysteries

Forms
- Picture books
- Plays
- Chapter books
- Series books
- Chapter books with sequels
- Short stories
- Diaries and logs

TEXT STRUCTURE

Fiction
- Narrative structure including chapters with multiple episodes related to a single plot
- Plots with detailed episode
- Plots with subplots
- Some short stories with plots that intertwine

Nonfiction
- Underlying structures—description, compare/contrast, temporal sequence, problem/solution, cause/effect
- Underlying structures often combined in complex ways
- Variety in organization and topic
- Some texts with several topics, organized categorically

CONTENT

- Topics that go well beyond readers' personal experiences
- Most of content carried by the print rather than pictures
- Content supported and/or extended by illustrations in most informational texts
- Content requiring the reader to take on diverse perspectives (race, language, culture)
- Fiction—settings requiring knowledge of content (history, geography, etc.)
- Content particularly appealing to preadolescents

THEMES AND IDEAS

- Many texts with complex themes focusing on human problems related to war, hardship, social class barriers, racism
- Some themes presenting mature issues and the problems of society, for example racism
- Themes focusing on the problems of preadolescents
- Themes that evoke alternative interpretations

LANGUAGE AND LITERARY FEATURES

- Long stretches of descriptive language, important to understanding setting and characters
- Complex plots, creating suspense and moving towards solution of the problem
- Multiple characters revealed by what they say, think, and do and what others say/think about them
- Multidimensional characters that develop over time
- Texts requiring inference to understand characters and why they change
- Many complex narratives that are highly literary
- Settings distant in time and space from students' experiences
- Some obvious symbolism in all types of fiction
- Fantasy and science fiction showing struggle of good and evil
- Include some literary devices, such as stories within stories, symbolism and figurative language

SENTENCE COMPLEXITY

- Longer (some 20+) complex sentence structures including dialogue and many embedded clauses and phrases
- Sentences with nouns, verbs, or adjectives in series, divided by commas
- Sentences with parenthetical material
- Wide range of declarative, imperative, interrogative sentences
- Complex sentences –phrases, clauses, compound

VOCABULARY

- Many new vocabulary words that readers must derive from context or use glossaries or dictionaries
- Many highly technical words that require background knowledge and are not defined in the text
- Many longer descriptive words—adjectives and adverbs
- Many words used figuratively—metaphor, simile, idiom
- Words with connotative meanings essential to understanding the text
- Words used in regional or historical dialects
- Some words from languages other than English

WORDS

- Many words with 3+ syllables
- Many compound words
- Many multisyllable proper nouns that are difficult to decode
- Many technical words that are difficult to decode
- Words with affixes (prefixes and suffixes)
- Words that are seldom used in oral language and are difficult to decode
- Long, multisyllable words requiring attention to roots to solve

ILLUSTRATIONS

Fiction
- Most texts with no illustrations other than cover jacket
- Some symbolic decoration on margins or at chapter headings

Nonfiction
- Full range of graphics (maps, charts, cutaways, tables, legends, scales)
- Some texts with graphics that are dense and challenging
- Many graphics requiring knowledge of how to use scales
- Many graphics requiring interpretation

BOOK AND PRINT FEATURES

Length
- Shorter (most approximately 24-48 pages of print) texts on single topics (usually nonfiction)
- Chapter books (most approximately 100-200 pages of print)
- Many lines of print on a page (5-30; more for fiction)

Print and Layout
- Large variation among print styles and font size (related to genre)
- Many texts with very small font
- Use of bold, larger font, or italics for emphasis or to indicate importance or level of information
- Variety in print color and background color
- Print and illustrations integrated in most texts, with print wrapping around pictures
- Spaces between lines varies, with some texts having dense print
- Variety in layout of nonfiction formats (question/answer; paragraphs; boxes; legends; call-outs) often occurring on a single page spread
- More difficult layout of informational text, with denser format
- Many sentences continuing over several lines or to the next page

Punctuation
- Full range of punctuation
- Occasional use of less common punctuation (colon, semicolon)

Tools
- Full range of readers' tools (table of contents, glossary, headings/subheadings, call-outs, pronunciation guides, index, references)

COLLIER AND COLLIER

"Where you coming from, boy?" he said in a low, scary voice.

I didn't want to tell them I was a runaway—there was no guessing what they'd do then. But I didn't have much of an idea where I was, so it was hard to make up a good lie. "I was trying to find my friends, sir, but I got lost in the dark."

"What friends? Where do they live?" still keeping his voice low.

I decided to come as close to the truth as I could. "Stratford, sir."

"You're a long way from Stratford, boy. What're you doing way down here?"

"Like I said, sir, I must have slid past it in the dark. I was just putting into shore to ask somebody."

"He's a spy," a low voice in the dark said. "The niggers are all for the British. Throw him in the water and be done with it."

"Honest, I ain't a spy," I said.

"Hold up a minute, Ned," the man hunkered beside me said. "What were you going down to Stratford for?"

I knew I'd better convince them I was on the American side. "My Pa, he got killed at Fort Griswold and my Ma got taken away by the British. I was going to Stratford to find my aunt."

Nobody said anything for a minute and I knew they was thinking if they should believe it. Finally the man beside me said in that low voice, "That's the truth?"

60

WAR COMES TO WILLY FREEMAN

"I saw it happen, sir," I said. "They stabbed him in the back and he flung his arms out, just so, and died."

The man beside me turned his head away. "Were there any niggers killed at Griswold, Ned?"

"There was some. Two or three, I think."

"All right, son. What time did the British get up there?"

"It was just around noon, I reckon, sir," I said. "They busted down the door and came pouring in, and when Colonel Ledyard tried to surrender, they ran him through with his own sword."

Nobody said anything for a minute. Then the one called Ned said, "That sounds right to me. I heard about it."

The man next to me rose up. "All right, son. You just lie there. Don't be moving around and don't make any noise. We'll decide what to do with you when we get back."

It was a raiding party, all right. They'd land somewheres on Long Island, bust something up, capture some British officers if they could, and run back across the Sound. I was going to find myself in the middle of a fight again.

And, of course, the chances was they'd take me back to Connecticut after the fight. There was no way of telling what would happen then. Maybe they'd find out I'd run off from Captain Ivers and send me back to him. Or maybe one of them would take me for a slave himself. Or I didn't know what all else. And then how

61

Figure 14–3. War Comes to Willy Freeman, *Level U*

compare/contrast (different kinds of pandas); many terms explained within the body of the text; numbered lists of facts; provides rich description of pandas, their characteristics, behaviors, history, and habitats; uses cause/effect and problem/solution (pandas as threatened species); uses chronological order (growth of Panda from cub); thorough coverage of the topic.

Other Text Descriptions at Level U

THE VIEW FROM SATURDAY [U]
Realistic fiction; 162 pages; 12 interconnected stories with recurring characters; each story told by a different character); long, complex sentences with full range of punctuation; many words from languages other than English; intriguing questions and answers at the end.

A GATHERING OF DAYS: NEW ENGLAND GIRL'S JOURNAL, 1830-32 [U]
Historical fiction—diary; 145 pages; diary entries from October 17, 1830 to March 8, 1832, with letters (date 1899) from the writer to her great granddaughter before and after the journal; first person narrative, requiring construction of events from entries; provides view of farm life from the perspective of a 14-year-old girl; some archaic

Folklore History

Giant pandas were first mentioned in historical records about 1,200 years ago. Two hundred years later, giant pandas were the rare and treasured possessions of emperors and other people of great importance. An emperor from the Han Dynasty (202 B.C. – A.D. 220) kept a panda in his palace, and an emperor from the Tang Dynasty (A.D. 616 – 907) sent two pandas to the emperor of Japan as a goodwill gesture. In these old records, the gifts are called "white bears." Nobody knows for certain whether these white bears were actually giant pandas. It does makes sense, however, that an animal as rare as the giant panda would become part of an emperor's treasure.

Since the Tang Dynasty, the panda has been considered a rare treasure. In 1972 the Chinese government gave two pandas to the Smithsonian Institute's National Zoo in Washington, D.C. The animals were a gesture of friendship between the Chinese and American governments.

A Tibetan Myth

Although giant pandas do not appear in many Chinese folktales, they do appear in a Tibetan myth. At the beginning of the story, four young shepherdesses are killed when they try to save a panda from a hungry leopard. When the other pandas hear what has happened, they decide to hold a funeral to honor the girls' sacrifice.

At this time, giant pandas were pure white, without a single black marking. To honor the deceased, the white pandas arrived at the funeral wearing black armbands. The pandas were so sad, and so moved by the ceremony, that they began to cry. As their tears rolled down, the dye from the black armbands began to run and mingle with their tears. As they rubbed their eyes, the black dye made big spots. In their grief, they clutched at their ears, and hugged one another closely. The black dye marked the areas where the giant pandas touched themselves and each other.

Although the pandas kept these black marks as a reminder of the girls, they also wanted their children to remember what happened. The pandas turned the four shepherdesses into a mountain with four peaks. This mountain stands in the Sichuan province near the Wolong Natural Reserve in China.

48

49

Figure 14–4. Giant Pandas, *Level U*

vocabulary, spelling, and sentence structure; ranges from stories of everyday life and work to serious topics such as death, slavery, and adjusting to a new stepmother; includes some poetry and documents of the time (for example, advertisement to sell a 17-year-old girl slave); symbolism in the form of a quilt given away to a runaway slave and another quilt pieced together over time; author's note at the end commenting on the construction of the story.

INSECTS [U]

Informational text; 58 pages; four chapters; main headings and two levels of subheadings; photographs, labeled drawings, illustrations of life cycles; life history chart, pronunciation guide, index; medium font; large number of technical words;

detailed information, with many unfamiliar concepts; descriptions of complex processes.

BEYOND THE SECRET GARDEN [U]

Biography; 128 pages; 13 chapters with dates and meaningful titles indicating phases of the subject's sometimes unconventional life; epilogue; references, index, and maps; many black and white photographs from the subject's life, most with additional information in the form of captions; presented chronologically; influences on the subject as well as her works unfamiliar to most readers; told in an interesting way; inclusion of some quotes from Burnett's books and others; interest greatly enhanced by knowledge of *The Secret Garden*; setting important to understanding (for example, divorce was scandalous at the time).

Level V

Text Characteristics

Biographies at this level go beyond simple narratives to provide a significant amount of historical information. Many biographies are not "fictionalized" for easier reading; they focus on harsh themes and difficult periods of history. Other longer biographies are told in narrative style but present complex themes.

Fiction includes science fiction that presents sophisticated ideas and concepts. In many of the works of realistic or historical fiction, the writer is conveying a significant message beyond the specific. Texts require readers to think critically. Full appreciation of texts requires noticing aspects of the writer's craft. Most long texts have print in a small font; texts may be 200 to 300 pages but contain many more words than texts with larger print. Text characteristics for level V are listed on the next page.

Examples

THE WOLVES OF WILLOUGHBY CHASE [V] (SEE FIGURE 14–5)

Historical fiction—series; 168 pages; 11 chapters; black and white scratchboard illustrations placed throughout; complex punctuation including many sentences with dashes; words in italics for emphasis; some archaic language (for example, *make haste, coursing swiftly, pipkins, wringer*); many multisyllable words (for example, *self-reproachfully, obliterated*); a great deal of long description; exaggerated plot and characters with moral lessons.

"No, ma'am."

He appeared, grinning broadly, planked a dry-looking loaf and a jug of water on the table, and then whispered, "Don't touch it, Miss Bonnie. Just as soon as the old cat's out of the way I'll bring something better!" And, sure enough, ten minutes later, he returned carrying a tray covered with a cloth which, when taken off, revealed two dear little roast partridges with bread sauce, red currant jelly, and vegetables.

"You'll not starve while I'm here to see after you," he whispered.

The children ate hungrily, and later James came back with a dish of trifle and took away the meat dishes, carefully covering them again with the cloth before venturing into the corridor.

"I wish I knew where the secret passage came out," he murmured. "Porson, the old steward, always used to say there was a sliding panel in this room and a passage that led down to the dairy. With that she-dragon on the prowl it would be rare and useful to have a secret way into here. You might have a bit of a search for it, Miss Bonnie."

"We'll begin at once!" exclaimed Bonnie. "It will be something to pass the time."

The moment James had taken away the pudding plates they began testing the walls for hidden springs.

"You start by the door, Sylvia, and I'll begin at the fireplace, and we'll each do two sides of the room," Bonnie suggested.

It was a big room, its walls covered in white linenfold paneling, decorated with carved garlands of roses painted blue. The children carefully pushed, pulled, and pressed each wooden rose, without result. An hour, two hours went by, and they were becoming disheartened and beginning to

74

feel that the story of the secret passage must have been merely an idle tale, when Sylvia suggested:

"We haven't tried the fireplace, Bonnie. Do you suppose it possible that part of the mantelpiece should be false?"

"Clever girl!" said Bonnie, giving her a hug. "Let us try it at once."

The mantel was large, and beautifully carved from some foreign stone and a gray, satiny surface. It extended for several feet on either side of the fireplace to form two wide panels on which were carved deer with elaborately branching antlers. The children ran to these and began fingering the antlers and trying to move them. Suddenly Sylvia gave an exclamation—as she pushed the deer's head to one side the whole panel slid away into the wall, leaving a dark aperture like a low, narrow doorway.

"You've found it!" breathed Bonnie. "Oh, what fun this is! Let us go in at once and see where it leads. Sylvia, you are the cleverest creature in the world, and I do not know what I should have done if you had not been here to keep me company. I could not have borne it!"

She was about to dart into the hole when the more prudent Sylvia said, "Should we not take lighted candles? I have heard that the air in this kind of disused passage is sometimes very foul and will put out a flame. If we had candles we should be warned in time."

"Very true! I did not think." Bonnie ran to a cupboard which held wax tapers in long silver holders and brought two each, which they kindled at the fire. Then they slipped cautiously through the narrow opening, Bonnie leading the way.

"We had better shut the panel behind us," she said. "Only imagine if Miss Slighcarp should come into the schoolroom and find it open!"

"What if we cannot open it again from the inside?"

75

Figure 14–5. The Wolves of Willoughby Chase, *Level V*

Text Characteristics: Level V

GENRES/FORMS

Genres
- Realistic fiction
- Fantasy and science fiction
- Informational texts
- Traditional literature, including myths and legends
- Biography, memoir, autobiography
- Historical fiction
- Genre combination (hybrids)
- Mysteries
- Satire

Forms
- Picture books
- Plays
- Chapter books
- Series books
- Chapter books with sequels
- Short stories
- Diaries and logs

TEXT STRUCTURE

Fiction
- Narrative structure including chapters with multiple episodes related to a single plot
- Plots with detailed episodes
- Plots with subplots
- Some short stories with plots that intertwine

Nonfiction
- Underlying structures—description, compare/contrast, temporal sequence, problem/solution, cause/effect
- Underlying structures often combined in complex ways
- Variety in organization and topic
- Some texts with several topics, organized categorically

CONTENT

- Heavy content load in many texts, both fiction and nonfiction, requiring study
- Critical thinking required to judge authenticity of informational texts, historical fiction and biography
- Content supported and/or extended by illustrations in most informational texts
- Content requiring the reader to take on diverse perspectives (race, language, culture)
- Many texts requiring knowledge of history
- Content particularly appealing to adolescents

THEMES AND IDEAS

- Many texts with complex themes focusing on human problems related to war, hardship, social class barriers, racism
- Some themes presenting mature issues and the problems of society, for example racism
- Themes focusing on the problems of preadolescents
- Themes that evoke alternative interpretations

LANGUAGE AND LITERARY FEATURES

- Long stretches of descriptive language, important to understanding setting and characters
- Complex plots, creating suspense and moving toward solution of the problem
- Multiple characters revealed by what they say, think, and do and what others say/think about them
- Understanding of multiple characters necessary for comprehending theme
- Multidimensional characters that develop over time, requiring inference to understand how and why they change
- Settings distant in time and space from students' experiences
- Many complex narratives that are highly literary
- Full range of literary devices, such as flashback, stories within stories, symbolism and figurative language

SENTENCE COMPLEXITY

- Longer (some 20+) complex sentence structures including dialogue and many embedded clauses and phrases
- Sentences with nouns, verbs, or adjectives in series, divided by commas
- Sentences with parenthetical material
- Wide range of declarative, imperative, interrogative sentences
- Complex sentences –phrases, clauses, compound

VOCABULARY

- Many new vocabulary words that readers must derive from context or use glossaries or dictionaries
- Many highly technical words that require background knowledge and are not defined in the text
- Many longer descriptive words—adjectives and adverbs
- Many words used figuratively or with connotative meanings essential to understanding the text
- Some words from languages other than English
- Words used in regional or historical dialects
- Some words from languages other than English

WORDS

- Many words with 3+ syllables
- Many compound words
- Many multisyllable proper nouns that are difficult to decode
- Many technical words that are difficult to decode
- Words with affixes (prefixes and suffixes)
- Words that are seldom used in oral language and are difficult to decode
- Long, multisyllable words requiring attention to roots to solve

ILLUSTRATIONS

Fiction
- Most texts with no illustrations other than cover jacket
- Some symbolic decoration on margins or at chapter headings

Nonfiction
- Full range of graphics (maps, charts, cutaways, tables, legends, scales)
- Some texts with graphics that are dense and challenging
- Many graphics requiring knowledge of how to use scales
- Many graphics requiring interpretation
- Many texts with graphics that are complex, dense and challenging

BOOK AND PRINT FEATURES

Length
- Shorter (most approximately 24-48 pages of print) texts on single topics (usually nonfiction)
- Chapter books (most approximately 100-200 pages of print)
- Many lines of print on a page (5-30; more for fiction)

Print and Layout
- Large variation among print styles and font size (related to genre)
- Many texts with very small font
- Use of bold, larger font, or italics for emphasis or to indicate importance or level of information
- Variety in print color and background color
- Print and illustrations integrated in most texts, with print wrapping around pictures
- Spaces between lines varies, with some texts having dense print
- Variety in layout of nonfiction formats (question/answer; paragraphs; boxes; legends; call-outs) often occurring on a single page spread
- More difficult layout of informational text, with denser format
- Many sentences continuing over several lines or to the next page

Punctuation
- Full range of punctuation
- Occasional use of less common punctuation (colon, semicolon)

Tools
- Full range of readers' tools (table of contents, glossary, headings/subheadings, call-outs, pronunciation guides, index, references)

THE CALIFORNIA GOLD RUSH [V] (SEE FIGURE 14–6)

Informational text; 32 pages; no sections or headings; glossary and timeline; maps; chronological account of the Gold Rush, beginning with Sutter's move to California; photographs and drawings with legends; technical vocabulary (for example, *motherlode; epidemics; homesteader, forty-niner, frontier, panning, transcontinental, sluice, boomtown, ghost town*); requires background knowledge of concepts like *vigilante*.

Other Text Descriptions at Level V

TUCK EVERLASTING [V]

Fantasy; 139 pages; 25 chapters; magical events; symbolism; layers of meaning; complex and literary language; epilogue; understanding enhanced by literary experience with traditional literature; themes of love, friendship, choices, death versus everlasting life.

THE FIGHTING GROUND [V]

Historical fiction; 157 pages (no chapters; takes place over a 24-hour period, and time designations break up book into sections); some German words, with guide in the back; some unassigned dialogue; traumatic experience and change of attitude for hero; narrative structure, with several episodes each section; themes of war, survival, and growing up.

BUT I'LL BE BACK AGAIN [V]

Autobiography; 64 pages; seven short chapters—not numbered; lyrics from Beatles' songs at the beginning of each chapter; events in the author's life told in chronological order; written in first person; photo collection in chronological order at the

And what of John Augustus Sutter, the man who was there when the gold rush began? By the time the gold rush was in full swing, Sutter's 50,000 acres of land were overrun with miners. They trampled his crops and orchards, muddied his streams, and slaughtered his cattle for food. "The country swarmed with lawless men," Sutter later wrote. "Talking with them did no good. I was alone and there was no law." Since he could not fight the waves of miners, Sutter decided to join them. Discarding his dreams of an empire, he bought mining gear and set out for the hills. He was unlucky, however, and never struck it rich. Years later, Sutter went to Washington, D.C., to reclaim his land in California. He appealed to Congress to recognize his claim to the land that Mexico had given him. On June 18, 1880, while Congress was considering his request, John Sutter died in a Washington hotel room.

The California Gold Rush was brief and furious. It began in 1848 and swept the nation in 1849. In 1850, California was admitted to the Union because of its huge population, and because it was so rich in gold profits. But the influx of gold seekers was already beginning to decline by 1851. Individual miners with pans and pickaxes could only get at the gold that was near the earth's surface and in riverbeds. By 1855, almost all the miners had vacated California and were hunting for gold and silver in other territories. Major gold rushes brought swarms of miners to such places as Tombstone, Arizona; Pikes Peak, Colorado; and Deadwood, South Dakota. Everywhere a gold rush hit, the

John Sutter lost control of his land when it was taken over by countless miners.

Denver, Colorado (left), was founded when gold was discovered there in 1858. It grew rapidly during the nearby Pikes Peak gold rush of 1859.

25

Figure 14–6. The California Gold Rush, *Level V*

end of the text; great variety in sentence length; many references to historical events; frank discussion of puberty, growing up, divorce and death.

Heart and Lungs [V] (See Figure 14–7)

Informational text; 32 words; 13 sections, table of contents, glossary, and index; much smaller font; many drawings and diagrams; additional information provided through insets with a smaller font than the body; points of information in numbered paragraphs; paragraph lead headings in bold; lists of information in paragraphs, identified by a), b), etc.; question/answer format; technical vocabulary (for example, *abdomen; atrium; olfactory nerve; pharynx; plasma; ventricle*); dense text with a great deal of information in each section.

Level W

Text Characteristics

Texts at level W have themes that explore the human condition, with the same kinds of challenges mentioned at earlier levels. Fiction and nonfiction texts present characters who suffer hardship and learn from it. The writing is sophisticated, with complex sentences, literary language, and symbolism. Texts vary in length; print is generally small. Comprehending texts at this level requires awareness of social and political issues; through these texts, readers come to understand social problems at deeper levels.

Fantasy and science fiction introduce heroic characters, moral questions, and contests between good and evil. Informational texts may present complex graphic information and require a wide range of content knowledge. Readers must understand all the basic nonfiction organizational structures. Narrative biographies include many details and prompt readers to make inferences about what motivated the subject's achievements. Text characteristics for level W are listed on the next page.

Examples

A Wrinkle in Time [W] (See Figure 14–7)

Fantasy—series; 211 pages; 12 chapters; introduction by the author; family tree in front; set in realistic modern world but with humans who have special abilities and some fantastic characters; technical vocabulary related to space science, some invented (for example, *tesseract*); other vocabulary including many multi-syllable words (*inexorable, suspiciously, indignantly, prodigious*, full range of dialogue, some in languages other than English; literary references; thoughts signaled by dashes at the beginning of the sentence; some words in italics or all capitals for emphasis; descriptive and figurative language; sophisticated concepts such as the conflict between good and evil, mind control.

The Life and Words of Martin Luther King Jr. [W] (See Figure 14–8)

Biography; 96 pages; 14 short chapters; foreword, table of contents; King's life told in chronological order from Chapter 2, with foreword revealing his assassination and Chapter 1 focusing on his move to Montgomery, AL, in 1954; black and white photographs throughout; many quotes from King speeches; focus on the Civil Rights struggle; many terms and concepts requiring background knowledge, for example *"Jim Crow," Emancipation Proclamation, civil rights, nonviolence, ghetto.*

Other Descriptions at Level W

Roll of Thunder, Hear Me Cry [W]

Historical fiction; 276 pages; 12 longer chapters; small font with single-spaced type; one black and white drawing at the beginning; dialogue in dialect of the time; use of metaphor ("the man was a human tree" p. 34); complex punctuation (for example, use of colon with explanation afterwards); many long and complex sentences with independent and dependent clauses as well as lists (for example, some over 45 words long); many vocabulary words related to the historical

Text Characteristics: Level W

GENRES/FORMS

Genres
- Realistic fiction
- Fantasy and science fiction
- Informational texts
- Traditional literature, including myths and legends
- Biography, memoir, autobiography
- Historical fiction
- Genre combination (hybrids)
- Mysteries
- Satire

Forms
- Picture books
- Plays
- Chapter books
- Series books
- Chapter books with sequels
- Short stories
- Diaries and logs
- Photo essays

TEXT STRUCTURE

Fiction
- Complex plots, many with multiple story lines
- Unusual text organizations such as flashbacks
- Plots with detailed episodes
- Plots with subplots
- Some short stories with plots that intertwine

Nonfiction
- Underlying structures—description, compare/contrast, temporal sequence, problem/solution, cause/effect
- Underlying structures often combined in complex ways
- Variety in organization and topic
- Some texts with several topics, organized categorically

CONTENT

- Heavy content load in many texts, fiction and nonfiction, requiring study
- Critical thinking required to judge authenticity of informational texts, historical fiction and biography.)
- Content supported and/or extended by illustrations in most informational texts
- Content requiring the reader to take on diverse perspectives (race, language, culture)
- Many texts requiring knowledge of history
- Content particularly appealing to adolescents

THEMES AND IDEAS

- Wide range of challenging themes that build social awareness and reveal insights into the human condition
- Many texts presenting multiple themes that may be understood in many layers
- Many texts presenting mature societal issues, especially those important to adolescents

LANGUAGE AND LITERARY FEATURES

- Long stretches of descriptive language, important to understanding setting and characters
- Some texts with archaic language
- Multiple characters revealed by what they say, think, and do and what others say/think about them
- Understanding of multiple characters necessary for comprehending theme
- Multidimensional characters that develop over time
- Texts requiring inference to understand characters and why they change
- Some texts with "heroic" or "larger than life" characters that represent the symbolic struggle of good and evil
- Many texts with settings distant in time and space from students' experiences
- Many complex narratives that are highly literary
- Fantasy requiring prior knowledge of classical motifs (such as the quest)
- Full range of literary devices, such as flashback, stories within stories, symbolism and figurative language

SENTENCE COMPLEXITY

- Longer (some 20+) complex sentence structures including dialogue and many embedded clauses and phrases
- Sentences with nouns, verbs, or adjectives in series, divided by commas
- Sentences with parenthetical material
- Wide range of declarative, imperative, interrogative sentences
- Complex sentences –phrases, clauses, compound

VOCABULARY

- Many new vocabulary words that readers must derive from context or use glossaries or dictionaries
- Many technical words requiring background knowledge or use of glossary or dictionary
- Many longer descriptive words—adjectives and adverbs
- Words used figuratively or with unusual connotations
- Words with multiple meanings within the same text
- Some words from languages other than English
- Words used in regional or historical dialects
- Some archaic words

WORDS

- Many words with 3+ syllables
- Many compound words
- Many multisyllable proper nouns that are difficult to decode
- Many technical words that are difficult to decode
- Words with affixes (prefixes and suffixes)
- Words that are seldom used in oral language and are difficult to decode
- Long, multisyllable words requiring attention to roots to solve
- Words that offer decoding challenges because they are archaic, come from regional dialect, or from languages other than English

ILLUSTRATIONS

Fiction
- Most texts with no illustrations other than cover jacket
- Some symbolic decoration on margins or at chapter headings

Nonfiction
- Full range of graphics (maps, charts, cutaways, tables, legends, scales)
- Some texts with graphics that are dense and challenging
- Many graphics requiring knowledge of how to use scales
- Many graphics requiring interpretation
- Many texts with graphics that are complex, dense and challenging

BOOK AND PRINT FEATURES

Length
- Shorter (most approximately 24-48 pages of print) texts on single topics (usually nonfiction)
- Chapter books (most approximately 100-300 pages of print)
- Many lines of print on a page (5-40; more for fiction)

Print and Layout
- Large variation among print styles and font size (related to genre)
- Many texts with very small font
- Use of bold, larger font, or italics for emphasis or to indicate importance or level of information
- Variety in print color and background color
- Print and illustrations integrated in most texts, with print wrapping around pictures
- Spaces between lines varies, with some texts having dense print
- Variety in layout of nonfiction formats (question/answer; paragraphs; boxes; legends; call-outs) often occurring on a single page spread
- More difficult layout of informational text, with denser format
- Many sentences continuing over several lines or to the next page
- Some texts laid out in columns

Punctuation
- Full range of punctuation
- Occasional use of less common punctuation (colon, semicolon)

Tools
- Full range of readers' tools (table of contents, glossary, headings/subheadings, call-outs, pronunciation guides, index, references)

A Wrinkle in Time   *The Man with Red Eyes*

"But it is only the little boy whose neurological system is complex enough. If you tried to conduct the necessary neurons your brains would explode."

"And Charles's wouldn't?"

"I think not."

"But there's a possibility?"

"There's always a possibility."

"Then he mustn't do it."

"I think you will have to grant him the right to make his own decisions."

But Meg, with the dogged tenacity that had so often caused her trouble, continued. "You mean Calvin and I can't know who you really are?"

"Oh, no, I didn't say that. You can't know it in the same way, nor is it as important to me to have you know. Ah, here we are!" From somewhere in the shadows appeared four more men in dark smocks carrying a table. It was covered with a white cloth, like the tables used by Room Service in hotels, and held a metal hot box containing something that smelled delicious, something that smelled like a turkey dinner.

There's something phoney in the whole setup, Meg thought. There is definitely something rotten in the state of Camazotz.

Again the thoughts seemed to break into laughter. "Of course it doesn't *really* smell, but isn't it as good as though it really did?"

"I don't smell anything," Charles Wallace said.

128

"I know, young man, and think how much you're missing. This will all taste to you as though you were eating sand. But I suggest that you force it down. I would rather not have your decisions come from the weakness of an empty stomach."

The table was set up in front of them, and the dark smocked men heaped their plates with turkey and dressing and mashed potatoes and gravy and little green peas with big yellow blobs of butter melting in them and cranberries and sweet potatoes topped with gooey browned marshmallows and olives and celery and rosebud radishes and—

Meg felt her stomach rumbling loudly. The saliva came to her mouth.

"Oh, Jeeminy—" Calvin mumbled.

Chairs appeared and the four men who had provided the feast slid back into the shadows.

Charles Wallace freed his hands from Meg and Calvin and plunked himself down on one of the chairs.

"Come on," he said. "If it's poisoned it's poisoned, but I don't think it is."

Calvin sat down. Meg continued to stand indecisively.

Calvin took a bite. He chewed. He swallowed. He looked at Meg. "If this isn't real, it's the best imitation you'll ever get."

Charles Wallace took a bite, made a face, and spit out his mouthful. "It's unfair!" he shouted at the man.

Laughter again. "Go on, little fellow. Eat."

Meg sighed and sat. "I don't think we should eat this

129

Figure 14–7.   A Wrinkle in Time, *Level W*

setting (for example, *chiffonier*); requires understanding of the historical setting, discrimination, prejudice; invites inference as to the symbolic nature of land ownership for African American families and strength of character needed to withstand oppression.

DRAGONWINGS [W]

Historical fiction; 248 pages; 12 chapters; no table of contents; afterword; language/tradition reflects Chinese culture; Chinese speech indicated by regular font, English speech indicated by italics; many multisyllable words; complex, literary language; requires background knowledge of social issues and historical events; adventure centering on themes of immigration, survival, prejudice, and poverty requires/expands understanding of diversity in language and culture.

HOWARD CARTER: SEARCHING FOR KING TUT [W]

Biography/archeologist; 63 pages (seven chapters); afterword, index/glossary, information about the author, references for further reading; chapters four to seven pages long; small font; short paragraphs; almost no dialogue; based on journals, diaries, and books by Carter; black and white illustrations throughout; symbolic presentation of ankh at

Rosa Parks, with E. D. Nixon (left), talks to a news reporter.

CHAPTER 4
THE JIM CROW BUSES

When Martin and Coretta moved to Montgomery, Alabama, in 1954, it was a peaceful town. But it was peaceful because hardly anyone there challenged the Jim Crow system. Some Negroes were afraid to challenge it — they might lose their jobs. Some just thought it was hopeless to fight the system. It was "peace," but it was an unjust peace, King said.

A few very brave men did speak out against Jim Crow. They were able to build a slow fire of discontent among some of Montgomery's Negroes. But so far, it was all beneath the surface.

There was one place in Montgomery where the "peace" was beginning to wear very thin. This was on the city's bus lines. There were no Negro bus drivers. Some white drivers were polite, but many were unpleasant. They often called Negro riders ugly

22

names. Negroes paid their dimes at the front door, like everyone else. But often they were forced to get off the bus and get on again at the back door. Sometimes the buses drove off before the Negro riders had time to reach the back door.

But that wasn't all. Suppose the Negro section at the back of the bus was full. A Negro still was not allowed to sit in the white section up front even if it was empty. He had to stand in the back. There was something that bothered the Negro riders even more. Suppose the white section was full and a few more white people got on the bus. The driver could order Negroes sitting behind the white section to give up their seats and move back. Then they might have to stand. If they said "No," they were arrested. Very few ever said "No."

In March, 1955, a Negro high school girl did refuse to give up her seat to a white person. She was pulled off the bus, handcuffed, and taken to jail. This aroused Montgomery's Negroes. There was talk of boycotting the buses. A committee of Negro leaders was formed to protest. One of the leaders was King.

The group met with the manager of the bus company and the police chief. Both men were polite. They said they were very sorry about the way the girl had been treated. They would talk to the bus driver about it. And they would try to make conditions fairer for Negro bus riders.

But nothing was done. Everything went along in the same way. Negro riders were still insulted. One important thing did happen. The Negro people of Montgomery began to throw off their fear. There was a new spirit of courage and pride among them.

This new spirit burst into the open when Rosa Parks was arrested. Mrs. Parks was well known and well liked among Montgomery's Negro people. She

23

Figure 14–8.   The Life and Words of Martin Luther King, Jr., *Level W*

beginning of each chapter; chronologically told story of Carter's struggle to find the tomb of King Tutankhamen and reveal its mysteries; some specialized vocabulary; updated information on cause of King's death available from National Geographic.

METEORITE! THE LAST DAYS OF THE DINOSAURS [W]

Informational text; 64 pages; eight sections, each explaining a different aspect of the significance of meteorites; table of contents, glossary, references, index, and acknowledgements; photographs and labeled drawings; extra information inserted in boxes; small font with single-spaced type; technical vocabulary (for example, *asteroid, atmosphere, crater, foraminifera, iridium, meteorite, ozone, pale-*

ontologist, tectites); assumes knowledge of much technical vocabulary (not defined in text or glossary); narrative style used to present some information; use of chronological sequence (history of dinosaurs and photographic essay of the expedition); use of description throughout; presentation of evidence to support theory; body of text written in first person, talking directly to reader; personalization of the text through photographs of and by the writer.

OCEAN DETECTIVES: SOLVING THE MYSTERIES OF THE SEA [W]

Informational text/science; 59 pages; six sections; five pages of support material (glossary, references, index, credentials of writer); small but varied fonts;

legends under illustrations; many photographs, charts, diagrams, and drawings; presents scientists by name along with reports of their research and their findings; cohesive and interrelated text, with some extra facts in insets; technical language (for example, *coho salmon, zooplankton, copepods*) and many names of animals; many complex sentences; clear, understandable style.

Levels X, Y, and Z

Books at the last three levels, X, Y, and Z, have many characteristics in common. Although we have placed books in these categories, based on using the leveling process, we caution that our team worked from their own knowledge of typical upper elementary and middle school children. Readers in these categories vary greatly. In fact, readers' ability to control these texts depends heavily on their:

- Previous reading experiences.
- Quantity of texts read in this genre and other genres.
- Background of processing the sophisticated language in written texts.
- Both general and specialized vocabulary.
- Experience in dealing with mature concepts and issues.
- Experience in reading texts with complex organizational patterns (many headings and subheadings; literary devices such as stories within stories).
- Background knowledge in content area of the text.
- Personal experiences in human relationships.
- Personal experiences in learning about the world (for example, travel or trips to museums).
- Interests and willingness to take on certain kinds of texts.
- Experience with reading the genre (wide reading of a variety of examples in the genre supports comprehending).

So, a student who has read a large number of fantasy texts might be able to process the most difficult of texts in that genre but find informational texts at the same level much more difficult. At the same time, a student with a passion for reptiles might read a very high level of text on the topic but be unable to process the same level in biography or on another topic.

Fortunately, upper elementary and middle school students can grow very skillful in judging whether a text is right for their independent reading; and they can also consciously stretch themselves, deliberately taking on harder texts and less familiar genres. Finally, you can teach them how to get help—to ask you for support and/or use references to help them understand tricky concepts.

In general, texts at X, Y, and Z include mature topics such as sex and violence even though the texts themselves may be easier. also included are texts that require a large amount of background knowledge and/or that are "unfriendly" to readers in that so much prior information is assumed or there are many difficult terms that are not defined within the text. Also included are texts that are extremely complex in structure and/or are unusually difficult to follow (such as many different stories told in first person by different characters or jumping around in time). They include texts that are very dense, providing a huge amount of difficult content within a shorter text.

Below, we address each of these three upper levels, with some comments about the characteristics of each.

Level X

Text Characteristics

Books at level X include science fiction that incorporates technical knowledge as well as high fantasy depicting quests and the struggle between good and evil. Readers are required to go beyond the literal meaning of the text to construct implied meaning

Text Characteristics: Level X

GENRES/FORMS

Genres
- Realistic fiction
- Fantasy and science fiction
- Informational texts
- Traditional literature, including myths and legends
- Biography, memoir, autobiography
- Historical fiction
- Genre combination (hybrids)
- Mysteries
- Satire

Forms
- Picture books
- Plays
- Chapter books
- Series books
- Chapter books with sequels
- Short stories
- Diaries and logs
- Photo essays

TEXT STRUCTURE

Fiction
- Complex plots, many with multiple story lines
- Unusual text organizations such as flashbacks
- Plots with detailed episodes
- Plots with subplots
- Some short stories with plots that intertwine

Nonfiction
- Underlying structures—description, compare/contrast, temporal sequence, problem/solution, cause/effect
- Underlying structures often combined in complex ways
- Variety in organization and topic
- Some texts with several topics, organized categorically

CONTENT
- Heavy content load in many texts, fiction and nonfiction, requiring study
- Critical thinking required to judge authenticity of informational texts, historical fiction and biography
- Content supported and/or extended by illustrations in most informational texts
- Content requiring the reader to take on diverse perspectives (race, language, culture)
- Many texts requiring knowledge of history
- Content particularly appealing to adolescents

THEMES AND IDEAS
- Wide range of challenging themes that build social awareness and reveal insights into the human condition
- Many texts presenting multiple themes that may be understood in many layers
- Many texts presenting mature societal issues, especially those important to adolescents

LANGUAGE AND LITERARY FEATURES
- Long stretches of descriptive language, important to understanding setting and characters
- Many texts with archaic language
- Multiple characters revealed by what they say, think, and do and what others say/think about them
- Understanding of multiple characters necessary for comprehending theme
- Multidimensional characters that develop over time
- Texts requiring inference to understand characters and why they change
- Some texts with "heroic" or "larger than life" characters that represent the symbolic struggle of good and evil
- Many texts with settings distant in time and space from students' experiences
- Many complex narratives that are highly literary
- Fantasy requiring prior knowledge of classical motifs (such as the quest)
- Full range of literary devices, such as flashback, stories within stories, symbolism and figurative language

SENTENCE COMPLEXITY
- Some very long sentences (some 30+) with complex sentence structures including dialogue and many embedded phrases
- Sentences with nouns, verbs, or adjectives in series, divided by commas
- Sentences with parenthetical material
- Wide range of declarative, imperative, interrogative sentences
- Complex sentences –phrases, clauses, compound

VOCABULARY
- Many new vocabulary words that readers must derive from context or use glossaries or dictionaries
- Many technical words requiring background knowledge or use of glossary or dictionary
- Many longer descriptive words—adjectives and adverbs
- Words used figuratively or with unusual connotations
- Words with multiple meanings within the text
- Words used in regional or historical dialects
- Some words from languages other than English
- Many archaic words

WORDS
- Many words with 3+ syllables
- Many compound words
- Many multisyllable proper nouns that are difficult to decode
- Many technical words that are difficult to decode
- Words with affixes (prefixes and suffixes)
- Words that are seldom used in oral language and are difficult to decode
- Long, multisyllable words requiring attention to roots to solve
- Words that offer decoding challenges because they are archaic, come from regional dialect, or from languages other than English

ILLUSTRATIONS

Fiction
- Most texts with no illustrations other than cover jacket
- Some symbolic decoration on margins or at chapter headings

Nonfiction
- Full range of graphics (maps, charts, cutaways, tables, legends, scales)
- Some texts with graphics that are dense and challenging
- Many graphics requiring knowledge of how to use scales
- Many graphics requiring interpretation
- Many texts with graphics that are complex, dense and challenging

BOOK AND PRINT FEATURES

Length
- Shorter (most approximately 24-48 pages of print) texts on single topics (usually nonfiction)
- Chapter books (most approximately 100-300 pages of print)
- Many lines of print on a page (5-30; more for fiction)

Print and Layout
- Large variation among print styles and font size (related to genre)
- Many texts with very small font
- Use of bold, larger font, or italics for emphasis or to indicate importance or level of information
- Variety in print color and background color
- Print and illustrations integrated in most texts, with print wrapping around pictures
- Spaces between lines varies, with some texts having dense print
- Variety in layout of nonfiction formats (question/answer; paragraphs; boxes; legends; call-outs) often occurring on a single page spread
- More difficult layout of informational text, with denser format
- Many sentences continuing over several lines or to the next page
- Some texts laid out in columns

Punctuation
- Full range of punctuation
- Occasional use of less common punctuation (colon, semicolon)

Tools
- Full range of readers' tools (table of contents, glossary, headings/subheadings, call-outs, pronunciation guides, index, references)

by a writer's use of symbolism. There is a continuing increase in the sophistication of vocabulary, language, and topic. Some characteristics of texts at levels X, are listed on the preceding page.

Examples of texts at level X are presented next.

Examples

THE EGYPT GAME [X] (SEE FIGURE 14–9)

Realistic fiction—series; 215 pages; 23 chapters; author's note in beginning; black and white drawings at various places in the text; some content knowledge required to understand the role-playing "Egypt game" the children are playing; some challenging vocabulary (for example, *solemnity, exalted, enthusiastic, mysterious*); several subplots in addition to the mystery; growth and development of characters over time; mystery involving a serial child killer.

GROWING UP IN COAL COUNTRY [X] (SEE FIGURE 14–10)

Informational text; 127 pages; eight sections and conclusion with headings and subheadings; table of contents, conclusion, bibliography, and acknowledgments; black and white photographs (with credits) and some drawings; very small font and single-spaced type; quotes for each section that interject personal histories; technical vocabulary (for example, *shopkeeper, culm, suffocating*); much narrative text; compilation of many stories to create the entire picture of coal country; requires readers to think across stories to derive meaning; inference require to understand setting and circumstances in which coal miners were placed, including "company

---

The Egypt Game

be easier to get away. That meant they were the last ones up to each home, and sometimes most of the good stuff was already taken; but they hardly noticed. They were too busy looking for an omen.

At the last house before they turned off Elm Street, the Egypt gang started up the front walk and collided with two other trick-or-treaters who also seemed to be hanging behind the main group—a monster and a walking pile of boxes. "Hey," the monster said, "it's Ross and February. What are you supposed to be?"

The rubber monster mask completely covered the speaker's head, but the voice was familiar; and besides, the sixth-grade boys were the only ones who called April, February. Then the walking boxes said, "Hey man! It's a whole herd of Egyptians." He poked Marshall in the stomach and said, "Hi there, King Tut."

"Okay, Mr. Wise-Guy Alvillar," Melanie said. "I know who you are." She turned to April with an exasperated shrug. "It's Kamata and Alvillar."

Ken Kamata and Toby Alvillar were just about the most disgusting boys in the sixth grade, in a fascinating sort of way. They were best friends and always together, and everybody always voted for them for everything and wanted to be on their team. But not April and Melanie. April and Melanie always told each other that Ken and Toby were just ordinary

92

The Return to Egypt

(ugh) boys, and it was stupid the way everybody treated them so special. April and Melanie just couldn't figure out what people saw in them.

Of course, Toby had a special talent for getting people off the hook by making the teacher laugh. Just when Mrs. Granger was really building up a head of steam over something, Toby would make some little remark and Mrs. Granger would start choking and have to turn her back. Sometimes she'd try to pick things up where she left off, but all that lost momentum made a big difference.

Ken *was* sort of cute in a big blunt cocky way. He had a clean-cut all-American-Asian look about him, and he walked with a high-school swagger. Toby was thinner, with big ears that stuck out of his shaggy hair and enormous brown eyes that were always up to something, like a pair of TV screens turned on full blast. But right now you couldn't see what either one of them really looked like at all.

Ken had a man's old overcoat on over a pillow-padded hunchback, and (wouldn't you know it) rubber monster hands and feet, too, as well as the mask. Ken's father sold a lot of real estate and he could afford expensive stuff like that. Toby was the box man. He had a small box over his head, with a Saran Wrap–covered opening shaped like a TV screen to look out through. The rest of him was covered with all sorts of other boxes all strung together and painted

93

Figure 14–9. The Egypt Game *Level X*

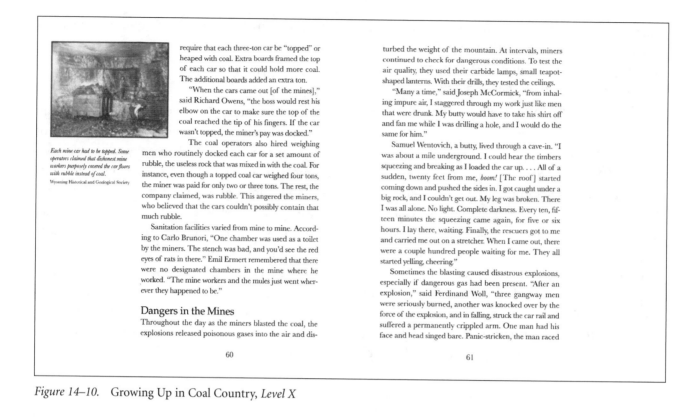

require that each three-ton car be "topped" or heaped with coal. Extra boards framed the top of each car so that it could hold more coal. The additional boards added an extra ton.

"When the cars came out [of the mines]," said Richard Owens, "the boss would rest his elbow on the car to make sure the top of the coal reached the tip of his fingers. If the car wasn't topped, the miner's pay was docked."

The coal operators also hired weighing men who routinely docked each car for a set amount of rubble, the useless rock that was mixed in with the coal. For instance, even though a topped coal car weighed four tons, the miner was paid for only two or three tons. The rest, the company claimed, was rubble. This angered the miners, who believed that the cars couldn't possibly contain that much rubble.

Sanitation facilities varied from mine to mine. According to Carlo Brunori, "One chamber was used as a toilet by the miners. The stench was bad, and you'd see the red eyes of rats in there." Emil Ermert remembered that there were no designated chambers in the mine where he worked. "The mine workers and the mules just went wherever they happened to be."

Dangers in the Mines

Throughout the day as the miners blasted the coal, the explosions released poisonous gases into the air and dis-

turbed the weight of the mountain. At intervals, miners continued to check for dangerous conditions. To test the air quality, they used their carbide lamps, small teapot-shaped lanterns. With their drills, they tested the ceilings.

"Many a time," said Joseph McCormick, "from inhaling impure air, I staggered through my work just like men that were drunk. My butty would have to take his shirt off and fan me while I was drilling a hole, and I would do the same for him."

Samuel Wentovich, a butty, lived through a cave-in. "I was about a mile underground. I could hear the timbers squeezing and breaking as I loaded the car up. . . . All of a sudden, twenty feet from me, *boom!* [The roof] started coming down and pushed the sides in. I got caught under a big rock, and I couldn't get out. My leg was broken. There I was all alone. No light. Complete darkness. Every ten, fifteen minutes the squeezing came again, for five or six hours. I lay there, waiting. Finally, the rescuers got to me and carried me out on a stretcher. When I came out, there were a couple hundred people waiting for me. They all started yelling, cheering."

Sometimes the blasting caused disastrous explosions, especially if dangerous gas had been present. "After an explosion," said Ferdinand Woll, "three gangway men were seriously burned, another was knocked over by the force of the explosion, and in falling, struck the car rail and suffered a permanently crippled arm. One man had his face and head singed bare. Panic-stricken, the man raced

Each mine car had to be topped. Some operators claimed that dishonest mine workers purposely covered the car floors with rubble instead of coal.
Wyoming Historical and Geological Society

60

61

Figure 14–10. Growing Up in Coal Country, *Level X*

stores" and child labor; inference required to understand why coal minors' children quit school and entered the mines.

Other Text Descriptions at Level X

WHERE THE RED FERN GROWS [X]

Realistic fiction; 261 pages; 20 chapters; of varying lengths; story about a boy and his dog told in flashback; has the quality of a memoir; poetic language and description; shows setting that will be unfamiliar for most students; mystical quality; themes of family relationships, hunting, death; many ideas implied rather than told.

BLACK PEARL [X]

Realistic fiction (qualifies as historical fiction because of 1960s setting); 96 pages; 18 chapters; set in La Paz, Baja California, and includes many Spanish words; flashback to a tale told by the story narrator, a young boy; implicit conflict between older legends and Christian religion; full range of

dialogue but mostly assigned; language structure often reflecting formal or ceremonial speech; involves death and coming of age.

HARRIET BEECHER STOWE AND THE BEECHER PREACHERS [X]

Biography; 131 pages; nine chapters; family tree; afterword, author's notes, bibliography, index; well researched; no dialogue but text slightly fictionalized for interest; many facts and historical characters; black-and-white portraits and photographs; many quotes from the subject; sophisticated and scholarly language; setting important to understanding the text (*slavery, abolitionists, war*).

MUMMIES AND THEIR MYSTERIES [X]

Informational text; 64 pages; eight sections; table of contents, glossary, listing of "mummy sites," index, and acknowledgments; technical vocabulary (for example, *mummification, bitumen, embalming, hieroglyphs, natron, resin*); many technical words not included in glossary or defined in the text; photographs with paragraphs of information, as well as maps, explores mummies (human- and naturally-preserved bodies) across the world; provides chemical explanations for mummification; requires readers to examine many different ancient peoples and their customs.

Level Y

Text Characteristics

Books categorized as level Y present subtle themes and complex plots. As with earlier levels, they include a whole range of social problems as themes, but more explicit details (for example, about death or prejudice) are provided. Texts also include irony and satire, literary devices that require readers to think beyond the literal meaning of the text. Books at level Y include many more complex works of fantasy that depict hero figures and heroic journeys. Readers are required to discern underlying lessons and may also analyze texts for traditional elements. A list of characteristics for level Y follows on the next page.

---

him. "Rum for General Wooster, boy," one of the aides said. Then he looked at Mother. "You're the taverner, m'am?"

"Yes, sir."

"We'll need some dinner."

There went my stew. But I didn't care. General David Wooster was head of the Connecticut militia. I'd never seen a general up close before, and as I brought the rum and water I looked him over. I was disappointed: he wasn't very glorious-looking—just a tired old man who was worried and frowning. As I stared he yawned and rubbed his eyes. "Timothy," Mother snapped. "Bring the gentlemen their dinners."

Suddenly the wounded man began to struggle to his feet, and saluted.

"Who are you?" General Wooster said.

"Private Hodge, sir. I took a British ball this afternoon."

"They were here, then?"

"Yes, sir. They've gone on toward Danbury about eight hours ago."

General Wooster ran his hand across his eyes. "Eight hours," he said softly. "Damn." He took his hand off his eyes. "Sit down, sir," he said. "Was there any attempt made to stop them?"

The wounded man struggled to the floor. "No, sir. Not that I could see, sir."

I stepped forward. "Sir, some of the trainband fired

[152]

on them from a house just down the road. The Redcoats killed them all and burned Starr's house." I remembered Ned's head jumping off his shoulders.

"How many men in the house, son?"

"I don't know, sir. Maybe five or six."

Suddenly the door banged open again. Another Continental officer stood there, gazing around the room. Then he walked in, followed by his aides, and crossed the room to General Wooster. In a moment I saw the insignia on his shoulder. He was a general, too. He walked over to General Wooster, followed by his aides. General Wooster got up. "Ben," he said. "It's good to see you. Boy, a glass of rum for General Arnold."

So General Arnold was in Redding. I brought the rum, and water and some bread, and we scraped out the bottom of the stew pot to feed General Arnold and his aides. As they ate, they talked, and I stood back ready to serve, and listened. They talked about routes and marching orders and other military things I didn't understand. Twice they mentioned William Heron in a friendly way. I thought that was strange; but I didn't worry about it much, because I couldn't get it out of my mind that right at that moment Sam might be in Redding somewhere. But what was I going to do about it? Of course he didn't know that Father was gone, and it worried me that he might be afraid to come home. Then there was the other side of it, which was that the chances were that Sam wasn't in General Arnold's

[153]

Figure 14–11. My Brother Sam Is Dead *Y*

Text Characteristics: Level Y

GENRES/FORMS

Genres

- Realistic fiction
- Fantasy and science fiction
- Informational texts
- Traditional literature, including myths and legends
- Biography, memoir, autobiography
- Historical fiction
- Genre combination (hybrids)
- Mysteries
- Satire

Forms

- Picture books
- Plays
- Chapter books
- Series books
- Chapter books with sequels
- Short stories
- Diaries and logs
- Photo essays

TEXT STRUCTURE

Fiction

- Many texts with the complex structure of adult level reading
- Texts with unusual structures for presenting information (combination of different genres)
- Some collections of short stories that have interrelated themes or build a single plot across the book
- Complex plots, many with multiple story lines and subplots

Nonfiction

- Underlying structures—description, compare/contrast, temporal sequence, problem/solution, cause/effect
- Underlying structures often combined in complex ways

CONTENT

- Heavy content load in many texts, fiction and nonfiction, requiring study
- Critical thinking required to judge authenticity of informational texts, historical fiction and biography
- Content supported and/or extended by illustrations in most informational texts
- Content requiring the reader to take on diverse perspectives (race, language, culture)
- Many texts requiring knowledge of history
- Content particularly appealing to adolescents

THEMES AND IDEAS

- Wide range of challenging themes that build social awareness and reveal insights into the human condition
- Many texts presenting multiple themes that may be understood in many layers
- Many texts presenting mature societal issues, especially those important to adolescents

LANGUAGE AND LITERARY FEATURES

- Long stretches of descriptive language, important to understanding setting and characters
- Many texts with archaic language
- Many highly literary texts, including the use of language in satirical or ironic ways
- Multiple characters revealed by what they say, think, and do and what others say/think about them
- Understanding of multiple characters necessary for comprehending theme
- Multidimensional characters that develop over time
- Some texts with "heroic" or "larger than life" characters that represent the symbolic struggle of good and evil
- Texts requiring inference to understand characters and why they change
- Many texts with settings distant in time and space from students' experiences
- Fantasy requiring prior knowledge of classical motifs (such as the quest)
- Full range of literary devices, such as flashback, stories within stories, symbolism and figurative language

SENTENCE COMPLEXITY

- Some very long sentences (some 30+) with complex sentence structures including dialogue and many embedded phrases
- Sentences with nouns, verbs, or adjectives in series, divided by commas
- Complex sentences with compound sentences joined by semicolons
- Sentences with parenthetical material
- Wide range of declarative, imperative, interrogative sentences
- Complex sentences –phrases, clauses, compound

VOCABULARY

- Many new vocabulary words that readers must derive from context or use glossaries or dictionaries
- Many technical words requiring background knowledge or use of glossary or dictionary
- Many longer descriptive words—adjectives and adverbs
- Words used figuratively or with unusual connotations
- Words with multiple meanings within the text
- Some words from languages other than English
- Words used in regional dialects
- Many archaic words

WORDS

- Many words with 3+ syllables
- Many compound words
- Many multisyllable proper nouns that are difficult to decode
- Many technical words that are difficult to decode
- Words with affixes (prefixes and suffixes)
- Words that are seldom used in oral language and are difficult to decode

- Long, multisyllable words requiring attention to roots to solve
- Words that offer decoding challenges because they are archaic, come from regional dialect, or from languages other than English

ILLUSTRATIONS

Fiction

- Most texts with no illustrations other than cover jacket
- Some symbolic decoration on margins or at chapter headings

Nonfiction

- Full range of graphics (maps, charts, cutaways, tables, legends, scales)
- Some texts with graphics that are dense and challenging
- Many graphics requiring knowledge of how to use scales
- Many graphics requiring interpretation
- Many texts with graphics that are complex, dense and challenging

BOOK AND PRINT FEATURES

Length

- Shorter (most approximately 24-48 pages of print) texts on single topics (usually nonfiction)
- Chapter books (most approximately 100-300 pages of print)
- Many lines of print on a page (5-40; more for fiction)

Print and Layout

- Large variation among print styles and font size (related to genre)
- Many texts with very small font
- Use of bold, larger font, or italics for emphasis or to indicate importance or level of information
- Variety in print color and background color
- Print and illustrations integrated in most texts, with print wrapping around pictures
- Spaces between lines varies, with some texts having dense print
- Variety in layout of nonfiction formats (question/answer; paragraphs; boxes; legends; call-outs) often occurring on a single page spread
- More difficult layout of informational text, with denser format
- Many sentences continuing over several lines or to the next page
- Some texts laid out in columns

Punctuation

- Full range of punctuation
- Occasional use of less common punctuation (colon, semicolon)

Tools

- Full range of readers' tools (table of contents, glossary, headings/subheadings, call-outs, pronunciation guides, index, references)

This Czechoslovakian woman was forced to witness the occupation of the Sudetenland and to salute the German Army.

4

"There were flames throughout the city"

Nazi policy wasn't just to harass Jews. It was to force them out of Germany. On the night of Friday, October 28, 1938, thousands of Polish-born Jews were chased out of Germany into Poland. At certain points along the border, Polish guards would not allow the Jews to enter Poland. Many Jews spent a sleepless night at the border in empty railway freight cars, crowded railroad stations, and open fields. Many waited near the border, hoping that an agreement between Polish and German authorities would allow them to return to their homes in Germany. Among the Jews deported to Poland was the Grynszpan family.

Berta Grynszpan sent a postcard to her seventeen-year-old brother Herschel, who was studying in Paris. She wrote that a policeman came to their house at night and told them to take their passports and report to the police station. From there they were taken in a police car to the town hall. They were held there and given orders to leave Germany within four days. "We are penniless," she wrote her brother. "Please send some money to us at Lodz. Love to you from us all, Berta."

Hitler's demands in exchange for his promise of peace. The agreement called for Czechoslovakian armed forces to leave the Sudetenland beginning October 1 and for German troops to replace them.

The Czechoslovakian people were not represented at the conference. They felt betrayed. Some threatened to revolt. But Neville Chamberlain returned to England waving the agreement and declared that by appeasing Germany he had brought "peace for our time."

32

33

Figure 14–12. We Remember the Holocaust, *Level Y*

Examples

MY BROTHER SAM IS DEAD [Y] (SEE FIGURE 14–11)

Historical fiction; 216 pages; setting in the Revolutionary War; no illustrations except historical maps in the front; small font with dense print; many long and complex sentences; vocabulary specific to the time (*Lobsterbacks; Minutemen; subversion; mumble-the-peg*); some profanity; many long paragraphs; explanations of opposing arguments regarding underlying causes for the war; complex issues requiring readers to see perspectives; mature themes such as war, death, and family conflict.

WE REMEMBER THE HOLOCAUST [Y] (SEE FIGURE 14–12)

Informational text; 148 pages; nine sections, each title with a quote from a survivor (or as the author suggests, "witness"); table of contents, preface, chronology, glossary, references and suggested reading; acknowledgments, and index; historical account of the Holocaust over a ten-year period (from Hitler's rise to the Nuremberg Trials; vocabulary related to the setting (*death march; Final Solution*); text made personal through quotes from Jewish survivors and others who remember the events; black and white photographs throughout; contrast shown in photographs (before and during the Holocaust); mature themes such as war and mass murder.

Other Text Descriptions at Level Y

THE GIVER [Y]

Fantasy/science fiction; 180 pages; 23 chapters; setting—a world some time in the future; very small font with dense text; some words used in new ways that reader must infer; requires reader to relate a strange new society to the present one; generic words like *dwelling* in relation to the new society require reader to infer what led to structuring the society; many layers of meaning; uncertain ending.

Where the Lilies Bloom [Y]

Historical fiction; 213 pages; 15 chapters and authors' note; first person narrative; long strings of unassigned dialogue; much figurative language; dialect particular to Appalachian area; requires background knowledge to understand the perspective of the narrator, Mary Call, who is extremely loyal to her father; mature topics such as poverty, death of a father (kept secret by his dying wish), and a family of children surviving on their own by gathering and selling herbs; character development as Mary Call learns and changes from her experiences.

Insects and Spiders [Y]

Informational text; 64 pages; 24 sections, each on a different topic related to insects; table of contents, glossary and index; headings and subheadings; text inset in boxes; some bulleted lists; varying size of font; many words in bold; questions posed on many pages; photographs and drawings; dense information on each page; use of compare/contrast and description, and chronological sequence (life cycles); invites readers to "browse around," looking for interesting facts.

Anne Frank: The Diary of a Young Girl [Y]

Informational text/diary (Anne's reflections presented chronologically in the order in which she wrote them); 283 pages (no chapters, entries vary in length); small font; sample of Anne's handwriting, diagram of room, and cover and frontispiece pictures; requires background knowledge of historical events and social issues; requires interpreting events from diary entries; no dialogue; fast-moving; short and long sentences; some fragments.

The Day Martin Luther King Was Shot: A Photo History of the Civil Rights Movement [Y]

Informational text; 96 pages; 24 sections; timeline, and table of contents; small font, single spaced; layout in columns; begins with Martin Luther King's assassination in 1968, then goes back to a descrip-

tion of slave ships words in italics to reflect King's emphasis in speeches; focuses on slave resistance and contributions of African Americans and of churches and abolitionists; uses cause and effect (explanations of the complicated underlying reasons for the war between the states); organized in chronological order with explanations for the events at each point in history; many narratives of prominent African Americans; use of chronological sequence (African American history in America).

Level Z

Text Characteristics

Informational books deal with controversial social concepts and political issues and include detailed historical accounts of periods that are less well known generally as well as events and people that are controversial. They also provide a great deal of technical information; readers learn new ways of finding technical information and encounter complex examples of the basic organizational structures for informational texts. Fiction texts explore a wide range of mature themes relative to the human condition. High fantasy presents heroic quests, symbolism, and complex characters. Some texts provide graphic details of hardship and violence.

Examples

The Bomb [Z] (See Figure 14–13)

Historical fiction; 161 pages; presented in three "books," the first with 12 chapters, the second with 16 chapters, and the third as a count down to the explosion of an atomic bomb; true story of Bikini islanders who were occupied by the Japanese and then by United States during WWII and were displaced for atomic bomb testing; factual information on the building of the atomic bomb at the beginning of each chapter; many words from languages other than English; very small font; written by a man who was in the Navy and participated in 1946; factual note and author note at the end; told

Text Characteristics: Level Z

Genres/Forms

Genres
- Realistic fiction
- Fantasy and science fiction
- Informational texts
- Traditional literature, including myths and legends
- Biography, memoir, autobiography
- Historical fiction
- Genre combination (hybrids)
- Mysteries
- Satire

Forms
- Picture books
- Plays
- Chapter books
- Series books
- Chapter books with sequels
- Short stories
- Diaries and logs
- Photo essays

Text Structure

Fiction
- Many texts with the complex structure of adult level reading
- Texts with unusual structures for presenting information (combination of different genres)
- Some collections of short stories that have interrelated themes or build a single plot across the book
- Complex plots, many with multiple story lines and subplots

Nonfiction
- Underlying structures—description, compare/contrast, temporal sequence, problem/solution, cause/effect
- Underlying structures often combined in complex ways

Content
- Heavy content load in many texts, fiction and nonfiction, requiring study
- Critical thinking required to judge authenticity of informational texts, historical fiction and biography
- Content supported and/or extended by illustrations in most informational texts
- Content requiring the reader to take on diverse perspectives (race, language, culture)
- Many texts requiring knowledge of history
- Content particularly appealing to adolescents

Themes and Ideas
- Wide range of challenging themes that build social awareness and reveal insights into the human condition
- Many texts presenting multiple themes that may be understood in many layers
- Many texts presenting mature societal issues, especially those important to adolescents
- Texts that explicitly present mature issues such as sexuality, murder, abuse, nuclear war

Language and Literary Features
- Long stretches of descriptive language, important to understanding setting and characters
- Many highly literary texts, including the use of language in satirical or ironic ways
- Many texts with archaic language
- Multiple characters revealed by what they say, think, and do and what others say/think about them
- Understanding of multiple characters necessary for comprehending theme
- Multidimensional characters that develop over time
- Texts requiring inference to understand characters and why they change
- Some texts with "heroic" or "larger than life" characters that represent the symbolic struggle of good and evil
- Many texts with settings distant in time and space from students' experiences
- Fantasy requiring prior knowledge of classical motifs (such as the quest)
- Full range of literary devices, such as flashback, stories within stories, symbolism and figurative language

Sentence Complexity
- Some very long sentences (some 30+) with complex sentence structures including dialogue and many embedded phrases
- Sentences with nouns, verbs, or adjectives in series, divided by commas
- Complex sentences with compound sentences joined by semicolons
- Sentences with parenthetical material
- Wide range of declarative, imperative, interrogative sentences
- Complex sentences –phrases, clauses, compound

Vocabulary
- Many new vocabulary words that readers must derive from context or use glossaries or dictionaries
- Many technical words requiring background knowledge or use of glossary or dictionary
- Many longer descriptive words—adjectives and adverbs
- Words used figuratively or with unusual connotations
- Words with multiple meanings within the text
- Many words from languages other than English
- Many archaic words

Words
- Many words with 3+ syllables
- Many compound words
- Many multisyllable proper nouns that are difficult to decode
- Many technical words that are difficult to decode
- Words with affixes (prefixes and suffixes)
- Words that are seldom used in oral language and are difficult to decode
- Long, multisyllable words requiring attention to roots to solve

- Words that offer decoding challenges because they are archaic, come from regional dialect, or from languages other than English

Illustrations

Fiction
- Most texts with no illustrations other than cover jacket
- Some symbolic decoration on margins or at chapter headings

Nonfiction
- Full range of graphics (maps, charts, cutaways, tables, legends, scales)
- Some texts with graphics that are dense and challenging
- Many graphics requiring knowledge of how to use scales
- Many graphics requiring interpretation
- Many texts with graphics that are complex, dense and challenging

Book and Print Features

Length
- Shorter (most approximately 24-48 pages of print) texts on single topics (usually nonfiction)
- Chapter books (most approximately 100-300 pages of print)
- Many lines of print on a page (5-40; more for fiction)

Print and Layout
- Large variation among print styles and font size (related to genre)
- Many texts with very small font
- Use of bold, larger font, or italics for emphasis or to indicate importance or level of information
- Variety in print color and background color
- Print and illustrations integrated in most texts, with print wrapping around pictures
- Spaces between lines varies, with some texts having dense print
- Variety in layout of nonfiction formats (question/answer; paragraphs; boxes; legends; call-outs) often occurring on a single page spread
- More difficult layout of informational text, with denser format
- Many sentences continuing over several lines or to the next page
- Some texts laid out in columns

Punctuation
- Full range of punctuation
- Occasional use of less common punctuation (colon, semicolon)

Tools
- Full range of readers' tools (table of contents, glossary, headings/subheadings, call-outs, pronunciation guides, index, references)

In July 1945, the cruiser USS *Indianapolis* sailed from San Francisco, carrying elements of an atomic bomb named Little Boy. She delivered her top-secret cargo to the island of Tinian, in the Marianas group, a long-range bomber base.

ELEVEN

Sorry and Abram pulled the Eniwetok outrigger from the canoe shed and slid it down to the water, setting sail to go south past Bokantuak and Eomalan, then around Rojkora, leaving the lagoon to head along the barrier reef and look for the tiger over the steep underwater cliff that dropped almost straight into dark ocean depths.

The wind was light but steady a few minutes past sunrise, and the double-end canoe, under the lateen sail, cut a path through the water. Abram sharpened the steel harpoon head with a stone as they glided along. The *zisst, zisst, zisst* made a pleasing sound, adding to the song of the water and the low hum of the wind on the sail.

"Mother told me about the tiger shark."

Abram lifted his eyes from the gleaming tip of Sorry's father's favorite harpoon. "Someone might have sent him to fish heaven by now. But I doubt it. Not that one. Tigers are as bad as the great white shark of colder water. Both are killers."

Sorry nodded. Jonjen had seen a tiger slice a man

56

in half off Lokwor. "How big was he when he bit you?"

"Seven feet, perhaps. A young one," Abram said thoughtfully. Then he added, with a laugh, "He wouldn't let me measure him."

"If he's alive, how big is he now?"

"Eleven or twelve feet, I'd guess. Maybe more."

Sorry had seen them seven or eight feet long. The young ones had dark stripes, but as they became older the stripes faded to a mottled gray. Their bellies were stark white. Their noses were not as sharp as the makos', and their mouths stretched from one side of their blunt heads to the other. They had spike teeth. Just the sight of them sent a hot stab of fear into swimmers or men in outriggers.

"Do they stay near home?"

"I think they do," Abram said. "Why?"

"I've always believed a tiger killed my father. There was no trace of him along the reef."

"That's the mark of a tiger, all right."

Sorry was thoughtful for a moment. "And if you spear the same one again?"

Abram chuckled. "I won't let the line get around my feet, you may be sure. I won't make that mistake twice. And I want you to stay in the stern, feet up, if I do hit him."

The line was coiled at the bow. It was strong, new line taken from the Japanese barracks.

"I hope we find him," Sorry said.

Abram nodded and ran a thumb over the harpoon head, testing its sharpness. A razor-thin line of blood came up. It was ready.

"Uncle Abram, have you killed any men in the war?"

"Me? No. I've only been on merchant ships, not

57

Figure 14–13. The Bomb, *Level Z*

from the perspective of a 14-year-old boy who tries to stop the bomb; little known modern "trail of tears," includes themes such as war and peace, death, powerlessness, and self-sacrifice.

POWERHOUSE: INSIDE A NUCLEAR POWER PLANT [Z] (SEE FIGURE 14–14)

Informational text; 48 pages; nine sections; table of contents, glossary, and index; section headings and subheadings; photographs with legends; diagrams; with extensive text; key words in bold; technical vocabulary (for example, *neutron, ore, plutonium,* *radiation, transformer, turbine, electron*); complex sentence structure; assumes that readers have a great deal of background information, with many concepts and vocabulary not explained within the text; description of complex processes; uses cause and effect (three mile island explanation).

Other Text Descriptions at Level Z

THE HERO AND THE CROWN [Z]

Sophisticated fantasy; 246 pages (25 chapters, most nine to twelve pages each.) Extensive detail; long complex sentence structure; very challenging

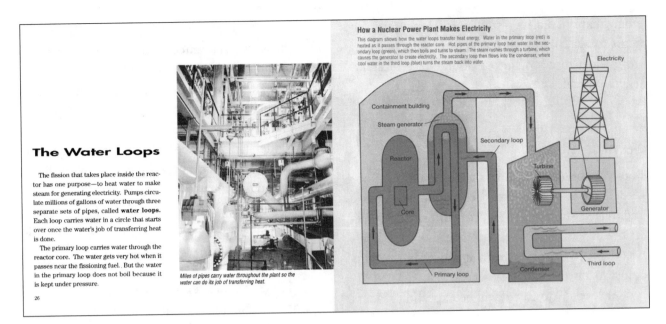

The Water Loops

The fission that takes place inside the reactor has one purpose—to heat water to make steam for generating electricity. Pumps circulate millions of gallons of water through three separate sets of pipes, called **water loops.** Each loop carries water in a circle that starts over once the water's job of transferring heat is done.

The primary loop carries water through the reactor core. The water gets very hot when it passes near the fissioning fuel. But the water in the primary loop does not boil because it is kept under pressure.

26

Miles of pipes carry water throughout the plant so the water can do its job of transferring heat.

How a Nuclear Power Plant Makes Electricity

This diagram shows how the water loops transfer heat energy. Water in the primary loop (red) is heated as it passes through the reactor core. Hot pipes of the primary loop heat water in the secondary loop (green), which then boils and turns to steam. The steam rushes through a turbine, which causes the generator to create electricity. The secondary loop then flows into the condenser, where cool water in the third loop (blue) turns the steam back into water.

Figure 14–14. Powerhouse: Inside a Nuclear Power Plant, *Level Z*

vocabulary; flashbacks and dream sequences; mature themes around a strong heroine who battles dragons, pain, and rejection.

ACROSS FIVE APRILS [Z]

Historical fiction; 190 pages; 12 chapters; story of the life of a boy from age nine to thirteen during the Civil War; very small font and dense print; use of archaic language and dialect; recounts historical events; requires knowledge of the setting; includes letters from the times; many difficult place names; author's note at the end documenting authenticity; mature themes such as war and death.

WE SHALL NOT BE MOVED: THE WOMEN'S FACTORY STRIKE OF 1909 [Z]

Informational text/history; 165 pages; 11 chapters; epilogue, bibliography, index; describes New York setting at the time; requires understanding of social issues not usually familiar to students; no dialogue; not fictionalized; well researched; black-and-white photographs with legends; detailed accounts.

MARIEL OF REDWALL [Z]

Fantasy—series book; 387 pages; 42 chapters; many invented vocabulary words specific to the culture as well as archaic language adapted to the culture; long, unfamiliar names of people and places; black and white map at the beginning and small, symbolic pictures at the beginning of each chapter; many four- and five-syllable words; long and complex sentences; a large amount of dialect by animals who have different economic stations and occupations within the created medieval-like culture; complex plot with many different characters and settings and multiple events taking place simultaneously in different places; inclusion of a large amount of poetry as well as legends and histories of the culture.

TO BE A SLAVE [Z]

Informational text/history; 160 pages; seven chapters; epilogue, foreword, and prologue; many archaic words; author commentary in italics; many quotes or "stories" from former slaves organized into categories such as resistance to slavery and

191

emancipation; dialect represented, some quite difficult to read; requires readers to build meaning from short pieces of information; voice of storytellers evident.

Summary

Books at the upper end of the continuum call for readers to use extensive background knowledge and varied strategies to process information presented in a variety of ways. Readers at these levels become truly advanced as their processing systems adjust to a broad range of genres.

At levels T to Z, we will be expecting readers to:

- Sustain reading over many long and complex texts, switching frequently and easily adjusting.
- Notice, understand, and discuss a wide range of literary devices, such as flashbacks and stories within stories.
- Understand idioms that are embedded within a text; understand how idioms can bring life to dialogue.
- Demonstrate understanding of a wide variety of human problems, global issues, and many different cultures and races.
- Demonstrate understanding of people different from oneself by culture, period of history, or other variation.
- Deal and construct understanding of mature themes such as war, prejudice, death, survival, and poverty, and discuss them in relation to one's own experiences.
- Understand the complexities of human characters as they develop and change; discuss one's own point of view and relationship to characters.

- Flexibly and automatically use tools such as glossary, reference index, credentials for authors, legends, charts, and diagrams.
- Use descriptive text as a way to understand settings and their importance to the plot or character development.
- Understand and be able to use the sophisticated, scholarly, and technical language that is found in informational texts.
- Argue to defend opinions about texts.
- Demonstrate critical thinking about a wide range of texts.

These complex texts can be read at several levels of understanding. Upper elementary students may read and enjoy them and derive rich understanding, yet miss some of the more obscure and symbolic meaning. Many adult readers will enjoy, learn from, and even be challenged by books at these levels.

Suggestions for Professional Development: Analyzing the Demands of Text T to Z

Continue exploring leveled texts with colleagues in your school. Again, we encourage working in cross-grade-level groups. Use the collection of books at levels J through X that you gathered for your Chapter 5 professional development discussions. This time, focus on levels T, U, V, and W, and add titles at levels X, Y and Z. You will need at least three titles per level. Try to include one nonfiction book for each level.

1. Before the meeting, divide your group into pairs and assign a level or levels to each pair. Distribute the books you have collected and

ask the group members to read the texts they have been given. (If you have a very small group, have the whole group do one level at a time and use only two titles at each level.)

2. Have each group create a list: What does this text call for readers to do? If you used the professional development suggestions at the end of Chapters 12 and 13, you have analyzed texts and also become familiar with the kinds of changes in text demands along the gradient. Now, simply brainstorm a list of demands, looking at the books you have read. Consider the ten characteristics: genre/form, text structure, content, themes/ideas, language and literary features, sentence complexity, vocabulary, words, illustrations, and book and print features.

3. Bring the entire group together and compare the grids. Ask:
   - What variety is there within levels in what texts call on readers to do?
   - What variety is there across levels in what texts call on readers to do?
   - What significant changes do you notice from level T through level Z? If you like, you can record these statements on a chart with two columns, one labeled *From* and the other labeled *To.*

4. Complete the discussion by asking the group to make some concluding statements about texts at levels T through Z.

CHAPTER FIFTEEN

THE CLASSROOM LIBRARY FOR INDEPENDENT READING

A strong collection of books is the foundation for the effective instruction that helps students become competent readers. In times past, most classroom libraries were filled with books that featured primarily European (Caucasian) characters and gave us a limited view of society. Now, many wonderful books are available featuring all cultures, and this diversity is reflected in the lists in this book. You will want to be sure that the fiction and nonfiction texts your students choose to read and that you read to them reflect a wide range of sociocultural and linguistic groups—Latino, Native American, African and African American, Asian, Middle-Eastern, Pacific Islanders—in a positive way. Also be sure to include books *written* by members of many diverse cultures.

You do not need a complete classroom library before you implement a reading workshop. In fact, we recommend that you assemble a basic collection of books and then build it over time. Think of your classroom library just as you would any other collection of books, each one carefully selected because it meets a need and provides enjoyment and learning. You'll want to build your collection throughout your career as a teacher, always discarding those books that are uninteresting, worn out, or inappropriate for your students and acquiring others that meet their needs and capture their interests. (If you're concerned about the cost of assembling a library, Chapter 18 provides some specific suggestions for how to acquire books with little or no money.)

Organization of the Classroom Library

The purpose of the classroom library is to encourage and motivate students to read. It is most important that books be attractively displayed and accessible (see Figure 15–1). You can make your classroom collection inviting by:

- Displaying books in baskets or tubs so they are easy to see and look through (rather than tightly packed in a bookcase with spines out).

- Being sure books you have talked about or students have recommended are included.

- Organizing books in categories so they can be found easily.

- Including both short and long texts.

- Allowing students to suggest titles to add to the classroom library.

- Providing a way for students to recommend books to others.

- Offering a range of texts from easy to difficult so that every student will find something "just right" to read.

The key to an efficient and interesting classroom library is organization. Figure 15–2 lists eight steps for organizing your library effectively.

Start by acquiring colorful plastic tubs or baskets, preferably all the same size (at least shoebox size or larger). These containers should be large enough so that you can place books in them with the front cover facing out. Don't cram the books into them. There should be room to flip through the books, seeing each title quickly.

Compare browsing through books in this fashion with searching through books tightly packed in a bookcase in alphabetical order, spines facing out. In the latter case, instead of browsing, you laboriously take out one title after another and put it

back. You bump up against other readers who are slipping out books and looking at them. It's hard to find the kind of books you like, because genres are mixed in willy-nilly. Inevitably, the shelves become untidy and the books are no longer in alphabetical order. Think too about your own browsing in a bookstore on a Saturday morning—the books are categorized by topic and genre so that you can find the kinds of books you want. "New" books are prominently displayed. You want your students to have a similar experience, but with more support than adults need.

Identify a large shelf area where you can place many baskets at levels students can reach—three shelves, one at table height, one higher, and one lower, work well. (If you have empty space on top of the shelves, display attractive hardcover picture books that will engage readers.) Several students should be able to browse through the books simultaneously without disturbing other students or interfering with your small-group instruction.

Figure 15–1. The Classroom Library

Steps for Organizing the Classroom Library

1. Acquire colorful plastic baskets or tubs of a uniform size.

2. Identify a large section of shelving that is accessible to students.

3. Identify the categories of books you want to display and label the baskets accordingly with large, clear print.

4. Place selected books, in categories, in the baskets. The books should face out so that students can flip through them, getting a clear view of the front of each one.

5. Add baskets and categories as you need them.

6. Change categories as needed (when studying different authors, genres, or topics, for example).

7. Revise collections (take away titles and add new ones) in the baskets as students read them.

8. Acquire and add duplicate copies of the most popular titles.

Figure 15–2. Steps for Organizing the Classroom Library for Intermediate Grades

Next, identify the categories of books you want to display and label the bins or baskets (see Figures 15–3 and 15–4).

In Figures 15–3 and 15–4, you will see a diagram showing an arrangement of books for primary grades and one for intermediate grades and middle school. Display books in attractive, clearly labeled bins or baskets with the fronts facing out so that students can flip through them easily.

In preparing the classroom library, categories will arise from your curriculum and, your work with students.

Favorite Authors

Some favorite authors for intermediate or middle grades might include Judy Blume, Avi, Gary Paulsen, Madeleine L'Engle, Gary Soto, Mildred Taylor, Karen Hesse, or Katherine Paterson. You will have introduced these authors through book talks, reading aloud, and literature discussion. Primary students can also develop a list of authors they like, especially if you emphasize the name of the author each time you read aloud and help students make connections among texts by the same author. Some favorite authors might be Tomie dePaola, James Marshall, Donald Crews, Eric Carle, or Gail Gibbons.

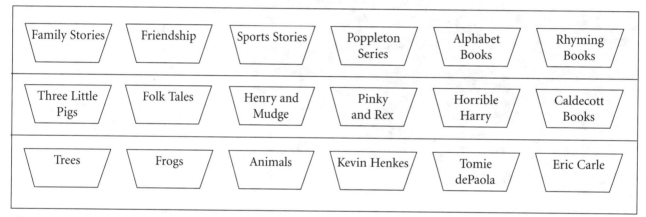

Figure 15–3. Labeled Baskets for Primary Children

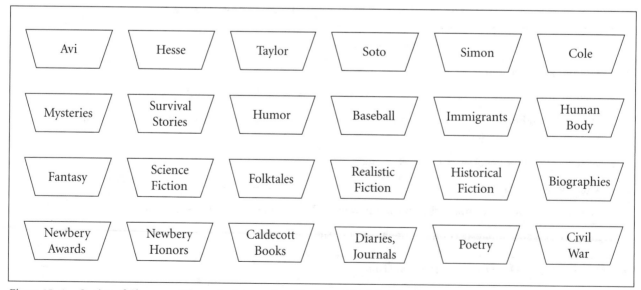

Figure 15–4. Section of Classroom Library for Intermediate Grades and Middle School

Favorite Illustrators

Favorite illustrators or styles of illustration can captivate students. For intermediate students, for example, the Pinckneys have created some wonderful illustrations for biographies. Other wonderful illustrators include Susan Jeffers and Ed Young. Primary students love James Marshall's whimsical folk tales and Jan Brett's richly illuminated illustrations, such as those in *The Mitten*. Patricia Polacco has provided a large number of illustrated stories that are appreciated across all grades.

The illustrations in many picture books are of high quality. Readers are presented with a wide variety of styles and media. The art enhances the meaning of the text and adds to its enjoyment, but high quality illustrations do more. They offer the opportunity to develop aesthetic appreciation of the artist's work.

Genres

Include genres that students already like and those they are learning about (traditional literature, fantasy, science fiction, realistic fiction, historical fiction, biography, autobiography, memoir, informational books). You can read aloud and discuss with students texts that represent new genres for them. After experiencing quite a few examples, students will become more comfortable with the genre.

Using picture books that can be read in one session is an efficient and enjoyable way to broaden your students' experience with various genres. For example, biographies such as *Wilma Unlimited* (Krull) or *Ellington Was Not a Street* (Shange, Nelson) provide good examples of how biographies are organized. *Abraham Lincoln and Me* (Borden & Lewin) is fiction but provides interesting facts about Lincoln that will interest primary students. You can set up a special display that offers them more choices (at a range of difficulty levels) and encourage them to explore more examples in the particular genre.

Characters, Formats, Topics

Students at all ages will come to select texts according to their interests, and they will also be developing particular tastes as readers. They will be drawn to particular types or categories of books. For example, primary children may like books about certain animals or characters such as Poppleton. They may like ABC books, rhyming books, flap books, or books that offer puzzles to be solved.

Some popular categories for older readers might be survival stories, friendship stories, series books, stories about strong women, biographies of famous women or men, sports stories, humorous books, books about family problems, or texts that explore social issues such as war or prejudice. As you detect students' interests growing, establish a basket to hold these types of books so that students can follow their interests. Often, students will "catch" interests from each other!

Traditional Literature

You can find many different versions of the same folktale or fairy tale ("Cinderella", "Sleeping Beauty", "Beauty and the Beast"). These versions range from the simple, straightforward stories that capture primary children's interest to much more complex stories that will be interesting for older readers to compare and use to probe deeper meanings. In addition, it is good to remember that fantasy, which is a very challenging genre, has its roots in traditional literature. Knowledge of motifs such as the quest or "threes" are learned through exploring simple stories like "The Three Little Pigs" or "Jack and the Beanstalk", and this awareness provides a foundation for understanding the complex texts such as Lloyd Alexander's *The Dark Is Rising*.

Informational Books

Across primary, elementary, and middle school, students will be interested in exploring a wide variety of content areas. Informational books are appealing to students, and in recent years, a large number of high-quality, illustrated books have become available. These are far more appealing to students than traditional textbooks and they provide excellent, up-to-date information in an interesting way. In addition, you will want to correlate your classroom library with the content areas your students are required to study (for example, dinosaurs, insects, wolves, dolphins, ecology, space, the ocean, health and the human body, the earth, historical events or people, rocks, volcanoes).

Series Books

Primary students love to meet the same characters again and again. Some popular reading systems will provide several books with the same characters; for example, Beverly Randell's *Baby Bear Goes Fishing* is followed by *Baby Bear's Present*. Children love reading all of the silly stories about Amelia Bedelia (Parish). *Henry and Mudge* (Rylant) is a high-quality series of beginning chapter books that are enjoyed by first and second graders.

As they grow older, students will search for series books, often reading a large number in a series such as Matt Christopher or Amber Brown. Once they have experienced and liked the first book in a series, they will enjoy others because they will bring a great deal of prior knowledge to their reading.

Series books are especially attractive to many students in grades 2–8. After you have introduced one or two books in a series (through book talks or in guided reading), you can put out a basket labeled for the series and point out that several more are available for choosing. Intermediate students enjoy books with sequels.

You can add baskets and categories as you acquire more books and/or as you introduce new areas of learning. Your social studies and science curriculum will undoubtedly lead to baskets of books on those topics. You can also change categories as needed. For example, students will move beyond a particular series or may have read all or most of the books by an author and will be ready for something new. Take away titles when they are

not needed and add new ones. You'll also want to keep an eye on students' reading lists and their reading interests. Find a way to acquire and add duplicate copies of the most popular titles. In these ways, you can keep the library fresh and interesting.

How Many Books Do You Need?

The classroom collection should contain many different kinds of titles to meet students' interests, broaden their scope of reading, and enable them to read massive amounts of material, thus building "mileage" as readers. An excellent classroom library should contain between 300 and 500 books. Unless you have extra resources, however, it will take several years to build a collection like that.

Also keep in mind that you will not put out all your books at once. Always keep "fresh" books coming into the library—not newly purchased, necessarily, but new to the students. By introducing "new" books with book talks, you can pique their interest anew. At any given time, there should be enough titles for all students to have good choices of books that interest them *and* that they can read successfully.

The charts in this section provide an estimated number of books for starter, basic, and expanded libraries, broken out into a range of levels, for grades K through 8. We have included levels only to ensure that you will purchase or acquire a range of books. You may need to adjust these estimates and ranges if you have large numbers of students reading substantially lower or higher than grade level. The book list organized by title alphabetically as well as by level and by genre (see *fountasandpinnellleveledbooks.com*) will be very helpful in selecting individual titles at levels appropriate for your students. To select titles in a variety of genres, refer to the list organized by genre. You will also add many unleveled books to your library for students to choose for independent reading.

Getting Started

First, look at the books you already have in your classroom and those that might be available in the school. The charts in this section assume you are starting from zero, and that is not usually the case. If you subtract the books you already have from the numbers on the charts, you'll have a more accurate estimate of what you need. The charts also assume a class size of between 25 and 30 students. If you have fewer students, you may not need as many titles, but you will still want to have good variety.

Then, think about the resources you will need. Paperback books purchased from a supplier who offers school discounts will cost between $4.00 and $5.00 each on average. With that price in mind, we have listed an estimated cost for starter, basic, and expanded classroom libraries. Since you probably already have some paperback books, your costs will be less than those we have listed. We have used $4.00 per book at levels A to J, and $5.00 per book for levels K to Z. The suggestions for acquiring books in Chapters 18 and 19 will help reduce costs further, but first you need to know what you need.

For primary classrooms, you will need a large collection of picture books that are not leveled. As an independent activity, children will enjoy looking at and talking about these books even if they are beyond their reading levels. Remember that the books you read aloud make a big impression on students. As they look through the volumes, they will remember language and notice aspects of print and illustrations. In this chapter, we discuss the number of leveled texts needed for browsing boxes and other independent reading.

Figures 15–5 through 15–11 are purchasing guides for starter, basic, and expanded classroom libraries for grades K through 8. The numbers on these chart indicate single titles, but you may want to acquire two or three copies of very popular books. A basic guideline for a starter library is to go for vari-ety rather than multiple copies or many titles in a series. The largest number of titles suggested are at the levels associated with each grade level. Slightly smaller numbers are suggested at the levels just below and above the grade level. This plan allows for many books at levels generally considered appropriate for the grade level. The assumption is that you have the greatest number of students reading at that level. You will want to adjust these numbers if your class varies from this pattern.

Suggestions for Professional Development: Evaluating the Classroom Library

Evaluate your classroom library to determine your needs and make an action plan. You may want to ask grade-level colleagues to work with you and make suggestions. Or you may want to work together as a faculty to improve all grade-level libraries.

1. Begin by taking an inventory of the books you currently possess. Organize and count them by category. Ask:
   - What genres are represented? Do I have enough variety?
   - How many of these titles are suitable for my students' reading levels?
   - How many of these titles are so interesting to my students that they want to read them?
   - Are my students' cultures, languages, and communities represented?
   - Are *all* kinds of diversity represented?
   - Does the library allow readers in my room to pursue an interest in a topic? An author? A type of book? Can they read in depth?
2. Share your findings with your colleagues and discuss next steps.
3. Next, look at the way books are displayed in the room. Use the list of steps and suggestions in this chapter to determine:
   - How accessible are books to students?

- To what extent do the book displays invite readers?

4. Now, use the charts in this book to estimate how many books you need. Consider:
   - The levels at which you need to acquire more books and how many.
   - The categories or genres in which you have fewer books and would like to acquire more.

- Authors, topics, and types of books that are popular with your students and represent purchases you would like to make.

5. Discuss your findings with colleagues and then make a "short list" of the numbers and types of books you want to acquire. Use the book lists organized by title and level as a resource (see *fountasandpinnellleveledbooks.com*).

Single-Title Classroom Library, Grade K			
LEVEL	STARTER	BASIC	EXPANDED
A	20	30	40
B	20	30	40
C	20	30	40
D	20	30	40
E	10	30	20
Total Number of Titles	**90 titles**	**150 titles**	**180 titles**
Estimated total cost*	**$360**	**$600**	**$720**
*Assumes starting with no books in the classroom			

Figure 15–5. Single-Title Classroom Library, Kindergarten

Single-Title Classroom Library, Grade 1			
LEVEL	STARTER	BASIC	EXPANDED
A	10	20	30
B	10	20	30
C	15	30	45
D	15	30	45
E	15	30	45
F	15	30	45
G	20	40	60
H	20	40	60
I	20	40	60
J	15	30	45
K	10	20	30
Total Number of Titles	**165 titles**	**330 titles**	**495 titles**
Estimated total cost*	**$670**	**$1,340**	**$2,010**
*Assumes starting with no books in the classroom			

Figure 15–6. Single-Title Classroom Library, Grade 1

Single-Title Classroom Library, Grade 2			
Level	**Starter**	**Basic**	**Expanded**
D	10	20	30
E	10	20	30
F	10	20	30
G	15	30	45
H	15	30	45
I	20	40	60
J	20	40	60
K	20	40	60
L	20	40	60
M	20	40	60
N	10	20	30
O	10	20	30
Total Number of Titles	**180 titles**	**360 titles**	**540 titles**
Estimated total cost*	**$800**	**$1,600**	**$2,400**

*Assumes starting with no books in the classroom

Figure 15–7. Single-Title Classroom Library, Grade 2

Single-Title Classroom Library, Grade 3			
Level	**Starter**	**Basic**	**Expanded**
I	10	20	30
J	10	20	30
K	10	20	30
L	15	30	45
M	15	30	45
N	20	40	60
O	20	40	60
P	20	40	60
Q	15	30	45
R	15	30	45
Total Number of Titles	**150 titles**	**300 titles**	**450 titles**
Estimated total cost*	**$730**	**$1,460**	**$2,190**

*Assumes starting with no books in the classroom

Figure 15–8. Single-Title Classroom Library, Grade 3

Single-Title Classroom Library, Grade 4			
LEVEL	STARTER	BASIC	EXPANDED
K	10	20	30
L	10	20	30
M	10	20	30
N	15	30	45
O	15	30	45
P	20	40	60
Q	20	40	60
R	20	40	60
S	15	30	45
T	15	30	45
Total Number of Titles	150 titles	300 titles	450 titles
Estimated total cost*	$750	$1,500	$2,250

*Assumes starting with no books in the classroom

Figure 15–9.   Single-Title Classroom Library, Grade 4

Single-Title Classroom Library, Grade 5			
LEVEL	STARTER	BASIC	EXPANDED
O	10	20	30
P	10	20	30
Q	10	20	30
R	15	30	45
S	15	30	45
T	20	40	60
U	20	40	60
V	20	40	60
W	15	30	45
X	15	30	45
Total Number of Titles	150 titles	300 titles	450 titles
Estimated total cost*	$750	$1,500	$2,250

*Assumes starting with no books in the classroom

Figure 15–10.   Single-Title Classroom Library, Grade 5

Single-Title Classroom Library, Grade 6, 7, 8			
LEVEL	STARTER	BASIC	EXPANDED
P	10	20	30
Q	10	20	30
R	10	20	30
S	15	30	45
T	15	30	45
U	15	30	45
V	20	40	60
W	20	40	60
X	20	40	60
Y	15	30	45
Total Number of Titles	**150 titles**	**300 titles**	**450 titles**
Estimated total cost*	**$750**	**$1,500**	**$2,250**

*Assumes starting with no books in the classroom

Figure 15–11.   *Single-Title Classroom Library, Grade 6, 7, 8*

CHAPTER SIXTEEN

THE CLASSROOM COLLECTION FOR GUIDED READING

Having a collection of leveled books is essential for effective teaching in guided reading. Your goal is to help readers expand their strategies and apply them to increasingly challenging texts. For the experience to have positive instructional and emotional value, difficulty must increase consistently but gradually. Just think what it would be like to select books from shelves of hundreds with no guide as to the approximate level of challenge they provide. Therefore, you will need access to a good leveled book collection, with multiple copies of titles, to support your teaching in guided reading.

The leveled collection makes it possible to:

- Quickly survey the choices available to you.

- Narrow your choices to those students are most likely to be able to read successfully.

- Keep books in order for efficient access.

- Have a concrete and visible way to monitor students' reading progress.

The guidance in this chapter is directed to the individual teacher in a single classroom. As soon as you can, however, you'll want to begin sharing a book collection with other teachers across the grades. If many or most of the staff at a grade level or in several grades are using books for guided reading, you will want to create a school bookroom, as described in Chapter 17. The school bookroom is the most economical option and provides the greatest variety of texts to meet students' needs.

Organization of the Leveled Collection in a Classroom

The leveled collection is a tool for the teacher. Effective organization of these books can save valuable time during the instructional day as well as planning time.

Location

First, think about a good location for your leveled books. Students will not be choosing these books on their own, so find a location that is very convenient for you—perhaps a shelf close to your reading table or desk, so that as you think about students' reading and go over your records, you'll have easy access to the books.

You can set up a small rolling office cart, or rolling cart with two or three shelves. You can organize all the supplies you need for guided reading. The cart holds your clipboard with student records, a dry-erase whiteboard, markers, a Magnadoodle, a tray of magnetic letters, stick-on notes, writing pads, and multiple copies of the books you've selected for students to read next. If students are reading longer books, they will keep those in their own book boxes until they are finished, but you will still have one book for yourself on the cart. You can roll this cart over to your storage place when you are returning books and selecting new ones.

Storage and Retrieval

You can use plastic tubs or boxes similar to those recommended for your classroom library, or you may want to use shoe boxes or magazine boxes. You can also cut down large cereal boxes and cover them with colored paper. These boxes can be stored on bookshelves; it will help if you can see titles easily without pulling out each box. A complicated index isn't necessary; simply scan what's available when you're selecting books.

Multiple Copies

You will need multiple copies of each title, which should be kept together to increase efficiency and reduce wear and tear. For thin books, elastic bands work well. Another technique is to put multiple copies of individual titles in gallon-size resealable plastic storage bags. Don't label the bags—the titles will be visible—and you'll be able to reuse them as needed.

Labeling and Arrangement

Label the boxes with the letter representing the level (see Figure 16–1). Also, place the level letter in an unobtrusive place on the book, perhaps on the back cover, or inside the back cover as a quick reference when you are returning books to your storage area.

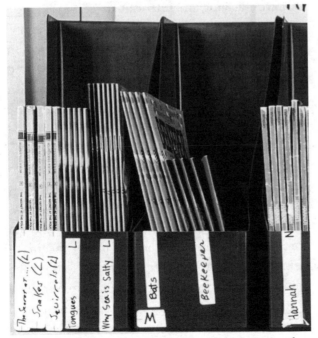

Figure 16–1. Labeled Boxes Containing Multiple Copies of Each Title

Arrange the boxes along the shelf in order of level. As you build the collection, you will identify the levels where you need the most books and you can add more storage units.

Within each box, arrange books alphabetically by title or author. You'll want a variety of titles at each level. If you have an adequate collection, no one student will read every book at the level, and you will also be using short stories and articles.

Connections Between the Classroom Guided Reading Collection and the Classroom Library

There will be some overlap between your leveled collection and your classroom library because you would not want to reserve all the good books for guided reading. For the most part, however, students will not have read a text you choose for them for a guided reading lesson because it will be at a slightly higher level than the books they can read independently. If, on occasion, a student says, "I read this," he probably will not have done so with the same kind of teaching support you can provide and there will be more learning through rereading and discussing the book with others. Tell students that when you reread a book, you notice things you didn't notice the first time. This should not happen too often, of course, or reading will not be interesting.

Getting Started

For grades K and 1, many of the leveled books in browsing boxes will be the same books children have read in guided reading groups, but you will also want to include some new books on slightly lower levels that children have not previously read.

During the transitions in grade two, you will want to use some browsing boxes, but also provide many more books in categories that children can read for themselves.

For grades three and up, it will be important to have differences between the books you use for guided reading and those for independent reading.

Select titles for your guided reading collection first, before you create your classroom library for independent reading, and try to avoid having the same titles in both collections. A little overlap is not a serious problem, but you wouldn't want them to be almost identical.

Carefully choose excellent titles at each level, paying attention to variety—you want fiction and nonfiction in a range of genres. You'll also want a number of short story collections, because short reads are good opportunities to develop students' processing strategies. They can then apply their learning to longer texts that they read independently.

How Many Books Do You Need?

Discovering just how many books you need for guided reading is a matter of trial and error. The number relates to your class size, the reading levels of your students, and how many guided reading groups you have.

Suggested here are the approximate levels, titles, numbers of copies, and cost for a basic and expanded classroom collection. Remember that your first step is to inventory the books you already have. For example, you may already have three or four copies of a title. If you are building a collection with a colleague, you may be able to assemble five or six copies between you. You can then purchase a few more to make the basic collection.

We have suggested quantities of books by level, but you will want to adjust these recommendations based on your assessment of the students in your class. Also, things change over a period of years. In schools where teachers, kindergarten through the upper grades, have been delivering a dynamic literacy program for several years, the average *level* of reading shifts over time. The point of guided reading is not to "push" students beyond their interests or age-appropriate topics and

themes; nevertheless, in schools that have used guided reading for a number of years, benchmark testing shows more students reading at or above grade level (Scharer, Williams, and Pinnell 2001). This increase is especially evident in schools where a large number of students are reading well below grade level when the language and literacy framework, which includes guided reading, is first implemented.

The bottom line: it's not economically feasible to have multiple copies of leveled books that are outside your grade's usual range of reading. You can borrow titles from teachers at other grades to meet the needs of your students who read substantially (more than one year) below grade level or who are very advanced. The reading groups created for these students will be smaller and you won't need as many copies.

Basic and Expanded Collections of Leveled Books for Grade K

Most kindergarten children are emergent readers who are just beginning to explore print. They need a great deal of experience reading very easy books that are engaging and interesting.

Kindergarten teachers typically "phase in" guided reading as they notice groups of children who are closely attending to print during shared reading, know some letters and related sounds, and recognize a few high-frequency words.

The number of books needed for guided reading in kindergarten depends on how many children are ready to work in a small group and to read a book for themselves. Based on continuous assessment of their students' understandings about print, alphabet letters, writing, and so forth, kindergarten teachers typically begin to bring together small groups of readers about the middle of the school year. Some children may be ready for group reading earlier and some much later. By the end of the year, however, we would expect all the children in kindergarten to be able to read levels A, B, or C with some teacher support. Children do not need to know all the letters of the alphabet or all the sounds, but before they are involved in guided reading they should have a good grounding in activities with high group support, such as shared reading and interactive writing, and they should have some understandings of how print works.

For kindergarten, we suggest a range of levels available from A to E, though a few children will be reading beyond these levels. You will not need to fully provide leveled books for unusually advanced readers because you can simply borrow them from other teachers. Movement up levels

will not be the only goal for advanced readers; discussion and opportunities for writing about reading will be even more important.

In the charts presented in Figures 16–2 through 16–5, we provide recommendations for a basic collection and an expanded collection of guided reading books for kindergarten. A basic collection provides the minimal resources needed to support a guided reading program—purchase this collection to begin your program. Estimates for the number of books have been based on a class of twenty-five children; two half-day kindergarten classes need the same number of books as

Basic Collection with Four Copies of Each Title, Kindergarten			
LEVEL	NUMBER OF TITLES EACH LEVEL	NUMBER OF BOOKS	ESTIMATED COST @ $4.00 PER BOOK
A	10	40	$160
B	15	60	$240
C	15	60	$240
D	5	20	$80
E	5	20	$80
TOTALS	**50**	**200**	**$800**

Figure 16–2. *Basic Collection with Four Copies of Each Title, Kindergarten*

Basic Collection with Six Copies of Each Title, Kindergarten			
LEVEL	NUMBER OF TITLES EACH LEVEL	NUMBER OF BOOKS	ESTIMATED COST @ $4.00 PER BOOK
A	10	60	$240
B	15	90	$360
C	15	90	$360
D	5	30	$120
E	5	30	$120
TOTALS	**50**	**300**	**$1,200**

Figure 16–3. *Basic Collection with Six Copies of Each Title, Kindergarten*

one full-time class, but if you let children take books home, you need a few extra books. If you have a limited amount of money to spend, just purchase a few of the titles each year, and build the collection over time. As illustrated in the figures, you might want to purchase more titles at the earlier levels and fewer titles at higher levels. We have provided information on collections with four copies or six copies of each title.

You will probably be working with groups of three to six children on any given level. Smaller groups of three or four are more effective with kindergartners who are just beginning to read for

themselves because you need to observe behaviors very closely and prompt them to support their early reading strategies (for example, pointing to assist one-to-one matching). Guided reading sessions will be quite brief; you may have two or more groups on the same level.

You will want to take into account typical reading patterns across your group of children. For example, if a large number of children typically enter your kindergarten with rich literacy experiences, you'll still need copies of books at level A, but children may move quickly to B, C, and even D levels.

Expanded Collection with Four Copies of Each Title, Kindergarten

LEVEL	NUMBER OF TITLES EACH LEVEL	NUMBER OF BOOKS	ESTIMATED COST @ $4.00 PER BOOK
A	20	80	$320
B	20	80	$320
C	20	80	$320
D	5	20	$80
E	5	20	$80
TOTALS	70	280	$1,120

Figure 16–4.   Expanded Collection with Four Copies of Each Title, Kindergarten

Expanded Collection with Six Copies of Each Title, Kindergarten

LEVEL	NUMBER OF TITLES EACH LEVEL	NUMBER OF BOOKS	ESTIMATED COST @ $4.00 PER BOOK
A	20	120	$480
B	20	120	$480
C	20	120	$480
D	5	30	$120
E	5	30	$120
TOTALS	70	420	$1,680

Figure 16–5.   Expanded Collection with Six Copies of Each Title, Kindergarten

It is not necessary *or even desirable* to push for higher text levels for those young readers. By processing easy texts they can soundly establish foundational understandings of how words "work" and also learn that reading is purposeful and enjoyable.

If you have a large number of children who need many first experiences with simple books, you'll want a large number of titles at levels A and B, so that your students can firm up early behaviors such as word-by-word matching and moving left to right. These early books are also helpful in establishing a core reading vocabulary of high-frequency words, and they make it possible for inexperienced children to notice critical aspects of words, such as letter-sound relationships and spelling patterns. Thus, you'll need to fine-tune our example not only in terms of the numbers of children you have but also in terms of their needs. Books on levels A and B can also be used for shared reading, with children having their own copies, a teaching approach sometimes used as a transition to guided reading. Remember that as teaching becomes more effective, needs for books at higher levels will increase.

Basic and Expanded Collections of Leveled Books for Grade 1

Guided reading is a key instructional context for grade 1. The easiest texts, levels A and B, are needed because some children will be emergent readers. Most will move quickly to the more complex texts at levels C, D, E, and F.

At first grade, we estimate that you will need a span of at least eleven levels (A through K). You will have some children reading beyond level K, but for that small group you can borrow books to enrich their experience. The bulk of reading for first grade, typically, is at levels C through H or I. A good standard is to have all first graders reading independently at level I by the end of the year. The charts presented in Figures 16–6 through 16–9 provide an estimate of the number and costs of guided reading books for a basic collection and an expanded collection, with four or six copies of each title, for the first grade. Make adjustments for the average reading levels of children as they enter reading, at midyear, and at the end of the year.

If children enter first grade with very little experience with print, you will need more books at level A or B; however, with daily instruction and strong teaching to establish early behaviors and concepts, they will move quickly to levels C and D. For children who are having difficulty reading levels A and B, the school will need to provide supplementary one-to-one tutoring, such as Reading Recovery or small group supplementary support, in addition to daily guided reading in the classroom. Typically, children make rapid progress in the tutorial program, so communication about the child's instructional reading level is essential between the Reading Recovery teacher and the classroom teacher so that classroom groupings can be readjusted to new levels. The same kind of communication is needed between the teacher who provides small group support and the classroom teachers.

Basic and Expanded Collections of Leveled Books for Grade 2

The range of reading experience will be even wider in grade 2. Some children will need to participate in guided reading every day. They need to begin at levels they can read with good teaching support because only by successful processing can they learn how to use the strategic actions they need to read more difficult texts.

The reading for most second graders will be from about levels H through M or N, with some children reading well beyond those levels. You will want to check children's understanding of these advanced texts if they show they can read the words. There may be concepts and ideas in the texts that are beyond their present understandings. Also, longer texts may become tedious for young children to plow through. In these cases, children are unlikely to find reading meaningful and enjoyable even if they are advanced in their skills.

Being able to read level L or M with fluency and understanding is a good standard for independent reading at the end of second grade. You may have some second graders who require intensive teaching at lower levels (perhaps D, E, and F). You will want to meet with those children in guided reading groups every day, and they will likely need some additional help.

As children read longer chapter books, they will spend more time in silent, independent reading. A guided reading lesson will involve introducing the book and asking children to read a unified part of it—not necessarily a chapter but simply a manageable amount of text that will form the basis for later discussion. Children can read together at the same location or at their own desks and come together again to talk about the parts that they have read. It will be necessary to allocate time for them to perform this individual reading. We estimate that fewer titles will be needed at levels N and O, but there may well be a group of children who are more advanced and will like to read books at that level. Make adjustments for the average reading levels of children as they enter reading, at midyear, and at the end of the year.

In the charts presented in Figures 16–10 through 16–13, we provide an example of a basic collection and a expanded collection, with four or six copies of each title, for second grade.

Basic and Expanded Collections of Leveled Books for Grade 3

In third grade, the variety of student reading material greatly increases. Students will be reading chapter books and many kinds of informational books. You will want to include biographies and informational texts in your collection and provide explicit teaching on how they are organized. Fiction will expand to include historical fiction and some simple fantasy. Students will be building reading stamina by taking on longer chapter books.

Third grade is also a time when students will become very much aware of their own tastes and interests as readers. They will gravitate to realistic fiction, and it is good for them to read a wide range of it. They like series books such as the *Kids of Polk Street School* series (Giff) and the *Ramona* series (Cleary). With your encouragement and instructional support, they can explore a wider range of genres. Guided reading is the place where they can meet new fiction and nonfiction genres and learn to enjoy them. You'll also want to promote a great deal of independent reading along with your guided reading lessons.

In third grade, you will need to cover a span of at least eight levels, K through R, with the largest number of titles needed at levels N, O, and P. Figures 16–14 and 16–15 suggest levels, number of titles, and estimated cost for basic collections with six and eight copies of each title. An expanded collection concentrates on the same span of levels, with more titles per level. Number of books and estimated cost for an expanded collection with six copies and eight copies are shown in Figures 16–16 and 16–17.

Basic and Expanded Collections of Leveled Books for Grade 4

Like third graders, fourth graders will tend to select mostly realistic fiction, but instructional support in guided reading can help them continue to explore other genres as well. At this age the peer group is becoming much more important; for independent reading, they will enjoy trading books with friends and forming book clubs. The *Ramona* series continues to be popular, as well as series like *Jenny Archer* and the *Boxcar Children*. Students enjoy informational books and "blended" genres like the *Magic School Bus* series. They enjoy history from a personal point of view, as in the *If You Lived in the Time of* series, as well as historical fiction, such as Jean Fritz's *The Cabin Faced West* or Mildred Taylor's *Mississippi Bridge*. Through guided reading, you can help them gain deeper understanding of themselves and others by reading about times, places, and people distant from themselves.

For a typical fourth-grade classroom, you will need a span of eight levels, N through U; most students will be reading at levels Q, R, and S. Figures 16–18 and 16–19 present suggested levels, number of titles, and estimated cost for basic collections with six and eight copies of each title. Numbers of books and estimated costs for an expanded collection with six copies and eight copies are shown in Figures 16–20 and 16–21.

Basic and Expanded Collections of Leveled Books for Grade 5

Through reading, fifth graders explore important and serious social issues such as war, prejudice, and poverty (for example, Yoshiko Uchida's *Journey to Topaz* or Lois Lowry's *Number the Stars*). As they approach teenage years, they may challenge their parents' authority and find books about growing up very appealing. They enjoy a wide range of biography as well as historical fiction, such as Katherine Paterson's *Lyddie*, and use it to learn about the past. Since students are expected to learn content by reading, you will want to be sure to include a range of informational books to help them learn about organizational features as well as to use reference tools and interpret graphic features.

For a typical fifth-grade classroom, you will need a span of eight levels, Q through X; most students will be reading at levels T, U, and V. Figures 16–22 and 16–23 present suggested levels, number of titles, and estimated cost for basic collections with six and eight copies of each title. Number of books and estimated cost for an expanded collection with six copies and eight copies are shown in Figures 16–24 and 16–25.

Basic and Expanded Collections of Leveled Books for Grade 6, 7, 8

In sixth grade, students are poised to enter adolescence. Their bodies are changing, although there is wide variation in physical development. They are searching for identity and a sense of self, and use reading as a way to broaden understanding of life.

Books like Karen Hesse's *Out of the Dust*, Cynthia Voigt's *Dicey's Song*, Cynthia Rylant's *Missing May*, and Mildred Taylor's *Roll of Thunder, Hear My Cry* capture their attention because they show early adolescents meeting and dealing with tragedy and hardship. Sixth and seventh graders also explore complex works of fantasy, often in series by authors such as Madeline L'Engle, Susan Cooper, and Ursula Le Guin and Orson Scott Card. Many students are ready to explore mature themes such as sexuality or abuse.

Figures 16–26 and 16–27 suggest levels, number of titles, and estimated cost for basic collections with six and eight copies of each title. Number of books and estimated cost for an expanded collection with six copies and eight copies are shown in Figures 16–28 and 16–29.

Sharing and Expanding Classroom Book Collections

At first glance it may seem impossible to bring together the kind of collection you need to support guided reading in your classroom, but the goal is reachable in time. Simply purchase some books each year, and build the collection over time. It is not even desirable to acquire all of the books at once, because you need to get to know the books over time and to make decisions based on the needs of the children. The approach is highly cost effective because the collection is reusable for many years, only requiring some replacement books on occasion.

First, take an inventory of your existing books to see what you already have at the levels you need. Don't forget that the stories in your basal readers, if appropriate for guided reading, can be leveled and used. With the explosion of reading material in the last few years, you may already have a pretty good range of books; the problem will be multiple copies. If another teacher in your building is interested in guided reading, work out an informal sharing arrangement. With some preliminary investigation and organization, you can work together to get started.

The development of an effective book collection is an ongoing professional responsibility and undertaking, one that offers strong support for your teaching and your students' learning. For this reason, it's a goal well worth achieving.

Making the Most of Limited Resources

The single-classroom leveled collection isn't the most cost-effective way to go. Many of the sets will be sitting unused because they either have already been read or won't be read until later in the year. Shared resources are always more economical. Even sharing between two or three classrooms greatly reduces the cost of a collection and increases its variety. For example, there's no need for both fifth-grade classrooms in your school to have eight copies of Avi's *Blue Heron*, a book that would take a group of fifth graders about a week to read. The multiple copies can move back and forth between the classrooms. Even if you place a single copy in the book rack for independent reading in each classroom, you have purchased ten copies instead of sixteen and saved approximately $30.00, which is enough to buy seven copies of another title. Sharing a leveled collection takes a little more cooperation, but the payoff is great.

Final Thoughts

Get to know the books slowly as you acquire them and explore them with students. You will discover those that appeal to students and offer a great deal to learn, and you can increase the number of copies you have of those texts. Also, you'll always want to add new books to the collection to keep your own teaching interesting and fresh. Adjust your collection as you think about the number of students in your classes, their present reading levels, and their predicted progress over the year.

The leveled collection is used primarily to support guided reading, but remember that you can always draw from this resource to create a special basket of books for students who need more guidance in finding "just right" books for their independent reading, at school or at home. In addition, students may have read good books in guided reading that they will explore more deeply in a literature discussion group.

Suggestions for Professional Development: Evaluating the Classroom Leveled Collection

1. Evaluate and organize your classroom collection so that you can get started. Begin by collecting in one place all of the books you have in the classroom that you think would be appropriate for guided reading.

2. Using the lists in this book and/or your own analysis (as guided by the prototypes in Chapters 5, 6, and 7), write the guided reading levels on the inside cover of each book or on a sticker on the front or back.

3. Organize the books in labeled boxes or baskets.

4. Locate a good place in your classroom for your collection. The books should be easily accessible to you but not to the students.

5. Consult the charts in this book and make some judgments about the levels you need most.

6. Now, look at your collection. The gaps will be obvious. Make a list of the levels where you need to add titles.

7. Keep this list handy so that you can add to it constantly. When you have the opportunity to order books, you will be ready! Also, you can use books clubs strategically to add quality to your collection.

8. Look through the lists on the website *fountasandpinnellleveledbooks.com* or the printed list, *Leveled Book List* (Fountas and Pinnell 2006) and identify some titles you either have read at these levels or that others have recommended. Add specific titles to your list.

Basic Collection with Four Copies of Each Title, Grade 1			
LEVEL	NUMBER OF TITLES EACH LEVEL	NUMBER OF BOOKS	ESTIMATED COST @ $4.00 PER BOOK A–J AND $5.00 PER BOOK K–Z
A	5	20	$80
B	5	20	$80
C	6	24	$96
D	6	24	$96
E	6	24	$96
F	6	24	$96
G	6	24	$96
H	6	24	$96
I	6	24	$96
J	5	20	$80
K	5	20	$100
TOTALS	62	248	$1,012

Figure 16–6. *Example of a Basic Collection for First-Grade Classroom with Four Copies of Each Title*

Basic Collection with Six Copies of Each Title, Grade 1			
LEVEL	NUMBER OF TITLES EACH LEVEL	NUMBER OF BOOKS	ESTIMATED COST @ $4.00 PER BOOK A–J AND $5.00 PER BOOK K–Z
A	5	30	$120
B	5	30	$120
C	6	36	$144
D	6	36	$144
E	6	36	$144
F	6	36	$144
G	6	36	$144
H	6	36	$144
I	6	36	$144
J	5	30	$120
K	5	30	$150
TOTALS	62	372	$1,518

Figure 16–7. *Example of a Basic Collection for First-Grade Classroom with Six Copies of Each Title*

Expanded Collection with Four Copies of Each Title, Grade 1			
LEVEL	NUMBER OF TITLES EACH LEVEL	NUMBER OF BOOKS	ESTIMATED COST @ $4.00 PER BOOK A–J AND $5.00 PER BOOK K–Z
A	8	32	$128
B	8	32	$128
C	10	40	$160
D	10	40	$160
E	10	40	$160
F	10	40	$160
G	10	40	$160
H	10	40	$160
I	10	40	$160
J	8	32	$128
K	5	20	$100
TOTALS	99	396	$1,604

Figure 16–8. Example of an Expanded Collection for First-Grade Classroom with Four Copies of Each Title

Expanded Collection with Six Copies of Each Title, Grade 1			
LEVEL	NUMBER OF TITLES EACH LEVEL	NUMBER OF BOOKS	ESTIMATED COST @ $4.00 PER BOOK A–J AND $5.00 PER BOOK K–Z
A	8	48	$192
B	8	48	$192
C	10	60	$240
D	10	60	$240
E	10	60	$240
F	10	60	$240
G	10	60	$240
H	10	60	$240
I	10	60	$240
J	8	48	$192
K	5	30	$150
TOTALS	99	594	$2,406

Figure 16–9.   Example of an Expanded Collection for First-Grade Classroom with Six Copies of Each Title

Basic Collection with Four Copies of Each Title, Grade 2			
LEVEL	NUMBER OF TITLES EACH LEVEL	NUMBER OF BOOKS	ESTIMATED COST @ $4.00[A–J] & $5.00 [K+]
E	5	20	$80
F	5	20	$80
G	5	20	$80
H	5	20	$80
I	8	32	$128
J	8	32	$128
K	8	32	$160
L	8	32	$160
M	5	20	$100
N	5	20	$100
O	5	20	$100
TOTALS	67	268	$1,196

Figure 16–10. Example of a Basic Collection for Second-Grade Classroom with Four Copies of Each Title

Basic Collection with Six Copies of Each Title, Grade 2			
LEVEL	NUMBER OF TITLES EACH LEVEL	NUMBER OF BOOKS	ESTIMATED COST @ $4.00[A–J] & $5.00 [K+]
E	5	30	$120
F	5	30	$120
G	5	30	$120
H	5	30	$120
I	8	48	$192
J	8	48	$192
K	8	48	$240
L	8	48	$240
M	5	30	$150
N	5	30	$150
O	5	30	$150
TOTALS	67	402	$1,794

Figure 16–11. Example of a Basic Collection for Second-Grade Classroom with Six Copies of Each Title

Expanded Collection with Four Copies of Each Title, Grade 2			
LEVEL	NUMBER OF TITLES EACH LEVEL	NUMBER OF BOOKS	ESTIMATED COST @ $4.00[A–J] & $5.00 [K+]
E	5	20	$80
F	5	20	$80
G	5	20	$80
H	5	20	$80
I	8	32	$128
J	8	32	$128
K	8	32	$160
L	8	32	$160
M	5	20	$100
N	5	20	$100
O	5	20	$100
TOTALS	67	268	$1,196

Figure 16–12. *Example of an Expanded Collection for Second-Grade Classroom with Four Copies of Each Title*

Expanded Collection with Six Copies of Each Title, Grade 2			
LEVEL	NUMBER OF TITLES EACH LEVEL	NUMBER OF BOOKS	ESTIMATED COST @ $5.00 PER BOOK
K	5	30	$150
L	5	30	$150
M	10	60	$300
N	10	60	$300
O	10	60	$300
P	10	60	$300
Q	5	60	$300
R	5	30	$150
TOTALS	65	390	$1,950

Figure 16–13. *Example of an Expanded Collection for Second-Grade Classroom with Six Copies of Each Title*

Basic Collection with Six Copies of Each Title, Grade 3			
LEVEL	NUMBER OF TITLES EACH LEVEL	NUMBER OF BOOKS	ESTIMATED COST @ $5.00 PER BOOK
K	5	30	$150
L	5	30	$150
M	5	30	$150
N	8	48	$240
O	8	48	$240
P	8	48	$240
Q	5	30	$150
R	5	30	$150
TOTALS	**49**	**294**	**$1,470**

Figure 16–14. *Example of a Basic Collection for Third-Grade Classroom with Six Copies of Each Title*

Basic Collection with Eight Copies of Each Title, Grade 3			
LEVEL	NUMBER OF TITLES EACH LEVEL	NUMBER OF BOOKS	ESTIMATED COST @ $5.00 PER BOOK
K	5	40	$200
L	5	40	$200
M	5	40	$200
N	8	64	$320
O	8	64	$320
P	8	64	$320
Q	5	40	$200
R	5	40	$200
TOTALS	**49**	**392**	**$1,960**

Figure 16–15. *Example of a Basic Collection for Third-Grade Classroom with Eight Copies of Each Title*

\multicolumn{4}{c}{**Expanded Collection with Six Copies of Each Title, Grade 3**}			
LEVEL	*NUMBER OF TITLES EACH LEVEL*	*NUMBER OF BOOKS*	*ESTIMATED COST @ $5.00 PER BOOK*
K	5	30	$150
L	5	30	$150
M	10	60	$300
N	10	60	$300
O	10	60	$300
P	10	60	$300
Q	10	60	$300
R	5	30	$150
TOTALS	**65**	**390**	**$1,950**

Figure 16–16. *Example of an Expanded Collection for Third-Grade Classroom with Six Copies of Each Title*

\multicolumn{4}{c}{**Expanded Collection with Eight Copies of Each Title, Grade 3**}			
LEVEL	*NUMBER OF TITLES EACH LEVEL*	*NUMBER OF BOOKS*	*ESTIMATED COST @ $5.00 PER BOOK*
K	5	40	$200
L	5	40	$200
M	10	80	$400
N	10	80	$400
O	10	80	$400
P	10	80	$400
Q	10	80	$400
R	5	40	$200
TOTALS	**65**	**520**	**$2,600**

Figure 16–17. *Example of an Expanded Collection for Third-Grade Classroom with Eight Copies of Each Title*

Basic Collection with Six Copies of Each Title, Grade 4			
LEVEL	NUMBER OF TITLES EACH LEVEL	NUMBER OF BOOKS	ESTIMATED COST @ $5.00 PER BOOK
N	5	30	$150
O	5	30	$150
P	5	30	$150
Q	8	48	$240
R	8	48	$240
S	8	48	$240
T	5	30	$150
U	5	30	$150
TOTALS	49	294	$1,470

Figure 16–18.   Example of a Basic Collection for Fourth-Grade Classroom with Six Copies of Each Title

Basic Collection with Eight Copies of Each Title, Grade 4			
LEVEL	NUMBER OF TITLES EACH LEVEL	NUMBER OF BOOKS	ESTIMATED COST @ $5.00 PER BOOK
N	5	40	$200
O	5	40	$200
P	5	40	$200
Q	8	64	$320
R	8	64	$320
S	8	64	$320
T	5	40	$200
U	5	40	$200
TOTALS	49	392	$1,960

Figure 16–19.   Example of a Basic Collection for Fourth-Grade Classroom with Eight Copies of Each Title

Expanded Collection with Six Copies of Each Title, Grade 4			
LEVEL	NUMBER OF TITLES EACH LEVEL	NUMBER OF BOOKS	ESTIMATED COST @ $5.00 PER BOOK
N	5	30	$150
O	5	30	$150
P	10	60	$300
Q	10	60	$300
R	10	60	$300
S	10	60	$300
T	10	60	$300
U	5	30	$150
TOTALS	65	390	$1,950

Figure 16–20. Example of an Expanded Collection for Fourth-Grade Classroom with Six Copies of Each Title

Expanded Collection with Eight Copies of Each Title, Grade 4			
LEVEL	NUMBER OF TITLES EACH LEVEL	NUMBER OF BOOKS	ESTIMATED COST @ $5.00 PER BOOK
N	5	40	$200
O	5	40	$200
P	10	80	$400
Q	10	80	$400
R	10	80	$400
S	10	80	$400
T	10	80	$400
U	5	40	$200
TOTALS	65	520	$2,600

Figure 16–21. Example of an Expanded Collection for Fourth-Grade Classroom with Eight Copies of Each Title

Basic Collection with Six Copies of Each Title, Grade 5			
LEVEL	NUMBER OF TITLES EACH LEVEL	NUMBER OF BOOKS	ESTIMATED COST @ $5.00 PER BOOK
Q	5	30	$150
R	5	30	$150
S	5	30	$150
T	8	48	$240
U	8	48	$240
V	8	48	$240
W	5	30	$150
X	5	30	$150
TOTALS	49	294	$1,470

Figure 16–22. Example of a Basic Collection for Fifth-Grade Classroom with Six Copies of Each Title

Basic Collection with Eight Copies of Each Title, Grade 5			
LEVEL	NUMBER OF TITLES EACH LEVEL	NUMBER OF BOOKS	ESTIMATED COST @ $5.00 PER BOOK
Q	5	40	$200
R	5	40	$200
S	5	40	$200
T	8	64	$320
U	8	64	$320
V	8	64	$320
W	5	40	$200
X	5	40	$200
TOTALS	49	392	$1,960

Figure 16–23. Example of a Basic Collection for Fifth-Grade Classroom with Eight Copies of Each Title

Expanded Collection with Six Copies of Each Title, Grade 5			
LEVEL	NUMBER OF TITLES EACH LEVEL	NUMBER OF BOOKS	ESTIMATED COST @ $5.00 PER BOOK
Q	5	30	$150
R	5	30	$150
S	10	60	$300
T	10	60	$300
U	10	60	$300
V	10	60	$300
W	10	60	$300
X	5	30	$150
TOTALS	65	390	$1,950

Figure 16–24. Example of an Expanded Collection for Fifth-Grade Classroom with Six Copies of Each Title

Expanded Collection with Eight Copies of Each Title, Grade 5			
LEVEL	NUMBER OF TITLES EACH LEVEL	NUMBER OF BOOKS	ESTIMATED COST @ $5.00 PER BOOK
Q	5	40	$200
R	5	40	$200
S	10	80	$400
T	10	80	$400
U	10	80	$400
V	10	80	$400
W	10	80	$400
X	5	40	$200
TOTALS	65	520	$2,600

Figure 16–25. Example of an Expanded Collection for Fifth-Grade Classroom with Eight Copies of Each Title

Basic Collection with Six Copies of Each Title, Grades 6, 7, 8			
LEVEL	NUMBER OF TITLES EACH LEVEL	NUMBER OF BOOKS	ESTIMATED COST @ $5.00 PER BOOK
R	5	30	$150
S	5	30	$150
T	5	30	$150
U	8	48	$240
V	8	48	$240
W	8	48	$240
X	5	30	$150
Y	5	30	$150
TOTALS	49	294	$1,470

Figure 16–26. Example of a Basic Collection for Sixth to Eighth-Grade Classrooms with Six Copies of Each Title

Basic Collection with Eight Copies of Each Title, Grades 6, 7, 8			
LEVEL	NUMBER OF TITLES EACH LEVEL	NUMBER OF BOOKS	ESTIMATED COST @ $5.00 PER BOOK
R	5	40	$200
S	5	40	$200
Y	5	40	$200
U	8	64	$320
V	8	64	$320
W	8	64	$320
X	5	40	$200
Y	5	40	$200
TOTALS	49	392	$1,960

Figure 16–27. Example of a Basic Collection for Sixth to Eighth-Grade Classrooms with Eight Copies of Each Title

Expanded Collection with Six Copies of Each Title, Grades 6, 7, 8			
LEVEL	NUMBER OF TITLES EACH LEVEL	NUMBER OF BOOKS	ESTIMATED COST @ $5.00 PER BOOK
R	5	30	$150
S	5	30	$150
T	10	60	$300
U	10	60	$300
V	10	60	$300
W	10	60	$300
X	10	60	$300
Y	5	30	$150
TOTALS	65	390	$1,950

Figure 16–28. *Example of an Expanded Collection for Sixth to Eighth-Grade Classrooms with Six Copies of Each Title*

Expanded Collection with Eight Copies of Each Title, Grades 6, 7, 8			
LEVEL	NUMBER OF TITLES EACH LEVEL	NUMBER OF BOOKS	ESTIMATED COST @ $5.00 PER BOOK
R	5	40	$200
S	5	40	$200
T	10	80	$400
U	10	80	$400
V	10	80	$400
W	10	80	$400
X	10	80	$400
Y	5	40	$200
TOTALS	65	520	$2,600

Figure 16–29. *Example of an Expanded Collection for Sixth to Eighth-Grade Classrooms with Eight Copies of Each Title*

CHAPTER SEVENTEEN

CREATING AND USING A SCHOOL BOOKROOM

While the cost and time entailed in creating a leveled book collection may seem daunting, we can offer a strategic tip that will make all the difference: work with your colleagues! The most efficient and cost-effective system for acquiring and using a collection involves a group of colleagues sharing books that are housed in a school bookroom or closet. In this chapter, we describe ways that you and your colleagues, working together, can create a valuable resource for the children in your school.

Planning a school bookroom will undoubtedly mean purchasing a large number of books; however, you will want to approach the task strategically and acquire the books over time. Acquiring a guided reading collection depends on the:

■ Number of classrooms and number of children in the school.

■ Number of teachers sharing the collection.

■ Typical reading levels for the majority of children at each grade level at different points in time.

■ Books you already have.

■ Financial resources available from year to year.

You may not have all the answers immediately; accordingly, we do not advise buying the guided reading collection in its entirety the first year. Also, if you have a limited amount of money to spend, you can limit your purchases to one-fourth or one-third of the titles the first year, or start with a sample of lower levels and build the collection over time.

A school bookroom is, of course, a room in which multiple copies of leveled books are arranged from levels A through Z. But it is much more than that. It is a place where you and your colleagues can share insights about the supports and challenges in texts, revise and enrich the text support for your guided reading instruction, discuss your common vision for reading progress and standards throughout the grades, and discuss books, authors, and readers.

The bookroom may serve teachers at one, several, or even all grade levels. Given the wide range of levels and materials needed within even one grade, it makes much more economic sense to share a good collection across the grades. If you can find a space in the school to house leveled books, and if you and your colleagues work together, you can create a rich resource for the guided reading program. The gradient of text, with many copies of a large number of titles, is also the foundation for talking about students' reading progress and for planning part of your system of assessment.

Getting Started

As with classroom libraries and classroom leveled collections, you will want to acquire a schoolwide collection gradually. First, gather together all the books for guided reading that you have in the current school bookroom and in classrooms. (Leave the books teachers and students need to support independent reading in classrooms.) You can also check the school library for multiple copies of books that would be useful for guided reading. At first, it may be hard for teachers to take books *out* of their classroom—they've very likely been hard to come by—but a smoothly functioning school bookroom will benefit everyone. Organize the books by level, noting:

- The numbers of titles you have for each level.
- The numbers of copies of each title.

Compare your current supply with the "starter" tables presented later in this chapter. Considering the range of reading levels of students in the school, make some hard decisions about levels where more books are needed and direct any resources toward those purchases.

We have estimated the average cost of a paperback at $4.00 through grade two, and $5.00 from grade three on, but you may be able to acquire them at up to a 20 percent or even higher discount. As you look at the numbers, you will see that it is worth a little trouble to find suppliers who will give you a discount. You are submitting large orders over time, so don't hesitate to ask for good prices. (Chapter 18 provides many suggestions for acquiring free books.)

Location

An important decision to make is where the school bookroom will be located. Space is always at a premium in elementary schools, and your first inclination will be to settle for a closet or some other place no one else wants. Nevertheless, we urge you to compete for the best possible space. You will need ample room for shelves so that your collection can grow.

The bookroom is often where teachers have their most interesting conversations. If you can, locate your books in a central area with good lighting and ventilation. Have some open space in the middle where you can place a table for browsing and reading, sorting and organizing books, and talking about books over lunch or during planning periods.

Books should be placed on shelves that are easily accessible so that teachers can pull out the boxes, look through them, and return them. If books are hard to take out and return, people in a hurry will leave them out of order. A neat, organized room will attract teachers to congregate there and will highlight the value of the collection.

In many schools, teachers have found a way to create a meeting room that combines many functions:

- Meeting together for professional development.
- Coming together to plan and talk.
- Housing the leveled book collection, with procedures for using and returning books.
- Displaying student work.
- Showcasing a professional book collection.
- Housing videotapes, DVDs, CDs, or other professional development support materials.
- Housing curriculum documents and standards documents.

Such a room is highly valuable in creating a professional learning community in your school. Your materials are easily accessible in an attractive and inviting place.

An alternative is to house the leveled book collection in the school library—the shelves are already there—but you'll need a congenial relationship with the school librarian. Since students do not need to use the leveled book collection, it can be in a less accessible part of the library. An added benefit is that teachers monitoring their students on assigned trips to the library can examine and select books from the leveled book collection at the same time.

Organizing and Using the Bookroom

Place all books for each guided reading level in consecutive order (A–Z) so that you will have an instant and concrete picture of reading progress over time. Getting to know these books well is a goal every staff member will achieve over time. You'll find that once you have used them for guided reading over a year or two, just a glance at the title or front cover will summon a mental map of the supports and challenges in the text and you will be able to consider this information in relation to the students you teach.

You may want to place all copies of a title in a labeled magazine box or covered cereal or shoe box. Label the box with title, genre, and level. If books are relatively thin, you may be able to put multiple copies of two or more titles in one box (see Figure 17–1). Place all boxes together by level so that when you look at the shelves, you can instantly find

Figure 17–1. *Labeled Book Boxes*

the levels you need (in the photo in Figure 17–2, notice how the books are arranged so as to be accessible to everyone).

You will also need to develop a way to use the bookroom cooperatively. It is terrific if an instructional assistant or parent volunteer can monitor the bookroom and keep it in order, but that's not always possible. If you don't have extra support, responsibility for overseeing the room can rotate each month. And even if you have help like this, you still want the staff to "own" the room and take care of it. Figure 17–3 shows the guidelines one group of teachers created.

A good system for keeping track of who has which set of books is to give

Figure 17–2. A School Bookroom

Guidelines for Using a School Bookroom

1. When you check books out, please leave a clothespin or place an index card with your name in the box.

2. For grades K–2 teachers: please keep the books for only two weeks and then return them so that others can use them.

3. For grades 3–8 teachers: please keep the books for only three weeks. Be sure to return them so that others can use them.

4. Everyone is responsible for refiling the books returned.

5. Assigned teachers agree to check the room for order the first of each month.

Here is our schedule:

September: Grade 8 teachers [names]

October: Grade 7 teachers [names]

November: Grade 6 teachers [names]

December: Grade 5 teachers [names]

January: Grade 4 teachers [names]

February: Grade 3 teachers [names]

March: Grade 2 teachers [names]

April: Kindergarten and Grade 1 teachers [names]

May: Meeting of all staff to evaluate bookroom use and suggest new titles.

June: Final check and celebration lunch!

Figure 17–3. Guidelines for Using a School Bookroom

each teacher a tub of clothespins with his or her name on them. After taking a set of books to use with students in your classroom, you simply attach a clothespin to the box containing the books. You may also use checkout cards (drop a card with your name on it in the box when you take the books, for example) or write down in a notebook the title of the set you've taken. When you return the books, you retrieve the card or clothespin or mark through the entry in the notebook.

Bookrooms that degenerate into a shambles because no one is responsible for them will seriously undermine your guided reading program. Periodically, meet in the bookroom to evaluate how it's going. Take an inventory of books; replace those that are worn out; determine what levels need new acquisitions.

Coordinating Between the Classroom and the Bookroom

In one school we visited, each teacher had a plastic basket with a handle to help collect and carry books to and from the bookroom. When they returned to their classrooms, the teachers kept the books for guided reading in the basket. They also had a particular spot in the classroom for storing the basket. Over several days, the teachers used the basket to gather the books that had been used in their classrooms and needed to be returned to the book collection. Then, they carried the basket to the bookroom and exchanged the books they had used for new books. In one school, the teachers place the basket with books to return outside the door on Wednesdays, and parent volunteers collect the baskets, refile the books and return the empty baskets to teachers. How long should teachers keep particular titles in their classroom? This is another decision you and your colleagues will need to make. We have found that a return cycle of about two to three weeks seems to work best.

After your students have read and enjoyed a particular title, you might want to keep one or two copies for your browsing box and return the others to the bookroom. One of the reasons we recommend having about eight copies of each book is to enable the classroom teacher to keep one or two in the browsing box for a few weeks. Eventually, all copies will be returned. In well-provisioned classrooms, one or two copies of the more frequently used titles might be available in a personal collection for the teacher. Then, teachers can use these copies to plan book selection and introductions as well as for independent reading.

Advantages of a School Bookroom

While creating a school collection requires more time and a great deal of cooperation, you will find it well worth the time and effort for the following reasons:

- The system is far more economical than individual classroom collections because all levels can be available all of the time, instead of many copies being stored in individual classrooms without availability to others.

- Replacing worn titles and adding new ones is a continual process.

- A larger variety of titles is available at each level.

- Working together to select and care for the book collection promotes collaboration and a shared vision for continuous achievement in the school.

- The book collection is an integral part of the ongoing assessment system.

- The book collection creates a feeling of sharing in the school, and people are more willing to work together to pool resources and acquire more funds for books.

- The bookroom is a gathering place for casual but important conversation about books and learning.

- All teachers become familiar with the full range of books being used across the grades.

- Teachers at lower grade levels become more aware of what children will be expected to read in the later grades.

- Rather than regarding books as "belonging" only to one grade level, teachers have visible evidence of a continuum of reading achievement.

- The book collection is highly cost effective.

Teaching becomes easier and children learn more when both teachers and children have plentiful access to high-quality books. Enlist the assistance of administrators and community members in building this invaluable resource for children. With the system we have presented here, a child from kindergarten to second grade will read more than 200 different books in guided reading, independent reading, and home reading. Intermediate and middle school students will read over 50 texts a year in guided and independent reading. This type of resourcing makes good sense. Children become effective readers only if they spend lots of time reading at school and at home. Our cherished goal, always, is more reading, and a rich book collection in a school will make it possible.

Estimated Costs of the School Bookroom Collection

Figures 17–4 through 17–9 suggest levels, number of books, and costs to support leveled reading in grades K through 8 for starter, basic, and expanded collections, first with eight copies of each title, then with twelve. These charts are based on two classes of 25 to 30 students at each grade level, for a total of

350 to 420 students. Adjust these estimates as necessary to reflect your particular situation.

A starter collection will help you get underway with guided reading; you can add to the collection as you go. As outlined in Figure 17–4, a starter collection would include ten different titles each for the most frequently used levels, with eight copies of each title. The total cost of the starter collection for a K–8 school with twelve classrooms is approximately $9,200 (eight copies of each title) or $14,700 (12 copies of each title [see Figure 17–5]). This starter set concentrates on variety, so you shouldn't purchase more than one or two titles in a series. Remembering that reading series books often affects reading power and motivation, ask your students to look in the school library or their community library for other books in a series to read independently.

The basic collection allows for more titles. With the basic collection, students will be able to read a wider variety of genres as well as more series books. As shown in Figures 17–6 and 17–7, a basic collection for a school bookroom will cost approximately $17,600 (eight copies of each title) to $26,400 (12 copies of each title). *These costs do not reflect possible discounts.*

The expanded collection shown in Figures 17–8 and 17–9 provides a rich variety of titles, allowing you to cover a range of genres and provide for students' extensive reading.

Remember that the books in these collections will be used over many years. The starter collection costs about $368 (25 students per class) or $300 (30 students per class) per current student. But since the students will be using the collection at least four years, the costs are actually $92 to $75 per student. And even those figures are more than the actual cost per student. You will be using this collection over many years for different groups of students. Of course, there will be replacement costs for books that wear out or are lost. You'll also want

to add new resources to the collection gradually. But if you assume just two cycles of students using the books over an eight-year period, the costs shrink to between $38 to $46 per student. We hope these figures will help you convince administrators to support your collection and also help you acquire outside funding.

Suggestions for Professional Development: Planning for a School Bookroom

Work as a team to plan and organize your bookroom. Again, the school librarian can offer excellent advice. The book list at *fountasandpinnellleveledbooks.com* and in printed version—*Leveled Book List K–8* (Fountas and Pinnell 2006) will be a resource, but remember you can also add books that do not appear on the lists. Begin by getting to know some books at each level.

1. Hold a meeting with colleagues to assess your current situation and make a plan.
   - Ask teachers to come with a list of all the books in their classrooms and the number of copies they could contribute to the shared collection. (They should bring with them a copy of any title of which they have more than one copy. Books can be designated by the teacher's name on the inside back cover just in case you decide later to break up the collection.)
   - Collect one copy of any books you already have in a shared book collection and bring these copies to the meeting.
   - Spend some time placing the books in leveled categories.
   - Then make a chart (similar to the charts in this chapter) of the number of titles and copies of each title at each level.

- You may also want to assess the range of genres by counting fiction and nonfiction or simply entering an evaluative comment (for example, "good variety," or "predominantly realistic fiction").

2. Now you are ready to begin your planning.
   - Decide what your goals are for the first year and the number of titles you need at each level.
   - Divide into teams to look for titles at each level.
   - Bring your findings back to another meeting and formulate a beginning book order.

3. After you have a minimal starter collection physically on hand, hold a meeting to organize the bookroom.

   - Decide on your location and how you will clear out other materials that are currently in the space.
   - Decide how you will store books and make a plan for acquiring magazine boxes, shoe boxes, or other containers.
   - Create a plan for getting help from volunteers if needed.
   - Create a time line for setting up the bookroom.
   - Decide how books will be taken from and returned to the bookroom by teachers.

4. Schedule a regular series of short meetings (perhaps every two weeks during lunch) to monitor how well the bookroom is functioning.

Example of a Starter Book Collection for a School Bookroom, Grades K–8, Eight Copies of Each Title

LEVEL	NUMBER OF TITLES EACH LEVEL	NUMBER OF BOOKS	ESTIMATED COST @ $4.00 [A–J] AND $5 [K+]
A	10	80	$320
B	10	80	$320
C	10	80	$320
D	10	80	$320
E	10	80	$320
F	10	80	$320
G	10	80	$320
H	10	80	$320
I	10	80	$320
J	10	80	$320
K	10	80	$400
L	10	80	$400
M	10	80	$400
N	10	80	$400
O	10	80	$400
P	10	80	$400
Q	10	80	$400
R	10	80	$400
S	10	80	$400
T	10	80	$400
U	10	80	$400
V	10	80	$400
W	10	80	$400
X	5	40	$200
Total Grades K–5	**235**	**1,880**	**$8,600**
Additional titles for elementary schools where grades 6, 7, and 8 are included:			
X	5	40	$200
Y, Z	10	80	$400
Total Grades 6, 7, 8	**15**	**120**	**$600**
Total Grades K–8	**250**	**2,000**	**$9,200**

Figure 17–4.   Starter Book Collection for a School Bookroom, Grades K–8, Eight Copies of Each Title

Example of a Starter Book Collection for a School Bookroom, Grades K–8, Twelve Copies of Each Title			
LEVEL	NUMBER OF TITLES EACH LEVEL	NUMBER OF BOOKS	ESTIMATED COST @ $4.00 [A–J] AND $5 [K+]
A	10	120	$480
B	10	120	$480
C	10	120	$480
D	10	120	$480
E	10	120	$480
F	10	120	$480
G	10	120	$480
H	10	120	$480
I	10	120	$480
J	10	120	$480
K	10	120	$600
L	10	120	$600
M	10	120	$600
N	10	120	$600
O	10	120	$600
P	10	120	$600
Q	10	120	$600
R	10	120	$600
S	10	120	$600
T	10	120	$600
U	10	120	$600
V	10	120	$600
W	10	120	$600
X	5	60	$300
Total Grades K–5	235	2,820	$12,900
Additional titles for elementary schools where grades 6, 7, and 8 are included:			
X	10	120	$600
Y, Z	20	240	$1,200
Total Grades 6, 7, 8	30	360	$1,800
Total Grades K–8	265	3,180	$14,700

Figure 17–5.   Example of a Starter Book Collection for a School Bookroom, Grades K–8, Twelve Copies of Each Title

	Example of a Basic Book Collection for a School Bookroom, Grades K–8, Eight Copies of Each Title		
LEVEL	NUMBER OF TITLES EACH LEVEL	NUMBER OF BOOKS	ESTIMATED COST @ $4.00 [A–J] AND $5 [K+]
A	20	160	$640
B	20	160	$640
C	20	160	$640
D	20	160	$640
E	20	160	$640
F	20	160	$640
G	20	160	$640
H	20	160	$640
I	20	160	$640
J	20	160	$640
K	10	80	$400
L	20	160	$800
M	20	160	$800
N	20	160	$800
O	20	160	$800
P	20	160	$800
Q	20	160	$800
R	20	160	$800
S	20	160	$800
T	20	160	$800
U	20	160	$800
V	20	160	$800
W	10	80	$400
X	10	80	$400
Total Grades K–5	**450**	**3,600**	**$16,400**
Additional titles for elementary schools where grades 6, 7, and 8 are included:			
W	10	80	$400
X	10	80	$400
Y, Z	10	80	$400
Total Grades 6, 7, 8	**30**	**240**	**$1,200**
Total Grades K–8	**480**	**3,840**	**$17,600**

Figure 17–6. Example of a Basic Book Collection for a School Bookroom, Grades K–8, Eight Copies of Each Title

LEVEL	NUMBER OF TITLES EACH LEVEL	NUMBER OF BOOKS	ESTIMATED COST @ $4.00 [A–J] AND $5 [K+]
Example of a Basic Book Collection for a School Bookroom, Grades K–8, Twelve Copies of Each Title			
A	20	240	$960
B	20	240	$960
C	20	240	$960
D	20	240	$960
E	20	240	$960
F	20	240	$960
G	20	240	$960
H	20	240	$960
I	20	240	$960
J	20	240	$960
K	10	120	$600
L	20	240	$1,200
M	20	240	$1,200
N	20	240	$1,200
O	20	240	$1,200
P	20	240	$1,200
Q	20	240	$1,200
R	20	240	$1,200
S	20	240	$1,200
T	20	240	$1,200
U	20	240	$1,200
V	20	240	$1,200
W	10	120	$600
X	10	120	$600
Total Grades K–5	**450**	**5,400**	**$24,600**
Additional titles for elementary schools where grades 6, 7, and 8 are included:			
W	10	120	$600
X	10	120	$600
Y, Z	10	120	$600
Total Grades 6, 7, 8	**30**	**360**	**$1,800**
Total Grades K–8	**480**	**5,760**	**$26,400**

Figure 17–7.   Example of a Basic Book Collection for a School Bookroom, Grades K–8, Twelve Copies of Each Title

Example of an Expanded Book Collection for a School Bookroom, Grades K–8, Eight Copies of Each Title

LEVEL	NUMBER OF TITLES EACH LEVEL	NUMBER OF BOOKS	ESTIMATED COST @ $4.00 [A–J] AND $5 [K+]
A	25	200	$800
B	25	200	$800
C	25	200	$800
D	25	200	$800
E	25	200	$800
F	25	200	$800
G	25	200	$800
H	25	200	$800
I	25	200	$800
J	25	200	$800
K	15	120	$600
L	25	200	$1,000
M	25	200	$1,000
N	25	200	$1,000
O	25	200	$1,000
P	25	200	$1,000
Q	25	200	$1,000
R	25	200	$1,000
S	25	200	$1,000
T	25	200	$1,000
U	25	200	$1,000
V	25	200	$1,000
W	20	160	$800
X	20	160	$800
Total Grades K–5	**580**	**4,640**	**$21,200**
Additional titles for elementary schools where grades 6, 7, and 8 are included:			
W	5	40	$200
X	5	40	$200
Y, Z	25	200	$1,000
Total Grades 6, 7, 8	**35**	**200**	**$1,400**
Total Grades K–8	**615**	**4,920**	**$22,600**

Figure 17–8. Example of an Expanded Book Collection for a School Bookroom, Grades K–8, Eight Copies of Each Title

LEVEL	NUMBER OF TITLES EACH LEVEL	NUMBER OF BOOKS	ESTIMATED COST @ $4.00 [A–J] AND $5 [K+]
Example of an Expanded Book Collection for a School Bookroom, Grades K–8, Twelve Copies of Each Title			
A	25	300	$1,200
B	25	300	$1,200
C	25	300	$1,200
D	25	300	$1,200
E	25	300	$1,200
F	25	300	$1,200
G	25	300	$1,200
H	25	300	$1,200
I	25	300	$1,200
J	25	300	$1,200
K	15	180	$900
L	25	300	$1,500
M	25	300	$1,500
N	25	300	$1,500
O	25	300	$1,500
P	25	300	$1,500
Q	25	300	$1,500
R	25	300	$1,500
S	25	300	$1,500
T	25	300	$1,500
U	25	300	$1,500
V	25	300	$1,500
W	20	240	$1,200
X	20	240	$1,200
Total Grades K–5	**580**	**6,960**	**$31,800**
Additional titles for elementary schools where grades 6, 7, and 8 are included:			
W	5	60	$300
X	5	60	$300
Y, Z	25	300	$1,500
Total Grades 6, 7, 8	**35**	**420**	**$2,100**
Total Grades K–8	**590**	**7,380**	**$33,900**

Figure 17–9. Example of an Expanded Book Collection for a School Bookroom, Grades K–8, Twelve Copies of Each Title

CHAPTER EIGHTEEN

BOOK CLUBS, GIFTS, AND COST-EFFECTIVE PLANNING

There are never enough books to supply classrooms where children love to read. You'll find that even after you conduct an inventory of your current supply and spend as much money as you can on the initial collection, you will want to acquire still more books. In this chapter, we briefly describe some approaches to bolstering your collection that have worked for many teachers.

Like any valuable collection, good book collections are gathered over time. Receiving a grant will give your book collection a big boost, and it is helpful in the beginning to acquire a critical mass of books, at least the starter collection described in Chapter 17. But sometimes those funds are hard to come by and require a lot of effort. Even if you have a starter or basic collection, you will still need to increase your number of books. Your classroom needs a rich collection of single titles, and you need access to multiple copies for guided reading and literature study. You'll need to make the most of the resources you have and explore creative ways to acquire books at little or no cost.

Using Internal Resources Strategically

As we've seen, the school bookroom is the most economical option for acquiring the multiple copies of titles needed for guided reading and literature study. For classroom libraries you will need single copies of a range of titles, but you may find that you can get better prices if a group of teachers coordinate their orders, putting them together to make a larger purchase.

Internal resources are likely to be combinations of:

- Yearly textbook allocations.
- Yearly materials budgets.
- Donations of cash from the parents' association or a local business.
- Special funds provided specifically for purchasing books.
- Gifts of books.

Sometimes districts will purchase large quantities of books to support guided and independent reading; the deep discounts possible with large orders like this really help. Also, almost every school has some discretion in terms of its yearly budget for books and materials. While restrictions are usually attached to these funds, it is often possible to direct some portion of the money to buying books for the collection—after all, they are your textbooks for teaching reading. And these days, with literacy receiving national attention, state or local funding is often designated specifically for purchasing books. This funding is different from the resources described in the next chapter because you do not have to write proposals to receive it. Local individuals and businesses may also make gifts of books. In general, never turn down any good books someone offers to give you, but do remember that not all books are appropriate for guided reading.

Becoming Involved in Purchasing

Unfortunately, large sums of money are often spent on books without much thought. Ordering books is a difficult and time-consuming job, and busy administrators have little time to spend doing so. You and your colleagues may want to volunteer to examine and order books. Your time will be well spent—you will not only have a better chance of acquiring quality resources for your students but also become more familiar with the texts and thus use them more effectively.

You may want to purchase some individual titles of book series rather than sets. Kits will no doubt include some high-quality books, and they may be economical, but they may also include books that you won't wish to use or that will not interest your students. In addition, be cautious about the levels assigned to books by their publisher. Leveling books is an inexact science, a complex process in which many factors must be considered. A given publisher uses particular scales that are not necessarily the same as those of other publishers and that may not necessarily apply to your students. The gradient of text we have described here can guide your selection but it, too, is not the final authority. The best authority is you, based on your own analysis. You and your colleagues can best decide the specific books your students need.

Spending Resources Strategically

You may or may not be able to make suggestions on the way funds are spent, but it is wise to be prepared. In other words, know the books you want to order *before* the funds become available. You will be ready at a moment's notice to place your order!

Titles for a starter set should be identified by school personnel who know the students and their interests and needs—therefore we do not provide a "short list." You can easily make your own wish list, however. After you have made an inventory of the books you already have, take your list to a local bookstore that has a large collection of children's books.

(If there are no large children's bookstores in your area, plan this visit in conjunction with an out-of-town trip to a conference or a social event.) Spend some time browsing through and even reading sections of these books and place check marks after titles you especially like. Often, the owner or manager will be happy to work with you and advise you, since they know you may become a very good customer.

You can also look up books on the Internet on bookseller websites; you'll be able to see a facsimile of the front cover of the book, read summary material and reviews by customers, and even read some pages. Unfortunately, though, you cannot examine the books in enough depth to think about them in relation to your own students. Another place you will find collections of books to examine is at bookseller displays set up at local state and national reading conferences. Some of these books are sold as kits, and it's important to examine each book individually, not buy a collection blindly. Booksellers will sometimes also bring collections of books to your school or a central office so that teachers can look at them.

Whatever your strategy, this knowledge of the titles you need gives you power. Sometimes small sums of money must be spent very quickly, and administrators will be grateful for a "ready-to-go" order.

Money Saved Is Money Earned

Any money you save is money you can use to buy more books. When you purchase books, maximize your purchasing power—large orders receive bigger discounts and are more likely to include free or reduced shipping costs. Another way to save money is to reduce your photocopying costs. Think carefully before you duplicate those worksheets—ask your students to write in their reader's notebooks and writer's notebooks instead. If you and your colleagues promise your principal that you will decrease photocopying costs by at least 25 percent, you will have a surprising amount of money to spend on books. (A teacher recently told us how much students liked and took pride in writing in their notebooks and how much time she saved by no longer having to stand at the copy machine.) Also, if you can eliminate the need for one consumable workbook or unnecessary textbook, you will save more dollars.

Look for ways to conserve costs across the board:

- Produce larger book orders by placing them once a year or once every two years.

- Develop an action plan for making the best use of supplies.

- Involve students in conserving supplies.

Don't do without supplies you and your students need, but carefully evaluate all purchases. Sometimes "homemade" versions of expensive items can be just as effective. Eliminate expensive items that have no proven value and pour the resources into something that does have value—promoting students' engagement with high-quality texts.

Acquiring Leveled Texts Without Spending Money

If you are just beginning to implement reading workshop and guided reading, getting enough books may seem like a daunting task. And it is true that good collections are built over several years. There are ways, though, to get enough texts to begin even if you have limited resources.

Reshape and Reuse What You Already Have

All schools have books. Chances are, you have the thick anthologies typically used in basal reading systems. These anthologies are full of information selections and stories that may be excellent texts for guided reading. Here are some suggestions:

1. Gather anthologies used at several grade levels appropriate for your range of students.
2. Go through each anthology, identifying selections that have potential. Using the characteristics and prototypes provided in this book, identify a level for each selection.
3. Pencil in the level in the table of contents or make an "index" for the selections.
4. Use the selections exactly as you would leveled books. Each teacher will need only eight to twelve copies of the anthology.
5. Try the leveled selections over time and adjust them as you use them with students.

One enterprising group of teachers received permission from the administration to "razor blade" selections out of old anthologies that were no longer used. With simple bindings the information selections and short stories became individual texts in their leveled book collections.

You may find treasures by visiting the book storage room in your school or your district's warehouse. Old children's magazines may be a source for good short stories and informational pieces as well, although you will want to be sure that the information is not dated. Consult your school librarian in every step of building a school book collection. Texts or funds may be available to make the link between the school library and the leveled book collection. In some schools the teachers' leveled book collection is a special section of the school library.

Work with Public Libraries

Many public libraries allow teachers to check out large numbers of books for as many as 20 or 30 days. You can certainly get many good read-aloud selections from libraries and use public library books to supplement your individual titles, leaving your own funds free to acquire multiple titles. Very well resourced libraries may even let you check out multiple copies of books to supplement your guided reading program. Visit the public library in the same way you visit a bookstore—get to know what is there and find out what their regulations allow you to do.

Using a public library in this way does require some special organizational procedures in your classroom. You can identify these books with a colorful sticky note and/or place them in a special basket or area and enlist your students' help in caring for them. On the classroom calendar, place a red ring around the date for returning or renewing books. Students who select public library books for individual reading will need to watch the calendar carefully and be sure the books are back in the classroom a day or two before they need to be returned.

Use Book Clubs

Book clubs are an excellent source for texts. Most book clubs give free books to the teacher when students order a certain number. Also, your students have the opportunity to purchase books at a reasonable cost. Owning a book you have selected yourself is strong motivation to increase home

Book Clubs for Elementary Students		
Scholastic Book Clubs Call 1-800-SCHOLASTIC (1-800-724-6527) *scholastic.com*	Bonus points are accumulated. Use bonus points to order free books from the catalogs.	
CLUB	LEVEL	DESCRIPTION
Firefly	Preschool	Paperback and hardback. Beginning readers.
See-Saw	K–1	Paperback picture books. Beginning readers. Math and science books.
Lucky	2–3	Fiction and nonfiction titles. Picture books. Early chapter books. Junior novels.
Arrow	4–5–6	Award-winning titles. Fiction, nonfiction (biography, history, informational). Variety of themes.
Club de Lectura	Pre K–5	Spanish and bilingual books. Spanish cassettes. From picture books and beginning readers to chapter books. Translations and original literature in Spanish.
Troll Book Club Call 1-800-541-1097 1-888-99-TROLL (1-888-718-7655) Fax 1-888-71-TROLL (1-888-718-7655) Troll Book Clubs 2 Lethbridge Plaza Mahwah, NJ 07430 *www.troll.com* [call 800 number for password]	Use bonus points to order any selection in catalogs. Paperback selections at different grade levels. Selections range from picture books to longer chapter books. Select grade level: Pre-K–K, K–1, 2–3, 4–6.	

Figure 18–1. Book Clubs for Elementary Students

reading. In Figure 18–1 we have listed some popular book clubs and some of their features.

Book clubs will send students a colorful flier/order form at regular intervals. Since these books are popular trade books, you are likely to know some of them—especially the series books. Look at the book club flier yourself before handing it out so that you can plan some book talks (see Chapter 1) to get students interested in a variety of good books. Without taking over the process, you can guide students' selection through discussion.

Students can read the books they purchase for independent reading and then, if they choose, can lend them to their friends or to the classroom library or include them on the rack or shelf of student-recommended books. As students order books, you will be able to choose free books. Again, using your inventory and the lists in this book, order those books that meet your needs.

Hold Book Fairs at the School

A local bookseller will often be happy to hold a book fair at your school, bringing in a large number of books to sell at a discount. Typically, students at all grade levels participate. Advertise the book fair well in advance, giving parents an idea of the kinds of books that will be available and how much they will cost. Remind students the night before so that they remember to bring money if they are going to purchase a book. During the day of the fair, different groups of students are allowed to browse the books and make purchases.

If you can, visit the fair before your students do so that you have an idea of the books that will be sold. Sometimes, you can even give the bookseller a list of books you would like to see. As with the book clubs, you can give book talks before the fair. Often, the school gets deep discounts or free books in proportion to student purchases for sponsoring the fair. Again, stu-

dents can elect to lend books to the class after reading them. You can place their names insider the front cover and they can take them home at the end of the school year.

Work with Parents to Hold Fund-Raisers

Fund-raising events can generate resources to support book purchases. Remember that it only takes about $250 to supply one level of a basic collection for a school bookroom. People who attend fund-raising events such as entertainment shows, bake sales, or fairs like to know that their dollars will be used for something as worthwhile as buying books for the students to read.

Make Donations, Loans, and Gifts Possible

There are many creative ways that individuals can contribute to a classroom or school book collection.

A "Lending" Program

One teacher invited parents to lend books to the class for a year (Figure 18–2 is the letter she sent home with her students). As the books came in, she made a list of the lenders and their addresses. She had students write a brief thank-you note to send home with the lenders' child. At the end of the year, lenders were contacted and asked whether they would like to have the books returned or to leave them in the classroom for next year's group. Many parents decided to donate the books permanently.

A "Birthday" Present for the Class

Sometimes schools establish a new student-birthday tradition by suggesting that parents or family members purchase a book for the school or classroom collection instead of bringing cupcakes or other refreshments. The student's name is written on the title page as an acknowledgment of the gift. You can even provide a master list of titles from which caregivers can choose.

Example of a Letter Requesting the Loan of Books

Dear Parents,

This year, students in our class will be reading a great deal. They will read biographies, informational books, and a variety of novels. We need a large number of books in our classroom library so that everyone can find books that are interesting and that will help them learn.

We have already collected several hundred books but we need more because our class will read over 1,000 books this year!

Can you help us by lending us some books that your children have already read? We will treat these books with care and return them at the end of the year, unless you decide to leave them in the room for next year's students.

We are looking for paperback and hardback books that are in good condition and suitable for children age __ to __.[1] To lend us books, write your name and address on the inside back cover of each book and send it to school with your child. We will return it to you at the end of the school year if you write "please return" inside the back cover.

Students will be reading these books at school and at home. We will make every effort to take good care of the books, but sometimes there are unavoidable accidents, so please do not lend us any book that is precious or irreplaceable and you would be very upset to lose.

Thank you for your help. You will be providing valuable learning opportunities for the students in our class.

Sincerely,

Teacher and Grade 5 Students

[1]Put in an age range that will not seem out of line to parents but will help you match the range of reading levels in your class.

Figure 18–2.   Example of a Letter Requesting the Loan of Books

"ADOPT A SCHOOL"

In many communities, local businesses "adopt" a particular school to sponsor and help. The company may send volunteers to the school to work with students or provide other kinds of administrative or custodial services, and these volunteers can be quite helpful in organizing and caring for the bookroom. Sometimes employees of a business may be interested in sponsoring one student's reading for a year. If you consider that the basic collection is used by many students over several years, the cost is quite reasonable.

Contributions to the classroom collection or the school bookroom are concrete demonstrations of support. From businesspeople's point of view, it is a way to contribute to the community and have that contribution recognized. You can place a bookplate inside the front cover acknowledging the gift. You can also have students write thank-you notes, mentioning a specific book as appropriate. Expressing appreciation and letting the business know how important the contribution is to students' learning builds a tremendous amount of goodwill in the community.

Summary

Just as you prioritize your time, you need to prioritize your resources. Deciding where to spend the money (even a small amount) you have at your discretion helps you realize what you think is important. Buying high-quality books for your classroom or school will positively affect your students' reading achievement, thereby giving them an essential tool for a successful future.

Suggestions for Professional Development: Expanding the Book Collection

Take some further steps down the road to a good classroom or school book collection by creating that starter list or "wish list" for yourself at either the classroom or the school level (better still, do it for both). Knowing what you need is the first step to acquiring a high-quality book collection.

1. If you have prepared an inventory, look at it again. If not, make an inventory of the books you currently have and the number of copies of each title. Notice the number of titles you have at each level.

2. Compare your current inventory with the recommendations for number of titles and copies of titles in Chapters 16 and 17.

3. If you are working on a classroom set, compare your inventory to the suggestions for your grade level for a basic and expanded set.

4. If you are working toward a school bookroom, decide whether your goal is a starter, basic, or expanded set and make comparisons with your inventory.

5. Set goals for:
   - The number of copies you need of titles you already have.
   - The number of additional titles you need at each level.
   - The number of copies you need for the additional titles.

6. Browse through the lists in this book and visit some bookstores to identify titles you would like to have. Then make your "short list."

7. Next, set some goals for the year and create an action plan. If you can add even one or two levels to your book collection or fifty single titles to a classroom collection, you will have accomplished a great deal during the year.

8. Think back over the suggestions in this chapter and consider:
   - Ways to save money.
   - Some texts you already have that can be reshaped and used to enhance the collection.
   - Ways to acquire books without money.

9. Establish a time line for your action plan and assign responsibilities for accomplishing your goals.

CHAPTER NINETEEN

How to Write Grant Proposals to Acquire More Books

When you begin a dynamic reading program, you will need and want more books. Your beginning inventory will give you an idea how many *more* books you need. That's definitely the place to start: you'll be ready when an administrator, the parents' association, or a local business asks you how you would spend available funds. Having very specific plans even for smaller amounts of money will build others' confidence in your ability to use resources wisely.

After you exhaust all your internal sources, you may decide to seek outside funding, perhaps by writing a proposal to receive a grant. There are three levels to this process: (1) a letter either seeking funds or opening a conversation about funding to support book acquisition; (2) *a concept paper,* a brief form of a proposal and often sufficient for the funding agency's purposes; and (3) a full proposal for a grant to support the purchase of books. Grant proposals may of course be far more encompassing than simply purchasing books; you may find that building your book collection is one very important component of a larger, long-term project for improving your literacy program.

Getting Started

A successful proposal is not produced just by sitting down and writing. All well-conceived, successful plans take a good bit of thinking and planning. It is good for teachers to work together because mutual effort adds to the creativity and is also persuasive to sponsors. Before you even begin, you will want to think about some basic essentials, some sources of funding.

Essential Elements

Almost all guides to proposal writing will tell you that there are two essential elements in seeking funds:

- You need a good idea.

- You need to relate your idea to a problem that it solves.

When you write a proposal for a good book collection, your "good idea" is to provide a large amount of high-quality reading material for the students in your school. Your short-term goal is to increase the amount and quality of reading your students do, and the long-term goal is to raise reading achievement. You may think your cause is so worthy that the reasons for funding are self-evident, but that is not the case. Funding agencies will want to know the specifics—what the problems are and how your idea will solve them. You need to make a logical argument. For example:

- A large number of students are reading below grade level and/or are uninterested in reading.

- There is evidence that increasing the amount of reading (or the variety/quality of reading) is one factor in increasing reading achievement.

- To increase reading (or the variety of reading), we need many books (or a variety of books) in classrooms.

- Currently, there are not enough books (or enough variety of books).

- Therefore, we need more books and we know which ones will be effective.

Requesting funding is like applying for a job; your proposal is a persuasive document assuring the sponsor that:

- Your plan is well conceived.

- You have considered effectiveness and efficiency.

- The plan is cost-effective.

- The people who will implement the plan are knowledgeable, qualified, and committed to the goals.

- This funding will make a measurable difference in students' achievement in literacy.

- You will be accountable for the outcomes of the program.

Following the Guidelines of the Sponsoring Agency

You should usually identify your potential sponsor before you begin writing your proposal, because funding agencies have different procedures, preferences, and requirements. Some agencies have a specific vision and mission, and all funds must be expended to serve that mission; agency personnel and board members do not want to waste their time reading thousands of proposals that may or may not fit that mission.

Sponsors who have definite agendas for giving away dollars will tell you exactly what they expect to see in a proposal. Government and state agencies will usually issue a "request for proposals" (RFP) that provides very specific guidelines. For others, the guidelines are less specific. Some require an initial letter and a series of interim approvals before you are permitted to submit a proposal. Often, a proposal that does not follow

the RFP or guidelines will simply be discarded, and no one will read and consider it. All your hard work will have been wasted.

Some steps you can take toward making an effective proposal are:

1. Identify one or more potential funding agencies.
2. Contact the agency and ask for their guidelines, mission statement, and descriptions of projects previously funded. (All of this information will be available on a website and in an annual report.)
3. Read the guidelines and other documents very carefully.
4. Decide what step to take first—a letter of inquiry, a concept paper, or a proposal.
5. Outline your proposal, following the guidelines precisely.

In some cases, you may even want to use some of the specific language that you find in the RFP. There may be an "evaluation section" that lets you know how the proposals will be judged, and this is very valuable information. For example, if an RFP, in a section called "Impact on Students," asks this:

Describe the evidence to be used to assess impact on students for the proposed project. Specify measures and procedures for data collection and reporting.

You wouldn't want to say something vague like this:

We will look at how students are progressing in reading.

Instead, respond appropriately and thoroughly, like this:

Several forms of evidence will be gathered to document the impact on students of the proposed reading program. Students' oral reading performance on a specified set of benchmark texts will be gathered using a standardized procedure (see attached example[1]). Performance will be rated for fluency, rate (words per minute), and accuracy. A rubric for measuring fluency is also attached to this proposal. After the oral reading, students will be asked to respond to several questions designed to assess comprehension. Data will include level of text read successfully (that is, above 95 percent accuracy), rate of reading (words per minute), fluency rating, and number of comprehension questions answered successfully. Scores will be recorded at the beginning, middle, and end of the academic year. A standardized test, the [name of test], will be administered at the beginning of grade 2. Scores on the state proficiency test [name of test] will be administered and collected at [time]. Additionally, classroom teachers will be asked to rate students' performance on classroom reading tasks. Parents will be surveyed to gather evidence that students are reading more at home. The survey is attached to this proposal. Student scores will be collected each year to determine trends in achievement. Scores on standardized test scores will be compared over a three-year period to students' scores in schools that are similar in demographic characteristics but do not have the infusion of books.

A small project would not require such an elaborate documentation system; you could use any *one* of the kinds of data listed above. The key is to demonstrate that you will be evaluating your efforts in a responsible way. Be specific; tell the funding agency exactly what you are prepared to do and use the language that they suggest.

Here's another example. The directions in the RFP say:

> The [Foundation or Government Agency] seeks proposals to fund projects designed to enhance the reading comprehension abilities of at-risk students. Proposals that show potential for helping students extend the meaning of fictional and expository texts are encouraged.

Your proposal could incorporate some of the language in the above two sentences—for example:

> A key to higher achievement is engaging intermediate-level students in large amounts of reading of a wide variety of texts, both fiction and nonfiction. Our book collection, and the program we propose to implement, will provide specific instruction and a large amount of reading of a wide variety of texts. The book collection will be composed of many high-quality fiction and expository texts. Through specific and explicit instruction directed toward developing comprehension strategies, teachers will assist students in extending the meaning of these texts through writing and oral discussion. Since most of the students in our school are "at risk"—that is, their family incomes are below the poverty level—this instruction and opportunity to read fiction and expository texts is of critical importance.

You will not be submitting the proposal if your plan does not fit into the mission of the funding agency, but if it does, you want to make that clear. Those who read the proposal will be looking for precisely that information.

Sources of Funding

A critical decision in getting started is selecting a prospective sponsor. There are many different sources of funding, private and public, individual and corporate, and the funding source to which

---

[1] You would attach relevant documents. The benchmark testing example in Chapter 9 contains one such procedure, and you can also find help in the assessment chapter (Chapter 28) of *Guiding Readers and Writers Grades 3–6* (Fountas and Pinnell 2001).

you apply has general implications for the form your request will take. Some ways to identify funding sources are:

- Work through your network of friends and acquaintances, especially those outside education. Let them know you are hoping to obtain more books for the students in your school to read. If you have a good idea, people will keep you in mind when they hear about a source of funding to support your work. After all, you are not seeking these funds for yourself but to support your students.

- Your public library will have lists and directories of philanthropic foundations. Look through the foundations' documents, and read their mission statements; look carefully at organizations that fund education.

- Keep in touch with your state education agency so that you will be informed about any special allocations of funds that will fit your goals. State education agencies issue RFPs for such funding.

- Check the *Federal Register,* a document published by the U.S. Office of Education that describes federal programs The *Federal Register* will be available in libraries as well as on the government website (*www.gpoaccess.gov/fr*).

- Surf the Internet for possible funding sources.

- Become involved in partnerships with a local university where the teachers are interested in beginning new projects and have skills and resources to apply for funding. A good match is a university professor who wants to do research and a classroom teacher interested in improving instruction.

- Join professional associations like the International Reading Association and the National Council of Teachers of English. Both national and state organizations often offer small grants for teachers.

GOVERNMENT SOURCES

Since reading and writing are critical skills for productive citizenship, it is in the state and national interest to improve literacy education. Often, special funds to support literacy learning are allocated by the state and federal government and are distributed by state education agencies or the U.S. Department of Education. Dispersal of these funds must follow the legal guidelines specified in the related legislation. Usually, application for state and federal funding requires an elaborate proposal; it would be difficult for an individual classroom teacher to attempt such a project. Also, there are usually strict guidelines regarding the eligibility of individuals and organizations. For example, state agencies accept proposals from schools, but those applications usually must be approved at the district level before they are sent.

Grant opportunities at the national level are listed in the *Federal Register.* The RFP will specify who is eligible to apply for funds, the approximate amount to be provided, and guidelines for writing the proposal. Your district may have a grants office where you can obtain information about grant opportunities. It is a good idea to keep in constant touch with your grants office or the superintendent's office. Opportunities sometimes arise quickly and the deadlines are tight. Those in the know are ahead of the game.

It may seem daunting to apply for funds at this level; organizing and preparing an elaborate grant proposal takes a lot of effort. But good communication is the key. If your school is applying for school reform money, or literacy improvement funds, you may be able to include resources for more books within the scope of a larger, more comprehensive effort. Check the guidelines to see whether and what amount of materials will be allowed as part of the funding effort.

PRIVATE FOUNDATIONS

There are many different kinds of foundations. Individuals or families may establish foundations for particular purposes. It will be important to read the background information about the foundation so that you understand how your work can fit within its mission.

Foundations usually prefer that you send a letter of inquiry or a "concept paper," which is a brief (usually two or three pages) description of your proposed project. Foundation staff members will usually read your letter or concept paper and may have it reviewed by outside consultants. Based on that preliminary examination, you may be invited to submit a more detailed proposal (structured according to foundation guidelines) and/or to meet with someone from the foundation.

An individual or group of individuals may establish a foundation to serve a particular community. In this case, the foundation seeks ongoing contributions from citizens and outlines a broad program of funding to support community improvement—health, environment, education, and so on. The foundation is usually governed by a board of community members. Its mission is to make the community a better place to live. A community foundation will have guidelines that tell you the categories of activity they seek to fund. If your proposal fits within a category, ask for the procedures for grant application.

Many large corporations also establish philanthropic branches. Sometimes the mission of the corporate foundation is related to the business; for example, a software company might fund technology in education or a publishing company's foundation might fund projects related to literacy. Alternately, the corporate foundation may wish to fund efforts within certain geographic areas (where their plants or offices are located, for example). A good way to start is to call the large companies in your area to find out if they have programs that fund educational efforts. If they do, ask for the guidelines.

It may help to know someone who is an officer or employee of the corporation. For example, one teacher had a good friend who worked for a large grocery chain. The African American employees of the chain were looking for a good cause. After communication and deliberation, they got together to provide funding over a period of years to support young African American children in Reading Recovery.

SERVICE CLUB ORGANIZATIONS

Service clubs offer a way for community leaders to get together to improve life in the community. A few examples are:

- The Junior League.
- The Lions Club.
- The Kiwanis Club.
- The Rotary Club.
- The Optimist Club (arm of the Optimist International Organization).
- Your school district may have its own versions of service organizations—Parent Teacher Associations, for example, or "booster" clubs, which are usually connected to sports but may be formed to support other activities such as music or literacy. These service clubs may be tapped to supply books for in-class reading or for home and summer reading programs.

INDIVIDUALS

Often, individuals form their own giving programs and are known for generous contributions to initiatives that help children. If you know someone who is interested in literacy and makes a practice of donating to special projects, you can start with a courteous letter to the person or to an assistant to introduce your idea. If you have a mutual friend or acquaintance, ask for advice on how to approach the individual; you may even be able to arrange a meeting.

Achieving a "Fit" Between Sponsors and Your Project

To be successful in securing funding, you need to look at what you do from the perspective of the potential sponsor. The sponsor will be asking questions like this:

- Does this proposal fit within our mission?

- Is it worthwhile?

- Is there research to support it?

- Will it benefit the population we want to serve?

- Will the benefit be supplemental (rather than replacing what the school should do anyway)?

- Are the applicants qualified?

- Do they have a good plan?

- Will the dollars be efficiently used?

- How do they plan to show us that the dollars made a difference?

Frankly, it is hard for sponsors to do a good job giving away money. Funding agencies are besieged with requests, all serving different agendae. They need assurance that their dollars will make a difference rather than just support someone's pet project. Increasing the number, variety, and quality of the books that students read, within a program that provides good instruction from a skilled and committed teacher, is well worth funding.

The Personal Touch

There are formal actions involved in seeking funding, but funding agencies like a personal touch. You want to maintain a respectful but friendly relationship with your potential sponsors. Many individuals and companies prefer not to be contacted personally, so a letter will be the only way to present your case. When possible, though, try to manage a personal introduction to the decision makers for the funding agency or staff members who inform them.

Meet with the Sponsor

Ask for a meeting and put your best foot forward. Chances are, you will get no more than thirty minutes or an hour to state your case. Prepare to make clear, concise descriptions of your problem and your plan to solve it. Some specific suggestions for a successful meeting are presented in Figure 19–1. In general, simply follow the rules of social courtesy. Be on time and well prepared. Leave at the designated time unless invited to remain.

You want to inform the funding agency of your work, but you also want to be sure that you listen and learn. Let your enthusiasm show, but going into long monologues or deluging the potential sponsor with stacks of paper will generally work against your cause. Have one or two very well prepared pieces of paper; emphasize research and your own staff's commitment; and be prepared to offer more details and/or reports if asked.

Be as specific as you can about what you are doing. Potential sponsors prefer simple reports of the results for individual students or identified groups of students rather than jargon. They are especially responsive to results from their own community or possibilities for students in the local region. Bringing the voices of your students and their parents into the conversation is very effective. Consider very brief vignettes or video segments (for example, a "before and after" portrait of a reader or writer). Bring a sample or two of the kinds of books you need to buy, photographs of classrooms richly supplied with books, or one student's reading list for the year showing a great and varied amount of reading.

Invite the Sponsor to Visit Your School

If the potential sponsor is interested in your work, a representative might be persuaded to visit the school. Usually, these visits are brief, so you'll need to plan very carefully. You want the person to experience the essence of your program. Walking through several classrooms gives the impression of a large number of students highly

Suggestions for Successful Meetings with Potential Sponsors

1. Be sure that your principal or appropriate administrators in your district are informed on an ongoing basis about your efforts to secure funds.

2. If you have a personal contact with the sponsoring agency, ask that person to introduce you and your proposed ideas and to "feel out" whether a meeting would be possible and/or appropriate. Your contact can attest to your sincerity, trustworthiness, and commitment.

3. Prepare and send any advance materials requested by the funding agency.

4. Work collaboratively with staff support people in the funding agency's office to schedule convenient times and places for the meeting.

5. Prepare carefully for the meeting by practicing what you want to say and asking others for feedback.

6. Funding agency representatives will usually prefer to meet with one person (or two or three) rather than a large group.

7. Don't deluge the representative with paper but have one excellent, concise, and well-prepared page that clearly shows what you plan to do and why.

8. Try to bring your students' lives and voices into the conversation. Your potential sponsor needs to know that these dollars will make a difference for them and to have a vision of what that difference will be.

9. Listen carefully to the comments and questions of the funding agency representative. These statements offer you insight into the agency's vision and priorities.

10. Follow basic rules of conversation. Answer all questions clearly, specifically, honestly, and concisely. Don't hedge or gush. Avoid long monologues; pause to allow for comments or questions.

11. Be on time (a little early) for the meeting. Be prepared to leave graciously when time is up unless you are invited to stay longer.

12. Invite the agency representative to visit your school, see you working, and meet the students.

Figure 19–1. Suggestions for Successful Meetings with Potential Sponsors

engaged in reading. In addition, you may want to have the visitor observe part of a lesson or a conference. Have the building administrator and key staff members available to answer questions, but keep the visit as informal as possible. You want to communicate that you are well prepared for the visit and are serious about what you want to do, but you don't want a visitor to think you are putting on a show. As much as possible, provide an authentic picture of what life is like in this building every day—what teachers and students are doing. As in any meeting, answer questions as clearly and honestly as you can. Make the visitor feel at home.

Developing a Letter Requesting Funds

Applying for funds often starts with a letter. For small local grants a letter may be all that is required. The letter in Figure 19–2 is an example of an introductory letter to a funding agency or individual. (The left-hand column identifies the goal of each part of the letter.) Notice that the letter specifically identifies the problem and proposes a clear solution. The request is supported by research; the contributions the school staff are prepared to make are documented; and, the qualifications of those who will lead the effort are presented. Funding agencies need to know that their funds will be well used.

Components of a Letter Seeking Support for a School Book Collection

COMPONENT	EXAMPLE OF A STATEMENT
Greeting	Dear _____ [Be certain that you have the appropriate individual to address. Be sure that you have his/her accurate name and title and that you spell the name of the funding agency correctly.]
Introduce yourself and your idea.	As the teachers and staff of Greensview Elementary School, we are committed to raising our students' achievement in reading. We are seeking sponsorship for a plan to dramatically increase the amount of reading students do at school and at home.
Recognize the funding agency or individual. [Mention any specific contributions made.]	In the past, you have made many important contributions to the education of students in our school. Your partnership has made a significant difference. We are especially appreciate of your sponsoring our subscription to *Time for Kids*.
Provide background information. [Discuss important features of your school. Establish general need if appropriate.]	At Greensview, we serve a population of 425 children, 200 in grades K–2 and 225 in grades 3 to 5. Our school is located in an urban area where there are high levels of unemployment and poverty. Over 95 percent of our students are eligible for free and reduced-price lunch. Many of our students are vulnerable to membership in neighborhood gangs, which can be prevented by success in school.

Identify the problem. [Be as specific as you can in documenting the problem.]	We are most concerned about our students' progress in reading. While our scores have shown improvement, more is necessary if Greensview students are to become highly proficient readers who can use reading for a variety of purposes. Current reading levels of 57 percent of our students are below recommended national standards.[1]
	    The number of our fourth graders meeting state standards on the proficiency test improved from 37 percent to 46 percent over the last two years, but we continue to dedicate ourselves to a 100 percent passing rate.
	    Finally, a recent study showed that many of our students do not read voluntarily at home. This situation must change if our students are to succeed in school and later life.

Establish your commitment and that of your colleagues. [Indicate specific "in kind" contributions the school community has made and is prepared to make.]	We have developed a plan of action to make the most of any resources we receive. Members of our staff have reserved and committed extra time in the summer to organize the collection. Parents have formed a volunteer group and are prepared to help us maintain the collection and assure efficient use. We have placed the highest priority on these books for students. We used available funds from the district, as well as a small grant from the state. We held a book fair that helped us to obtain some books. Teachers and parents have already contributed over 300 books. A local office supply store has agreed to donate 60 cardboard library book boxes to protect our books.

[1]The recommended national standards from the Center on Education and the Economy are described in "New Standards." *Performance Standards: Volume 1—Elementary School: English Language Arts, Mathematics, Science, Applied Learning.* 1998. National Center on Education and the Economy and the University of Pittsburgh. Printed in the United States of America by Harcourt Brace Educational Measurement.

Figure 19–2.   Components of a Letter Seeking Support for a School Book Collection

Components of a Letter Seeking Support for a School Book Collection (continued)

COMPONENT	EXAMPLE OF A STATEMENT
Propose your solution. [Make a clear summary statement of what you propose to do. Back it with evidence. Cite research in the text or in footnotes.]	This year we are implementing an intensive, research-based instructional program in reading and it is already making a difference. Research has shown that the amount of reading students do is related to increased achievement.[2] The approach combines explicit teaching in small groups and a large amount of independent reading. As teachers, we select books that students can read successfully and, through instruction, gradually increase the difficulty and variety. We want all of our students to read many kinds of fiction and nonfiction and expand their skills. Our students are reading at school and at home every day, and we are running out of books!
Describe the solution. [Be concise in describing your plan of action. If the sponsor wants a more detailed plan, you can provide it later.]	We propose to increase the number and variety of books available to students by building a school book collection to support guided reading (small group instruction), independent reading, and home reading. This collection is efficient and cost-effective because it is shared among teachers and students at all grades. The collection will ensure that every student has sufficient books to read massively and widely.
Establish your credibility. [Persuade the sponsor that you can do the job.]	All of the teachers on our staff have successfully completed an intensive training course to improve their instruction. They are highly knowledgeable about selecting books for instruction. We have made an inventory of our current collection and have a plan for acquiring precisely those volumes we need to support good instruction.
Describe how you will tell whether your project is making a difference. [Assure the sponsor that you will document and report the outcomes of your program. Be sure that you include student achievement measures.]	We expect the implementation of our instructional program to have positive outcomes for students' reading achievement. We have designed a rigorous evaluation system that is consistent with national [or state] standards. We will document the number of students who meet grade-level standards, as measured by passage reading and assessment of comprehension. We will also document and report the number of students who meet criteria on the state proficiency test in reading.
End with a summary statement about impact. [Be specific about the significance of the investment.]	This project, if funded, will make a difference in reading achievement for 425 students during the coming school year. The collection will be used for many years to come. It will never need replacing in entirety. Over eight years, about 700 children will have read selected books from the collection at a cost of about [ ] per child.

[2]Researchers found that children who scored in the 98th percentile read 65 books per year; children who scored in the 90th percentile read 21.2 books per year; children who scored in the 20th percentile read .7 books per year; and children who scored in the 2nd percentile read 0 books per year (see Anderson, R.C., P.T. Wilson, L.G. Fielding, 1998, "Growth in Reading and How Children Spend Their Time Outside of School," *Reading Research Quarterly* 23: 285–303).

Figure 19–2.   Components of a Letter Seeking Support for a School Book Collection (continued)

Components of a Letter Seeking Support for a School Book Collection (continued)	
COMPONENT	EXAMPLE OF A STATEMENT
End with willingness to provide more information.	We would be happy to show you the collection we have started as well as to have you visit our school and observe reading instruction. We hope that your [company, agency] priorities can include this positive contribution to our students' literacy learning.
Signature	Principal, School Leadership Team, Parent Volunteer Coordinator

Figure 19–2. *Components of a Letter Seeking Support for a School Book Collection* (continued)

Of course, you will want to modify and personalize this letter to accomplish your own purposes. Also, if you know the addressee very well, you may find the letter a bit too formal. In general, shorter is better, so you may want to eliminate one of the sections. When in doubt, write a very professional letter that presents a formal, supported request.

Developing a Concept Paper Proposing a Funded Project

A concept paper is a brief description of your proposed project. A concept paper for a small grant to support a book collection would be no more than three pages. Sometimes the concept paper is a preliminary proposal; if it is well received, you will be invited to submit a more detailed proposal. Occasionally, your project will be funded on the basis of the concept paper alone, and all you will be expected to submit is a detailed budget. In any case, a concept paper is well worth developing because it forces you to put your ideas into concise form. The example of a concept paper presented in Figure 19–3 is less than 1,500 words.

In this example, the different components of the concept paper have identifying headings, but you wouldn't necessarily need them. Notice that the concept paper is roughly parallel to the letter of application but provides slightly more information. It begins with a statement of rationale and purpose. Be sure that you demonstrate that you know the demographic details describing students in your school.

If you have completed any informal studies that show need, you can refer to them here. Knowing the students adds to your credibility. Specific objectives let the funding agency know precisely what you plan to do, and the plan of action that follows demonstrates that you have thought through the process and are well prepared. The time line provides the details of your schedule for carrying out your plan. Finally, a few sentences about evaluation show how you will document outcomes. A summary statement brings the application to a close but offers further details if there is interest.

Writing a Proposal

Effective proposals present your ideas in clear language. When in doubt, use plain language rather than educational jargon. Often, you will be communicating with persons outside the field of education. You may need to use "insider" words like *guided reading*, but be sure to define them in your text.

Another mistake proposal writers sometimes make is to use sweeping generalizations that are not supported by specific evidence. The more you can make *supported* rather than general statements, the more credibility your proposal will have. (Figure 19–4 contains some examples of supported

Example of a Concept Paper

INTRODUCTION AND RATIONALE

As a school staff, our primary goal is to raise achievement in reading for students in all grades at Greensview School, in Urban City. Reading is the most important skill our students will develop in elementary school. Our goal is to assure that every one of our students enters middle school with the high level of proficiency in reading that is essential for later school success and a quality life. We are especially committed to our students' developing the ability to read with good comprehension and to use fiction and nonfiction texts as tools for learning. This goal is possible given the preparation we have undertaken and the commitment of our staff.

PURPOSE

Over the last year we have investigated research-based best practice in reading instruction and prepared our staff to implement a dynamic reading program that will massively increase time for teaching reading as well as students' independent reading. Our proposal provides for a 100 percent increase in the time for daily reading instruction and a 300 percent increase in the amount of school and home reading students do. A high-quality school book collection, with both fiction and nonfiction materials, is essential to support our program, which includes small-group reading, independent individual reading, and home reading. In this proposal, we seek funds in the amount of [amount], to support the acquisition of classroom books and a school book collection that will provide the rich text resources that our students need.

POPULATION TO BE SERVED

At Greensview, we serve a population of 530 children. Our school is located in an urban area where there are high levels of unemployment and poverty. Over ninety-five percent of our students are eligible for free and reduced-price lunch. Many of our students are vulnerable to membership in neighborhood gangs, which can be prevented by success in school. While we have made very good progress in starting Greensview children on the road to reading, but more work is needed to start children on the road to habitual home reading. In grades K–2, we must start children on the way to competent reading. The demands of reading in grades three to five are even greater. We want our students to become highly proficient readers who can use reading for a variety of purposes. Current reading levels of fifty-seven percent are below recommended national standards.[1]

The number of our fourth graders meeting state standards on the proficiency test improved from thirty-seven percent to forty-six percent over the last two years, but we continue to dedicate ourselves to a one-hundred percent passing rate. Finally, a recent study showed that many of our students do not read voluntarily at home. This situation must change if our students are to succeed in school and later life.

SPECIFIC OBJECTIVES

We propose to dramatically increase[2] the number of students who meet national standards for reading achievement. We also seek to increase the number of fourth graders students who meet state criteria on the proficiency test in reading. Finally, our goal is to increase the amount of reading students do at school and at home to at least one chapter book per week.

(Continued)

Figure 19–3. Example of a Concept Paper

Example of a Concept Paper (continued)

PLAN OF ACTION

Four years ago, the teachers in our school undertook an extensive project to improve classroom instruction. They established small-group guided reading as well as a systematic and intensive phonics and spelling program. Reading and writing in kindergarten were greatly increased. As a result, we find that our students coming into third grade are reading more and at higher levels of text. For example, using a systematic end-of-year assessment, we test our students using nationally recommended benchmarks for reading.[3] In fall 1998 only twenty-five percent of entering third graders were able to read level M, the national recommended standard. Further, only fifteen percent of those students performed successfully on assessment of comprehension of the same passages. In fall 2001 forty-seven percent of entering third graders were able to read level M with high accuracy and satisfactory performance on comprehension.

We see this increase as evidence of a dramatic improvement in our program, and we expect scores to rise further as we improve our work. We must sustain progress in primary grades and make further progress in the intermediate grades and middle school, especially as the demands for performance rise sharply and much more sophisticated skills in reading and writing are required.

Research indicates that students who do not become highly proficient readers are unlikely to do so throughout their lives. In addition, these elementary years are the time when students build up a large volume of reading and develop important habits. Research has shown that the amount of reading students do makes a difference in achievement.[4]

Last year, all of our teachers took steps to examine the literacy program and to expand their skills. A leadership team, including the principal and teachers in grades three to five, participated in a year of training; in addition, a literacy facilitator has been employed and trained to work with the staff over the next two years. We will dedicate one hour of instructional time per day for reading. All teachers will participate in ongoing training and coaching to improve classroom instruction. Our approach combines explicit teaching in small groups and a large amount of independent reading. In classrooms where we have implemented this approach, our primary students are reading several books a day; our intermediate students are reading at least one chapter book per week. They are reading at school and at home every day, and we are running out of books!

As teachers, we select books that students can read successfully and, through instruction, gradually increase the difficulty and variety. We want intermediate students to read many kinds of fiction and nonfiction and expand their skills. Our teachers are highly knowledgeable about selecting books for instruction. We have already done a great deal of investigation to assure that we acquire a collection that will support acceleration of progress in reading. We have made an inventory of our current collection and have a plan for acquiring precisely those volumes we need to support good instruction.

We have developed a plan of action to make the most of any resources we receive. Members of our staff have reserved and committed extra time in the summer to organize the collection. Parents have formed a volunteer group and are prepared to help us maintain the collection and assure efficient use.

We have placed the highest priority on these books for students. We used available funds from the district, as well as a small grant from the state. We held a book fair that helped us to obtain some books. Teachers and parents have already contributed over 300 books. A local office supply store has agreed to donate 30 cardboard library book boxes to protect our books. Our staff has committed volunteer time in the summer to organize the collection.

(Continued)

Figure 19–3. Example of a Concept Paper (continued)

Example of a Concept Paper (continued)

TIME LINE

Given the plans that we have already put into action, we will be able to complete the organizational work to have the book collection ready for use in September 200_. With the assistance of parent volunteers, the collection will be maintained and evaluated during the 200_–200_ academic year. During that time, all teachers will participate in ongoing training and coaching (at least 40 hours). This training is sponsored through a local university-school partnership documented by the attached letter. In summer 200_, more books will be added to the collection, which will provide the full basic collection for teachers' use in 200_–200_.

EVALUATION PLAN

In spring 200_, 200_, and 200_, we will collect and report scores on a systematic benchmark assessment that we use to determine the percentage of students who meet national standards for reading level at every grade, K–8. We will also collect and report the percentages of [third] graders who successfully meet criteria for the state proficiency test in reading. In addition, we will collect and compile data on students' weekly reading to determine the amount and kind of reading that they do. These data will be considered by the entire school staff at an evaluation meet each fall.

SUMMARY STATEMENT

In this concept paper, we have described a plan of action for expanding the reading skills of students at Greensview, an urban school serving a high-risk population. Our plan will put books into students' hands and engage them through motivation and intensive reading instruction. Our goals are to increase the number of students who meet standards for proficient reading as well as to increase the amount students read at school and at home. A basic school book collection, with over 3,000 books, varied by fiction and nonfiction, is essential to support our plans. This collection will serve over 400 students during the next three years, and will be an important component of our reading instruction for years to come. We will be happy to provide a more detailed proposal for this plan.

---

[1] The recommended national standards from the Center on Education and the Economy are described in "New Standards." *Performance Standards: Volume 1 – Elementary School: English Language Arts, Mathematics, Science, Applied Learning*. 1997. National Center on Education and the Economy and the University of Pittsburgh. Printed in the United States of America by Harcourt Brace Educational Measurement.

[2] If possible, consult with the funding agency to determine whether a specific percentage (for example, to 85 percent) is required.

[3] "New Standards."

[4] Researchers found that children who scored in the ninety-eighth percentile read 65 books per year; children who scored in the ninety percentile read 21.2 books per year; children who scored in the twentieth percentile read .7 books per year; and children who scored in the second percentile read no books per year (see Anderson, R.C., P.T. Wilson, L.G. Fielding. 1998. Growth in Reading and How Children Spend Their Time Outside of School, "*Reading Research Quarterly* 23: 285–303).

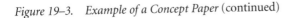

Figure 19–3.   Example of a Concept Paper (continued)

Grounding Statements in Evidence	
GENERAL STATEMENTS	**SUPPORTED STATEMENTS**
Students in grades three, four, and five need more help in reading.	Our yearly assessment revealed that sixty-five percent of our third graders, fifty-seven percent of fourth graders, and fifty-one percent of fifth graders do not meet national standards for reading performance at the end of the year. We are concerned that forty-nine percent of our fifth graders are going on to middle school lacking the necessary reading skills to succeed.
Students in our school are falling behind in reading.	In fall of this year, systematic assessment revealed that thirty-five percent of entering third graders are reading at least ten points below grade-level standards.
Students in our school are reluctant to read.	A survey of parents revealed that the average time our students spend reading at home is only ten minutes. For fifty-seven percent of students surveyed, the time is less than three minutes! Our analysis of our school reading program revealed that students read an average of only ten books per year. Reading practice is critically important for upper elementary students. We propose to increase the number of books read by 300 percent.

Figure 19–4.   Grounding Statements in Evidence

statements.) Making supported statements is especially important when you are talking about the problems and issues in your school. You'll want to provide evidence that those problems exist and document their severity.

Proposals also tend to have specific guidelines as to the length of each section, the overall length, and the number of appendices allowed. Follow these guidelines precisely; your proposal could be disqualified if you do not follow them. More is not necessarily better when it comes to a proposal; too many words can get in the way of your message.

Components of a Proposal

Figure 19–5 lists the components of a full proposal for a grant to provide books for guided, independent, and home reading.

- The first component, an abstract or summary, is very important. Indeed, the prospective sponsor may read nothing else! An example of an abstract is presented in Figure 19–6. This abstract is 150 words long and provides the important information about the proposal.

- Next, write an introduction and rationale. Your purpose here is to convince the potential sponsor of the importance of your idea.

- Provide a clear statement of purpose.

- Describe the students to be served by the project. Here, you can clearly establish the fact that your students need more books and that the funds can make a difference for a large number of them.

- Next, state the specific objectives of the proposal. There is sometimes confusion between goals and objectives. Goals are broader, overall statements, while objectives are more specific and can be measured. Some examples of goals and their related objectives are presented in Figure 19–7.

- In the plan of action, present exactly what you plan to do. While you do not want to include unimportant details (such as the colors of boxes), you do need enough detail to convince the sponsor that you know what you are doing.

- Your evaluation plan should detail precisely what you will do to determine whether the program is working or not. Both the plan of action and the evaluation plan should be more detailed than you presented in your concept paper, but be sure to adhere to any stated length restrictions.

- Both plan of action and evaluation design should be reflected in the time line. A simple way to present a time line is to detail briefly the actions during each month of the time period proposed. (A sample time line is presented in Figure 19–8.)

- At the end of the proposal proper, present a statement of impact that summarizes the potential this proposal has for making a difference. Refer to student outcomes. Include specific numbers when possible.

- Develop a budget (an example is presented in Figure 19–9).

- Include appendices that extend the proposal. One appendix might be a bibliography if you have supported your rationale with research.

Another could contain the curriculum vitae or brief biographical sketches of project personnel; still another can provide letters of support from credible people who can testify to your efforts.

These components may vary from proposal to proposal. Sometimes you will be responding to a specific RFP, and in that case, you will follow those directions rather than these general guidelines.

Writing a complete proposal is a lengthy process. The good news is that once you have prepared one of these proposals, you can draw from it to write others for different sponsors and use it as a source of language for letters of application and/or concept papers. Figure 19–10 summarizes the steps in preparing a proposal. Obviously you need to begin well ahead of your deadline and revise and refine as you go. Establishing clear deadlines for each step of work will help you avoid as much last-minute stress as possible.

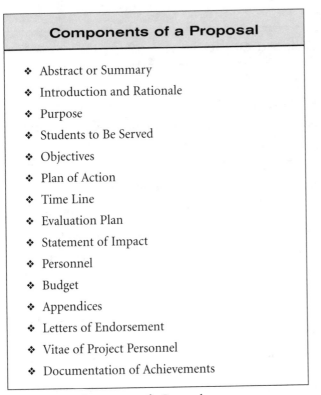

Components of a Proposal

- ❖ Abstract or Summary
- ❖ Introduction and Rationale
- ❖ Purpose
- ❖ Students to Be Served
- ❖ Objectives
- ❖ Plan of Action
- ❖ Time Line
- ❖ Evaluation Plan
- ❖ Statement of Impact
- ❖ Personnel
- ❖ Budget
- ❖ Appendices
- ❖ Letters of Endorsement
- ❖ Vitae of Project Personnel
- ❖ Documentation of Achievements

Figure 19–5.   Components of a Proposal

Example of an Abstract

We propose to increase the reading opportunities and reading achievement for students in grades K–8 at Greensview School. In this proposal, we describe a plan of action for establishing an efficient, economical, high-quality book collection to support small-group reading instruction and independent and home reading. Students will read appropriate fiction and nonfiction books daily and expand their skills as they read with greater variety. Our goal is to provide high-quality instruction that will assure that students are highly proficient readers of fiction and nonfiction as they leave elementary school. The requested funds would provide over 3,000 books for instructional and home reading and influence the reading achievement of 700 children over the next eight years. The effectiveness of the project will be evaluated through documentation of the number of books read and collection of scores on individual and standardized tests for all students involved.

Figure 19–6.   Example of an Abstract

Summary

There are a number of ways to apply for funding to support your book collection, ranging from person-to-person contact with potential sponsors to writing a letter of application or concept paper to preparing a full proposal. While it is a great deal of work and effort to produce a proposal, the process sometimes brings colleagues together around important problems. Securing funding means that someone important recognizes the importance of your work, so it is a real boost for the success of your project. If you go about it the right way, you can deepen the vision you share with your colleagues and even have some fun doing it.

Suggestions for Professional Development: Creating a Proposal

1. Prior to a staff meeting, identify one or two potential sponsors for building classroom collections and/or a school bookroom collection.

2. As a whole group, generate ideas.

3. Form teams to write a letter of inquiry, a concept paper, or a full proposal. If you have two sources, form two teams. (If you have only one source, form teams to prepare specific components.)

4. Have teams read the guidelines of the funding agency carefully and use the examples and suggestions in this chapter to prepare the documents.

5. Have members of the staff not on the writing teams review the documents and make suggestions.

6. Revise the documents.

7. Ask outsiders to read your letters, papers, or proposals and provide suggestions. You might consider people from the business community or any person familiar with funded projects.

8. Finalize your letters, concept papers, or proposals and submit them to the potential funding agencies.

9. Celebrate together if grants or application is funded!

Sample Goals and Related Objectives

GOAL 1. *To increase grade three, four, and five students' reading.*

- ❖ Objective 1. To increase the number of books read during small-group reading instruction.
- ❖ Objective 2. To increase the number of books students read independently during the reading block of time.
- ❖ Objective 3. To increase the time and number of books that students read at home.

GOAL 2. *To improve the effectiveness of reading instruction for students in grades three, four, and five.*

- ❖ Objective 1. To increase the time for small-group reading instruction during the reading block of time.
- ❖ Objective 2. To provide appropriate materials to support effective small-group reading instruction.
- ❖ Objective 3. To increase the number, quality, and variety of texts to support small-group reading instruction.

GOAL 3. *To raise reading achievement of upper elementary grade students at Greensview School.*

- ❖ Objective 1. To increase the number of students who meet established grade-level standards for reading at the end of grade three, four, and five.
- ❖ Objective 2. To increase the number of fourth-grade students who meet criteria for satisfactory performance on the state proficiency test.

Figure 19–7. Sample Goals and Related Objectives

Sample Time Line for Establishing Classroom and School Book Collections

MONTH	TASKS	PERSONNEL RESPONSIBLE
March	Complete long-range plans for staff training and reserve dates.	Principal Literacy team[1]
April	Make inventory of current collection. Complete lists of books to order. Contact publisher representatives and negotiate for best prices.	Literacy team
May	Make final selections and create orders. Involve total staff providing input. Plan staff training.	Literacy team All staff Principal
June	Hold day of staff training to prepare for organizing and using the collection and to use instructional techniques.	Staff development coordinator All staff
July	Unpack books, label, and organize them. Place books for classroom collections in classrooms. Create system for using the collection.	Literacy team Volunteers
August	Hold two days of staff training on instruction. Use books as part of training. Organize and label classroom collections. Train volunteers to assist in maintaining the book collection.	Staff development coordinator All staff Volunteers
September	Implement instructional program. Assess students' reading and form reading groups. Hold two meetings to discuss use of classroom collections and school book collection.	School staff development coordinator All staff
Monthly	Hold monthly meetings for further professional development. Midyear—collect evaluation data on students.	School staff development coordinator Literacy team All staff
April	Assess classroom collections and school book collection. Evaluate levels; note needs for next year. Have appreciation lunch for volunteers.	Literacy team All staff Volunteers
May	Place new book orders. Collect final evaluation data on students.	Literacy team All staff
June	Analyze evaluation data. Prepare final report. Hold project evaluation meeting.	Literacy team All staff Principal

[1]The literacy team consists of one teacher from each grade level, the principal, the school staff developer, and the Reading Recovery teacher and/or special education teacher. At the middle school it may include one content area teacher as well.

Figure 19–8. *Sample Time Line for Establishing Classroom and School Book Collections*

Sample Budget for a Proposal

Item	Description	Funds Requested		
		Year 1	Year 2	Total
1	*Personnel*			
a.	Project Director and Committee	Donated	Donated	-0-
b.	Clerical Support (Yr. 1 = 80 hours @ $16.00) (Yr. 2 = 40 hours @ $16.00)	$1,280	$ 640	$1,920
c.	Volunteer Support	Donated	Donated	-0-
	Total Personnel	**$1,280**	**$640**	**$1,920**
2.	*Materials and Supplies*			
a.	Boxes for Books (Yr. 1 = 200 @ $2.00) (Yr. 2 = 100 @ $2.00)	$400	$200	$600
b.	Supplies	$50	$25	$75
	Total for Materials and Supplies	**$450**	**$225**	**$675**
3.	*Books*			

a.	Single Titles for Independent Reading in Classrooms
	Grade K (Levels A–B) = 40 single titles x 2 classrooms=
	  80 books x $4.00
	Grade 1 (Levels B–I) = 80 single titles x 3 classrooms =
	  240 books x $4.00
	Grade 2 (Levels J–M) = 40 single titles x 3 classrooms =
	  120 books x $4.00 to M
	Grade 3 (Levels K–R) = 75 single titles x 3 classrooms=
	  225 books x $5.00
	Grade 4 (Levels N–U) = 75 single titles x 3 classrooms =
	  225 books x $5.00
	Grades 5, 6 (Levels Q–X) = 100 single titles x 2 classrooms =
	  200 books x $5.00
	Grades 7, 8 (Levels S–Z) = 100 single titles x 2 classrooms =
	  200 books x $5.00
		$6,100
		
		[1,290 books]
			$3,050
			
			[645 books]
				$9,150
				
				[1,935 books]

b.	Basic Collection for Grades K to 5* Additional 7 copies of 67 titles @ $5.00 = $2,345 Additional 203 titles, 12 copies each = $12,180	$7,265 [1,453 books]	$7,260 [1,452 books]	$14,525 [2,905 books]
	Total for Books	**$9,515**	**$8,260**	**$17,775**
4.	*Other*			
a.	Miscellaneous Expenses	$100	$100	$200
b.	Overhead	Donated	Donated	-0-
	Total Other	**$100**	**$100**	**$200**
	TOTAL REQUESTED	**$11,345**	**$9,225**	**$20,570**

Half of the book collection is purchased each year, so that selections may be tested and evaluated carefully.

Figure 19–9.   *Sample Budget for a Proposal*

Sample Budget for a Proposal (continued)

NOTES TO THE BUDGET:

1a. Our school's literacy coordinator, assisted by a voluntary committee of teachers, will provide leadership by acting as a steering committee to acquire and organize the collection for use. The committee members are: [NAMES]. The school librarian, [NAME], will assist in providing for a convenient space to house the collection. These individuals have made a commitment to the project and have reserved four days in the summer to work on the project.

1b. In year 1, the equivalent of two weeks of clerical support is needed to unpack, organize, and label books and to establish the check-out system so that the collection can be efficiently used. In year 2, the equivalent of one week of clerical support is needed to expand the collection and house new books.

1c. Parent volunteers have been secured to maintain the collection during the next two years. On a regular basis, parents will file any new books that are ordered, refile books that are used, and check the order of the collection. Volunteer efforts will be coordinated by [NAME].

2a. To keep the collection in an orderly and attractive way, heavy cardboard "magazine" boxes will be used. These boxes may be purchased at a discount from a school supplier. Boxes will hold an average of ten books each and will be needed for the entire collection, including those titles in the current inventory.

2b. General supplies will be needed to label books and magazine boxes and to create the check-out system, for example, tape, a labeling system, markers, and library cards.

3a. With our current average class size of 28 students per class, our analysis indicates that primary classrooms need at least 200 single titles and a library of single titles of at least 100 books is needed for grades two through five. This classroom library of single titles will be supplemented by the school library resources as well as by borrowing some single titles from the basic school collection (3b). Grade 3 and 4 classrooms already have an average of 25 books, but grade 5 classrooms are not at all well supplied. We propose supplying classrooms with 500 titles during year 1 and 200 additional titles during year 2.

3b. Our goal over the two-year period is to create a basic collection to be shared across grades. Currently, in addition to the single-title classroom copies, we possess 107 titles with multiple copies from levels H to X that we consider suitable for the collection, but we do not have enough copies of some of these titles. We especially need titles at levels P through U to support readers in grades 4 and 5. We propose to add an average of six books per title to expand to sets of twelve copies each for the 67 titles. To expand the shared book collection, we propose to add 203 titles, with six copies of each in year 1 and 6 more copies in year 2. The total collection will house 6,240 books in all and will be used by 672 students over a nine-year period. Free shipping costs will be negotiated with book suppliers.

4a. It is anticipated that some funds will be needed for miscellaneous expenses (for example, providing refreshments for parent volunteers or making telephone calls to books suppliers). A small amount is included in the budget to support these expenses.

4b. Administrative or "overhead" costs of 8 percent are usually built into grant applications. These costs have been waived by the superintendent and board in order to maximize the use of funds to buy books for students.

Figure 19–9. *Sample Budget for a Proposal* (continued)

Steps in Writing a Proposal for a Grant to Support Guided, Independent, and Home Reading

1. Prepare some clear statements about:

   ❖ What you need.

   ❖ Why you need it.

   ❖ What problem it addresses.

   ❖ How it will solve the problem.

   ❖ Specific details such as number of books and levels.

2. Determine total costs and cost per student.

3. Identify local, state, and federal funding sources.

4. Select one funding source to begin.

5. Research and obtain guidelines if available.

6. Read the guidelines to determine the priorities of the funding agency. Seek advice from individuals if possible.

7. Using the guidelines and the specific statements you have prepared, generate ideas, design the proposal, and outline the budget.

8. Develop a work plan for writing the proposal; share jobs.

9. Perform any research needed to write the proposal (such as documentation of student performance in past years).

10. Write the first draft of the proposal.

11. Complete the budget.

12. Assemble attachments, if appropriate. Ask for letters of support well before your deadline.

13. Complete forms for the funding agency, if applicable.

14. Review and edit the draft, involving several outside people who can give feedback.

15. Prepare final copy, being sure that it is businesslike, professional, and attractive.

16. Write a cover letter.

17. Submit proposal by the deadline.

Figure 19–10.   Steps in Writing a Proposal for a Grant to Support Guided, Independent, and Home Reading

Appendices

Evaluation Response for Text Gradient

DIRECTIONS:

Since any text gradient is always in the process of construction as it is used with varying groups of children, we expect our list to change every year. We encourage you to try the levels with your students and to provide feedback based on your own experiences. Please suggest changes to existing book levels and suggest new books for the list. Please provide the information requested below.

Name: _____   Grade Level You Teach: _____

Telephone: (   ) _____   E-mail address: _____

Address (street, city, state): _____

BOOK EVALUATED:

Book Title: _____

Level: J   K   L   M   N   O   P   Q   R   S   T   U   V   W   X   Y   Z

Author: _____

Publisher: _____

THIS BOOK IS:

_____ A book listed on the gradient that I have evaluated with my class.
(Complete SECTION A and make comments in SECTION C.)

_____ A book listed on the gradient that I am recommending as a benchmark for a level.
(Complete SECTION A and make comments in SECTION C.)

_____ A new book that I suggest adding to the collection.
(Complete SECTION B and make comments in SECTION C.)

SECTION A: *(for an evaluation of a book currently included in the list)*

Is it appropriately placed on the level (explain)? _____

To what level should the book be moved? _____

J   K   L   M   N   O   P   Q   R   S   T   U   V   W   X   Y   Z

Are there points of difficulty that make it harder than it seems? _____

Is the text supportive in ways that might not be noticeable when examining the superficial characteristics?

_____

SECTION B: *(for the recommendation of a new book)* Indicate recommended level:

How does this book support readers at this level? _____

What challenges does it offer? _____

SECTION C: *Please place additional comments on the back or on another sheet.*

Mail this form to:

Irene Fountas, Lesley University, 1815 Massachusetts Ave., Suite 378, Cambridge, Massachusetts 02140. Fax: (617) 349-8490   E-mail: *ifountas@mail.lesley.edu*

Gay Su Pinnell, The Ohio State University, 200 Ramseyer Hall, 29 W. Woodruff Avenue, Columbus, Ohio 43210. Fax: (614) 292-4260   E-mail: *pinnell.1@osu.edu*

School Record of Book Reading Progress

Student's Name: _____   School: _____

Record book reading progress three or four times per year, as agreed upon with your school faculty. Note dates in bottom row. Put an open circle ○ at the child's instructional level on each date indicated. A filled in circle l indicates student is having some difficulty at the level. Mark the level ○* if additional teaching is also being provided by specialists. Give the year and descriptions of additional reading services on back.

Teacher																								
Book Level	K	K	K	K	1	1	1	1	2	2	2	2	3	3	3	3	4	4	4	4	5	5	5	5
Z (7-8)																								
Y																								
X																								
W (6+)																								
V																								
U																								
T (5)																								
S																								
R																								
Q (4)																								
P																								
O																								
N (3)																								
M																								
L																								
K																								
J (2)																								
I																								
H																								
G																								
F																								
E																								
D																								
C (1)																								
B																								
A																								
Date																								

School Record of Book Reading Progress

Name_____ Grades_____ 3 _____ 4 _____ 5 _____ 6

Title of Text, Accuracy Rate, SC Rate (● = above 90%; ○ = below 90%)

Book Level																
Z																
Y																
X																
W																
V																
U																
T																
S																
R																
Q																
P																
O																
N																
M																
L																
K																
J																
I																
H																
G																
F																
E																
D																
C																
B																
A																
DATE																

Professional References

ANDERSON, T. H., AND B. B. ARMBRUSTER. 1984. "Content Area Textbooks." In *Learning to Read in American Schools*, ed. R.C. Anderson, J. Osborn, and R.J. Tierney, 193-224. Hillsdale, NJ: Lawrence Erlbaum Associates.

ANDERSON, R. C., P. T. WILSON, AND L.G. FIELDING. 1998. Growth in Reading and How Children Spend Their Time Outside of School." *Reading Research Quarterly* 23: 285-303.

ARMBRUSTER, B. B. 1984. "The Problem of "Inconsiderate Texts." In *Theoretical Issues in Reading Comprehension*, ed. G. G. Duffy, L. R. Roehler, and J. Mason, 202-217. New York: Longman.

ARMBRUSTER, B. B., AND T. H. ANDERSON. 1981. "Content Area Textbooks." Reading Education Report NO. 23: Urbana: University of Illinois Center for the Study of Reading.

BECK, I., E. MCCASLIN, AND M. G. MCKEOWN. 1980. "The rational design of a program to teach vocabulary to fourth-grade students." Pittsburgh: University of Pittsburgh, Learning Research and Development Center.

BECK, I. L., M. G. MCKEOWN, AND E. W. GROMOLL. 1989. "Learning from social studies." *Cognition and Instruction* 6: 99-158.

CLAY, M. M. 2001. *Change over time in children's literacy development*. Auckland, New Zealand: Heinemann.

_____. 1991. *What Did I Write?* Portsmouth, NH: Heinemann.

_____. *Becoming Literate: The Construction of Inner Control*. Portsmouth, NH: Heinemann.

_____. 1993. *A Guidebook for Reading Recovery Teachers*. Portsmouth, NH: Heinemann.

_____. (2002). *An Observation Survey of Early Literacy Achievement*. Portsmouth, NH: Heinemann.

CALFEE, ROBERT AND MARILYN CHAMBLISS. 1998. *Textbooks for Learning: Nurturing Children's Minds*. Malden, MA: Blackwell Publishers.

FOUNTAS, I. C., AND G. S. PINNELL. 2001. *Guiding Readers and Writers: Teaching Comprehension, Genre, and Content Literacy*. Portsmouth, NH: Heinemann.

_____.1996. *Guided Reading: Good First Teaching for All Children*. Portsmouth, NH: Heinemann.

_____.1999. *Matching Books to Readers*. Portsmouth, NH: Heinemann.

_____, eds. 1999. *Voices on Word Matters: Learning About Phonics and Spelling in the Literacy Classroom*. Portsmouth, NH: Heinemann.

FRY, E. 1977. "Fry's readability graphs: Clarifications, validity, and extension to level 1", *Journal of Reading* 21, 242-252.

Metametrics, Inc. (Accessed October 28, 2005.) The Lexile Framework® for Reading. http://www.lexile.com/EntrancePageHtml.aspx.

New Standards. 1998. *Performance Standards: Volume 1-Elementary School*. National Center on Education and the Economy and the University of Pittsburgh.

PINNELL, G.S., AND I.C. FOUNTAS. 1998. *Word Matters: Teaching Phonics and Spelling in the Reading/Writing Classroom*. Portsmouth: NH: Heinemann.

Scharer, P., J. Williams, and G.S. Pinnell. 2001. Literacy Collaborative: 2001 Research Report. Columbus, OH: The Ohio State University.

Singer, H. 1992. "Friendly Texts: Description and Criteria". In *Reading in the Content Areas*. 3rd Edition, ed. E. K. Dishner, T.W. Bean, J.E. Readence, and D.W. Moore, 156-168. Dubuque, IA: Kendall/Hunt.

SELECTED BOOKS FOR GRADES K–8, FICTION AND NONFICTION

ADLER, DAVID. 1989. *Remember the Holocaust*. New York: Henry Holt and Company.

AIKEN, JOAN. 1962. *The Wolves of Willoughby Chase*. New York: Bantam, Doubleday, Dell.

ALTER, JUDY. 1997. *Wild West Shows: Rough Riders and Sure Shots*. New York: Franklin Watts.

BARTOLLI, SUSAN CAMPBELL. 1996. *Growing Up in Coal Country*. Boston: Houghton Mifflin.

BIDDULPH, FRED AND JEAN. 1992. *Earth and Moon*. Bothel, WA: The Wright Group.

BRYSON, THERESA. 2003. *Balloon Ride*. Pelham, NY: Benchmark Education.

BURTON, MARGIE, CATHY FRENCH, & TAMMY JONES. 1999. *Big Rocks, Little Rocks*. Pelham, NY: Benchmark Education.

CLEARY, BEVERLY. 1957. *Henry and the Paper Route*. New York: Avon Books.

COLLIER, JAMES LINCOLN. 1974. *My Brother Sam Is Dead*. New York: Scholastic.

COLLIER, JAMES LINCOLN. 1983. *War Comes to Willy Freeman*. New York: Bantam, Doubleday, Dell.

CONFORD, ELLEN. 1989. *What's Cooking, Jenny Archer?* Boston: Little, Brown & Company.

CUMPIANO, IDA. 1992. *Weather Watch*. Carmel, CA: Hampton-Brown Books.

DANZINGER, PAULA. 1996. *Amber Brown Wants Extra Credit*. New York: Scholastic.

DUDLEY, KAREN. 1997. *Giant Pandas*. Austin, TX: Raintree Steck;Vaughn.

FLETCHER, RALPH. 1997. *Spider Boy*. New York: Bantam, Doubleday, Dell Books for Young Readers.

FROST, HELEN. 1999. *Going to the Dentist*. Mankato, MN: Capstone Press.

GIBSON, MARIE. 2000. *Alice's Diary: Living with Diabetes*. Huntington Beach, CA: Pacific Learning.

GIFF, PATRICIA REILLY. 2000. *Nory Ryan's Song*. New York: Scholastic.

HARTLEY, LINDA. 2004. *Landslides*. Boston: Houghton Mifflin.

HARVEY, MILES. 1999. *Look What Came from Russia*. New York: Franklin Watts.

HESSE, KAREN. 1964. *Letters from Rifka*. New York: Hyperion Books for Children.

HURWITZ, JOHANNA. 1992. *Aldo Peanut Butter*. New York: Puffin Books.

KING-SMITH, DICK. 1984. *Harry's Mad*. New York: Alfred A. Knopf.

KLINE, SUZY. 1988. *Horrible Harry in Room 2B*. New York: Puffin Books.

L'ENGLE, MADELEINE. 1962. *A Wrinkle in Time*. New York: Bantam, Doubleday, Dell Books for Young Readers.

LOBEL, ARNOLD. 1970. *Frog and Toad Are Friends*. New York: HarperCollins.

LOWRY, LOIS. 1957. *Anastasia Krupnik*. Boston: Houghton Mifflin.

LUNIS, NATALIE. 2002. *Baking Bread*. Pelham, NY: Benchmark Education Company.

MAHY, MARGARET. 1984. *A Good Knee for a Cat*. Huntington Beach, CA: Learning Media.

MCPHERSON, JAN. 1996. *Under a Microscope*. Bothell: WA: The Wright Group.

MELSER, JUNE. 1998. *The Mirror*. Bothell, WA: The Wright Group.

MURDOCH, KATH AND STEPHEN RAY. 1997. *Creatures in the Night*. New York: Mondo Publishing.

National Geographic Society. 2001. *Cactuses*. Washington, DC: National Geographic Society,

Nayer, Judy. 1996. *Summer at Cove Lake*. Parsippany, NJ: Modern Curriculum.

PETERS, ELLEN JEAN. 2004. *Rachel Carson.* Boston: Houghton Mifflin

RANDELL, BEVERLEY, JENNY GILES, & ANNETTE SMITH. 1996. *Look at Me.* Barrington, IL: Rigby Education.

RANDELL, BEVERLEY, JENNY GILES, & ANNETTE SMITH. 1996. *Me.* Barrington, IL: Rigby Education.

Randell, Beverley. 1994. THE BIG KICK. BARRINGTON, IL: Rigby Education.

————.1994. *The Lion and the Rabbit.* Barrington, IL: Rigby Education.

————.1996. *Baby Bear Goes Fishing.* Barrington, IL: Rigby Education.

RILEY, KANA. 1995. *Peaches the Pig.* Lexington, MA: D.C. Heath and Company.

RYLANT, CYNTHIA. 1990. *Henry and Mudge: The First Book of Their Adventures.* New York: Simon and Schuster.

SIGMAN, MARGIE. 2004. *Grandparents Are Great.* Boston: Houghton Mifflin.

SMITH, ANNETTE. 1996. *Sally's New Shoes.* Barrington, IL: Rigby Education.

SNYDER, ZILPHA KEATLEY. 1967. *The Egypt Game.* New York: Bantam, Doubleday, Dell Books for Young Readers.

STEIN, CONRAD. 1998. *The California Gold Rush.* Chicago: The Children's Press.

SWAIN, CYNTHIA. 2003. *Batteries.* Pelham, NY: Benchmark Education.

TAYLOR, THEODORE. 1995. *The Bomb.* New York: Avon Books.

WATERS, CARRIE. 2004. *The Sleepover.* Boston: Houghton Mifflin.

WEBER, REBECCA. *Making a House.* Pelham, NY: Benchmark Education.

WELDON OWEN. 1999. *Ocean Life.* Denver, CO: Shortland Publications, Inc.

WILCOX, CHARLOTTE. 1996. *Powerhouse: Inside a Nuclear Power Plant.* Minneapolis, MN: Carolrhoda Books, Inc.

WILDCATS. 1999. *Incredible Places.* Bothell, WA: The Wright Group.